Jewish Marital Status

Jewish Marital Status

A Hadassah Study
Edited by Carol Diament

JASON ARONSON INC.
Northvale, New Jersey
London

10 9 8 7 6 5 4 3 2

Library of Congress Cataloging-in-Publication Data

Jewish marital status / edited by Carol Diament.
    p.   cm.
  Bibliography: p.
  Includes index.
  ISBN 0-87668-870-9
    1. Women, Jewish—United States.   2. Jews—United States—
Families.   3. Women in Judaism.   I. Diament, Carol.
HQ1172.J46   1989
306.81'089924—dc20   89-32974
                                                               CIP

A comprehensive program guide is available to complement *Jewish Marital Status*.
Each chapter in the book is covered through detailed discussion questions and other
programming ideas. The program guide also contains extensive resources and
bibliographic references, and is an ideal tool for your study groups, education events,
and outreach efforts. The program guide is available from the Hadassah National
Order Department, 50 West 58th Street, New York, New York 10019.

Manufactured in the United States of America. Jason Aronson Inc. offers books and
cassettes. For information and catalog write to Jason Aronson Inc., 230 Livingston
Street, Northvale, New Jersey 07647.

*To Doris Oxenhorn, Rose Oved Binder,
and Leora Tanenbaum, without whose
devotion this book would have remained
but a dream*

Contents

IV. SINGLE AGAIN

A. Widowed

B. Abandoned

C. Divorced

V. REMARRIED

VI. INTERMARRIED

VII. GAY OR LESBIAN

VIII. CHILDLESS

Acknowledgments

In acknowledging the contributions made to this work, I begin with the men and women who opened their hearts and minds to write about their lives. Their willingness to discuss their experiences is the *sine qua non* of this book.

I want to thank those who wrote about the Jewish tradition, from which we have much to learn and be proud. If presented to young people with compassion and understanding, the teachings of Judaism might engender more respect for their heritage and ultimately create a new climate within which we can all live.

I am indebted also to the courageous social scientists and lay persons who, within the framework of this book, made suggestions for creative policy planning. Illuminating needs is not enough. The Jewish community must respond by implementing appropriate programs.

This book could not have come into being without the faith of two individuals: One is my former chairperson, Sue Mizrahi, who was excited about the idea from its inception and whose sharp literary sense is evidenced throughout the book. The other is Ruth Cole, my current chair, whose provocative comments inspired me, as I sat at my editor's desk, to strive for a work that would honestly reflect the state of modern Jewish relationships.

Among the persons who championed this project from the start were Carmela Kalmanson, Aileen Novick, Charlotte Jacobson,

Sylvia Doppelt, Edith Zamost, Barbara Goldstein, Ruth Kaslove, Efrat Levy, and Marc Brandriss.

Thanks are due to Ruth B. Hurwitz and James C. Lee for tackling the promotion of the book.

I owe a great debt of gratitude to the editors and publishers at Jason Aronson Inc., Arthur Kurzweil, Muriel Jorgensen, Nancy Goodman, and Jason Aronson, whose ideas and perceptions made them invaluable advocates; to my children, who patiently tolerated their mother's preoccupation with this book for almost two years; and to my husband Paul for his conception of the cover, chapter divisions, and for his constant assurances of the importance of the work.

Finally, it is to Doris Oxenhorn, Rose Oved Binder, and Leora Tanenbaum to whom I owe the greatest debt of all. Doris, our administrative assistant, has sustained me throughout. Her faith and objectivity shaped my vision for this book. Rose, our editorial secretary, typed and retyped this manuscript, and, as always, provided me with wise counsel and heartening encouragement throughout the process. Leora came to Hadassah's Jewish Education Department as a Ramaz High School intern in the spring of 1987 and worked diligently as our Jewish Education assistant in the intervening summers. She researched and summarized numerous articles on Jewish marital status and saw this project through from its very commencement until the final galleys were received two years later. The choice of articles was often a collaborative effort.

It is to them that I have dedicated this book.

Grateful acknowledgment is made to the following for permission to reprint previously published material:

I. SINGLE

Moment: "Are Good Jewish Men a Vanishing Breed?" by William Novak, Jan/Feb 1980, vol. 5, no. 2. © 1980 by *Moment*. "Dating Ourselves" by William Novak, Jan 1984, vol. 9, no. 2. © 1984 by *Moment*. With permission of the author.

II. NOT QUITE MARRIED

Reconstructionist: "Sex and the Single God" by Harold M. Schulweis, Nov 1981. © 1981 by *Reconstructionist*. With permission of the author.

Response: "An Interview with Rabbi Shlomo Riskin" by Neal Kaunfer and Zev Shanken, Spring 1976, vol. 10, no. 1. © 1976 by *Response*. "The Liberal Jew and Sex" by Ellen M. Umansky, Winter 1976–1977. © 1977 by *Response*. "The Kedushah of Monogamy" by "Tsuriel," Winter 1976–1977. © 1977 by *Response*. With permission of the authors.

III. MARRIED

From MARRIED PEOPLE: STAYING TOGETHER IN AN AGE OF DIVORCE by Francine Klagsbrun. Copyright © 1985 by Francine Klagsbrun. Reprinted by permission of Bantam Books. All rights reserved. With permission of the author.

Journal of Reform Judaism: "Reading the Jewish Tradition on Marital Sexuality" by Eugene B. Borowitz, Summer 1982. © 1982 by Eugene B. Borowitz.

Reuven P. Bulka: "Prelude to Marriage," adapted from JEWISH MARRIAGE: A HALAKHIC ETHIC (New York and Hoboken: Ktav Publishing House and Yeshiva University Press, 1986). © 1986 by Reuven P. Bulka.

IV. SINGLE AGAIN

B. ABANDONED

Moment: "A Different Kind of Hostage" by Robert Gordis, April 1987, vol. 12, no. 2. © 1987 by *Moment*. With permission of the author.

C. DIVORCED

American Jewish Committee: Excerpt from pamphlet SINGLE PARENT FAMILIES by Chaim I. Waxman (pp. 11–16). © 1980 by the American Jewish Committee. With permission of the author.

Selected paragraphs from *Jewish Women's Resource Center Newsletter* by Shaye J. D. Cohen, Fall 1986. © 1986 by Shaye J. D. Cohen.

Conservative Judaism: "Divorced Parent Family" by Barbara Kalin Bundt, Winter 1982. © 1982 by *Conservative Judaism*. With permission of the author.

Lilith: "Jewish Divorce Law" by Blu Greenberg, Summer 1977. Reprinted with permission from *Lilith*, the nation's only independent Jewish women's magazine. *Lilith* is published quarterly at 250 West 57 Street, Suite 2432, New York, NY 10107. With permission of the author.

Simon & Schuster: Selected paragraphs from HOW TO RUN A TRADITIONAL JEWISH HOUSEHOLD by Blu Greenberg (pp. 284–285). © 1985 by Simon & Schuster. With permission of the author.

Menorah: "One Single Jew" by Sheila Peltz Weinberg, Sep/Oct 1981, vol. 2, nos. 10–11. © 1981 by Sheila Peltz Weinberg.

VI. INTERMARRIED

Baltimore Jewish Times: "Peering Into the Limbo of Judeo-Christian" by Harold M. Schulweis, 12/18/87; "The Fruits of Experience," 9/18/87. © 1987 by *Baltimore Jewish Times*. With permission of the editor.

Excerpts from MIXED BLESSINGS: MARRIAGE BETWEEN JEWS AND CHRISTIANS by Paul and Rachel Cowan. © 1987 by Paul Cowan and Rachel Cowan. Reprinted by permission of Doubleday, a division of Bantam, Doubleday, Dell Publishing Group, Inc. With permission of the authors.

Jewish Spectator: "Coping with Intermarriage" by Jonathan D. Sarna, Summer 1982, vol. 47, no. 2. © 1982 by *Jewish Spectator*. With permission of the author.

Reform Judaism: "Mom, We're Just Dating" by Mark L. Winer, Summer 1987. © 1987 by Mark L. Winer.

Inside: "Intermarriage" by Joyce Eisenberg, Winter 1987. Reprinted with permission from *Inside Magazine* and the author.

VII. GAY or LESBIAN

Gay Community News: "A Taste of Heaven" by Liz Galst, 3/27/88–4/2/88. © 1988 by the author.

Keeping Posted, Leader's Edition: "Jewish and Gay" by Janet Marder, Nov 1986, vol. 32, no. 2. © 1986 by Janet Marder.

VIII. CHILDLESS

Sh'ma: "Some Jews Among Us—Akarah" by Sherry H. Blumberg, 12/12/86. © 1986 by the author. Reprinted with permission of the author.

"Saying No To Motherhood" by Vicki Lindner. © 1987 by Vicki Lindner. Originally published in *New Woman Magazine*, April 1987. Reprinted by permission of Berenice Hoffman Literary Agency.

Long Island Jewish World: "Where's Poppa? Bringing Up Baby, Sans Daddy" by Ruth Mason, June 12–18, 1987. © 1987 by *Long Island Jewish World*. With permission of the author.

Reconstructionist: "Jewish Population Growth," editorial, Oct/Nov 1984. © 1984 by *Reconstructionist*. With permission of the editor.

Response: "A Guide for the Jewish Adoptive Parent" by Dan Shevitz, Spring 1985, vol. 14, no. 4. © 1985 by *Response*. With permission of the author.

IX. EPILOGUE

Sh'ma: "Family or Community? A Response" by Martha A. Ackelsberg, March 20, 1987. Reprinted with permission of the author.

Sh'ma: "Family, A Religiously Mandated Ideal" by Susan Handelman, March 20, 1987. Reprinted with permission of the author.

Introduction

The Greeks were busy at the mating game when the Hadassah women came to the Fontainebleau Hotel in Miami Beach for their 72nd National Convention in August 1986. That was to be the start of a variety of projects responsive to the rise in nonconventional family units, including the book you have in front of you and the creation of Hadassah's new Outreach Department to young singles, single parents, and career women.

We came to the Fontainebleau on the heels of a conference held by AHEPA, a Greek cultural organization.[1] The Greeks were there in great numbers, young and old, proud middle-aged parents with their Adonises and Aphrodites, gray-haired grandmothers, wide-eyed children. The adults sat around tables in conference rooms and study halls, soaking up Greek culture and at times just conversing or playing cards. The young people in their 20s and 30s were all at the pool, assiduously pursuing one another.

Some of our members exclaimed in amazement, "Why don't *we* do this? Here we are, 2,000 women strong, with nary a man in sight and certainly no young ones at that." The question beckoned. When we asked one of the Greek women what the purpose of the conference was, she replied that the focus was cultural, but that in reality

[1]The American Helenic Educational Progressive Association and its auxiliary arms, the Daughters of Penelope, the Sons of Pericles, and the Maids of Athena.

the intent was matchmaking. "We want our young people to remain Greek Orthodox. This means everything to us; nothing else matters much."

I am not a sociologist, nor have I ever had any ambitions to become one, but it doesn't take much to see the pain in which many members of the Jewish community find themselves. As a Jewish community professional, but more as a mother of children in their 20s, I know that our young people are yearning. My daughter, when she started at Columbia College in 1983, often called me from her dorm room to tell me just that: "You don't know what it's like here, Mom. Some of my friends are in intensive monogamous relationships, a few of them sleep around, but if you want something in the middle, there's absolutely nothing."

Casual dating of several persons on a one-to-one basis, as it was in my generation, is apparently passé. Men and women are now friends; they go out on Saturday night in packs. This is not to say that the good old days of necking in the back seat of a car were idyllic, but at least there was "something in the middle." Certainly, we learned to make small talk and go to museums and theaters and parks, even if we didn't like any of the men we were dating, and they weren't particularly enamored of us. My son was taken aback when I recalled my youthful misadventures, most of them dull, some painful. "But at least I learned," I told him, "and your father knew how to pick up a phone and ask a girl out by Wednesday for a blind date on Saturday."

In our day, our parents, their friends, and assorted relatives were actively engaged in the matchmaking process. My father made six *shidukhim* (matches) in his life, and is therefore, according to tradition, twice guaranteed a place in the heavenly Garden of Eden. He did this not for money, but because he cared about people and about Jewish continuity. The *shadkhan* (matchmaker) of old, as now, was shunned in the heyday of the very modern '50s, but the responsibility of the older generation to its young and their determination that the children marry Jews were paramount. We, too, would brook no interference from our parents, but they were out there behind the scenes, trying, like the Greeks at the Fontainebleau.

Is it that Jews are a generation removed from the Greek community or other ethnic groups in the United States? Is it that we are moving away from hearth and home into the sophisticated mainstream of yuppiedom? Have we become more like our gentile American neighbors, among whom we study and dwell? Obviously, yes! The break with traditional family patterns brings us into the open society, which is at times far too open. Often we are lonely and isolated, and it is hard to find a Jewish connection.

The Hadassah Convention at Miami Beach was a beginning, and then came the World Conference on Jewish Demography in Jerusalem in October 1987, which made us realize that singles were not our only challenge. A Hadassah delegation of five was in attendance. Several Hadassah departments were represented, along with various Jewish federations and organizations throughout the world.

The sponsor of the Conference was the International Committee for the Demography of the Jewish People, established by the World Zionist Organization Executive. It gathered world Jewish community leaders, together with demographic experts and social scientists, to consider how modern social trends, the open society, the weakening of the traditional family, and the changing status of women affect Jewish life, and how major Jewish organizations should respond. We met in separate groups, coming together for major plenary sessions.

The sociological statistics were alarming. The Jewish population is shrinking. The most grimly and repeatedly circulated projection was that Jewish women in the Diaspora will bear, on average, no more than a Solomonic 1.6 to 1.7 children. There is growing singlehood. Cohabitation without marriage, delayed marriage, homosexuality, rising divorce, dual-career families, and childless marriages are among the barbs and hooks tearing at the fabric of Jewish society.

Perhaps the greatest threat of all to the future of Diaspora Jewry, we were warned, is intermarriage among young Jews. Rabbis and chief rabbis, from France and Denmark, rose to provide us with a litany of woes and to describe the disintegration of Jewish homes within their communities. This, they intoned, brings in its wake spiritual chaos and Jewish alienation.

The communal agenda for Israel is different from that of the Diaspora. At the Jerusalem Conference, the concern of the Israelis was to raise the Jewish birthrate. Evidence cited was that there were only two means of increasing the birthrate: "to enable those who want children but cannot produce them unaided to do so through modern medical means; to motivate couples of normal capacity to bear children to have more through an ideological vision or a new perception of their interests."[2] Many Israelis felt that greater mate-

---

[2] Rela Geffen Monson and Daniel J. Elazar, *Jerusalem Letter* #68, published by the Jerusalem Center for Public Affairs, Dec. 30, 1987.

rial incentives, such as larger dwellings, would help increase the birthrate.

For Israelis, the answer to demographic survival in the Diaspora was simple. Only increased *aliyah* would save Diaspora Jews from assimilation. World communal leaders saw this solution as naive and doctrinaire. Although *aliyah* as an ideal should be championed, they felt that it was not an honest way of dealing with the real demographic issues of intermarriage, delayed marriage, divorce, and childlessness that face world Jewish communities.

So where does that leave Hadassah? What role can we play in combating the demographic dilemma of the American Jewish Diaspora? The Education Department determined that Jewish demography would become the Education theme for 1988 to 1990. This would dovetail with the resolution passed at the Jerusalem Conference to do a demographic survey of world Jewish populations in 1990.

We invited Rela Geffen Monson, a noted sociologist and Dean at Gratz College, to our 1988 Midwinter Conference in New York to provide concrete suggestions for sustaining the Jewish family and background information on the state of world Jewish demography. She advised us that there are two routes to dealing with demographic issues: the ideological/rhetorical and the programmatic. "Rhetoric," she told us, "are ideas promulgated from the pulpit and in periodicals and in study guides, through radio, TV, and the videotaped lectures of inspiring teachers. It can be inherent in the symbols we choose, in the cover pictures and other illustrations for *Hadassah Magazine,* in the topics chosen to be dealt with at Jewish Education conferences and at regular meetings of groups and chapters."[3]

Rhetoric was perfect for the Jewish Education Department. Policy implementation (advocacy for flextime, parental leave, day care) and programmatics (outreach to singles, single parents, and dual-career families) would be left for other departments. We devoted our annual Jewish Education guide, *Bat Kol,* to Jewish demography and family. We planned seminars across the country on the changing Jewish family. Our biennial Brandeis Summer Institute dealt with Jewish family dynamics through the study of Jewish texts. "Outreach Through Intermarriage" and "The Jewish Family Through a Literary Looking Glass" were the topics addressed at the 74th National Convention in Chicago by various experts.

---

[3]Rela Geffen Monson, "The Vanishing Jews: Realities and Options," *Bat Kol,* Fall 1987, p. 16.

But our crowning achievement in the realm of rhetoric is this book, which we at Hadassah's Jewish Education Department had begun to think about as far back as 1986 in Florida. We wanted to emphasize the human aspect; we sought not just to present the dry sociological facts and extrapolate policy planning decisions from them, but to offer intimate essays of men and women within and outside the conventional family unit, to convey the essence of their lives and feelings. These pieces we interspersed with classical Jewish teachings in order to raise our readers' consciousness to the Jewish obligations of marriage and childbearing. At the same time we felt impelled to urge the Jewish community to reach out to those of us in alternative family lifestyles, because Judaism is for all Jews. We are all of us part of the whole.

Excessive emphasis on family can alienate people outside conventional family units. Holding ourselves up to an ideal of what the family once was is not always productive. Therefore, the history of the Jewish family, although not within the purview of this book, deserves some mention by way of background to the present struggles so vividly illustrated in the succeeding chapters.

The traditional family in biblical, talmudic, medieval, or even modern times was not nearly so perfect as we would like to believe. It was patriarchal and autocratic. Children had little to say about their own life choices. Every Jew was bound to the community from the time of his birth to his death, with little access to the gentile world. The extended family, the most vaunted feature of the traditional Jewish community unit, was perhaps overly glorified. The three-generational family living under one roof was far from ideal. The family instabilities we experience are also not a twentieth-century development. Emancipation in eighteenth-century Central Europe and nineteenth-century Eastern Europe gave rise to individualism, detachment from the Jewish community, and allegations of self-centered hedonistic lifestyles. *"Plus ça change, plus c'est la même chose."*

That is why we commissioned articles on all kinds of lifestyles and relationships, from single men and women to widows and gays, to remarrieds and intermarrieds. We combed the Jewish journals of the past decade, *Moment Magazine, Lilith,* the *Baltimore Jewish Times,* and a host of others, to better understand, to empathize, and to respond.

Jewish singles, we found, often don't like each other. William Novak, who wrote what has now become the classic "Are Good Jewish Men a Vanishing Breed?" in 1980, told us that only Jewish women were writing about their lives, their bitterness and grief at not being able to find good Jewish husbands. "If you could find Jewish men who would write and tell you why they're not marrying Jewish or not marrying at all, you will have achieved something important." David Greenwald and Rachi Shveel have provided some of the answers. They range from attraction to "outsiders," to rage at the dual standards of modern feminism, to avoidance of over-achieving Jews.

The Not-Quite-Married segment of the book presents arguments for and against alternatives to the traditional marriage relationship. Ellen Umansky writes of love and sharing as the most important elements in a good relationship; often these are not present in conventional marriages. Rabbis Shlomo Riskin and Harold Schul-weis, one a noted Orthodox rabbi and the other a revered Recon-structionist, address premarital sex from different vantage points. Yet both agree that there is no substitute for a Jewish home, sanctified by marriage, to engender commitment to self and to community.

Years ago most Jews married young, moved to suburbia, had children, and joined the Jewish community. Late marriage means postponement of this affiliation. "Good for the Jews, it can't be!" Classical Christianity regards love as pure, to the degree that it is uninvolved with sex; the new morality bespeaks just the opposite, that sex need have no connection to love. Judaism, however, views love and sex as inseparable. It is important for our young people to know this. Our hope is that we have presented this theme with sensitivity and understanding.

Marriage has been dealt with from a halakhic perspective, not through personal confidences. A good marriage nourishes the soul. But what makes a good marriage? The commitment and character of the individuals who share it, the values they profess, and the sacrifices they are willing to make for one another. A good marriage is a haven from the vicissitudes of modern living. And what makes a good *Jewish* marriage? How do we create a good Jewish home that, on the Jewish wedding day, is symbolized by the marriage canopy? This is effected through celebration and commitment; through Jewish ritual and ceremony; through education and example; and eventually through the presence, or at least the promise, of children. The home, even more than the synagogue, is the center for Jewish celebration.

But not everyone's home is based upon marriage. Some choose never to marry, others cannot find a suitable life partner, and still others have seen their marriage ravaged through death, divorce, or desertion. This is the subject of the next portion of the book, "Single

Again.'' Some of the most eloquent and poignant pieces are contained here. Gail Katz became a widow at 31, Rhoda Tagliacozzo at 45. Gail writes of her own private pain and what it means to raise four children alone, especially in the Orthodox world. Rhoda surveyed older widows and writes of their lives, which many of us will recognize as our own.

The divorced and deserted wife in Jewish law remains a thorny issue, which Blu Greenberg and Robert Gordis attempt to tackle humanely, without breaching the halakhah to which they are fervently committed. Others, like Sheila Peltz Weinberg and Shaye J.D. Cohen, describe their new lifestyles as single mother and father, respectively, while Barbara Kalin Bundt and Chaim I. Waxman look for strategies to integrate single-parent families within the Jewish community.

Yet many Jews don't stay ''single again'' forever. There are studies to prove that they remarry faster than other ethnic groups.[4] The book therefore addresses problems of blended families, long *bar* and *bat mitzvah* guest lists containing myriads of grandparents, relatives, and friends.

The greatest fear for the future of the American Jewish community stems not from divorce or late marriage but from the rising tide of intermarriage among young Jews. Egon Mayer, an expert on intermarriage, has found that assimilation is not necessarily a corollary to intermarriage. Frequently, the non-Jewish partner converts and the family practices a more committed Jewish way of life than do average American Jews. Even in nonconversionary marriages, the Jewish partner may be more tenacious of his or her ethnic traditions than is the non-Jewish spouse.

Harold Schulweis, in a searing essay on nonconversionary marriage, would disagree. ''For all the commonality between Christianity and Judaism, the hyphen between the cross and the star of David,'' he says, ''provides no sign of identity for the offspring of such a marriage. They are destined to live on the narrow edge of the hyphen, neither as Jews nor as Christians.'' Jonathan Sarna and Joyce Eisenberg write about coping with the *fait accompli* of intermarriage, while Rabbi Mark L. Winer warns parents that interdating leads to intermarriage. A fitting conclusion to the polemic on intermarriage should involve the voices of the progeny of an intermarriage. The intelligent views of the children of Rachel and the late Paul Cowan present just such an ending.

---

[4]*The Jewish Family: Myths & Reality,* edited by Steven M. Cohen and Paula E. Hyman (New York: Holmes and Meier, 1986), pp. 221–223.

There was resistance in some quarters of Hadassah to treating the relationship of gays and lesbians as part of Jewish marital status, but convincing arguments were made in favor of inclusion. There are, after all, Jewish gay and lesbian homes, whose residents have Jewish attitudes and needs. We felt it incumbent upon us to acknowledge those homes and hope that the component of the book that deals with this controversial lifestyle has been given a fair and balanced assessment.

Attention, too, must be paid to childless couples. Because of technological and sociocultural changes, birth control is more freely used now than ever before. Increasingly, American Jews are among those who choose to forego parenthood, in favor of improved career prospects. Some studies demonstrate that new parents tend to affiliate in the community and become more receptive to religious observance. Childless couples may therefore delay their integration into the community for years.[5] We chose an article that explored the pain of involuntary childlessness and followed that with one by a woman who eschewed childbearing. The obvious solution to childlessness is adoption, but the alternative of in vitro fertilization has been selected by some single women.

The epilogue of the book conveys the tension between conventional and nonconventional family units as the vital force in perpetuating Jewish life. Whereas one side views the traditional family as the most powerful agent in insuring Jewish survival, the other sees this as a biologically reductionist claim that ignores the crucial importance of the wider community and its contribution.

This tension, too, is not new. Nineteenth-century enlightenment, especially among the Jews of Eastern Europe, gave birth to two movements, socialism and Zionism. Socialists viewed the family as a narrow bourgeois creation and sought to restructure society into communes for the betterment of humankind. Zionism, which was also viewed by the socialists as bourgeois, battled for the soul of Eastern European Jewish youth by merging socialism with Zionism.[6] The socialist traditions, which the pioneers of the Second Aliyah brought with them from Russia to the land of Israel, resulted in the phenomenal success of the kibbutz. The kibbutz was originally and ideologically structured not along family lines, but rather as a commune. The New Left of the '60s once again sought to move

---

[5]Ibid.

[6]Socialist Zionism was one of many forms of Zionism, among them Religious, Revisionist, and Cultural Zionism.

in that direction. The *havurah* movement in the United States is an offshoot of this concept.

This book seeks to convey the interdependence of family and community. Both are crucial elements of Jewish living. Throughout this book our main thrust has been to bring the Jewish tradition to bear on all sorts of relationships in which Jews find themselves. Marriage, according to our tradition, is the finest institution in which men and women can structure their lives, and we at Hadassah are here to promote and encourage it. But in many cases it simply does not work. Here is where insight and outreach are needed to develop programs for action. We hope the pages of this book will inform and inspire critical reflection and thoughtful activity to that end. Thought and action are indeed essentials of our tradition.

Carol Diament, Ph.D.
July, 1989

Biographies of Contributors to Jewish Marital Status

MARTHA A. ACKELSBERG is professor of government at Smith College, Northampton, Massachusetts.

SHERRY H. BLUMBERG is a Ph.D. candidate in Jewish education at Hebrew Union College-Jewish Institute of Religion in Los Angeles and instructor of Jewish education at Hebrew Union College-Jewish Institute of Religion in New York. She is the author of *God the Eternal Challenge* (Alternatives in Religious Education, 1982), among other volumes. Since writing the article, she and her husband have adopted a son, Joshua.

RABBI EUGENE B. BOROWITZ, Ph.D., is professor of education and Jewish religious thought at the Hebrew Union College-Jewish Institute of Religion in New York. He is also Editor of *Sh'ma*, a journal of Jewish responsibility.

REUVEN P. BULKA, Ph.D., is rabbi of Congregation Machzikei Hadas in Ottawa, Canada. He is editor of the *Journal of Psychology and Judaism* and author of 17 books, including *The Jewish Pleasure Principle*.

BARBARA KALIN BUNDT, Ph.D., is manager of market research information for the Toro Company. A life member of Hadassah, she has four children, three of whom are in Israel.

MARGARET CHARYTAN is a Ph.D. candidate at the CUNY Graduate Center in Sociology. A former high school English teacher, she is married with two children.

SHAYE J.D. COHEN, Ph.D., is professor of Jewish history at the Jewish Theological Seminary and dean of its graduate school. He is author of *From the Maccabees to the Mishnah*. He is reportedly now quite good at knotting braids.

RUTH G. COLE, National Chair of the Jewish Education Department of Hadassah, is a professional counselor and teacher who lectures frequently on the Jewish family. She is vice president of Jewish Family Service of Bergen County, New Jersey.

PAUL COWAN, author of *An Orphan in History* (Doubleday, 1982), passed away September 26, 1988. RACHEL COWAN is a rabbinical student at Hebrew Union College-Jewish Institute of Religion. Paul and Rachel conducted workshops for interfaith couples and lectured widely.

CAROL DIAMENT, Ph.D., is the National Jewish Education Director of Hadassah. Editor of *Jewish Marital Status,* she is the first woman to have earned a doctorate in Jewish Studies at Yeshiva University. She has taught at Queens College and lectured throughout the United States on Eastern European Jewish culture, women, the Jewish family, and Zionism.

JOYCE EISENBERG is a freelance writer and editor based in Philadelphia.

LIZ GALST is a writer, filmmaker, and lover of Jewish cuisine. She lives in Somerville, Massachusetts.

BARBARA GOLDSTEIN is a member of the National Board of Hadassah, the Women's Zionist Organization of America, and a former National Jewish Education Chair.

ROBERT GORDIS, Ph.D., is editor of *Judaism,* a quarterly journal, and professor emeritus of Bible and the philosophies of religion at the Jewish Theological Seminary. He is the author of numerous books, including *Love and Sex: A Modern Jewish Perspective* (Farrar,

Straus & Giroux, 1978). Gordis served as chairman of the commission that prepared *Emet Ve'emunah,* the first official statement of the philosophy of the Conservative movement.

BLU GREENBERG lectures and writes about contemporary Jewish subjects. She is author of *On Women and Judaism* (Jewish Publication Society, 1982) and *How To Run a Traditional Jewish Household* (Simon & Schuster, 1985).

DAVID GREENWALD is a writer who lives in Hoboken, New Jersey.

SUSAN HANDELMAN is professor of English and Jewish Studies at University of Maryland, College Park.

GAIL KATZ teaches writing and literature at Edward R. Murrow High School in Brooklyn, New York, a communications arts school. She also teaches an English preparatory course at Kingsborough College in Brooklyn. She has taught folk dance in Temple sisterhoods and to senior citizens in East Flatbush.

RABBI NEAL KAUNFER is the director of the Principals' Center and education specialist, secondary education services at the Board of Jewish Education of Greater New York. He is one of the founders of the coalition for Alternatives in Jewish Education, Kibbutz Gezer-American Garin, the West Side Minyan, and the Lishma Adult Education Program and coffeehouse at Temple Ansche Chesed, Manhattan.

FRANCINE KLAGSBRUN is a writer whose articles have appeared in such national magazines as *The New York Times Book Review, Newsweek, Ms., Family Circle, McCalls,* and *Hadassah Magazine.* Two of her books are *Married People: Staying Together in the Age of Divorce* (Bantam, 1986) and *Voices of Wisdom: Jewish Ideals and Ethics for Everyday Living* (Pantheon, 1980).

DIANE LEVENBERG, Ph.D., is associate professor of English at Kutztown University in Pennsylvania. She is the author of *Out of the Desert,* a volume of poetry, and is a freelance journalist.

VICKI LINDNER has published articles on a wide variety of topics in magazines and is an author of both nonfiction and fiction books. She has been a recipient of the National Endowment of the Arts Award.

HASKEL LOOKSTEIN, Ph.D., is rabbi of Congregation Kehilath Jeshurun and principal of the Ramaz School in New York City. He is past president of the New York Board of Rabbis, vice president of the UJA Federation of New York, and vice chairman of the Coalition to Free Soviet Jews. He is the author of *Were We our Brothers' Keepers? The Public Response of American Jews to the Holocaust, 1938–1944* (Hartmore House, 1985).

RABBI JANET MARDER is assistant director, Pacific Southwest region, of the Union of American Hebrew Congregations.

RUTH MASON is a mother of two and a journalist living in New York City.

EGON MAYER, Ph.D., is author of *Love and Tradition: Marriage Between Jews and Christians* (Plenum, 1985) and *From Suburb to Shtetl.* He is professor of sociology at Brooklyn College and past president of the Association for the Social Scientific Study of Jewry.

WILLIAM NOVAK is the author of several books and has worked with Lee Iacocca, Tip O'Neill, Natan Sharansky, and Nancy Reagan on their memoirs.

VICKI ROSENSTREICH is a social worker and coordinator of the Jewish Family Life Education Program, an educational outreach program, at the Jewish Board of Family and Children's Services in New York City. She is married with three children.

HELEN RUBINSTEIN is a freelance trainer specializing in meeting management and communications and lives in New York City.

JONATHAN D. SARNA, Ph.D., is associate professor of American Jewish history at Hebrew Union College-Jewish Institute of Religion in Cincinnati and director of its Center for the Study of the American Jewish Experience. He is the editor of *The American Jewish Experience* (Holmes & Meier, 1986) and author of *JPS: The Americanization of Jewish Culture* (Jewish Publication Society, 1988).

SUSAN WEIDMAN SCHNEIDER is editor of *Lilith,* the nation's only independent Jewish women's magazine. She is the author of *Jewish and Female: Choices and Changes in Our Lives Today* (Simon &

Schuster, 1984) and *Intermarriage: The Challenge of Living with Differences* (The Free Press, Spring 1989).

HAROLD M. SCHULWEIS is rabbi of Valley Beth Shalom in Encino, California. He is the author of *Evil and the Morality of God* and of numerous articles published in such national Jewish magazines as *Sh'ma, Commentary, Baltimore Jewish Times,* and *Judaism.* He has been contributing editor of *Reconstructionist, Sh'ma,* and *Moment.* Recipient of the Akiba Award of the American Jewish Committee, among other awards, he is chairman and founder of the Foundation to Sustain the Righteous Christians.

ZEV SHANKEN is a writer and teacher who has recently developed an audio tape program for Women's League for Conservative Judaism and United Synagogue on "Jewish Parenting of the Adolescent."

RABBI DAN SHEVITZ has served since 1976 as Hillel director and Jewish chaplain at the Massachusetts Institute of Technology. He lives in Newton, Massachusetts, with his wife, Susan, and their two adopted children, Yehoshua Shimon and Noach Hanan.

RACHI SHVEEL (a pseudonym) is a writer and teacher who has been a Jewish activist, programming journalist, and *baal tefillah* (prayer leader) for many years.

RABBI DANIEL B. SYME is a vice president of the Union of American Hebrew Congregations. He oversees many of the Union's programs and committees, including the programs of outreach, education, television, and film production. For twelve years he authored a series in the UAHC's national newspaper, *The Jewish Home.* His latest book is *Finding God,* published by the UAHC.

RHODA TAGLIACOZZO is a writer who lives in New York. Her nonfiction has appeared in the *New York Times Sunday Magazine* and *New York Woman,* and she has had short stories in *McCall's, Ladies Home Journal, Cosmopolitan,* and other magazines. Her first novel was *Saving Graces* (St. Martin's Press, 1979).

LEORA TANENBAUM is an undergraduate at Brown University and an alumna of Ramaz High School in New York City. She is an assistant to the National Jewish Education Department of Hadassah.

YEROHAM TSURIEL (a pseudonym) is a teacher and freelance writer currently living in Jerusalem.

ELLEN M. UMANSKY, Ph.D., is associate professor of Bible and Hebrew at Emory University. She is the author of two books on Lily Montagu, founder and leader of the Liberal Jewish movement in England, and of numerous essays on women and Judaism, Jewish theology, and modern Jewish thought.

CHAIM I. WAXMAN, Ph.D., is associate professor at the department of sociology at Rutgers University. He is author of *America's Jews in Transition* (Temple University, 1983).

SHEILA PELTZ WEINBERG is rabbi of Congregation Beth Am Israel in Penn Valley, Pennsylvania.

MARK L. WINER is senior rabbi of the Jewish Community Center in White Plains, New York, and project director of the Research Task Force for the Future of Reform Judaism.

Jewish
∧ **Marital Status**

Jewish

∧ **Marital Status**

- ☑ Single
- ☐ Not quite married
- ☐ Married
- ☐ Single again
    - ☐ Widowed
    - ☐ Abandoned
    - ☐ Divorced
- ☐ Remarried
- ☐ Intermarried
- ☐ Gay or Lesbian
- ☐ Childless

1

Spinsters of the '80s

Helen Rubinstein

To be a single woman in America in the 1980s is no easy task. Especially if you read newspapers and magazines filled with articles on how you should be living, what you should be feeling . . . and most of all, what you should be doing to get and keep your man. On the one hand, we are told that if we give too much of ourselves to a man, we are repeating classically female masochistic tendencies. On the other hand, if we're really careful with our emotions, waiting for the right man, our expectations are too high. If we admit that we really would like to get married—yes, a career is good, but you can't hug a job—we're told that we're victims of our biological clocks. What about the woman who loves her work, the competition, and the fight for the top? She's headed for burnout.

Lots of people are getting awfully rich writing articles about us . . . the "Spinsters of the '80s." And suddenly it's "in" to be married. And married but good. But, are they serious when they write about Victoria Vice President, who suddenly sees the light, gives it all up for husband and baby, and moves herself, her family, and her thousands to the suburbs? Is she *really* going to replace those years of high-powered decision making with mother–child play circles and a machine full of suds? Victoria VP had the position, had the clout, has the man, has the kid, has the bucks, and now she's watching Phil Donahue? Where does that put all of us who actually have to work for a living and are single to boot? I'll tell you where it puts us:

searching frantically for that dream man who will get us out of this mess!

We didn't start out that way. Once upon a time, we were young soldiers in the ranks of the women's movement. Fighting our way through the thickets of relationships, we struggled to open doors for ourselves, we fought to pay restaurant bills, we overcame fear itself to ask a man out. And where did it get us? Today there are magazine articles with titles like "Romance Is In," "The New Dating Etiquette," "Holding Back to Keep the Romance in Your Relationship." And, insult of insults, an article in "*M*," a magazine for fashionable young men, which suggests that the marriageable woman is the one with a fast-paced, glamorous career to give up when the couple decides to have a child.

As is often the case in media reports of "changing lifestyles," the reality of life today, of singlehood today, gets completely lost. Where are these men who are supposed to be romancing us? How many of us have a glamorous career to give up? Who are we anyway?

A DAY IN THE LIFE

Rachel rises at 6:30 A.M., washes, dresses, and eats breakfast. She prepares the dry cleaning and her lunch, makes the bed, walks the dog. She drops off the dry cleaning on her way to work.

Rachel, a project director for an advertising agency in New York, is responsible for eight accounts. Two are due for presentation tomorrow, Friday. Her day is filled with meetings, telephone calls, and work on the two upcoming projects. She also makes several personal phone calls during the day. She calls the shades and shutters store to ask if her Levelors™ can be delivered on the weekend. Yes, they tell her, but only in three weeks and at an extra charge of $10.00. Frustrated, she okays the delivery. She calls the handyman to arrange for installation of the blinds.

Rachel makes several calls to arrange her weekend. She's got a date on Saturday night, so that takes care of that. She plans dinner with a friend for Friday night, lunch and a museum visit for Saturday afternoon. She decides to leave Sunday free for chores. She calls her mother to find out how her doctor's appointment went. It went well, but her mother asks that Rachel go with her to the doctor the next time, since it was hard for her to get there. Rachel suggests that she take a cab instead of public transportation and offers to pay for it. There is silence at the other end of the line. Her mother then invites her for Friday night dinner, telling her that her sister Beverly and her husband have other plans. "But Mom," she says, "today is Thursday and all my plans are made. I'd like to come, but why didn't you invite me sooner?" "Oh, you're going out?" Rachel's mother's voice rises slightly as she asks this question. "Yes, with Marilyn." "Oh well, I don't want you to spoil your plans for me."

Rachel ends the phone conversation, slightly angry, slightly guilty. She leaves the office at 6:00 P.M. and goes to work out for an hour. She stops off at the market, then goes home. She prepares her dinner and while it's cooking she walks the dog. Feeds the dog. Feeds herself. Washes the dishes. Pays some bills. Marilyn calls to cancel Friday night. Briefly, Rachel wonders whether she should call her mother. Rachel doesn't call her mother. At midnight, she goes to bed.

WHAT'S IMPORTANT?

Here is Rachel, still needing to legitimize her plans to her mother . . . dinner with a female friend doesn't quite make it.

But Rachel and all of us are no fools. We know what's important . . . meeting men and dating them. What we also know is that there are few things more painful than what's important . . . and seemingly unattainable. We're constantly being told "they're out there," if you know where to look, what to do, what to say, how to dress. . . . As usual, the onus of looking and finding is put on the woman . . . who is then accused of being aggressive if she does what she's expected to do.

Most of the personal ads placed in magazines are placed by Jewish women. We sometimes think that they are talking to themselves. "No, no," we're told. "There are lots of men out there. You're being too fussy." Or, "You're not trying." Well, we have tried and we're sure there are many men "out there," but the focus is on the women: It's *their* problem, it's *their* duty to "try." And we sometimes think that many men like it that way. It lets them abdicate responsibility in their own search for mates *and* it relieves them of any guilt they *may* be feeling about dating "outside." After all, it's those pushy Jewish women they can't stand, right?

How often have we heard, and said, that it is easier to talk to women than to men? That women can't communicate with their husbands? That men are often noncommunicative? Perhaps as children, men were so accepted for themselves, for just *being there*, that they didn't need to strive to please their mothers with clever verbal tricks or childish "repartee." Girls have to work harder to be noticed and appreciated . . . unless, of course, they're beautiful.

We often wonder, why can't Jewish mothers love their daughters as they do their sons? Or better yet, let go of both a bit more? Why can't their sons break away and form relationships with appropriate women?

Why are they so obvious in their retreat to the women who *least* remind them of their mothers? Or why do they insist on relating to Jewish women as though they *were* their mothers?

When we go to a French film, we always find ourselves relating better to the people on the screen than when we see an American film. The women look so much more real, so much more diverse. They have, dare we say it, an ethnic character. American films are the wet dreams of nice Jewish boys who now have the power to sell *their* fantasies of the WASP image that they crave.

John Updike wrote, in the novel *Couples*, "The Jews have inherited the middle classes . . . they're the only ones who want it." Our paraphrase is, "The Jews have inherited the WASP image ideal; they're the only ones who still want it." That's not completely accurate, we suppose, but we find it enraging that Jewish women are made to feel inferior and undesirable in films and the media, much of it controlled by Jewish men.

These are times of great ambiguity as far as sexual roles go, especially for people in their 30s—those caught between the dinosaurs of prefeminist times and the regressive "New Romance" of the younger generation. However, most women we know are aware of these ambivalences in themselves and their men and try to deal with them. Badly, sometimes, but nevertheless they are "there," present in the sexual arena. The most that men seem to require of themselves is that they allow themselves to be "caught." The community and the media, in their intense pressure on women, acquiesce.

AFTERWORD

What follows is part of a letter to the editor of a congregational newsletter somewhere in Massachusetts.

> Dear Editor,
>   Singles are a sad and serious dilemma for Jews today, both individually and collectively, which contributes to the staggering statistics pertaining to the high rate of intermarriage, the low birth rate, and non-affiliation with Jewish institutions. . . .

Sad to say, this letter reflects much of the thinking about the unmarried by the general Jewish community. And if there is a "problem," it is in this attitude.

Singles are seen by the Jewish community as deviant. As needing to be fixed . . . or fixed up. This feeling sometimes comes about as a result of the best intentions. Seeing bleak demographic figures before their eyes, leaders in the community want to help. We Jews have a tendency, and it has served us well, to look to our communal institutions for all kinds of help. But can the community help? Is there anything to help? Isn't the issue really dignity of choice? Haven't Rachel and others like us been deprived of our full adult status, not only in the overt way presented above, but in many more subtle ways?

Whether or not a single woman wishes to marry is irrelevant to the fact that, as an autonomous woman, she should be allowed the dignity accorded to all adults.

We're sorry that we can't come up with a wish list for the community. Frankly, we wish "the community" would get off our backs. Who knows? Maybe what's needed is a slick PR campaign. Sorry.

2

Are Good Jewish Men a Vanishing Breed?

William Novak

Suzanne, a close friend of my wife, has just turned thirty. She's smart, funny, friendly, generous—and very attractive. Suzanne enjoys a fine career as a social worker and heads a major department at a Jewish communal agency. Last year she was involved briefly with a lawyer who worked for consumer rights, but they decided to break it off when it was clear to both of them that the relationship was just not working out. This year Suzanne has no social life to speak of. "I'm not talking about meeting my prince," she jokes. "I can't even get a date with a guy I *wouldn't* go out with!"

Suzanne's complaint is hardly unique. Everywhere I look these days, I see terrific young women who are, as it's called, "looking." Sometimes I talk to these women and, perhaps because I'm married, and certainly because I'm inquisitive, they tell me things I didn't hear when I was single. Most of them, I find, describe variations on a single theme: There just don't seem to be many good, available men around with whom to have a relationship.

Of course, not all single women are interested in meeting men, and not all single women find it difficult to do so. But many, many women are in this situation, and the man shortage is doing strange things to them. It undermines their self-confidence, affects their emotional stability, and, worst of all, it causes them to blame themselves for a situation that is mostly beyond their control.

"Is there something wrong with me?" many of these women wonder privately. "After all, if I really am attractive and appealing and intelligent, then why am I not meeting anybody? It doesn't make sense that all the good men are married or gay. Maybe I'm doing something wrong. Maybe my standards are too high. Or maybe, as my mother keeps telling me, I'm just not doing enough to meet men."

So when I first started hearing these complaints from women I knew, I didn't pay too much attention and dismissed them as the self-indulgent laments of women who would rather be married than single. But as the stories began to pile up, and as I was able, temporarily, to set aside my traditional male biases, a different picture emerged. With few exceptions, the women who were telling me these stories were impressive and desirable. By no stretch of the imagination could they be considered "losers"—although, in truth, some were beginning to feel this way. Could it be that what they were telling me was objectively true? And, if it was, why was nobody else talking about it?

I decided to check with my male friends who were single, the counterparts to all these women, and the first thing I discovered is that I didn't have very many. This got me to wondering if the women weren't more right than I realized. The men I know who aren't gay or married tend to be single only in the literal sense of the word: many are in a solid relationship with a woman, while the rest have no trouble meeting good, available women—even if they haven't yet found the right one.

The women, I was starting to understand, were describing a real situation that has generally gone unrecognized in our society, even though it's a terribly important fact in the lives of millions of Americans. As Suzanne likes to put it, there is an elephant in the room and nobody is talking about it.

Well, not nobody, exactly. Whenever I get into one of these discussions with single women, the first thing that becomes clear is that the elephant is actually talked about all the time and in great detail. "You talk about it with very close friends and you get each other depressed," says Ellen, 29, a graduate student in history. "The idea that you might not have it someday is terrifying, a bit like thinking about death."

When these women are not laughing or getting depressed, they try to understand how things got this way, how the elephant ended up in the room in the first place. While they usually don't come up with satisfying answers, these discussions do serve an important purpose. They reinforce the idea that there really *is* an elephant in the room, even if the rest of the world is convinced that there isn't.

I think it's important that somebody who isn't a single woman comes forward to testify that he, too, can make out the bloated form of a large, grey, four-legged mammal. I realize that this testimony may be depressing to those women who still hold out the hope that what they think they are seeing is a mirage made out of their own unhappiness. On the other hand, perhaps this statement can be useful. "I really hope you write about this," one woman told me, "so I can send it to my mother with a note saying, 'See, it isn't just *me*.' "

I'm also naive enough to believe that talking about the elephant might also benefit men. Strictly speaking, this article is not about men, but about women's perceptions of men. And so in an objective sense, what I report about men is unfair to them, as they have no chance to reply to the women, and worse, they have no opportunity to emerge here as individuals. So this does not represent the whole story, but merely one aspect of it.

How can I risk being unfair to men? While part of me still believes that I'm just one more footsoldier slogging it out in the endless war between the sexes, and that my saying these things somehow constitutes an act of extreme disloyalty to my side, I also know that at this point in my life my chief concern is no longer with the members of my own sex, but rather my age group—my generation. And a lot of women in my generation are getting a raw deal.

Let me spell out the problem in more detail: Among educated people now in their late twenties or in their thirties, there are many who are single and who would prefer to be married. Within this group, women are at a significant disadvantage in two major respects.

The first part of the problem has to do with numbers, which are startling. Very simply, roughly 20 percent of all young Jewish women are not going to marry a Jewish man because there just isn't one available.

Here's why: First, in the 20–34 age bracket, there are 92 Jewish males for every 100 Jewish females. That's just an 8 percent difference, but then we have to take account of the intermarriage statistics. Out of every 92 male Jews who marry, roughly 24 are going to marry "out," a choice that only 12 out of every 100 Jewish women will make. And that reduces the number of Jewish males who are available as husbands from 92 to 68, as against 88 Jewish women who are available as wives. Sixty-eight men, 88 women, or 20 women who are a kind of remainder—20 out of every 100.

These numbers are rough estimates. Maybe they're off; maybe the figure is not 20 percent, but only 15 percent. Still, there is a very large group of Jewish women who are, for all practical purposes, stuck. They could intermarry, of course, but they don't. It's not clear why they don't. Perhaps they agree with my friend who says, "I sometimes think I could marry a Buddhist, if he were a genuinely nice person, but that's only a passing thought. I'm so socialized against marrying somebody who isn't Jewish that I really can't take my desperate thought seriously. I refuse to imagine *Shabbat* as a solo affair, or one that my sweet Buddhist will indulge me."

There are, in short, not enough men to go around. When all the sorting is done, some women are going to be left over, and they will most likely blame themselves, because nobody has bothered to tell them the harsh statistical truth.

Under these trying circumstances, you might expect that Jewish women would be so desperate that they'd settle for just anybody. But they don't, and won't. And that's the heart of the story, the part that doesn't show up in the charts and the tables. That's the part that has to do with women's expectations, with the shortage not of men but of *mentschen*. The men who *are* around, if they're not married, gay, or otherwise unavailable, are often disappointing as people. However successful they may be in their working lives, they seem (to these women, at least) to be lacking in the personal realm. Their range of interests is often narrow; more important, there seems to be something missing. Their emotional resources, their ability to enter into a committed relationship—these all seem underdeveloped. What's missing, in short, is a set of qualities that women find so readily in other women.

At this point I can hear some readers muttering that the scapegoat—or the criminal, depending upon one's point of view—is the women's movement. Both sides are right; the women's movement *is* at the heart of this new situation. Now that some of the dust has settled, we can pause for a moment to consider the effects of one of the fastest, most sweeping revolutions in modern history. The women's movement has achieved many important gains, but it must be pointed out that these gains have not come free of cost. There has been a stiff price to pay and a series of hidden injuries to both men and women that have yet to be acknowledged. And the current situation of single women in America—the very people who have also benefited the most from the women's movement—is perhaps the most obvious casualty.

It would be difficult to exaggerate the tremendous effects of feminism during the 1970s, even—or perhaps especially—on those women who have never seen themselves as "members" of the movement, but rather as fellow-travelers, a phenomenon which *Ms.* magazine has called the "I'm not a feminist—*but*" syndrome.

A decade ago, when feminism moved from rhetoric to real

action, one of its chief goals was to promote a kind of remedial effort among women. If men had good jobs, high salaries, positions of power, political clout, sexual freedom, the seemingly interesting life, then the suitable response was for women to pursue these goals in the same way that men did: by insisting on their rights, by attending professional and graduate schools, by learning to be ambitious and aggressive, by working hard, and all the rest. "All the rest," it turns out, was less important than the first part of the injunction, and it included such diverse tactics as participating more in the national culture, and in general paying more attention to the external world.

At the same time, however, and to its credit, feminism did not find it necessary to break the connection of women to their own *internal* worlds of who they were and how they felt. On the contrary: The women's movement built upon that base and actually strengthened the internal worlds of many women through a variety of means. These included consciousness-raising groups, as well as psychotherapy, the reading and writing of feminist literature, the development of feminist history, music, art, cinema, and theater, the keeping of journals, the general value placed on personal sharing, and the broad, common concerns of sisterhood—and above all, the accurate perception that political change arises directly out of the heartfelt truth of individual, personal experience. The women's movement, in other words, was, among other things, a political legitimization of what women always knew about themselves and each other: that despite their denigrated positions in the external world, they possessed large and important internal resources that could be the basis for a strong and powerful movement.

It was taken for granted, then, that in order to catch up to men, women had to work on these two different fronts: external and internal. But while this was going on, it turns out that there was very little to catch up *to*. While feminism was giving women higher expectations about themselves, nothing of the sort was taking place among men. So instead of narrowing the gap between men and women, the movement inadvertently widened it. Or, as Suzanne explains: "By now women have mastered the so-called masculine skills of how to succeed in a profession. Well, it turns out that any idiot can learn how to achieve, but it is apparently less easy for men to learn how to love and how to be emotionally supportive—especially if they're not even trying!" It is somewhat of an overstatement, but it is as though millions of women had trained earnestly for a race that most men never took seriously. Having won easily, the women now stand around the finish line, awkward and disappointed, looking in vain for suitable men to run not against—but *with*. But the men are nowhere in sight.

Some men, of course, *have* changed as a result of feminism, but this occurs most often by their being in an intimate relationship with a woman. And unless that relationship ends, those men are unavailable anyway. And there you have the problem in a nutshell. What has happened, then, to the men? Some really *are* gay, of course. Many women believe that there are more gay men than gay women, but there are no reliable statistics on the subject. It is particularly painful for single women to discover that gay men exist in larger numbers than they ever imagined—especially in New York. And although this has become a cultural stereotype, women often find that these gay men seem to be among the most talented, most sensitive, and most emotionally responsive men they have ever met. Another large group of men got married during the 1970s—often to younger women. And many women believe that this group includes some of the more emotionally stable and secure men, but unless they divorce, they remain elusive.

While women these days have various complaints about men, calling them self-centered, narcissistic, indecisive, afraid of making commitments, and all the rest, the word "emotional" invariably turns up during the first thirty seconds. The most common complaint is that a man is "emotionally immature," and from there the responses go out along a spectrum: emotionally underdeveloped, emotionally retarded, emotionally crippled—all the way to "emotional eunuch." Ironically, many women have begun psychotherapy or psychoanalysis because they have assumed that their not meeting men was their own fault—and in some cases, of course, they were right. But as a result, these women generally emerge from therapy or analysis with deeper insights into their emotional lives. And that, in turn, raises their standards when it comes to the men they are meeting, which makes the whole process even more difficult.

"You meet a 35-year-old man," Judy asserts, "and you assume you're meeting a man. But very often it's just an adult body with a little boy hiding inside it, saying 'me, me, me.' He doesn't know who he is, and he doesn't know what he wants. Can you imagine what it's like trying to give your love to such a man? And that's what really hurts: Maybe I'm wrong, but I think of myself as somebody with a lot of love to give, somebody who could really be good at loving—and I can't find anybody to give it to. I feel like I'm being wasted."

And Lois adds, "I hate stereotypes, but I can't stop feeling that maybe the stuff about the Jewish mother is right. *So* many of the men I meet are impossibly spoiled, and their success in their careers simply confirms what they've been taught to believe about themselves—that they are prizes. I know that somewhere under those layers of arrogance, there must be some fears, some areas of softness, the things that make a person human. Why is it so damned hard to get to them? I don't want to marry a career; I want to marry a person."

Are non-Jews any different? I ask. "Yes and no. They don't seem nearly as achievement-oriented, they don't seem to be constantly trying to prove something or to satisfy somebody else's expectations of them. But the differences turn out to be superficial. It just takes longer to find out that they're as shallow and as boring as everybody else."

Lois isn't an observant Jew, nor is she especially involved in Jewish life. For those of my friends who are, the problems are still further compounded. One single woman, active in a *havurah,* observes that she and her friends "all know the same nine bachelors." Another, dead serious, tells me that every night she says the *Shema*—and then adds a prayer that men will change. The special problems of those for whom the holidays matter, for whom the substance of Jewish life is a major concern, are very real. For them, the harrowing question is whether they are going to have to trade off, to sacrifice their beliefs and their concerns in order to marry. They attend the weddings of their friends—painful enough as it is—and then are subjected to the unintended cruelty of the well-wishers who greet them with, "*Im yirtzeh ha-Shem*—God willing—soon by you!" Often, these are women who have been prepared ever since birth for marriage and for having children. Sometimes deeply affected by the women's movement, sometimes untouched by it, they still see themselves as stunted; without marriage, and with the prospect that they may never marry beginning to haunt them, they live on the edge of panic. There's not much else they can do, as one said to me, "I want to meet a good man, but I'm not about to jump under the *huppah* with just anyone."

What these various complaints boil down to is that women today believe that a relationship can no longer get by on the traditional specialization, with men required to carry all the financial burdens of the relationship while women take responsibility for the emotional side. It's as simple as that.

When I started really listening to the complaints of single women, I kept hearing comments like these:

"The men I meet are selfish; they're princes. They want everything to revolve around them. They want you to be attractive, interesting, and entertaining, but if *you* have problems, they don't want to hear them."

"Men just want to be entertained. They want their egos bolstered. They want to take rather than to give. I'm reaching out and they're not there."

At this point I want to make clear that, surprising as it may seem in light of these comments, most of them are made without anger. All the women I spoke with were eager to be proved wrong in their perceptions of men. There was nothing ideological in their complaints about the opposite sex. True, I found plenty of disappointment and sadness and a certain amount of resignation. But conspicuously absent was the offensive man-hating that was so common five and ten years ago—the "men are shmucks" point of view.

"You should really talk to men," I was repeatedly told, but very few women could think of any I should talk to. One woman who was not interviewed heard about the article and called me to insist that I talk to her friend, this wonderful divorce lawyer with his own views on the matter. I tracked him down: A Harvard man in his mid-forties, married with a family, clearly thoughtful and sensitive, who proceeded to tell me about his clients. His own views coincided with everything else I was hearing, but his different perspective was useful. "The women I see are together and attractive," he told me, "while the men are into a different scene every week. Men are on a wholesale retreat from intimacy. Women are always asking me if I know anyone. If you find a man who's willing to talk about his feelings and his problems, and if he's also willing to listen, he'll be adored by women—and quickly snapped up."

He continued: "Riding into town each morning on the train, there are pockets of working men and women, and I sometimes listen to their conversation. The women talk about their lives, or other people, or families, relationships, personal experiences— things with emotional content. Men sometimes talk about their work, and occasionally about women, but most often they're talking about the Red Sox, the Patriots, the Bruins, or whatever team is currently breaking their hearts."

These days, too, nobody seems to know what the rules are anymore. Take the myth of initiating women. While it's true that some women are far more aggressive in the sexual marketplace than they used to be, in the overwhelming majority of cases it is still the man who makes the first phone call, who initiates the social overture. For most women, it's downright difficult to take the first step in social intercourse with men. The men, meanwhile, knowing that the women at least *have* this new option, and believing what they are told—that women are using it—have in many cases abdicated their traditional roles of initiation without adopting any new postures, thereby leading to an uncomfortable vacuum, a lack of momentum and energy. Women are afraid to call men, afraid to look foolish or needy. And men, for their part, are afraid of being rejected, or increasingly, of being *intimidated* by the New Woman they've heard so much about.

Like many women these days, Barbara, a 32-year-old teacher, is badgered by a mother who is convinced that her daughter isn't doing enough to meet men, that she isn't taking advantage of every conceivable opportunity. "Join the ACLU," Barbara's mother tells her every three weeks. "Once, thirty-five years ago," Barbara told me, "a man asked my mother to marry him. She turned him down. 'In that case,' he told her, 'I know somebody you'd like.' And that turned out to be my father. How would you like to grow up with that story?"

One of Barbara's mother's rules—and it isn't just Barbara's mother who says this—is that if you're a single woman, and a man asks you to go out, and you already have plans with another woman, you cancel those plans without a second thought. Today, most women will have none of that, although this doesn't mean they're not conflicted. "A guy called me a few weeks back," says Barbara, "and I told him I was busy Thursday night, having dinner with my roommate from college. And he wouldn't believe me. '*Seriously?*' he asked. 'Then change your plans.' Of course I didn't, but now I'm getting lonely and apprehensive about the future, and there's always that nagging thought that perhaps my mother was right."

One of the few bright spots in this whole picture, at least from the women's point of view, is that a few more men are now appearing on the scene as a result of divorce, or, as Suzanne calls it, "recycling." While most women are understandably cautious about recently divorced men, who often turn out to be totally uninterested in a stable, serious relationship, those who have been on their own for a couple of years or more are judged innocent until proven guilty. "You assume they've learned something from the trauma they went through," says Tina.

"When I'm at the beach," Carol says, "I keep an eye out for young children—accompanied by men who seem slightly lost." Carol has had bad experiences with newly divorced men, but she also feels that she doesn't have the luxury of waiting for the men to be ready to enter a new commitment; by that time they are invariably involved with somebody else. "Really," she says, "it's worse than looking for an apartment in Manhattan, where people read the obituaries to get a head start on the competition. Given how bad things are, you have to wonder if it isn't fair to intervene slowly in a bad marriage, once you know they're going to break up anyway."

But by and large it's a bleak picture for many women with a lot of love to give and nowhere to give it. While they're waiting for a solution to the problem, they give each other advice: "Be open to everything but don't appear to be looking too hard." "You've got to initiate; don't let a potential prospect get away. If he doesn't like the fact that you called him, you don't want him anyway." And "have a sense of humor about it all and cultivate your own life; don't be too down on yourself about something you can't control."

A cynic might point out that the solution may be for women to lower their expectations, to give up on the idea that men are going to turn up who will change their lives. The best response to that comes from Diane White, a columnist for the *Boston Globe,* who wrote: "We persist because we are women. We are romantic. We want to fall in love. We want to get married. We are embarrassed to admit these things, but they're true. We are supposed to want to be independent and self-sufficient and successful. We want all these things and we want a man, too. It's the heartbreak of heterosexuality."

It is true, of course, that men also have their problems, their anxieties, and their complaints around this issue. Certainly it does not take a woman to say, as one told me recently, "Can you imagine what it's like to light the *Shabbat* candles every Friday night and then, when you turn around, to see that there's nobody there with you?" The loneliness and vulnerability of single men is an important story, but it's not this story. *This* story is about women who are looking for men—and for *mentschlikhkeit,* both of which they find in short supply.

Nor is this the whole story. Some women, undoubtedly, choose to blame the shortage and the inadequacies of men rather than facing their own problems. Some women who think they want to get married are actually ambivalent in ways they don't recognize. And some women set such impossibly high standards that no man has a chance to live up to them. There are, in short, many individual exceptions to the general picture I have described here. But even when all these exceptions are accounted for and deducted from the total, there is still a major problem left.

Perhaps there are large numbers of Jewish women who prefer the single life, or who are terrified by the prospects of marriage. I did not find them, and I suspect that they do not exist in such large numbers as the media would have us believe. I found, instead, a profound moral yearning, a strong fear of being passed over, a fervent commitment to intimacy—and to family. And I found all of these emotions expressed more in sorrow than in anger, and, generally, with hope rather than resignation.

Given the numbers of people involved, and their quality, we're not talking here about a private problem. It would be painful enough if that were so. But some of the best young people that the Jewish community has produced are not getting married—although they very much want to. They feel strong pressures against intermarriage, but they also don't want to end up alone. They want, many of them, to bear children, and they watch the passing years with growing fear that they may not. What happens to these women—or what fails to happen—will matter significantly, not only to their own lives, but to the future of American Judaism.

POSTSCRIPT

While I certainly hoped that this article would find an audience when it appeared in the January 1980 issue of Moment, *nothing prepared me for the flood of attention and publicity that soon followed—and lasted for five years.*

Most of the women (and a few of the men) who contacted me said that I had "touched a nerve"—and almost everybody used that phrase. Apparently, I had openly stated what women often discussed among themselves, but—back in 1980, at least—had seldom been articulated in print, and certainly not by a male writer.

A number of women, both younger and older than the people I wrote about, let me know that the problems I described were all too familiar in their lives, too. And some readers, women as well as men, pointed out that my treatment of the subject was too one-sided and that I had said far too little about the legitimate grievances and frustrations of single men.

I resolved to address these and other shortcomings in a book that grew out of the Moment *article and was published three years later as* The Great American Man Shortage and Other Roadblocks to Romance. *But when I started looking for men to interview in order to represent their side of the story, I found only a handful who could speak intelligently on this topic. This, of course, was exactly what the women had complained about, although I had hoped they were exaggerating. In time, however, I realized that the men, too, had legitimate grievances, even if they couldn't always say exactly what those were.*

Here, unfairly reduced to a single paragraph, are the major complaints of the men: First, that although the statistics favor the men, once you pass the age of thirty, it becomes increasingly difficult to meet women in a dignified environment. Second, that single men feel guilty until proven innocent, as women seem to blame them for every sin that men have committed against women in the past fifty years. Third, that women tend to judge men by what jobs they hold and how much money they make, rather than by their more human qualities. Fourth, that women who are otherwise assertive are strangely and disappointingly passive when it comes to love and romance. And finally, that the stereotype of the Jewish American Princess, ugly though it be, is often rooted in reality.

In short, the whole question is more complex than I initially realized. Today, nine years later, the situation has only grown worse. Each year, thousands of Jewish women who had expected, among other achievements, to raise families of their own are becoming too old to have children. Here and there I see signs of hope, as the organized Jewish community, and a handful of private activists, have begun to initiate dating services, singles programs, and other responses to a difficult and depressing situation. But I'm afraid this has been both too little and too late.

3

Jewish, Single, and Male

David Greenwald

I am a single Jewish male who has never had a romantic involve-ment with a Jewish woman. In fact, I've had very few Jewish friends, male or female, since high school. While this hasn't been a conscious decision on my part, I'll readily admit there may be subconscious motives involved. The truth is that this avoidance probably reflects some of the deeply abiding ambivalences I feel toward my faith. It is perhaps paradoxical that, in recent years, while I've been wrestling with elusive questions concerning the significance of my Jewish identity, I've rarely, if ever, considered the reasons for my seeming alienation from my Jewish peers—particularly female. I'm now forcing myself to confront this issue in responding to an article sent to me by Hadassah's Education Department, entitled "Spinsters of the '80s," written by a single Jewish woman. I'm not interested in engaging in a polemic with the author, Helen Rubinstein, nor am I interested in being a spokesman for single Jewish men. I simply want to present the facts of my dilemma and, perhaps in doing so, come to some understanding of why I feel as I do.

This exercise is particularly timely for me because I've begun to feel domestic stirrings in the past year or so; and for reasons only dimly understood by me, aside from the obvious one of wanting to please my parents whom I love and respect, it's somehow important that my children be raised as Jews. This means either that I have to marry a Jewish woman or find a non-Jewish woman willing to convert. The first option would probably be the more likely one.

So I've been more receptive to the inevitable offers from family members and friends of the family to "fix me up with a nice Jewish girl." These ventures, although not disastrous, have not been particularly successful. It hasn't been that any of the women were unappealing; most were. It was just that they were so . . . so familiar to me.

I grew up in a Westchester community that comprised several ethnic groups including Jews; however, all but a very few of my classmates were Jewish. I was in the accelerated and AP classes throughout junior and senior high school, seeing the same faces every term. The kids I went to school with were not merely college-bound; they aimed directly toward the elite liberal arts institutions. They were driven and narrowly achievement-oriented, for whom anything less than an "A" was an embarrassment, and anything less than 1300 on the SATs was reason for panic. I shared in this hysteria—getting cramps before tests, anxiously comparing grades with classmates after the corrected tests were distributed, taking the college boards four times until I was satisfied with the results—although I was always in the lower echelon of my classes. I still remember the shame I felt in my junior year of being exiled from my math and science classmates, demoted to the regular senior, college-prep classes because I had slipped academically during my sophomore year.

Needless to say, when I arrived at college, I gravitated toward friends who had nothing much in common with the ones I had in high school; none was Jewish, none upper middle class suburbanites, and none obsessive about grade point averages. We formed a group of frustrated writers and musicians, reluctantly and infrequently attending classes, while spending a good part of our time reassuring ourselves over beers in local bars and getting high in dorm rooms, bawling our favorite songs. I felt liberated. I had left high school and the values and attitudes of my former classmates far behind.

In a sense, I've been avoiding those people ever since. Although I attended a school that more than lived up to their inflated standards, I've never been particularly success-oriented. And I certainly don't fall into the category of "professional." Only in the past year or so have I discovered any real ambition. I don't believe I've been a source of embarrassment to my parents, but they've probably had to do a little equivocating when asked by friends and acquaintances what I was up to. I suppose I'm an anomaly by middle-class Jewish standards, often feeling compelled to justify my existence. I've certainly never felt comfortable with my Jewish peers.

Don't get me wrong. I'm not claiming alienation from the
Jewish community in any way. I've had a Hebrew high school
education, though it was more a social than an educational experience. And I've been to Israel several times, each time making a
semi-successful attempt to learn the language—twice on *ulpanim.* I
was even engaged to a kibbutznik when I was in my early twenties,
considering at one point the possibility of making *aliyah.* I participate with my family in Jewish holiday rituals— *seders,* high holy
day services, and sporadic visits to *shul* on other occasions. And as
I mentioned, I'm serious about making sure my children grow up in
a Jewish household.

At the same time, I harbor more than a few doubts about the
meaning of my Jewish identity. I find myself becoming increasingly
disenchanted with Israel's political policies—its intransigence concerning the Palestinian question and the West Bank settlements. I
was last there when Israel invaded Lebanon in 1982, and I felt
obliged to leave, soon after, out of disgust; I have little desire to
return now. On a more personal level, I'm confused about God's
relevance to Judaism. I really don't know any Jews who consider a
belief in God's existence to be a necessary precondition to being
Jewish. For me and many other Jews, the rituals and ceremonies are
mere formalities, lacking in substance because they're not imbued
with true religious significance; God is not a presence. Is a cultural
tradition really enough to give them meaning? Naturally, I'm not
including the Orthodox faith in this description, but for me Orthodox
Judaism with its sexism and dogmatism has never really been an
option. I'm proud to be Jewish, to be part of a marvelous heritage,
but apart from a fortuitous birth, I can't really point to anything that
gives me a firm Jewish identity.

After several days of self-examination, I find that my feelings
about Jewish women are just as perplexing to me. In all honesty, I'm
not sexually attracted to them. In my experience, and I suspect this
is true for most men, whether or not they want to admit it, sexual
interest has to be present at the outset of any potential romantic
involvement, especially for younger men. Obviously, a lot of other
factors are involved, but if that sexual excitement doesn't exist, most
men won't be encouraged to look any further. That's not to say that
the whole matter is reduced to physical appearance—a sense of
humor, a lively intelligence, or more intangible sensual qualities
may ignite desire, as may many other things, of course.

The problem isn't that Jewish women lack any of these traits—
on the contrary, they may be found in abundance—but their presence might often be overlooked by Jewish men because of the

familiarity I alluded to. While it doesn't breed contempt, I think it's responsible for a certain lack of interest on our part.

Women are perhaps more sophisticated in their approach to relationships. They may tend to examine the whole package and even initially evaluate a man's potential as a mate, while men are mired in the sexual element. Only when they've established the fact that there is a possible sexual compatibility do they look further.

Jewish males and females are thrown together at an early age, and they never seem to escape each other. They're in the same classes in public school; they attend Hebrew and parochial schools together. They see each other at beach clubs and country clubs, summer camps and synagogue social functions, the Poconos and the Catskills. And in college they meet at Hillel-sponsored events. While they get to know each other quite well, something important is sacrificed—a certain air of mystery, of otherness that's necessary to stimulate romance. More often than not, I feel a brotherly affection for the Jewish women I meet, which excludes other emotions. They're just not exotic in any way.

Because of this enforced proximity between Jewish males and females throughout youth and young adulthood, there seems to be a certain underlying desperation when singles get together at Jewish social functions. I think it's the consequence of the vain effort being made to kindle sexual interest and of a desire to escape the feeling of being pressured to fulfill a duty. Spontaneity is stifled; romance cannot blossom when one's romantic options are so circumscribed. Rebellion is an obvious response.

I don't want to sound smug; I certainly don't pretend to have any answers. My confusion, though not nearly as poignant because I don't live with it every day, rivals that of the young single women in this country looking for available men with whom to have a relationship. The demographics are especially grim for Jewish women. According to William Novak (see Chapter 2), ". . . roughly 20 percent of all young Jewish women are not going to marry a Jewish man because there just isn't one available." My attempt to address the issue doesn't begin to do justice to the dimensions of this tragedy. And it is a tragedy when twenty of every one hundred Jewish women, desiring marriage, with much to offer a potential partner, will remain alone.

It's this frustration that leads to the understandable bitterness and anger of a Helen Rubinstein, who lashes out at Jewish mothers responsible for producing sons who feel compelled to "retreat to the women who *least* remind them of their mother"; the Jewish, male-controlled media that make Jewish women feel "inferior and undesirable in films and the media"; and the Jewish community, which places an insupportable burden on single Jewish women (as well as men) by labeling them deviants and depriving them of "full adult status"; as well as the women's movement, which created unreal expectations for women, particularly Jewish women who were in the forefront of the movement, only to leave these women vulnerable to the depredations of the retrogressive '80s.

I felt sadness when I read her article, sadness because I empathize and because I am helpless—I have no response. I realize how acute the problem is for Jewish women because of their standards. They demand men who are successful in their work lives and successful as human beings—interesting, intelligent, and emotionally resourceful enough to be able to enter confidently into a committed relationship. Straight single men who fit this description seem to be at a premium these days. These women deserve a better fate.

4

In the Desert

Rachi Shveel

It is characteristic of the spiritual obtuseness of contemporary feminism that it would have popularized so fatuous a slogan as "A woman without a man is . . . like a fish without a bicycle"—or whatever such inanity made the rounds of tee shirts not long ago. My own Jewish heritage teaches us something very different: that a woman without a husband is not a whole or fulfilled person, and that a man without a wife—I, for example—is equally incomplete, or even more so.

As I seek my promised land—does not the Talmud advise calling your wife your home? (perhaps, *l'havdil,* as God is called "The Place"?)—I am mindful of all the desert's traps: anxiety and fear, lack of faith, and the temptations of singleness. Feminism's special contribution to this perilous journey has been that of the *meraglim* (spies) of the Exodus: to spread fear and heighten anxiety; to demoralize us—men and women both—and undermine our belief in ourselves and in each other.

The result, at least for me, has been precisely a prolonging of Exile/*galut*—not only of singleness but of a sense of spiritual out-of-placeness: of feeling not at home in the world. I still have not entered the land—still not taken a wife—and so my body wanders the desert while my soul necessarily regresses into Egypt-space, or is it the reverse? Feminism, for me—and I don't mean, here, the need some pious Jewish women feel for new avenues of Divine service—has been a nearly unremitting source of *tzuris*—of *mitzrayim/*

Egypt—in the spiritual (midrashic) sense of constriction and enslavement.

That experience of straitening—of near-asphyxiation—is produced in me by Jewish women's unexamined contradictions and oppressive expectations of men; by feminism's loveless values and cultivation of anger; by its inability to trust or to be worthy of trust. Like our Egyptian taskmasters, feminists, themselves bitter, have embittered our lives—and they may have succeeded, as our oppressors of old sought to, in weakening our marriages and our readiness *to* marry, and in limiting our child-rearing.

It was not always such—or it did not always seem that it would be. The promise of feminism, wrote Susan Milligan in a severely critical article, was "the possibility of a society . . . where individual worth wouldn't be measured by the money one made or the prestige of the job one held." At its deepest, the vision was the humanistic one of the *Shabbat,* which, as Saul Berman has reminded us, teaches that what is most precious in us is what is *not* economically productive.

The reality could not be further apart—as one learns from reading "What Do Women Really Want?," a magazine adaptation from William Novak's *The Great American Man Shortage* that I wish Hadassah had reprinted here. The men Novak talked to—one would not guess it from the piece Hadassah *did* reprint—report that "women judge them by how much prestige, power, and money they have acquired"—they are "success objects," valued for their professional status and their paycheck. So as Jewish women—*especially* Jewish women—increasingly forsake vocations of service for cushiony tickets as lawyers, doctors, and brokers, the range of "respectable," i.e., sufficiently wealth- and status-generation options for men of quality, with ethical values and spiritual or artistic vocations, narrows: *mitzrayim.*

It is the ultimate contradiction of feminism—and a touchstone of feminists' lack of honorableness and integrity—that the movement has demanded of our society equal rights without requiring of its adherents equal responsibilities. Instead, in my experience, Jewish women of every level of professional and financial accomplishment, from psychologists and editors to well-paid union workers and corporate lawyers—expect men to pay for them—to "take them out," in the telling idiom, just as women, feminist or no, want—and presumably always will want—to be "taken" sexually.

"I'm an old-fashioned girl," one family therapist told reporter Susan Bolotin. "I like to be wined and dined." Indeed, *most* of the feminists she spoke to expected to be treated. She does not say whether she's old-fashioned enough to accept that the men who will be wining and dining her will, justly and fairly, be favored in hiring and promotions over the women they'll be treating—and will, with equal justice, be paid more than their treated peers.

For feminists, there *is* such a thing as a free lunch. A vice president at NBC, no less, tells the *New York Times,* "Every so often I pick up the check"; she does not say whether it is acceptable that women be hired and promoted "every so often" at NBC.

Such enslavement is, of course, not only a matter of dinners and theater tickets, but of entire lifestyles. "It's amazing," notes Jane Caprinato, a social worker who teaches a "Spouse Hunting" course in Boston, where in my experience and Bill Novak's, single Jewish women—or SJWs, in the language of the personals—are constantly complaining that there are too few "available" men. "Women who are very successful . . . want to marry someone who makes more than they do." Novak's wife, founder of a Boston area Jewish dating service, hears similar sentiments.

So I do not have Cynthia Ozick's option, a lifetime of good writing enabled by her generous, nonwriter husband, or my cousin's, whose comfortable suburban lifestyle is supported by her lawyer husband; feminist bombast notwithstanding, my options are *fewer* than my female contemporaries', my freedom less. The only corporate lawyer I was ever involved with paid her *own* way grudgingly and eventually married a psychiatrist. She never dreamed of treating *me,* as any man would have been expected to in her place; and the SJF M.D. advertising in a recent Jewish newspaper seeks a "wealthy, generous professional"—she is, or will be, wealthy but is not herself generous, having been encouraged by feminism to value selfishness and disdain relationships with men based on giving—the essence of love, according to Erich Fromm.

Another SJF is equally out-front: She seeks "an attorney or physician who wants to share love." She is, obviously, impoverished; but I am left feeling almost suffocated—the life squeezed out of my soul and body, as Arthur Waskow defines a *mitzrayim.*

Feminist narcissism and self-absorption, of course, run deeper. The strongest feminist I was ever involved with missed a date with me because she lost track of time—I am not making this up— lingering over an exhibition of vaginas. This should not, perhaps, be surprising: Rivka Haut writes that Roslyn Lacks, in *Women and Judaism,* "suggests the goddess cults as role models for today's women." No wonder feminists at international conferences are invariably anti-Semitic; it is a truism of history that idolators hate Jews.

The oppressiveness of feminists' expectations of men today runs deeper, too. It is not merely a matter of money, but of all those macho qualities, supposedly disdained by feminism but still prized by feminists, for which money is, in the '80s, a decadent symbol. Helene Deutsch's insight—that women are innately masochistic, and so need to be aware of that impulse, the better, perhaps, to subdue it—rings ever truer as feminist rhetoric masks but does not suppress female needs.

"I am an ardent feminist," runs a knowing Feiffer cartoon, "who is turned on by mean macho men my age . . . but who finds considerate, compassionate men my age *wimps.*" Paul Newman was advised that he would never make it as a sex symbol if he didn't convey a sense of *threat*—so he worked out with weights, until he did. Do I, I wonder? Must I?

"Right now I'm going with a furniture mover," reports one magazine editor. "He's kind of a rat, not very respectful of women . . . but sometimes I want something primitive." I, a confirmed paragraph mover, experience the masochism in a more modulated fashion: I am never more attractive to women than when I am not all that interested, not all that vulnerable. Intense interest is a turn-off; distance is as seductive as threat—and faking it works, too.

Gentleness, on the other hand, can only be disabling in the world Feiffer describes—a transparent turn-off. The feminists I know are turned on to men who were taken with the movie "Blue Velvet"—which I found revoltingly violent and sadistic. No wonder so many prominent Jewish male feminists are conspicuously promiscuous, usually with adoring Jewish female feminists, or boorish with women, or both; indeed, their sense of authority seems to derive from the contemptuous behavior toward women they confess. This is the same logic—apparently irresistible in our society—whereby sexually perverted preachers teach the requirements of a moral life, or the architects of the war in Vietnam offer sage counsel on foreign policy.

Alas, feminism, even as it has sought, often successfully, to suppress dissent (*Moment* magazine would not even print vigorous responses to Novak's piece), has lacked the emotional maturity to encourage the necessary soul-searching, the often painful introspection. Instead, Jewish women's organizations—Hadassah, I'm sorry to say, included—make ending JAP jokes a holy cause. Now I don't tell JAP jokes, nor do I like them, and the only time I hear the word, in fact, is from the mouths of Jewish *women*, admitting that "I have a lot of JAP in me" to explain why they expect to be treated on dates: why they want equal rights without equal responsibilities. But erasing the term from society's consciousness without changing Jewish women's "Jappy" behavior makes about as much sense as a campaign to eradicate lung cancer while insisting on people's right to smoke. Worse, focusing on JAP jokes obscures the more significant reality: the unceasing vomit of vicious anti-male stereotyping and vilification that feminists have indulged, and indulged in, for the last two decades.

Letty Cottin Pogrebin—sought-after spokeswoman among Jewish feminists—whines in the *New York Times* about the tolerance for what she calls casual "sexist" comments, her criteria for that designation being somewhat loose, but there is nothing casual about the vitriol that eludes her outrage. "Men love death," writes Andrea Dworkin; "men especially love murder." Susan Brownmiller, Robin Morgan, and Adrienne Rich—all speaking from what Rachel Flick has called "feminism's incredible bitterness"—echo her equation of sex with rape.

A book that Rich—a virtual *ima* (foremother) for innumerable Jewish feminists—admiringly calls "a microcosm of the American feminist movement" is summarized by Carolyn See as relating "how 32 prominent American feminists are sick to death of men." And Bill Novak himself, to his discredit, included in his *The Great American Man Shortage* an article of cheap insults and misandrous putdowns, subtitled "32 Kinds of Men to Avoid," which he would not dream of disseminating had it been written, of women, by a man.

Feminism has simply not valued—indeed, it has *dis*valued—the cultivation of compassion and empathy toward men's needs and men's pain. "Men continue to be important to me, not in themselves but in what they do to me," opines one feminist's role model in the *Times'* "Hers" column—expressing a virtually perfect repudiation of the humanistic Jewish values that sages from Hillel to Buber have taught us.

"To be a nurturing and empathetic mother and to be a loving and supportive wife," wrote Sylvia Ann Hewlett, "were seen [by feminism] as signs of weakness and inadequacy"—not, as in Judaism, as signs of spiritual perfection and mastery of womanly *midot* (spiritual qualities). To be "supportive" has, of course, a prized value status for feminists, when its meaning is, with characteristic self-centeredness, being "supportive" of feminists' struggles—with feminism, there is always a double standard.

Other *midot* fare no better. *Tzniyut*—the exquisite cultivation of innerness, of modesty, of reserve—is prized by traditional Jewish women, but Letty Cottin Pogrebin has a flip answer to women possessed of a *lev tov* (a good heart) and hence concerned about

needlessly distracting men with improperly provocative clothing:
"Don't blame the victim," she tells the *New York Times.* She is truly
a savant of feminism, having learned how easily one gains sympathy
by portraying the oppressors—here, teasing, hostile feminists—as
victims—much in the fashion of some black anti-Semites today, who
cloak their racism in "victims' " garb. And anyone who doesn't
think see-throughs mask hostility should read the candid comments
of "Weathermen" women on the subject.

Indeed, the overall discourse on "women's issues" increasingly
has the quality of a demented pseudoreality, like a U.N. debate on
Israel. Schools and employers are encouraged—or required—to give
preferential consideration to women who will expect me to support
them, and a women's magazine lists dozens of scholarships open
only to women—how is this not illegal?—but a congresswoman
whines that Geraldine Ferraro, that quintessential beneficiary of a
double standard, may not have been paid as much as comparable
males for her Pepsi commercial!

As I write, New York University Law School has formally
outlawed "sex bias," which it defines, in part, as "verbal . . . conduct
that denigrates . . . persons on the grounds of gender." Do they have
in mind Dworkin, or Brownmiller, or the contributors to an anthology of feminist theories whose theme, according to reviewer
Wendy McElroy, is "Men as a category oppress women," or more
simply, "Women—good, men—evil"?

Working Woman runs an article on "the male/female money
gap" in an issue boasting not a single male staffer on its masthead;
but a letter writer to the *Progressive* complains—I'm serious—that
the magazine had forty men and twenty-five women—he counted!—
contribute to one section in the course of a year.

Mademoiselle offers "The Good-Bye Guy: When You're in
Trouble, He Checks Out," and the author of a *Washington Post*
article obscenely titled "Wormboys" advises that men "cannot be
depended on during tough times," but the author of Novak's misandrous slurs once invited a male friend to "keep in touch, as long as
you don't have any problems." Donahue prates on today about
women abandoned by their husbands—but the Jewish lesbian feminist who left her husband and child for a woman is still honored in
havurah and Jewish feminist circles.

No women's magazine reports the simple findings of a woman
who dressed up like a man for three months, for NBC News "Over-
night": "People are warmer to women. . . . Men are not treated as
well as women, at least in my experience." Indeed, a recent international survey reveals that women are generally slightly happier than

men—would one imagine so from the incessant whining of these last
twenty years, or from many of the women quoted in the articles
here?

Instead, as I seek my own happiness—and to fulfill the Torah's
directives for family life—I am confronted with feminism's bitter
fruits: a generation of women so fearful of love, so incapable of
genuine equality or initiative (they expect to be courted as well as
treated, feminism having taught them a selectively useful, cost-free
notion of liberation), and so neurotically incapable of commitment
that they cannot manage so much as a timely phone call. One
personals advertiser, obviously interested in me but determined to
be "pursued," actually told me she couldn't commit to calling me
while in town—I was to call her, though she would be reachable only
with difficulty—because she "never had enough dimes on her";
better to wait for Bill Novak's call, the more urgently to decry the
lack of available men, than to see to the dimes and seriously pursue
the relationship. To court—me or anyone—would be to court anxiety—to risk intimacy.

They are, I realize when I step back from my own anger,
themselves victims of feminism: hungry for intimacy but incapable
of pursuing it without losing either feminine pride, which feminism
either denies or distorts, or feminist self-respect, which demands
that they define themselves, as they do men, by their jobs or careers;
desiring deep sexual love but primed by feminism to regard sex as
pornographic and men as invasive. Some will experience disappointment and even hostility if and when (God forbid?) they give birth to
male children—so reports Diane Ehrensaft in a dreadful book on
"co-parenting," though a visit to *P'nai Or*, the female-chauvinist
"New Age" community, is sufficient to confirm the phenomenon. All
but the strongest are unable to choose the life of a homemaker, if
they wish it, without embarrassment or apology.

I am left, talented and sensitive, as Novak would put it, creative
and intuitive, as Levenberg might, decidedly unshallow and unbor-
ing, as Novak's "Lois" will be relieved to hear, most definitely *not*
"gay"—and indeed, as "Marilyn" tells Diane Levenberg, "frightened, single, and lonely"—frightened, at least, of *being* single and
lonely when I am old. I am embittered—by feminist hypocrisy and
the obeisance paid it, by its insidious double standard, by its
vengeful intolerance—and I am impaired, of course, by my own
bitterness.

Inside, my heart sighs, with Suzanne Vega, "Hold me like a
baby/That will not fall asleep," but I dare not reveal that longing to
Novak's women, who, fearful of the vulnerability they think they

want, will defensively conclude that I am "emotionally underdeveloped." Other women I meet will doubtless answer with the perspective of a woman's magazine respondent: "In my next relationship, *my* pleasure comes first"—and, in any case, will, like Vega, look to *me* for cradling; women are allowed to be the child inside them, but I am always to be a rock, a pillar of strength, the proverbial shoulder. Then, perhaps, I can *be* rocked now and then—be allowed an occasional lapse of toughness—not equality at all.

Robert Kennedy, he of tough mind and tender heart, borrowed from the Greeks his desideratum of worthwhile political change: to tame the savageness of men and make gentle the life of this world. Feminism, weak-minded and hard-hearted, has failed, above all, in its savagery, its lack of gentleness. It has spoken with hate and told lies; it has dehumanized men and relationships; it has neither cultivated virtue in its adherents nor deepened their understanding. It has poisoned our world.

5

Single Jewish Women Ten Years Later

Diane Levenberg

During the cresting wave of the women's movement in October of 1978, two years before Novak's piece appeared in Moment, *Diane Levenberg wrote an article for the* National Jewish Monthly *entitled, "Either I'm Neurotic or I Haven't Found the Right One Yet." In it, she recorded interviews with numerous Jewish women in their 30s who lamented the search for mates as the pool of available Jewish men dwindled and their biological clocks ticked away.*

One of the women summed up the majority sentiment when she said, "Part of the price of our independence is that we're not home all day to counsel and console. Most men can accept this in us as friends. But they're still afraid to give up their need for a mothering wife by living with us as one independent person with another." The number crunch was also on their minds: "There are probably two Jewish women to every Jewish man in most large East Coast cities. I know, for example, that there are half a million more women than men in New York City alone."

Now it is over a decade later and these women are in their 40s. Has their situation changed much? Here is Levenberg's update.

A decade later, having spent the last ten years in therapy, women's groups, and in the company of psychologically astute and introspective women, one thing single Jewish women know is that if anyone is neurotic, it's the endless stream of men out there with whom they haven't been able to connect.

They've had breakfast with these men at *havurah* retreats,

they've shared the podium with them at conferences, they've watched the same brilliant sunset at the harmonic convergence, and still they all report a similar phenomenon. No connection. Jewish men and women seem to have lost the ability to relate, to be intimate, to really hear each other. There is always the hope that physical chemistry can produce a passionate bond, but the elements necessary for empathy and compassion seem to have disappeared through the hole in the ozone.

Also having disappeared into another mysterious black hole are the men. Where have they gone? No one is quite sure why, but there are fewer Jewish men out there in their late 30s and early 40s. Two possible reasons are that Jewish men intermarry more than women do, and they also have the option of dating younger women. It's a rare sort of woman who could take the risk of "marrying down"—a younger, possibly less professionally accomplished man.

What leaves absolutely no doubt in the minds and hearts of Jewish women is that whatever they have been able to accomplish within their control, a Ph.D., an executive directorship, even the continual enjoyment of their own company, their appropriate mate still hides in the arms of destiny and occasionally even in the arms of other women. The odds of finding him then begin to seem the equivalent of winning the jackpot from the one-armed bandit in a gambling casino.

What leaves these single Jewish women mystified, helpless, and hurt is that no matter how many degrees they have earned, no matter how much society rewards their careers, and no matter how many therapists pronounce them sane, there are still those ineluctable forces of fate to contend with. No matter how one tries to will it, the right Jewish man won't ride up to their door on a push-button stallion. He doesn't seem to offer them the magic potion at Jewish singles events, and after one turns 30, one's friends have a thinning list of single Jewish men to introduce them to.

Here are three very 1980s tales of single Jewish women who have hoped and despaired, entered the fray and retreated, and have, after years of strategizing and praying for the right answer, finally arrived at their unique ways of rattling their destinies.

Judy Schwartz will turn 38 in May. She is a psychologist in a large East Coast city—a "virtuoso listener"—as she describes herself. Between appointments, she lets me interview her in her spacious, well-furnished apartment. She assumes a comfortable position on her couch and begins her tale.

"I put all relationships on hold until I got my Ph.D. three years ago," she says. "I had a magical idea that there was a God and the right man would arrive when I finished it." However, she feels fortunate in that there were men in her life who held her hand during the ten years it took her to acquire her union card.

"I never had any problem attracting men," she says, "but without my having earned this degree they knew and I knew it wasn't appropriate. The entire time I was writing my dissertation, I believed in a benevolent God who would provide for me. The men I knew during that time were warm, fun, and exciting, and they contributed to this belief.

"The last three years I had one male friend who was supportive and also totally safe. Though he had a scholarship from Harvard, his emotional problems kept him on the fringe of society. He was a golf caddy who was devoted and committed to my well-being. He was also an Irish Catholic. Though he too believed that there was no future for us, he felt comfortable, as though he were launching me off. Like a good father putting a child to sleep, he would reiterate a happy story. Some day you'll be married, he'd say. Looking at my messy apartment, he gave me reassurance about that as well. He saw it as a metaphor for my hysteria. Some day, he said, you'll have a safe haven."

Then came the day of reckoning. Judy received her Ph.D., took a licensing exam in psychology, and passed it. And lo and behold, her benevolent God seemed to be bent on denying her a mate. There were absolutely no men around. This might have been due to the isolation she endured while working on her dissertation. Now, for almost two years, there was a new kind of pain.

"In your early 30s," she says wistfully, "it looks like the pain will end. But in your late 30s, it feels insidious. One sees no end to the pain and no way out. You know you're competent. You've pulled off everything you put your mind to. Now you come up against something over which you have no control. I can't tell you how devastating that feels.

"You're successful and accomplished and have everything you hoped for and now you're lonely and miserable. As a psychologist, I could make other people's lives happy—and, in fact, I did see a lot of movement in the lives of my clients. Coming home to discover that my own life hadn't moved was a shock. At one point, I saw someone through a bad marriage who ended up having a baby. In the end, I wished I were her. It was also painful that patients and colleagues saw me as a career woman who didn't want to get married. I know that some of my patients even assumed I was gay.

"Planning a more comprehensive strategy, I went to Jewish singles events, and even answered the personal ads in magazines.

There was no question in my mind that I was looking for a Jewish man. In my home town, my grandfather built the synagogue, my father was president, and my cousin was the architect. This coming *Shabbat* I'll be reading the Torah at my own synagogue. I have always had a strong Jewish identity and an urge to keep Judaism alive. More than anything, I want a Jewish home for my children.

"The Jewish men I dated, however, lacked a sincere spiritual identity. I have a sense of awe and the miracle of life that they just didn't share. Nor did I sense that they had achieved any real individuation from their families. Somehow, they were not men yet."

What these men did share, however, was a sort of egomania. Rarely listening, they simply droned on and on. Having received love and attention at home, Judy feels that she's able to give it herself. But these men offered her nothing in return. She went out with successful doctors and good looking businessmen—none of whom were able to make, as she says, "good quality contact." Then there was the wealthy dentist who, having no idea of how to make a life for himself, lived in an empty condominium and ate dinner every night at his mother's house.

As Judy sees it, her own father and brother were outstanding men—very communicative and sensitive. It was this sort of man she was holding out for. Finally, about to give up, she thought of having a child on her own. She was advised to wait until she was 40. In the meantime, so many things reminded her of her loneliness—families in malls, couples at the *minyan,* her own clients. On weekends, she continued her strategy, seeing each evening out as a "performance." But even for an attractive, successful woman, it was hard to maintain her usually excellent self-esteem. During the week, she sometimes went to the movies alone—to kill the pain and have some romance.

Sometimes she blamed herself, thinking that she had mishandled her life—that there was something wrong with her, that she was failing to make herself happy. Only her relationship with God and her work helped her function.

Despite all this anguish, Judy's story does have its own sort of happy ending. At a church dance near her home, she met a man she could finally talk to. Alive and immediately communicative, he began to discuss religion, God, and spirituality. Unfortunately, he wasn't Jewish. But to Judy there was a positive side to this. Unlike Jewish men, he didn't expect her to be warm; he merely appreciated it.

"Jewish men," she says, "have a resentment about giving that he doesn't have. He's had a hard life and now he pulls his own weight. I wish I could share my culture with him, all the Jewish words I so love, but he's learning. And it's all right with him to raise our children as Jews. Though he's Irish Catholic, he has his own form of spirituality and I share this with him. I feel that as a human being he captures the essence of Judaism more than any Jewish man I've dated. He's a *mentsch* and I feel as though we're soul mates. I think we'll be married soon, and I feel lucky that I have my parents' support. Even my mother finally agreed that this generation of Jewish men has a problem. What else can I say but that there was a benevolent God who brought me to him?''

Brenda Wolman is a director of a counseling center for women and a therapist in private practice. She is beautiful, brilliant, a well-known therapist in her small East Coast city, and still single at 38. We meet in her cozy office replete with *objets d'art* and a floor lamp that gives off a warm rosy glow.

"My fantasy was that I would be married between 25 and 28. I felt I would have more than one child because I was an only child and I hated that. I also thought my husband would earn more money than I did.

"When I was in graduate school I felt pretty helpless to do anything to make it happen. I was just supposed to meet Prince Charming, but I had no information on how to make this happen. Part of my frustration was that I didn't meet the love of my life in college and then, when I was out in the world, it still wasn't happening. All the while I was dating, I was anxious because I didn't know what I should be doing to meet the right man. I took a photography session and even went on some windjammer cruises to meet someone with mutual interests.

"Finally, when I was 23, I was very depressed, because my father had just died, and I went into therapy. I had an affair with the therapist and then was depressed for a number of years. When I was 26, I met a nice Jewish man, but he was just too unexciting. He reminded me too much of my father. But before I broke up with him I said to myself, 'You know, you may be giving up the possibility of having children. Are you prepared to do that?' I guess I was.

"When I was 29, I met another man at a feminist caucus, part of a retreat for progressive Jews. He was there because he was looking for women. He and I began to do Jewish organizing together and I was thrilled. I went to his house on a farm, addressed envelopes, ate *Shabbat* dinner, made love, and stayed involved with him for three years. He's a charismatic, larger-than-life, powerful figure. In those days, however, I still saw myself as a little woman who didn't have a sense of self and meaningful work. I was just a year out of graduate school and was a starving social worker. My own life didn't seem nearly as interesting as his, but this felt like a critical time to get married. He had a son and I saw that he was a good father. I wanted children very badly and I desperately wanted this relationship to work out.

"Soon I began to work on the issue of Jewish identity and singles groups. However, instead of being encouraging, he began to criticize me, and I felt very put down by him. I was in a therapist training group and he said, 'How can you be a therapist if you're so messed up we can't have a relationship?' Perhaps he was unaware of it, but he needed me to support and adore him, while at the same time he was threatened by my growth. He wanted me to meet all his dependency needs without his even needing to ask for what he really wanted.

"For years, I felt the pain of this relationship because, despite all the emotional abuse, we had a passionate sexual connection. After this, I went into therapy, again with a man, and this therapist helped me end the relationship. He showed me how the behavior didn't match the words.

"Then I plunged into a terrible depression. I was 32, unmarried, childless, and wasn't earning enough money to have my own apartment. At the same time, however, I was starting to have a sense of myself as a professional and to feel good about my work. And I had begun to connect with the Jewish women's movement.

"I became part of a Jewish women's group, and I think that they and my therapist saved my life. We had a consciousness-raising group that became a warm, nurturing place where we tried to support our own growth and make sense of our lives. None of us had lives we thought we would have by then. We were married, single, even lesbian women, all living lives that didn't resemble our own earlier fantasies. That was incredibly affirming. We were all questioning ourselves and began to give each other support, realizing that there wasn't a right way to do this.

"We're living through a period of profound social change in the way men and women relate. Gender roles are all being redefined, and this is having a crucial impact on coupling. I began to see that what was happening to me was happening to a whole generation. After that, I didn't trust myself to make a relationship work and I was depressed and lonely.

"Soon after, I fell in love with a woman in my group. The possibility of lesbianism became real to me. She had been a lesbian since she was a teenager. But I treated the living situation as though we were roommates, and we kept separate bedrooms. For her, however, to live with me was the result of an enormous decision. But I still couldn't get it out of my head that I wanted to try it again with a man. She felt the same way, so we were both ambivalent.

"Eventually, I left her to be with a man, knowing that I felt better about myself because of her. For me, this was a healing relationship. But I wasn't yet ready to choose her. I asked God to provide me with a Jewish man and so She did. He was European with an exotic history. But I failed to see that he was also conservative, overly rational, and uptight. He was distant and unconnected.

"Now I'm 38, have a really strong sense of myself, love my work, and can support myself. I have deep friendships with women, and my life has meaning and purpose. I'm not sure that I want children. I no longer have the 'let's get married and have kids' fantasy. But there's no other paradigm, and I find myself not quite knowing what I'm looking for. Right now, I'm involved with two men. One might want to marry me and have children. He's also a good friend. The other probably won't settle down. He's more exotic and passionate. So it might be neither of them. But for once I'm not anxious about the outcome. Right now, I'm getting what I need, even if it's not all in one place."

Nancy Katz is a tall, attractive, 40-year-old professor of English at a small eastern college. Literate, articulate, sensitive, she has devoted hours of thought to her single status.

"I had a fantasy," she says, "that I could do my work and live in peace with a man who cherished me, and we would have a couple of kids. But I made a series of dreadful choices. When I look back on it, I see that I was with men who were ultimately rejecting or devouring—almost all of them Jewish men.

"I finished my doctorate when I was 25 and began teaching at Tel Aviv University. I stayed there for three years, met a man who was also teaching—philosophy—and he looked perfect for me. He was very intellectual, attractive, virile, politically in the same camp—liberal left. We fell in love, went out together for a year, and everyone assumed we would marry. But he lived with his parents, who were opposed to me. They said I was the same age as he was, not an Israeli, and that I had no money. Now I see that he was basically narcissistic and unloving. I met him again two years ago in America and I was glad I hadn't married him.

"He too has never married. He got a doctorate from Oxford, had a terrible accident, and was in a coma for a long time. But none of these things has changed him. I could still see what a pathetic human being he was.

"I lived with another man for a year, when I was 28. He was a nuclear engineer, a dreamer, an extremely needy man. I lived with him because I wanted to settle down, love and be loved. But I discovered he was a misogynist and even threatened physical abuse. He scared me off men for a while.

"After Bernard, I tried to get together with a man who wouldn't marry me, and that went on for three or four years. He was a professor of English and he, too, has never married.

"My most positive experience was with an older man in his 50s. He was also a professor of English, and he lived 1,200 miles away. We spent summers together and vacations. We talked on the phone a lot. He wanted to marry me but I had three reasons for declining. Though he wanted me to show interest in his poetry, he was never interested in mine. And my poetry is the most important thing in my life. I resented his attitude—felt it as an assault on my being. We're still friends, but I still harbor the resentment.

"The second reason was that sexually I didn't find him that exciting. And lastly, he couldn't have any children. I would have given up too many things to marry him, but I was 32 before I stopped seeing him completely.

"Then I fell in love with another impossible man—another Israeli. He was a chemist and I thought he was really the right one. He was a Don Juan, brilliant, charming, seductive, appreciative of my mind, my poetry, but emotionally unavailable. I spent one weekend with him and kept that fantasy going for six years. That was my psychopathology. We saw each other sporadically over that period, and he was in a fantasy state as well. He has never married either.

"There have been other Jewish men who have offered to marry me, but they seemed to be needier than I am, and I was afraid they would devour me. I feel a tremendous tie to Judaism, which comes through in my writing. Recently I joined a synagogue and hoped that there I might meet a new man. But I'm afraid the Jewish establishment doesn't care about singleness or isolation. There is no singles group at this synagogue. The idea of family is still so intense that single Jews are still treated like second-class citizens.

"I've been in therapy for a long time and realize that my inability to find the right man is in part my own neurosis, but to some extent it's also a social condition. When I realized that I was addicted to relationships in the same way others are addicted to liquor, food, or drugs, I joined Alanon. There, in addressing the disease of co-dependence, I was able to break off with an unavailable man.

"Now, though I still have hope, I'm also in semi-retirement. I'm afraid of repeating my old mistakes. What keeps me going is my work, my mother, my program, and my dog. I still have faith, but I have also experienced so much pain, so much loneliness. I still want children, so I'm thinking of insemination and being a single mother. I think perhaps men suffer in the same way, but this culture tends to be much harder on women."

6

Single by Choice

Ruth Mason

Julia Falk[1] radiates a quiet self-assurance. She's the kind of woman who knows herself, knows what she wants, and, at 59, doesn't place much importance on the opinions of others. Though she admits to being a nonconformist, she doesn't look like one. If anything, her manner and appearance suggest conservatism. Her short hair is simply coiffed, her nail polish pink. She is soft-spoken and somewhat reserved, but one detects a contained energy. On a late summer morning, when many other Manhattanites have escaped the steamy city, she dons a pale pink pin-striped suit, black patent leather sandals, and simple gold jewelry, and walks the six blocks to her office. Her work, like her personal life, is something she created to suit her independent, intelligent, inquisitive temperament. Falk and Co. is a highly profitable, thirty-year-old management consulting firm with clients ranging from Fortune 500 companies to foreign governments. In work, as in her private life, Julia has arranged things so she doesn't have to answer to—or compromise for—any boss.

Julia's decision not to marry evolved slowly, over time. At 59, she can look back on that decision and thoughtfully analyze the reasons for it. But remaining single wasn't her original plan. Like all girls brought up in the 1930s and 1940s, she expected to grow up, get married, and have children. Julia was raised in what she calls a

---

[1]Ms. Falk's name and other identifying details have been changed to protect her privacy.

"typical home and family of the era," in which the father worked and the mother took care of her home and four children. She had a traditional Jewish upbringing, complete with Hebrew school, confirmation, and a kosher home. When she first tasted bacon, she confesses, she thought the heavens would open up. When they didn't, she "corrupted" the rest of the kids in the family and also learned a life-long lesson: You could take risks and not be punished.

Julia went to an Ivy League college on scholarship and was one of only six women in her class to graduate with a degree in economics. Despite her degree, she was offered only secretarial jobs with glorified titles. Throughout college she had considered work as an interim measure, something to do until she got married. But after one year as a secretary, she decided to get a graduate degree. She worked for the university during the day and did her course work, for free, at night. "By the time I decided to get my MBA," she recalls, "I was a little more oriented toward—not career, I didn't think of it that way—but—I wanted something more than what was being offered."

Julia's difficulty in articulating the evolution of her life choices reflects the consciousness of the era in which she grew to adulthood. She didn't feel discriminated against when potential employers only offered her low-level jobs. "It didn't occur to me that when they asked me if I was planning to get married and have children, they were waiting for me to say no . . . that they weren't going to invest in a woman who would leave to have a family."

There was no *Ms.* magazine in the 1950s to tell Julia Falk that she was a victim of unequal treatment or that she had other options available to her than the ones she saw all around her. In 1989, she calls herself a feminist ("but not a raving one"), but in 1959 she had only an inner conviction that she had not spent four years in college to be a secretary—or a housewife.

During her first job, Julia recalls, she stopped thinking of her work life as a stopgap that didn't really matter. "I realized I spent most of my waking hours at work and I had better like what I was doing. I thought an MBA would open things up."

It did in more ways than one. The business world could no longer ignore her talents, and she eventually rose to an executive position in a major firm. The MBA also allowed her to leave home respectably. "I couldn't figure out a way to move out of my parents' house and stay in Baltimore. You just didn't do that. So I looked for jobs in New York."

By her late 20s, Julia knew she did not want to have children and live in the suburbs. The two went together in her mind. She was bored with suburban topics of conversation and didn't like the groupings of women with women and men with men she saw there. When she visited friends in the suburbs, she would rent a car so she could get away when she wanted to. She also felt temperamentally unsuited to raising children. "Rightly or wrongly, I thought people should have children when they're young and don't know what they're doing. When you're older, you more fully realize the responsibility. Also, I thought I'd go crazy if I had to spend all day with babies. I couldn't even spend an hour with nieces and nephews before they could talk, and I adored them."

Being a mother and working was not an option Julia thought she had. "Remember, this was 1959 and mothers didn't work. I was enjoying myself, enjoying my work, and I had a nice social life. I thought it would be nice to be married without kids.

"But the men I met weren't right for me. They were looking for someone who would take care of the house, be a good hostess, and put *their* concerns first. Wouldn't anyone want to come home from work and find dinner cooked, the house clean, their laundry done, and their shoes repaired? I would have liked someone to do that for me, too."

Julia's decision not to marry evolved slowly. "By my early 30s, the decision was pretty much made, given who the candidates were. I had the feeling I was too old and too young at the same time. If I were older, I might have looked for companionship and not been as (she pauses here) *choosy*? If I were younger, I would have been less aware."

She of course felt the normal pressures—especially from her mother. "Everything I was doing was the antithesis of everything she understood. I tried to explain to some extent, but we'd get into arguments, so it was easier to talk about other things.

"I'd been living in my own apartment for fifteen years when I overheard my mother say, 'When Julia has her own home. . . .' Her attitude bothered me at first, but after fifteen years, I knew who I was and what I was doing. A certain amount of growing up helps you deal with your parents.

"I should be grateful to Betty Friedan (author of *The Feminine Mystique*, the book that launched the 1960s women's movement). Before all that started, my mother had a hard time explaining me to her friends.

"I don't feel pressure any more. I made my accommodation with my parents. I'm lucky they lived long enough for us to become friends."

Julia has had relationships with men, including one that lasted seven years. "He was smart, vigorous, and fun—and also very strong and domineering. I thought I would be in danger of becoming what I was supposed to be—an accommodating, sweet little lady with no opinions of my own."

Though she doesn't use these terms to describe herself, Julia's idealism and perfectionism also may have played a role in her remaining single. Her experience with piano lessons is illustrative. She took lessons and played seriously throughout her childhood but quit during her senior year of high school. "I was pretty advanced, but I stopped when I realized I wasn't going to make excellence." A three-page profile of her personality—the result of a computerized personality test on which her firm is working—reveals that she is "especially vulnerable to idealizing interpersonal relationships, raising these relationships to a plane that seldom can sustain the realities of human nature."

Julia's decision not to marry was not an ideological or a principled one. She is not opposed to marriage. But bad marriages are widespread, she says, and she can't understand why people stay in them. "People marry partly to be married. They say, 'Well, I'm in love, I'm supposed to be married, let's talk about the wedding' rather than consciously deciding, 'This is the right person for me.'" She defines a good marriage as one in which the couple are friends as well as lovers and are "equal in terms of helping each other and respecting who each is and what they do. I think this is very difficult to achieve and maintain.

"I think being single beats a bad marriage, but I don't think it beats a good marriage, especially if you can remain your own person. That seems easier to do now than it was when I was younger."

Julia muses that if there were enough space, she might consider living with a man. Margaret Sanger, the birth control pioneer, and her husband lived in separate apartments in the same building, and they would phone each other before visiting. That arrangement is Julia Falk's ideal.

Unlike many single women, Julia is happy with her life. She describes her work as "fascinating," and her social life is full. She likes "a little corner of turbulence" or excitement, and when it's not there, she creates it. Pressed for an example, she mentions discovering Brooklyn. "I'll realize I don't know Brooklyn at all and call some friends to see who wants to go on a tour with me. Of course no one wants to do a tour of Brooklyn, but by the time I've called fifteen people, all sorts of other things have come up."

Julia's main interest outside of work is music. She's an opera buff, loves chamber music and symphonies. She spends more of her spare time on music than anything else. While some single women might find vacationing alone a problem, Julia combines her vacations with business trips and relishes discovering new places.

While Julia is living proof of her contention that a single woman can have a happy, fulfilling life, she does feel the disadvantages of being single. Perhaps part of the secret of her success lies in the fact that she doesn't dwell on them. "You give things up because we live in a two-by-two society—but it's not so bad in Manhattan. I usually don't find myself in social situations where I'm the only single person."

She recalls that when she was in her 30s, some of her single friends desperately wanted to get married. "I found that strange. They were fun and interesting and doing interesting work, but they had this *thing.* Some people I know who have been married feel the same way. All they can think about is wanting to be married again. Thinking marriage will make you happy is like thinking a nose job will make you happy. Or like being a kid of 6 and wanting to be 14. Suddenly you're 14, and that's not so hot either. You have a whole life to do with as you want, and if you're going to sit around waiting for a man to make it complete, you'll miss out."

Obsessing about marriage, Julia says, prevents you from enjoying who you are and what your life is now. "Women who think this way should turn their attention to making something out of their lives. If they meet someone, fine. But if not, they won't feel like their lives have been wasted."

The advantages of being single? "You're in charge; you run your life to suit you. No one's going to tell you the house is a mess, or they don't like the colors you painted the walls."

Julia has a full life: She runs her own successful business, has close friends and family relationships, and she has her freedom. Does she have any regrets?

This is a hard question for Julia to answer. Clearly, it's not the type of question she herself broods over. She leans forward, her arms folded in front of her on a table. "I don't know," she answers after some thought. "It's hard to say. If all the circumstances would be the same, I'd have made the same choices. To some degree, I regret not having had a good marriage. But I don't think about it."

7

What's Happening on the Singles Scene?

Margaret Charytan

Let us be honest about it and stop playing games: the main goal in programming for singles is to be successful enough to lose the audience—to marriage. And let us admit that the main business in working with singles is to provide the means for them to meet, mingle, and (hopefully) marry. The reason for this somewhat obsessive concern is quite simple. According to many demographic studies, the Jewish community is at less than zero population growth. We are not having enough children to insure the survival of the Jewish people. It is understandable, therefore, that trying to increase the chances for Jews to marry and bear children should be foremost on the community agenda.

What age group of singles should we concentrate on? There are, of course, many kinds of singles with particular needs. There are single parents, older singles in their 40s, 50s, and 60s, there are widows and widowers—all of whom need to find a place within a Jewish community that stresses the family. But that problem is another story altogether. The focus of our particular concern is the young singles (21–25) who aren't necessarily interested in marriage yet, but are out of school and out of touch with each other, and those singles who are in their late 20s and 30s, immersed in their careers, but finding their social lives beginning to narrow.

How successful are the approaches used by our communal agencies? An informal survey conducted by this writer indicated that there are many difficulties faced by those who reach out to the singles, but there are many success stories, too.

The 92nd Street "Y" (YM-YWHA) in New York City runs a spectacular lecture series that attracts hundreds of singles—primarily those in their late 20s and 30s who do not usually attend synagogue services or functions. According to the program's coordinator, Julie Weissfuss, hundreds of people come to hear the speakers, both at the Tuesday evening coffeehouse series and the Sunday evening lectures. Both events are preceded and/or followed by refreshments to encourage socializing.

Weissfuss does not keep any statistics but has noticed that people do seem to meet and leave together. "Hearing a stimulating lecture gives people something to talk about," she says, "and that makes it easier for people to approach each other." One look at the roster of speakers that appear at the "Y" gives a clue to the program's success: Gail Sheehy, author of *Passages;* Chaim Potok, author of (among others) *The Chosen;* feminist writer Betty Friedan; poet Allen Ginsberg; Pulitzer Prize winning journalist David Halberstam; U.S. District Attorney Rudolph Giuliani—these are just the highlights of their program. It's no wonder, then, that the "Y" has no trouble getting a good crowd. But in truth, there are very few community centers around the country that can command the crowd that the 92nd Street "Y," a New York institution, attracts. And many singles feel that lecture series do not really provide them with much of an experience or the nonpressured environment they desire: "People listen, drink some coffee, and then they go home." "I feel awkward standing around dawdling over a cup of coffee waiting for someone to come over and begin a conversation." "Even though you've just heard the same lecture, it's hard to strike up a conversation with someone you've not been introduced to."

Jamie Field—who programs for the St. Louis, Missouri, Jewish Community Center—operates with a more realistic budget and finds that having "fun" lectures with a small group eases the situation for her audience. For an evening with a hypnotist or a psychic, twenty to forty people will show up: "With audience participation in the demonstrations, it's a lot easier to make people feel relaxed." Field doesn't just sit back and wait for participants. She, like Director Patsy Goldberg of the Atlanta, Georgia, J.C.C., makes phone call after phone call trying to get each of their contacts to bring four or five others to the Jewish Community Center events they run. Patsy Goldberg puts the problem succinctly: "We have to overcome the stigma of running a program for losers. Singles have the idea that if you have any social skills, you wouldn't have to come to singles events. Yet, once you are out of school and move to a new community, it's hard to meet people."

In Dallas, Texas, Ronett Sagman—who heads The Group (sponsored by the J.C.C.)—finds that people who are new to town call the number she places in the *Texas Jewish Post* along with her name. "That gives our events a personal touch. People can call me to find out how to dress, and if they give me their name, I can promise to introduce them around. We put their names on our mailing lists for all our future events." Sagman notes that a problem common to the smaller Jewish communities in the South and West is that after a year or two, people keep seeing the same faces and stop coming to events. Goldberg tries to combat this by organizing weekends she advertises in Jewish newspapers all over the country. "We held a Blue Jeans Weekend at a children's summer camp in Georgia that 200 people attended from all over the South," she reports. Participants shared accommodations, ate communal meals, went sailing, waterskiing, canoeing, and had a great time. Sagman has held a Texas Singles Camp outside of Austin, Texas, at a Young Judaea facility and reports that "five couples met and are now seeing each other; they were from different parts of Texas, so structuring a weekend that attracts people from other locations can be very rewarding in bringing new people together."

While Jewish community centers, especially those with full-time workers assigned to working with the singles, can provide Jewish singles with some involvement, many singles are turning to the synagogue for help in meeting their needs.

Rabbi Ephraim Buchwald, of the Lincoln Square Synagogue in New York City, reports that there have been an astounding number of marriages among participants in the Sabbath morning services he runs for beginners—those new to synagogue ritual: "Out of the fifty people who began with us this year, at least forty have married people they met in the kiddushes that follow the services. Perhaps their new commitment to becoming more observant gives them assistance in committing themselves to marriage and building a family."

The Beth Shalom Congregation in Elkins Park, Pennsylvania, designed by architect Frank Lloyd Wright, draws many people because of its unique beauty, but Rabbi Eric Lankin, who spearheads the singles programming at the synagogue, can take much of the credit for creating the right ambiance for singles. "I believe," he says firmly, "that singles should not be divided up into groups for separate services. It's much less pressured for them to join in with the regular congregational services. That way, they are an integral part of the community—not oddities. After services, the synagogue hosts a separate *Oneg Shabbat,* which about 150 singles attend. Special events centered around the holidays are planned—a dessert party in the *sukkah,* for example." Rabbi Lankin has encouraged the young marrieds in the community to plan *Shabbat* "retreats" where twenty couples and their children plus twenty singles go away together.

Another successful program is run by the Sutton Place Synagogue in New York. Rabbi David Kahane has been instrumental in making singles feel at home in turning to the synagogue for their social needs. Several different services are held for different age groups, and there are regularly scheduled Friday night dinners. "At first," explains Harriet Janower, who directs the synagogue's programs, "we had speakers at the dinners, but we found that everyone was just sharing a Friday night meal and sitting around talking with each other." The Sutton Place Synagogue also hosts dinners at restaurants and cocktail parties at art galleries, but it is their synagogue services that seem to appeal most to the singles—at least 1,500 people showed up for the High Holiday Services held at the Waldorf Astoria hotel in Manhattan.

Rabbi Buchwald has noted that "singles should get involved in community projects with the needy. Charity work would be a good vehicle for a healthier social involvement." Those who are involved with the Young Leadership Division of UJA-Federation find that fundraising and community leadership also have a positive social side. UJA-Federation reports that there are increasing numbers of singles attending their information meetings and participating in such "hands-on" activities as cleaning up synagogues in deteriorating neighborhoods or going out on mini-missions to recruit new members.

Less formally organized approaches are used with younger singles—those still in college or graduate school. Most of these young adults cannot be categorized as singles; yet they, too, should be provided with ways to maintain their social contacts among fellow Jews. Recognizing this need, the Combined Jewish Philanthropies of Boston, Massachusetts, awarded a grant to the Young Adult and Graduate Students Society, which is based in the Harvard University Hillel Center. Program director Rebecca Diamond finds that "food is the key. We hold Sunday morning brunches and about a hundred people come to eat, listen to our speakers, and meet each other." Boston has a number of different graduate schools, and Diamond feels that graduate students, as well as young adults ranging from the age of 22 to 27, aren't really ready to join a synagogue, but they do feel isolated and would like to have a social life. "It is essential," Diamond notes, "to get input from this age group before attempting to plan any events, but trying to form a committee of students from different schools can be very frustrating and time consuming. It's especially difficult in the fall. When they start graduate school, they don't want to jump in and start taking leadership roles." Diamond reiterates that the students and young people do need to be reached (her mailing list is derived from school registration packets with a check-off for religious preference). "After going to college for four years, leaving most of one's friends behind, and coming to a new place for graduate school or a job, it's very important to find a vehicle for meeting other Jews."

Out in the suburbs of New York, in Malverne, Long Island, the Mid-Nassau Jewish Community Council has been quietly sponsoring a Jewish coffeehouse for the past ten years. Café Gilah is the brainstorm of two dynamic community members—Ann Levine and Adele Katz—who contacted every Jewish organization and synagogue in the area and convinced them to join together in running this social center: "There were a lot of Christian missionary groups in the area, and many of them were attracting Jewish college students. We felt an obligation to provide an alternative social environment." Levine has found that most of the students weren't interested in attending lectures, even those given by well-known personalities. "All they wanted was a place to gather. We gave them ping pong tables, music, some board games and books, bagels and cream cheese, and they kept on coming around."

Acknowledging the serious implications of the singles scene, The Federation of Jewish Philanthropies in many cities has set up task forces to help their affiliated groups develop new approaches. Several area task forces have published a directory of programs and services available to singles, but perhaps the most innovative, albeit old-fashioned, method the task force has funded is a variation on the *shadkhan* (matchmaker) of old. Proposed by the Educational Alliance West, a New York organization that works for the continuity of the Jewish people, the program arranges interviews by social workers for those who apply. Director Deborah Rafalitz explains that references are carefully checked, and applicants get a minimum of six names to call. In addition, the Alliance arranges small dinner parties for eight, as well as larger parties. "So far," Rafalitz reports, "we've had about fourteen people married out of three hundred applicants."

The United Synagogue of America has also turned to a variation on the same theme. Open to the singles page of any Jewish newspaper throughout the country, from West Coast to New England, and you will see their ad for the Jewish Singles Computer Service. For a small fee, registrants get a form to fill out on which they list the personal characteristics they are looking for in a mate. Three lists of names and phone numbers are sent out at seven-week intervals. The United Synagogue is also contemplating a more personalized *shadkhan* service.

What seems like a throwback to our parents' generation may very well turn out to be the best approach, and perhaps it is the most effective approach that can be used by members of each synagogue community—personal introductions. It is all very well, as at least one Jewish organization in Louisville, Kentucky, has done, to produce a version of the "little black book"—a listing of the names of eligible Jewish men and women in the area (names were submitted voluntarily), but it's the personal introduction that seems to work best. One synagogue community in Great Neck reports that they have had couples invite their single friends over for a *Shabbat* in which various small dinners and luncheons were hosted to encourage the singles to meet.

Although many women are working full-time today, and few have time to give elaborate parties, there are still plenty of occasions for friends to gather together to share activities. And it just might add an extra *mitzvah* to the occasion to ask each couple to bring along an unmarried friend. There is nothing embarrassing in asking an unmarried friend (or your older married friends' children) to join you for skiing, for a book discussion group, or a lecture, as well as to meet some new people you think he or she might like to know. And it's easier for people to get acquainted when the conversation focuses on a particular activity shared by people with mutual interests. This is an approach that does not have to be left to the formal matchmaker, the rabbi, or the social director. It is a *mitzvah* we should all participate in if we care about the future of the Jewish community.

8

Dating Ourselves

William Novak

Just where are you supposed to go these days if you're single and you'd like to meet appropriate members of the opposite sex? To a singles group? Many of these are deadly, and even when they're not, most single people *assume* they are and keep their distance. Singles bars? Forget it. Anyone who's been to one knows that they're the *worst* place to initiate a serious relationship.

But what are the alternatives?

It's a persistent and troubling question. A couple of years ago I spent a few months interviewing single people for my book *The Great American Man Shortage and Other Roadblocks to Romance*. One evening, I met with a funny, articulate, divorced lawyer in his 30s. He began the conversation by informing me that there were two ways that I could become, in his words, "wealthy beyond belief." As I listened eagerly, he explained that the first route to riches lay in finding and marketing a successful cure for baldness.

"Forget it," I told him. "What's your second idea?"

"The other thing you could do," he said, "is to come up with a dignified and effective way for single people to meet each other."

He's right: It used to be much easier. Not so long ago, most people met their future partners in high school or college, in churches and synagogues, or through friends or relatives. Today, our lives are far more fragmented and disconnected, and a growing number of unmarried people are now spending money to make the kinds of connections that used to happen naturally.

There are currently more than fifty million unmarried adults in America—which means that singles constitute the largest minority group in the country. Recently, a variety of entrepreneurs have stepped in to help them connect with each other. Right now, the biggest success story in what is rapidly turning into a new industry isn't computer dating, or video dating, or any other technique based on the latest technology. On the contrary: Single people of all ages are flocking to dating services, where a sympathetic counselor using only her memory and her intuition arranges introductions for her clients.

While these dating services often are large (some are even franchised), what they offer—and what single people evidently want very much—is personal service and attention. At a dating service, your counselor takes the time to learn about your preferences, your romantic history, your hopes and expectations. Moreover, she (or occasionally, he) is somebody you can call after a date, somebody to report back to, somebody who can—and will—try again on your behalf.

Not every dating service is good, of course, but they all depend upon word-of-mouth reputation, and most make an honest effort to please their clients. Here's how they work: Normally, you sign up for either six months or a year, at a cost ranging from $200 to $500. You're then asked to fill out a lengthy questionnaire, and you're interviewed in some detail by a member of the staff. Over the next few months, the service provides a certain number of names and phone numbers and a brief description of each person they think you should meet. If you do meet someone promising, many dating services will let you put your membership on "hold" for a while.

Most of the newer dating services cater to successful, professional, attractive people who find it both time-consuming and difficult—if not downright embarrassing—to meet their counterparts of the opposite sex in the more conventional ways. And now, not surprisingly, we're beginning to see dating services that accept only Jewish clients.

I first became aware of this development when I was invited to talk about my book on The Phil Donahue Show. The other guests on the panel represented various types of dating services, and my role was to explain why this way of meeting people had become so popular—and so necessary.

One of them was Bobbie Goldfarb, an energetic woman in her mid-40s and one of the founders of The Jewish Dating Service (JDS) in Minneapolis. When it was her turn to be interviewed, Bobbie Goldfarb proudly announced that JDS had already produced forty marriages. Think about it: In a community of only 33,000 Jews, Goldfarb and her partners had been responsible for forty Jewish marriages in three years! (As of August 1988, JDS had arranged 110–120 marriages.)

It's too bad that Phil Donahue didn't ask Bobbie Goldfarb how she had met *her* husband, because he would have heard a good story. On a warm spring evening in 1962, Bobbie had a visit from Stephen Goldfarb, a law student and her oldest friend in the world. Bobbie and Stephen had been in kindergarten together and had remained close friends ever since.

"Just friends?" I asked.

"Just friends," Bobbie assured me. "There was no romantic involvement."

But on that night, Stephen said to her, "Listen. In a platonic relationship, one person is a coward. Who is it, you or me?" A few minutes later he asked Bobbie to marry him.

"But we've never gone out!" she replied.

"Look," said Stephen. "This whole thing is making me nervous. I've got finals coming up. I want you to let me know in three days."

Three days later, first thing in the morning, Bobbie called Stephen. His sister answered. "Stephen is sleeping," she said. "Do you want to leave a message?"

She replied, "Just tell him Bobbie says okay. He'll know what it's about."

A year later they were married. Today, Bobbie Goldfarb spends her days meeting with single people and making matches. Sometimes she tells them the story of how she came to marry Stephen. "Never underestimate the power of a platonic relationship," she tells her clients.

After Bobbie Goldfarb appeared on Phil Donahue, The Jewish Dating Service in Minneapolis received more than 150 letters. Roughly half of the inquiries came from individuals who said they wanted to set up a Jewish dating service in their own community. Goldfarb and her colleagues Sandy Olkon and Jean Bundt receive inquiries from all over the country, and they have helped start Jewish dating services in Dallas, Houston, and Atlanta.

There are a number of new Jewish dating services around the country, but Phil Donahue was right to invite The Jewish Dating Service in Minneapolis on the show, for this one is the grandmother of them all. JDS began ten years ago from a room in Temple Israel, the large Reform congregation in Minneapolis. Bobbie Goldfarb and her two partners each put in one morning a week, in addition to

Wednesdays from 4 to 11 P.M. and all day Sunday. (They now work 9:00 A.M.–12 noon, Mondays through Thursdays, although they occasionally come in as early as 7:00 A.M.) Nobody got paid.

The response was tremendous. In the first three months, JDS arranged 760 dates—at which point they stopped counting. The partners asked their clients to report to them after each new introduction, and before long the volume of calls was overwhelming. Many of those calls came to the women at home. "Finally," says Sandy Olkon, who met her husband through Bobbie Goldfarb and is one of the founders of JDS, "my husband put his foot down and said this had to get out of the house. We are getting calls at midnight Thursday from people who had tickets to a show on Friday night and wanted a date."

Before they moved into their office in suburban St. Louis Park, you could join JDS for free. Today, at $300, it's still a bargain. The cost includes an interview, a references check, a guarantee of meeting eight people at the end of six months, and $1 for a Polaroid photo. The photo is confidential, and it's used only to help the interviewers keep track of their many clients.

For Goldfarb and her two partners, and for everyone else I've spoken to who does this kind of work, matchmaking is a cause rather than a job. At JDS, the women take only pocket money. It's not that they object to earning a real income, but they're very concerned with keeping their fees affordable.

Who are their clients? "We've been finding people who the Jewish community doesn't know about," says Marilyn Weisberg. Many are recent arrivals in town who have been transferred to the Twin Cities for business reasons. JDS is an ideal place for them because, in addition to dates, the service also provides roommates, same-sex friends, professional connections, and even a place to have dinner on the Jewish holidays.

"The people we attract aren't the ones who show up at social gatherings," says Weisberg. "They're either too busy, or they don't like crowds, or they don't care for the people they've been meeting that way. Most of our clients are professional, including a number of women who are doctors and lawyers. Frankly, I'd like to see us attract more people without college degrees or fancy jobs."

Everyone who signs up with JDS has to provide three references to certify that he or she is Jewish, single, and of sound character. If a client is divorced, he has to show his papers. There's an application form that asks whether the client's mother is Jewish. What if a client considers himself Jewish, but isn't, according to *halakhah*? "We'll accept such clients," says Olkon, "but we point out that a Conservative or Orthodox rabbi won't marry them unless they go through a halakhic conversion.''

Because the atmosphere at JDS is homey and informal, new clients might think they're seeing a certain lack of professionalism. But it's only a cover. "You might walk in here and think we are three dizzy dames," says Goldfarb. "In fact, it's planned that way, because we want our clients to be relaxed. Many people who come to us are very nervous. Some of them still think that dating services are for losers and nerds. Sometimes they get as far as the parking lot, and then they turn around and go back home.''

Confidentiality is particularly important at JDS, given that the Jewish community in Minneapolis-St. Paul is relatively small. If the partners see one of their clients on the street or at a social event, they make no acknowledgment unless the client says hello first.

Each new client is interviewed at length, although "interview" may be the wrong word. Actually, it's more like a conversation over coffee. The partners ask about educational levels, religious obser-vance, interests, and values. The brief application form asks some basic questions, including one about drug use ("mostly marijuana, some cocaine, and the occasional mushroom," says Weisberg), but there are no questions about sex.

Before name and number are given out, the partners check to make sure that the other person is available and agreeable. That way, there are no disappointments about such surface details as height, weight, age, or occupation.

At JDS, as at all dating services these days, the two biggest complaints from clients have to do with smoking and fat. At least half simply refuse to go out with a smoker. When it comes to preferring a date who is slender, the women are fussy, and the men are even more so. Predictably, nobody has yet complained about meeting a date who's too thin. A new client who is grossly over-weight will be told that the chances of getting dates through JDS may be remote.

Who calls whom? The partners ask the men to call the women, but they report that the men—and a few of the women—believe that the task should be shared. "Most women still don't like to call men," says Weisberg. "Maybe after the first or second date, but they don't want to call a total stranger.''

This agrees with my own findings. Of the women I interviewed, even the boldest and most assertive told me that they preferred not to call men. "I'd rather man the phone than phone the man," was the way one woman put it. Most women I spoke with were con-vinced—or pretended to believe—that the men still preferred to do the calling. The men, meanwhile, seduced by media images of the New Woman, are still at home, waiting for the phone to ring, hoping that the lovely lady with the bottle of Harvey's Bristol Cream will finally take the first step.

In Minneapolis, too, the biggest problem is the shortage of men over 40. The Jewish Dating Service attracts a number of divorced women, but there are few men for them to meet. As Marilyn Weisberg explains it, their ex-husbands tend to be interested in younger women, or in women who aren't Jewish.

Although the great majority of its clients are upscale professionals, JDS also does its best to serve singles with special needs. "The Jewish community is very narrow about people who aren't in the mainstream," says Goldfarb, who has in mind a network that is not only for purposes of romance but also for simple companionship. (In fact, Goldfarb, who recently has been involved in starting a Jewish day school on the high school level, is already planning her next project: a communications center for Jews who are disabled.)

For Bobbie Goldfarb and her partners, The Jewish Dating Service is clearly God's work. "We change people's lives every day," she says. "I feel I'm doing something a lot more important than making money. There's never a day that I don't want to go to work."

I have described the matchmakers at some length in this article, with barely a word about—or from—their clients. Having previously written about the feelings and experiences of single people, I wanted to concentrate on the other side, on those who try to offer an alternative to loneliness.

Had I interviewed the clients who have signed up at these various dating services, I would have heard endless variations on the following theme: "I never thought I would do something like this, but nothing else seemed to be working. Dating services aren't really for people like me."

But they are. Two years ago, when I interviewed several hundred single people, I was struck by how many see themselves as different from the rest of the population. For example, although I rarely asked, many people felt it necessary to tell me that they never go to singles bars, with the clear inference that other single people go all the time, and that their own sense of alienation from such places is somehow unique or at least unusual. But as I spoke with single people all over the country, it became clear that almost nobody over the age of 30 who is interested in a serious relationship goes to singles bars expecting to find one, although many people apparently believe that everyone else does.

Similarly, many people told me that they would rather stay

home than date somebody who doesn't appeal to them. "I don't go out just for the sake of dating," I was told repeatedly, again with the implication that this attitude is unusual. It isn't. Along the same lines, most people were convinced that everybody else is enjoying more sex, going out on more dates, or generally having more fun than *they* are.

Given the large number of single people who are interested in an intimate relationship, it's too bad that so many feel isolated and different from a mythical norm. Which brings us back to the recent surge in dating services. The appeal of a dating service, after all, is that it treats each client as an individual. And if many of these individuals have a lot more in common than they suspect, this would help explain why dating services are not only popular these days, but sometimes even successful at what they do.

Matchmaking among Jews is as old as Judaism itself. The twenty-fourth chapter of Genesis describes in detail how Abraham sent his servant to choose a wife for Isaac. In more recent times, we have a long tradition of the *shadkhan*, and today's Jewish dating services clearly are a modern variation.

But if matchmaking is God's work, then it can't be left only to the professionals. Among amateurs, bringing together a man and a woman is often known as "fixing people up." That's a terrible expression; it implies that something is broken. "Blind dates" don't sound very appealing either, so let's call them "introductions" instead.

Introductions can work—I met my wife that way—so long as you keep in mind three simple rules: First, everyone involved should have low expectations. Decide in advance that there will be no hard feelings if things don't work out. Second, the initial meeting between two people should be brief and informal. And finally, never introduce two people unless you're doing both of them a favor.

Jewish

∧ **Marital Status**

- ☐ Single
- ☑ Not quite married
- ☐ Married
- ☐ Single again
    - ☐ Widowed
    - ☐ Abandoned
    - ☐ Divorced
- ☐ Remarried
- ☐ Intermarried
- ☐ Gay or Lesbian
- ☐ Childless

9

The *Kedushah* of Monogamy: A Personal Perspective

Yeroham Tsuriel

The seemingly irreconcilable conflict between the sexual norms of the Jewish tradition and contemporary mores and modes of behavior in this area is a problem with which an entire generation is wrestling and that, perhaps more than any other, causes the halakhic system to appear unlivable and irrelevant.

First, I wish to explain the stance from which I write. I am an Orthodox Jew, and as such I am totally committed to the authority of the traditional *halakhah* and its interpretation through the institutions of *Torah she-be'al peh.* My obedience to the norms of personal modesty and chastity derive from that source. At the same time, I have wrestled with this problem and understand the dilemma of this generation from within. While it is not customary among Jews to engage in public confession of sin, I must state that I have acted out a deep split within my own life: For nearly five years, I lived a pious Jewish life in all respects but the sexual. As one who has become a *ba'al teshuvah* in the classic sense of having knowingly and willfully sinned, and subsequently returning to the full demands of the Torah, I hope it will not seem presumptuous for me to say that I possess a certain understanding of both poles of this question and of how the gap between the modernist and traditionalist positions may be spanned.

A few more words of background. During my college years, I lived an urbane and open life style, which included many friendships with young women of greatly varied backgrounds. I remember feeling at that time that my adherence to the norms of the *halakhah* with respect to physical intimacy helped to create an atmosphere of dignity and respect in my relationships with the opposite sex. Subsequently, I moved to another city, one of the centers of the emergent youth culture, and there, under the combined pressures of a personal religious crisis and the free values prevalent in my environment, my sexual morality began to crumble. I found a certain social nexus within the *havurah* movement, with people for whom praying together, celebrating *Shabbat,* studying classical texts, etc., were perceived as freely chosen, nonobligatory vehicles for their personal religious sensitivities. (Years later, I came to a realization as to how alien this mode of perception is to the tradition.) Within this context, more or less free sexual unions were the order of the day.

Looking at that world in retrospect, it is no longer clear to me that single adulthood in and of itself is responsible for the relaxed sexual morality of our generation. The reverse is true as well. Free sex encourages a casual attitude toward relationships generally, which, in turn, further discourages early marriages. The prevailing cultural prejudice that marriage is not necessary, and that a young couple ought to live together for a considerable time before considering marriage, discouraged me, for example, from cultivating relationships with those women who still adhered to the "outmoded" norm of premarital chastity. Furthermore, I found that this attitude encourages predatory and exploitative approaches toward sexual partners, particularly on the part of men.

What can be done to civilize this jungle? I would contend that it is in the nature of this jungle to be a jungle. The chaotic irresponsible elements within sexuality are so close to the surface even among sensitive, gentle, cultured individuals that any such enterprise seems doomed to failure.

A letter from a friend of mine—a young woman who grew up in the atmosphere of the youth culture of the late '60s and, by a long and tortuous path, found her way to Judaism—portrays some of the issues involved in striking and eloquent terms.

When I beat *al het* for the lack of mental and academic discipline that have left me without vessels for my now somewhat mature speculations, it is not so separate from the obligation I feel is necessary for some of the other holes I've poked in my soul with men. . . . At every moment when a hint of method was clear, a man appeared and I felt he embodied the knowledge I sought. I exchanged being lost from myself for being lost in him. This is so clearly a lack of perception for the Divine Image within me, and such a belittling of my privilege and responsibility of choice. . . . Both the refusal to achieve clarity of thought and action through orderly work, and the sacrifice of the end for the worship of one of the means—i.e., becoming a "macrobiotic" or "frummie" or "artistic" type—are idolatry and a murdering of the human possibility to encompass the creation, but they're not the only way to do it. *Z'nut* (promiscuity) is way number three to make *ha-Shem*'s name have a foreign sound in His own world. A relationship whose commitment does not allow full expression of both people without fear of overstepping the boundaries . . . can only be a fragmentation, creating a contradiction between one's soul and one's actions. Any lack of commitment in sexuality, which plumbs the depths of each, can make a habit of taking those discoveries lightly, releasing their energy into the air instead of embodying it in work that honors God's name. . . . Just as saying *ha-Shem* is He who has power to rule over all of "these" does not exclude any of the creation, so great is His oneness, so too *kedushah* in sexuality does not limit one's ability to love or to give, but includes every possible relationship in its higher focus. It includes it and contains it in manageable, usable form. Only then can one avoid killing the Godly spark in oneself or another.

Kedushah, restraint, monogamy, seen not as puritanical restrictions or hatred of the human life force, but as a focusing of that energy. Perhaps here lies the beginning of an answer to the problem. There is a paradox in sexuality. It touches that which is most human in us, in binding us intimately to another person, and in bringing us close to the mysteries of our mortality; and at one and the same time it appears as a blind, chaotic drive, crying for release in any form. The modern view, based on a bowdlerized version of Freud, teaches that repression or sublimation of sexual energy is unhealthy and that orgasm is a value in itself. In contrast, the traditional Jewish view is based on the premise that this energy must be channeled and harnessed, in creating the bonds of the couple and the family, and through them, the larger community. To leave this energy at the level of mere pleasure-seeking is to fail in our task as human beings.

Perhaps it is this insight that the Kabbalists express when they speak of the importance of *shemirat ha-brit*—guarding the covenant of circumcision—and the seriousness of sexual sins in terms of the flow of Divine energy between the *sefirot* of *yesod* and *malkhut*, which are the deepest sources of energy.

If sexuality as experience goes to the depths of each individual's being, so does the teaching about sexuality touch cords that are close to the essence of the Jewish world view. Traditionally, the notion of *kedushah,* holiness, which is the highest rung of spiritual development that a human being can reach, is tied to the idea of self-restraint and discipline. In Judaism, this discipline is applied not only to the mind and to people's higher faculties, but to their basic biological drives as well. Moreover, *"kedoshim tihyu,"* "you shall be holy," is addressed not only to spiritual giants, but to every single Jew. These demands are not easy, and they cannot be explained simply in rationalistic terms. One central idea in Judaism is that of the *hukkah*—that law that we obey even though we do not understand the reason for it—through which we surrender our reason and will to that of the Almighty. Perhaps one of the motifs underlying this is a profound awareness of the limits of the human intellect and of the ease with which the thinking processes of even the most sophisticated may be bent by the promptings of the *yetzer ha-ra.* This is the essential point of departure of Judaism from Western culture. For us, man is not the measure of all things.

Milton Himmelfarb, in an essay entitled "Paganism," observes that Judaism is defined by the sages as "denial of paganism" (*kefirah ba'avodah zarah*). He notes that two of the outstanding elements in paganism are its orgiastic approach to sex and its fascination with bloodshed. These three elements—idolatry, licentiousness, and murder—are linked together as the three acts for which a Jew is commanded to die in *kiddush ha-Shem,* and they are also linked together in the passage from Leviticus 18 read on Yom Kippur afternoon. "Unchastity is the piety of paganism. The things that are 'abominations' for Israel are the 'statutes' for the people of Egypt and Canaan. . . . Bloodshed is likewise the piety of paganism." Himmelfarb goes on to speculate as to whether the current mode of sexual libertarianism, which goes under the banner of gentleness and kindness ("Make Love, Not War"), won't, in the end, carry in its wake a new wave of paganism and irrationality that will involve not only unchastity, but cruelty and contempt for human life as well.

At one time, I believed that the *halakhah* ought to respond to current sexual morality through a liberalization of norms—opening the *mikvaot* to unmarried women, and exploring the possibility of a limited *heter* for premarital relations. In fact, the nature of the prohibition on premarital intercourse, provided that the woman is not a *niddah,* is rather ambiguous. It is a point of debate among the *rishonim* whether the verse, "there shall not be a *kedeshah* among the daughters of Israel" (Deuteronomy 23:18), refers only to those who engage in incestuous or adulterous liaisons (Ramban), to those who are generally promiscuous (Ravad), or to any woman who engages in intercourse without benefit of *huppah* and *kiddushin*

(Rambam). Rabbi Yaakov Emden, in a responsum published in the mid-eighteenth century, deals with this problem and concludes that, under carefully delineated circumstances, sexual relations without marriage are permissible. Among the preconditions that he stipulates are: (1) that the woman observe all the laws of *niddah;* (2) that, for the duration of the relationship, known as *pilagshut* (concubinage, or half-marriage), both lovers be faithful to one another; (3) that the relationship be a public one, in which the man and his mistress live together; (4) that a rabbi be consulted in each individual case. Emden adds that those who teach this *heter* perform a great *mitzvah* for, inasmuch as certain people will engage in relations without marriage in any event, it is better that they should do so in some form of halakhically legitimate context.

While Emden's view does define one valid option within the *halakhah,* and must be respected as the considered opinion of a major halakhic figure, I can no longer see this as the desired solution for our generation, convenient as it might be. The entire Jewish people rejected this view. Rav Hayyim of Brisk, when asked about this responsum, described Emden as a "knave within the bounds of Torah." At best, this solution was intended to be used after the fact and not as an expression of what God's will as expressed in the Torah wants and demands of Jews.

How does one live this way in the real world? There is no easy answer. The forces against it are many: the person's own sexual urge, the sexual stimuli that are ubiquitous in our culture; the need for human warmth and closeness that is expressed in the physical embrace; the social pressures urging one not to be "uptight" or "hung up," which, repeated often enough, lead one to doubt one's own position. Basically, the only way to preserve sexual purity is to build a strong, clear awareness that this is the true Jewish path and that only through it may one achieve *kedushah* and *toharah.*

Maimonides sums up the seriousness of the laws of *arayot* and the difficulty they pose in the *Mishneh Torah.* Perhaps we may gain strength from his words.

> There are no laws in the entire Torah which are as difficult for the majority of the people as those concerning *arayot.* The sages said that when Israel was commanded about *arayot* they wept and accepted the mitzvah grudgingly . . . and they further said that one can not find any community, at any time, in which there were not those who were guilty of illicit relations.
>
> Therefore, a man ought to bend his impulse in this matter and accustom himself to extra holiness, purity of thought, and

proper views in order to be saved from sin. . . . And he should avoid frivolity and drunkenness and sexual talk, for those are great factors leading to *arayot*. And he oughtn't to live without a wife, for by marriage he will attain greater purity. But greater than all of these, he should turn himself and his thoughts to words of Torah and broaden his mind in its wisdom, for sexual thoughts only grow strong in a mind which is empty of wisdom.

POSTSCRIPT

Rereading "The Kedushah of Monogamy" after more than a dozen years is a strange experience. The author of the article was a young, earnest, unmarried man in his late twenties, who could devote most of his waking hours to study of Torah and reflection upon matters of Jewish philosophy and spirituality. The author of these lines is a man in his early forties, his everyday life filled with the responsibilities of family and profession. The former was rather naive, innocent, and optimistic about life, while the latter has both experienced and seen in others some of the pain and suffering that can be felt, perhaps more than in any other area, in the realm of intimate relationships.

While I still agree, in substance, with both the theoretical principles and the halakhic conclusions outlined in that article, I cannot avoid the feeling that there is more than a bit of self-righteousness in the tone of the article. I find a certain lack of compassion or understanding for a person who cannot live up to the high standards of sexual morality I championed there. To put matters quite simply: the dream in which one marries as a young adult and settles down to live "happily ever after" with one's life partner is one that, for many people, does not seem to work. The social context in which there are more and more unmarried adults—whether due to divorce, homosexuality, or the simple inability to find a suitable partner—is one that cannot simply be ignored in a serious discussion of "sex and the tradition in the contemporary world." The needs, both for intimacy and love, and for sexual expression on whatever level, are among the most fundamental human needs. The two are of course interrelated. Sex is ideally expressed in a loving, caring, committed relationship, while feelings of love, which are in essence spiritual, are quite properly expressed in the realm of the physical (it is significant that our Rabbis always accepted this point and never developed concepts of "platonic" or "chaste" love such as are found in the medieval courtly or romantic traditions). Given this, can one realistically say, "Let the Law pierce the mountain," and condemn those who are unable, for whatever reason, to live "normal" family lives, to live a life of extended celibacy? And if they can't or won't lead such a life, accuse them of living in bad faith with the halakhah?

I do not have any easy answers. To describe is not necessarily to condone or to permit in halakhic or moral terms. As a Jew committed to the framework of the halakhah, I can perhaps advocate a liberal pesak permitting sexual relations between unmarried people under certain clearly defined conditions (i.e., sexual faithfulness for the duration of the relationship and observance of immersion in the mikvah), following R. Moses Isserles' gloss on Even ha-Ezer 26:1. But I am aware of the woeful inadequacy and irrelevance of such a ruling for the woman stuck in a loveless, destructive marriage whose husband spitefully refuses to give a get, or for the individual who in good faith finds himself or herself drawn to members of the same sex. As an Orthodox rabbi, there is no possible way for me to give a heter for either adultery or homosexuality, but nor, at the risk of sounding Christian, do I feel it my right to cast stones at them.

Those of us living in the latter part of the twentieth century may have a stronger sense than our forebears of the fragility and transient nature of human relationships, the pain and loneliness of life without love and intimacy, and the peculiar difficulties of finding one's way in life as a moral being in the contemporary world. Loyalty to the integrity of the halakhah and sympathy for one's fellow human being must therefore constitute "two verses that come as one" (shnei ketuvim ha-ba'im ke-ehad). Together with the lofty ideals and calls for personal holiness, there must be compassion, love, and understanding for another human being and his/her quandary in this confusing and value-shattering age.

10

The Liberal Jew and Sex

Ellen M. Umansky

The following is a response to Yeroham Tsuriel:

In his article, "Sex and Jewish Tradition," Yeroham Tsuriel maintains that the halakhic Jew can best respond to the crumbling sexual morality of modern society by following those traditional Jewish sources that have understood "*kedushah* (holiness), restraint, and monogamy" to represent the Will of God. Although he states that his intent is to span "the gap between the modernist and traditionalist positions," Tsuriel's rejection of what he considers to be "contemporary mores and modes of behavior," and similarly, his rejection of any liberalization of halakhic norms, leads him to a reaffirmation of the traditionalist position as the only "true Jewish path." Tsuriel may feel that his conclusions are not "pious restatement(s) of the Orthodox position" because they emerge out of a long period of personal struggle, self-questioning, and doubt. However, the desired solution he claims to have discovered for "an entire generation" is, in fact, the position of the *Shulhan Arukh* first presented by Maimonides in his *Mishneh Torah*. Tsuriel does not really offer us a way of spanning the gap between modernist and traditionalist outlooks. Instead, he admonishes us to turn our backs on contemporary sexual mores and, as he has done, return "to the full demands of the Torah."

As a nonhalakhic Jew, it is difficult for me to accept Tsuriel's solution as my own. My source of ethics derives neither from the Talmud, commentators such as Maimonides, nor the *Shulhan*

Arukh. Although I believe that there are ethical imperatives that each Jew must follow, I see these demands as rooted in the ethical autonomy of the individual and not in any external code of law. Careful thought, responsible decision making, and the conviction that what I have decided is "right"—and would also be "right" for others in a similar situation—are all important components in setting up an ethical standard of behavior. While Jewish tradition does influence my concept of morality, like Mordecai Kaplan, I recognize this tradition as having a voice but not a veto. Thus, ultimately, I must take the reasoned judgment of individuals as seriously as I do the demands of *halakhah*.

Orthodox Jews frequently remark that it is easier to be a liberal Jew than it is to be "fully observant." This kind of observation betrays a failure to take the demands of liberal Judaism seriously. For the liberal Jew who, like myself, is committed both to the rational capacity and ethical autonomy of individual persons as well as the preservation of Jewish religion and culture, making one's ethical standard both personal *and* Jewish, is often a difficult and painful process. Moreover, the inner struggle and lack of conviction that one's "mores and modes of behavior" are unquestionably right continues even after decisions have been made. While Tsuriel maintains that he too has struggled to reach the ethical (identified with God's Will), his admission that as an Orthodox Jew he feels "totally committed to the authority of traditional *halakhah* and its traditional interpretation" makes his decision to follow the precepts of the *Shulhan Arukh* a foregone conclusion.

Essentially, I see Tsuriel's self-proclaimed struggle not as an attempt to discover the ethical, but as a growing recognition that one cannot be a pious Jew "in all respects but the sexual." If one is genuinely committed to Orthodoxy and sees this commitment as presupposing an adherence to the authority of traditional *halakhah,* then one cannot accept halakhic decisions only when it is convenient or desirable to do so. The fact that, as Tsuriel admits, "the nature of the (halakhic) prohibition on premarital intercourse, provided that the woman is not ritually unclean, is rather ambiguous" somewhat weakens but does not negate Tsuriel's conclusions. He rejects the liberalization of halakhic norms because he feels that such a measure would only be a compromising, convenient solution. He therefore states that "the test of our generation" is an affirmation of premarital chastity, faithfulness within marriage, and adherence to the laws of family purity. Believing that God expects us to live up to these sexual standards, Tsuriel asserts that only those Jews who do so can attain a life that is both holy and pure.

As a liberal Jew, I can react to Tsuriel's article, but I cannot fully respond to it. Neither do I think that Tsuriel can fully respond to my own stance on sexual ethics. While both of us are Jews, our sense of what is Jewish vastly differs. Therefore, any attempt at real communication would have little chance of success. For Tsuriel, a position on sexuality that claims to be Jewish must follow "traditional *halakhah* and its traditional interpretation." For me, any sexual standard that aims at achieving moral excellence can also be defended as Jewish. While, obviously, Jews are not the only people capable of positing a morally excellent sexual standard, God's command to be holy gives us a special obligation to strive toward the highest level of ethical behavior. In formulating my own sexual ethic, then, I too have taken seriously God's command to be holy. However, I cannot believe that only by adhering to the norms of *halakhah* does one begin to make life sacred.

My standard of ethical sexual behavior stresses not the sexual purity of the individual, but rather the sexual *relationship* between two human beings. Its moral criterion rests with Martin Buber's concept of personhood and what it means to be fully human. While recognizing that "self-restraint and discipline" are important means of hallowing life, the sexual standard to which I adhere rejects the notion that premarital intercourse and the decision not to observe the family purity laws labels one undisciplined and without self-restraint. Instead, it maintains that by treating someone as a whole person and not as a sex object, in Buber's language, as a "Thou" and not an "It," one transforms physical and potentially animalistic and exploitive behavior into expressions of warmth, caring, feeling, and love. This kind of physical intimacy is qualitatively different from acts of rape, sex performed only to satisfy one's sexual urges, and intercourse based not on mutual desire but on feelings of obligation. The extent to which it is transforming depends both on the depth of emotion involved and the degree to which the other's individuality and self-worth are considered.

Because my criterion of ethical sexual behavior is based on personhood, a relationship that most fully recognizes the humanity of the persons involved is necessarily on a higher ethical level than that sexual relationship based only on mutual consent. Premarital sex becomes unethical when an individual treats another solely as a sex partner, an "It" instead of a "Thou." Intercourse between two people who love each other is more ethical than intercourse based on mutual agreement, and intercourse within marriage (if entering into a marital relationship is the deepest expression of love that two people can offer) represents the highest level of human sexual intimacy. To strive toward moral excellence, however, this relationship should be monogamous. Extramarital affairs jeopardize feelings of trust, honesty, and closeness, and indicate a weakening of one's marital (or what Eugene Borowitz calls a "love for life") commitment. Therefore, moral excellence is incompatible with marital infidelity because such affairs reduce the strength, and significance, of the marital bond. This is as true of premarital relations as of intercourse within marriage.

While, as human beings, we have an obligation to strive toward that which is morally excellent, even if one formulates an ideal standard of sexual behavior, it may not be possible to attain that ideal at every stage of one's life. An I-Thou relationship based on mutual love and a desire to spend one's life together necessitates that the individual first find a Thou to whom this kind of commitment can be made. Moreover, even if one has found such a person, he or she may not be ready to enter into a marital relationship. Instead, that individual may choose to spend some time discovering his or her own set of values, self-identity, and personal sense of direction. Undoubtedly, it is possible to achieve these ends within marriage. However, the independence and greater flexibility that singleness affords make single adulthood a stage in one's life that should neither be minimized nor, I think, missed.

The liberal Jew knows of no pre-established path to holiness. Thus, in order to seriously consider God's command to be holy, he or she must first recognize that which can make life sacred. To me, one hallows life when one regards others as persons. As Buber states, we must often perceive the world and those people within it as objects of our experience. Yet when we encounter another human being as a Thou, "we are touched by a breath of eternal life," for all of us have been created in God's image.

An Interview with Rabbi Shlomo Riskin

Neal Kaunfer and Zev Shanken

Neal Kaunfer and Zev Shanken: Sometimes Jews have difficulty finding answers to their personal problems within the *halakhah.* Certain problems are particularly difficult to deal with. One such example is the issue of nonmarital sex. Many persons, including committed Jews, have discovered that sex is important not only for pleasure, but for the maintenance of physical and mental health. Yet today we are experiencing a period of extended adolescence in which large numbers of Jews must wait until their 20s or 30s to get married (if at all). What kind of response can you give them?

Shlomo Riskin:[1] As in all issues, we first have to consider what the halakhic view is on nonmarital sex, and why. I can give you a little exegesis, here. In describing the creation of Adam, the Bible records God's statement, *"Lo tov heyot adam levado,"* "It is not good for man to be alone." To me, this is one of the most profound and one of the most significant statements in the Bible. It speaks about the tragedy of the human predicament. The Bible then says: It's not good for man to be alone. . . . I'm going to make a helpmate

---

[1]Rabbi Shlomo Riskin, Ph.D., oversees a bustling labyrinth of Jewish educational and spiritual institutions. He is Founder of Lincoln Square Synagogue in New York, Founder and Chief Rabbi of Efrat, Israel, and Founder and Dean of the Ohr Torah Institutions. He is committed to the modern applications of Jewish law and is a leading figure in reaching out to "not yet religious" Jews.

for man, an alter ego, somebody who's going to be a help, but also be an opposite. Then a very fascinating thing happens. God brings all the animals to man to name. After Adam names all the animals, he doesn't find this alter ego. God puts him to sleep and from his rib creates Eve. The *Midrash* says that Adam had relations with every one of the animals and it didn't work. Only with woman could he say, "Bone of my bone and flesh of my flesh." I believe what the Bible is saying is that for the human being, sex is far deeper than merely a physical, biological expression. In order to be meaningful, sex must be accompanied by a sense of commitment to another. The individual must really feel that the woman with whom he is becoming one flesh is someone who cares about him deeply, not just a one-night stand. I don't believe that one-night stands can be ultimately satisfying, and I say this through clinical experience with the religious and nonreligious, observant and nonobservant.

Marriage is truly our way of guaranteeing that the sexual expression will be concomitant with commitment. That's what marriage really is: a statement of commitment by two people. It's not something that is eternal and can never be broken, but nevertheless it's an honest realization of commitment.

Certainly I understand all the pressures and all the difficulties. I was 23 before I was married. I'm very well aware of the problems of a prolonged adolescence. I don't think it's so healthy, by the way. It's very damaging to society. I think we are making a very big mistake educationally by extending the period of adolescence. But I don't think the answer lies in sexual relationships, because I've seen too many broken hearts.

It's too easy. You know, Freud said, "When it comes to self-deception, every person is a genius." And it's too easy because of the very strong biological drive to talk oneself into a commitment that isn't there. And it's very simple to talk oneself into a commitment if one has not made a statement of commitment other than perhaps "I love you." I've seen too many broken hearts on both ends. I believe that despite all the pressures and all the difficulties, the place of sex is within marriage. Seeing sex as an expression of sanctity and an expression of commitment of one person to another I think *ultimately* is what helps in the society.

Kaunfer and Shanken: Many people are not able to find that committed relationship easily. They're searching it out. Yet, during that period of time sexuality becomes part of that ongoing search for a permanent relationship.

Riskin: They're afraid of commitment. We've created a society that is very individualistically centered. Very selfish. And *frightened* to make commitment. The relationships without marriage very often are an expression of this fear of commitment. There's something wrong with the whole educational level. There's something wrong with the products in modern society. And I think something un-healthy. And rather than encourage *more* relationships without commitment, I would much prefer to unlock the key to the creation of healthy human beings who are not frightened of commitment.

Kaunfer and Shanken: And do you think that that's being done here?

Riskin: I have. I've started a yeshivah high school. I'm thinking of beginning a teacher's seminary.

Kaunfer and Shanken: That's not a mixed group, though. Are they separated?

Riskin: Well, we have a boy's high school. In September we're starting a sister school. The two high schools are separated, yes, but they have some activities in common. We do this in order to teach boys and girls how to relate to one another without the social stress that will make individual development difficult. I can try to educate in the best way I know how, but I think there's a real problem that runs against the basic grain of Judaism. Judaism *does* insist on commitment. The fact that there is a circumcision on an eight-day-old boy tells the youngster, even before he is ready to realize it, that he is committed. We have created a society of people who find it very difficult to commit themselves to anything. I believe that we have to create intensive Jewish environments and urge young people to make the commitment. I think marriage is a very impor-tant part of Jewish life. In addition to everything else, if we don't create little Jews, we are not going to be able to survive. That's as important as halakhic commitment.

Kaunfer and Shanken: The problem is that there are other traditions of knowledge and truth. Many people say that their commitment is to an individual search for an identity.

Riskin: I understand. But here I would have to say that there are certain times when Judaism has to say forthrightly, "Here's where we part company." There is room for a tremendous amount of individual search, but within a certain context. The individual must understand that he is part of a nation. Freud had a marvelous book, *Civilization and Its Discontents,* in which he points out that the very structuring of the society means that the individual must overlook, under certain circumstances, his own personal needs for the good of the community. Otherwise you cannot have a valid society emerg-ing. This is also true within a family context: I live with my wife and my four children, and each of us has to make certain sacrifices for the good of the group.

Kaunfer and Shanken: When you said, "This is where we part company," what does that mean in terms of the individual?

Riskin: I am not judgmental. None of us, certainly not I, would claim that we keep all the ideals of Judaism. I do the best I can; I try very hard. Keeping only part of the law is not to be a hypocrite; it's merely to be inconsistent. Do we understand that people will fall while they're groping, while they're developing, while they're growing? Of course. The only thing to which I object is making an *ideal* of the faltering. It's one thing to say: "Because of my educational background and because of my emotional, psychological needs, I can't get married and I'm involved in a sexual liaison. I'm developing, I'm thinking, I'm groping, and I will be as constructive a member of the Jewish community as I can." Then one is accepted completely. It's something else to say, "Because I'm groping and *I* can't make it within the marital context, there's something wrong with the whole marital context, and Judaism as a religion should now sanction premarital sexual relations." The first I understand very well. With the second I have to strongly part company.

Kaunfer and Shanken: Do you foresee the necessity for any actual change in Jewish law?

Riskin: In terms especially of my clinical experience, of dealing with people who have gotten married after living together, I believe not only that there should be no relaxation, but perhaps there ought to be even an intensification of halakhic restrictions.

I want to tell you something. The Bible understands balance very well. "You shall love your neighbor as yourself" is a very important principle. And many people live by the love ethic. The balance to that is "Thou shalt not commit adultery." Adultery is the death knell of tradition in Jewish society. I'll tell you of a very interesting experience that I had last year at a rabbinic conference that met to discuss the problems of divorces amongst the members of the rabbinate. Their wives claimed that their husbands were having adulterous relationships with members of their community. It is very easy for something like this to happen. A rabbi often sees his congregants in very vulnerable positions. Jewish law has guards against this. In my particular synagogue adulterous relationships are unheard of. People don't greet each other with a kiss. I don't stay in rooms alone with women congregants. I believe these laws are very clever and very necessary. They speak in depth to the human condition. And I think that we need these safeguards.

Kaunfer and Shanken: So what you're asking for is a process of reeducation away from the kind of society we live in.

Riskin: That's precisely it. And we have to be able to create—in unabashed fashion—intensive Jewish communities that will live with Jewish values.

Kaunfer and Shanken: From what you said, you seem to imply that there really is no contradiction between the Jewish way of living and contemporary findings in the area of mental health.

Riskin: Absolutely. I think that the more people thoroughly understand Judaism and the more proficient we become in mental health, the more we will see that when the Bible says "*Le-tov lakh,*" there's a system ultimately for your good.

JONI FRIEDMAN[2] COMMENTS

Rabbi Riskin's views on sex and marriage are not surprising. But I do not understand one thing: If a lack of maturity is leading young Jews into nonmarital sexual relationships, is marriage at an earlier age the solution? Will this lead to more stable marriages? I agree with him that there are far too many unhealthy sexual relationships being carried on and that we ought to do something about that. But tell me: Where is the value in universal virginity until marriage, outside of the fact that Jewish law says it is a value? (Don't say it's *mi-d'oraita*—that was only for women, to keep their market value up.) Is there another answer besides, "It's a sin"?

LEONARD LEVIN[3] COMMENTS

Rabbi Riskin's equation of the sexual norms of Judaism with mental health is two-faceted: on the one hand, the society that lives strictly by those norms really *is* healthy; on the other hand, where there is discrepancy between current Orthodoxy and the consensus of enlightened opinion, you would be surprised "how much room there is within Jewish law to meet the legitimate needs of now."

---

[2]Joni Friedman was a rabbinical student at Hebrew Union College-Jewish Institute of Religion at the time of her response.

[3]Leonard Levin is a veteran of the *havurah* movement and is currently a systems analyst in Chicago. He is also writing a book, *The Schizophrenic Society*. He was on the editorial board of *Response* from 1973–1976.

What makes for social health? We should beware at the outset of the fallacy that application of any one set of social norms, *regardless of the prevailing cultural context,* is "for your good."

Now, early marriage, for example, is a disastrous prescription for today's young, because they *need* "prolonged adolescence" to sort out their own commitments *to themselves,* before they are in a position to make permanent commitments to others. (The alternative of prolonged celibacy, which Riskin also entertains, was properly recognized as "unhealthy" by the Jewish tradition when it advocated early marriage in the strongest terms.) The norm "marry early" was healthy within the context of traditional Jewish culture because it was consistent with the entire pattern of expectations to which traditional Jews were subjected; it is pernicious today as judged by the same standard of compatibility with prevailing social–cultural facts. The same applies, in greater or lesser degree, to wholesale application of *any* of the more specific norms of traditional Jewish sexual behavior to today's society.

At times, Rabbi Riskin seems to imply that the way to solve this problem is to create a subsociety that governs itself solely by the traditional norms and dissociates itself from the reigning anarchy of the rest of the society. If this is his aim, it is a noble one but doomed to failure. The very appeal to the "mental health" standard shows that the power of modern norms is manifest within Riskin's own thinking; the traditional norms can never claim the absolute hegemony they once had, at least not among present company. We are all two-souled, even today's Orthodox.

The other possible implication of Rabbi Riskin's position is that in the present crisis of values, those who confess from the outset their dual identification with modern society and with the Jewish tradition may find in the structure-giving aspect of Jewish values the *clue* to resolving the incoherence of today's societal norms in the direction of positive, sane rules of conduct in sexual and other areas. I say "clue," because traditional *halakhah* can at best serve us as exemplar and paradigm, not as absolute binding authority—first, for the reasons mentioned; second, because "Accept *halakhah* as authority!" coupled with "Be modern!" is a classic illustration of the kind of inconsistent sets of expectations that have led us to the very trouble we find ourselves in.

Unless, of course, the *halakhah* does exhibit the kind of flexibility that would adequately adjust for today's needs. This Rabbi Riskin does assert. Many of us have hoped, for a century and a half, that this would prove to be the case. If by "*halakhah*" is meant authoritative Orthodox interpretations of *halakhah,* there is every indication that we shall have to continue waiting until the coming of the Messiah—may he come soon!

RABBI RISKIN'S AFTERWORD

Both Joni Friedman and Leonard Levin questioned my prescription for early marriage in the society of today. However, my premise rests on our ability to educate a generation of young Jews who—despite the healthy tensions that emerge from the desire for self and societal improvement and development—are at relative peace with themselves and are therefore ready to make a commitment to another person. It is to this end that I am dedicating whatever strength God gives me. This certainly does imply our creation of a subsociety where values derive from Jewish tradition and *its* concepts of mental health. It similarly implies the ability of halakhic Judaism to meet the needs and concerns of most Jews—as I am convinced to be the case if only given the opportunity. I would suggest that Jewish tradition must first—*mitzvah* by *mitzvah*—be explored and experienced, tested and tasted. As the Shpolyer Zayde taught, "If one feels God's love, there are ultimately no questions, and if one does not, there are ultimately no answers." Halakhic tradition reflects the path that has expressed that love for over three thousand years, both from God to His people and from the people to their God. It's at least worth a try for our generation, which is no less in need of love.

12

Jewish Silence on Sexuality

Harold M. Schulweis

In recent decades sexual matters have been discussed in terms of the perils of detection, infection, and conception. These warnings have been countered with technological arguments concerning the efficacy of the pill and other pharmaceutical devices. These days the threat of the dreaded AIDS epidemic is brandished about as the latest argument for "safe sex." But what if a medical cure is found? Does the moral and religious stance collapse with the development of new vaccines and prophylactic devices? Is there a religious view of sexuality independent of pragmatic and utilitarian arguments, pro and con? While all religions take stands on sexual behavior, love, and marriage, not all are in agreement with each other. The differences are significant for the understanding of the faiths.

Jews do not normally speak about sexuality in the synagogue because they feel it to be somehow an inappropriate subject. Matters of sex are aired outside the sanctuary, given over to psychologists, sociologists, talk show guests, and not to those who traditionally deal with spiritual matters. But sexual silence in the synagogue is both un-Jewish and unwise. Jews are not the children of Paul or Augustine or Luther. They are not the inheritors of a classic Christian or gnostic tradition that associates sexuality with concupiscence. The Jewish tradition is far more open to the imperatives of the body. On the most awesome of all days, Jews read out loud about sodomy, transvestism, and adultery. On Yom Kippur afternoon Jews in the synagogue read the 18th chapter of Leviticus. The rabbis were remarkably astute in picking that section for a holy day when Jews behave like the angels, neither eating nor drinking. The reading selected on the holiest day reminds the worshipers that they all have bodies. As the Jewish prayer reads, "*Ha-guf shelakh v'ha-neshamah shelakh,*" the body is Thine and the soul is Thine.

Jews are rooted in a biblical and rabbinic tradition that deals explicitly and frankly with human sexual relations. Not to speak about the Jewish view of sexuality creates a vacuum more likely to be filled by Christian perspectives that vary significantly from the Jewish outlook. The generic blanket "Western religion" serves only to weigh Judaism down with burdens that are not hers. For example, Judaism is no stranger to the affirmation of life and its celebration. That includes the joys of sexuality. Yet Kinsey in his *Sexual Behavior in the Human Male* argues that the duplicity of the contemporary stands on sexual morality is the product of an original Judeo-Christian code reflecting "the pervading asceticism of Hebrew philosophy." Hopefully Kinsey knew more about sexuality than he knew about Hebrew philosophy. If there is anything that differentiates the attitudes of Christianity and Judaism, it is their respective attitudes toward sexuality and the status of the body.

The classic text in the New Testament's treatment of marriage is found in the 6th and 7th chapters of the first book of Corinthians. There, the Pauline idea of celibacy and of virginity is unambiguously articulated. "It is good for a man not to touch a woman . . . I say, therefore, to the unmarried and widows, it is good for them if they abide even as I. But if they cannot contain, let them marry for it is better to marry than to burn." Based on such New Testament scriptural statements, the church fathers and figures like Augustine viewed marriage as "the hospital for the sick" (Luther). Augustine saw marriage as "medicine for immorality," and Tertullian, one of Christianity's great theologians of the third century, opposed digamy. (Digamy refers to the remarriage of widows and widowers.) Addressing those who had experienced "the fortunate disease of a mate," he urged the survivors to take advantage of the opportunity to break their carnal desires and not remarry. That position is found as well in Jerome and Origen. Not long ago, Pope Paul restated the decree of mandatory celibacy for priests and single deacons and prohibited the remarriage for married deacons once they have become widowers.

Why, according to classic Christianity, is the flesh of passion to be crucified? Why, according to Matthew, is the spiritual man to make himself "a eunuch for the sake of heaven?" In the 7th chapter

Paul further declares, "For I would have you without carefulness. He that is unmarried careth for all things that belongeth to the Lord, how he may please the Lord, but he that is married careth for all things which are of the world how he may please his wife." Paul argues that when a man marries, his interests are divided. Paul sees this conflict of interests to be detrimental to the service of the Lord. The choices are either/or. Will you serve God or man? Will you serve your Savior or your family? Will your salvation come in another world and through an otherworldly agency, or in this world and through the human effort to transform? In classic Christian teaching the world is bifurcated; a serious caesura divides the body and the soul, the sensate and the spiritual, the inner and the outer, the human and the divine, the law and the spirit. Salvation is not of this world, through this world, or by this world. This world is to be overcome and transcended. The Christian ideal of celibacy reflects man's decision to withdraw from Eve, the matrix of life and reproductivity, so as better to serve God. Ideally one is to come to God unencumbered by the concerns and responsibilities for the human family.

KIERKEGAARD AND BUBER

Such a marital ideal is enacted in the life of the spiritual father of Christian existentialism, Søren Kierkegaard. After betrothing his beloved Regina Olson, he gives her up out of his exclusive fidelity to God. Martin Buber's response to the great Danish theologian articulates the Jewish understanding of marriage. Buber insists that God wants us to come to Him precisely through the Reginas He has created. Divinity draws closer not by the subtraction but by the addition of the human other to the self. God and humans are not rivals. If in the classic Christian view the ideal is celibacy, in the classic Jewish view the ideal is marriage. For a Jew the task is to be connected with the world, and marriage is the human way to enter the world of care and responsibility. The Jewish blessing naming the infant includes *huppah*, the consecration of marriage alongside the goals of Torah study and the practice of good deeds. Divinity and humanity are not competitors. Human beings are co-sanctifiers, co-creators with God in the repair of the world. To marry, to have children, are religious acts reflecting the commitment to mend the torn fabric of this world. To have a child is to have a flesh-and-blood connection with the future. Childless we may sing *après moi le déluge.* But when we know that our children may be caught in that deluge, there is less likelihood to speak glibly of the chaos in our wake. Through our children and our children's children we have an investment in the future. Marriage is not understood privatistically, but rather it echoes the theological and moral resonance of our tradition. The sanctity of marriage and the blessing of procreation are vital elements in Judaism's struggle against *shtei reshuyot,* the belief in the existence of two primordial powers that divide the world. Judaism still battles against the varieties of polarizing dualism that would bifurcate the universe.

THE JEWISH VIEW OF THE "YETZER"

The opposition to a polarized view of the world is exhibited in Judaism's approach to the *yetzer* of man. *Yetzer* is the amoral energy of drives, desires, wants, and needs within us. It expresses the ambivalent character of libidinal energy. The *yetzer* is far from being condemned as irredeemably evil. Alien to the Jewish tradition is Matthew's counsel "to pluck out one's eye before the shapely form of a woman whom you desire. He who looketh at a woman to lust after her, hath committed adultery with her already in his heart." Nowhere in Jewish literature is the self-sacrificing act of Origen's self-castration for the sake of escaping the temptation for lust deemed praiseworthy.

Characteristic of the Jewish view is the legend found in the tractate *Yoma* (69b). For three days and nights the rabbis fasted, seeking to capture the *yetzer ha-ra,* the evil inclination that appeared to them in the form of a fiery lion circling the Holy of Holies. When they at last captured and imprisoned the *yetzer ha-ra,* they were warned that should they destroy it, they would be destroying the world with it. The captors then devised to imprison the evil impulse for three days. "And for three days they searched throughout the entire land and could not find a freshly laid egg." It is to instruct us that without the energies of libido, there is little left of civilization. Following the wisdom of the sages, the strong is one who can control his libido, not one who denies it or seeks its suffocation. Even in the eras of pogrom and persecution, when ascetic practices were more common among Jewish mystics, sexual asceticism was not countenanced. One of the distinguishing marks differentiating Jewish mysticism from non-Jewish mysticism, Gershom Scholem informs us, is the absence of sexual asceticism in the former.

THE MANY MOTIVATIONS OF
CONSECRATED LOVE

What in Judaism is the major motivation for marriage? It centers on the primary *mitzvah* to assure the preservation of the world. The supporting text used by rabbinic commentators comes from Isaiah 45:18: "He created it not a waste, He formed it to be inhabited." Interestingly, the Hebrew term for bachelor is *ravak,* which literally means emptiness, for the bachelor who willfully refuses marriage empties the world. Folk tradition further dramatized the point by denying the bachelor the prayer shawl, which made him something of a marked man.

But procreation is not the sole end of marriage. A statement from *Yevamot* (61b) reads, "Though a man may have many children (and has thus fulfilled the *mitzvah* of procreation), he is not to remain unmarried because it is not good for a man to be alone." To be alone is a dreaded condition. In Judaism, the love of a man for a woman and a woman for a man has to do with the body as well as the spirit. The notion of platonic love is alien. Jewish tradition has no marriage accommodation such as that of the *syneisaktism* of the church, wherein a man and a woman live together as a brother lives with his sister.

In the Jewish tradition, love is concerned with the whole being of the other and that whole being of the other is physical, psychological, economic, moral, and religious. To love entails loving the other with all our heart, with all our soul, with all our might. And with all our body. For a man or a woman to contract marriage vowing sexual abstinence violates the character of the marriage covenant, a violation of the meaning of marriage. Such a vow causes *tzarah d'gufah,* a pain of the body. Let the Nazarite observe his ascetic vows; let him not eat meat or drink wine; let him grow his hair long. But deliberate sexual abstinence is another matter. For it imposes suffering upon the other. The moral duty of the husband, the tradition declares, is *simhat ishto,* the rejoicing of his wife.

In a thirteenth-century treatise, *Menorat Ha-Maor,* written by Israel Ibn Nakawa and popularly attributed to Nachmanides, a chapter deals with the sanctity of sexuality in the relations between husband and wife. In the "Epistle of Holiness" addressed to the husband, the author writes: "Engage her first in conversation that puts her mind at ease and gladdens her. Thus, your mind and intent will be in harmony with hers. Speak words which arouse her to passion, union, love, and desire. Never may you force her, for in such a union the divine presence cannot abide. Quarrel not with her . . .

win her over with words of graciousness and seductiveness." With those, such as Maimonides, who fell under the influence of Aristotle and who deprecated the sense of touch, our author disagreed. "Let a man not consider sexual union as something ugly or repulsive; for this we blaspheme God. Hands which write a sacred Torah are exalted and praiseworthy; hands which steal are ugly." And so it is with the sexual organs of the body. All energies are ambivalent. There is nothing that is intrinsically contaminating or intrinsically holy. Sanctity and profanation depend upon the moral uses of these powers.

The non-Jewish contemporaries of Al Nakawa and Nachmanides, Peter Lombard and Pope Innocent III, insisted that the holy spirit absents itself from the room where a married couple have sexual relations and even for the sake of procreation. Such sexual relations shame God. There thus grew up a church tradition that one is to sexually abstain on Friday in memory of the death of the Savior, on Saturday in honor of the Virgin Mary, and on Sunday in memory of the Resurrection. In this Church tradition holiness and sexuality are contradictory. Contrast this view with that of *Sotah* (17a), which asserts, "When a husband and wife unite in holiness, there the divine presence abides." Inasmuch as the *Shabbat* celebrates the creation of the world, what more appropriate time for a husband to rejoice with his wife.

THE NEW CHALLENGE TO JEWISH SEXUAL MORALITY

The pendulum has swung the other way. Few people today struggle with the inhibitions of the Victorian era. If the Victorian morality proposed the ideal of loving without falling into sex, the new morality promotes sexuality without falling in love. For one, love is separated from sexuality; for the other, sexuality is separated from love. Both positions partake of dualism. Consequently, Judaism does battle with the dualism of the new morality as well as with the dualism of the old Victorian and Christian morality. It inveighs against sexless love in marriage and loveless sex without. Both dualisms oppose the Jewish passion for authenticity and organicity.

The new sexual morality derives much of its validity from its protest against the false prudery of our culture and the hypocrisy of double standards in which premarital relations for the male are evidence of his virility and for the female proof of her infidelity. In its bluntest form, the new morality was popularly articulated by the publisher of *Playboy* magazine, Hugh Hefner. Hefner put it on the line. "Sex is a function of the body, a drive which man shares with the animals, like eating, drinking and sleeping; it is a physical demand that must be satisfied. If you do not satisfy it, you will have all kinds of neuroses and repression psychoses. Sex is here to stay. Let us forget the prudery that makes us hide from it, throw away those inhibitions, find a girl who is like-minded and let yourself go." One of the typical cartoons in *Playboy* magazine depicts a boy and a girl locked in amorous embrace during which he cries out, "Why talk of love at a time like this?" The cartoon portrays Hefner's counsel of cultivated coolness toward the other.

SOME ARGUMENTS AGAINST FORMAL MARRIAGE

One conventional argument advocating the right and propriety of having sexual relations without commitment maintains that being in love is its own justification. The important thing is "to feel." Feeling is more important than the proforma protocol of the marriage license.

An accompanying argument avers that sexual relations openly arrived at by mutual consent are fine as long as "nobody gets hurt." Consequently, neither seduction nor coercion is condoned. If two people voluntarily wish to have such a relationship, and nobody gets hurt, there is nothing wrong with it. An auxiliary argument maintains that sexuality is morally neutral. It is a biological phenomenon and not really different today from yesterday's holding hands.

Response to such arguments requires examination of our own ideals of marriage and love. Do we accept the underlying presuppositions of these arguments, which entail the isolation of the body from the total self and the private self from the community? If sexuality is viewed as a bodily function alone, the purpose of which is to relieve the over-accumulation of tensions, then the body is seen as a machine. The body as machine is our governing metaphor. Clearly, before you invest in a machine, you try it out to see whether or not it works. If it doesn't work, you may discard it or trade it in or try to fix it up. Such mechanistic reductivism of sex is yet another manifestation of the depersonalization of man and woman. It is not surprising that so much of the literature dealing with happy marriages is replete with mechanical advice such as techniques and quantitative measurements, a veritable world of high frequency and low fidelity.

The body as a machine carries its own consequences. Psychiatrists report a rising concern with impotence and frigidity. Patients
no longer come to the psychiatrists with the old complaints of sexual
inhibitions. They now come with a complaint of "affectlessness," an
incapacity to feel, an inability to be moved. The complaint of these
overtly emancipated men and women is numbness. The heroes of
polymorphous sexuality cry, "I don't feel anything." The lyrics of
the anesthetized self echo the misery of "I don't feel anything." At
the core of Alexander Portnoy's complaint in the boudoir is awareness of his affectlessness. "God, how have I become such an enemy
and flayer of myself? And alone, so alone nothing but myself, locked
up in me." Why alone when there are so many others in bed? Why
no feeling from one who so celebrates feeling? Perhaps because there
is no real other in bed with the narcissistic self. When the other is an
appendage of your body, an instrument of your physiological gratification, one is alone with oneself engaged in autoeroticism. Philip
Roth's protagonist cannot feel anything because he will not or
cannot feel for another.

Jean-Paul Sartre illustrates *mauvais fois,* the fad faith of such
pseudo-relationships. A young man and woman go out on a date.
They sit in a cafe drinking coffee, and he seizes hold of her hand and
squeezes it. She is now beset by an embarrassing dilemma. Should
she squeeze back, she signals her acceptance of his advances.
Should she withdraw her hand, he stands rejected. She is prepared
for neither consequence. She resolves the dilemma by ignoring the
situation and continues the conversation as if nothing has happened.
Her hand hangs limp as if unattached to the rest of the body. It is
equally possible for the entire body to become disengaged, to become
so disassociated from the whole self as to render its presence
meaningless. The body then says nothing and feels nothing.

The strategy to touch and not be touched, to feel one's self but
not to feel for another, is in Buber's language to turn meeting into an
I-it relationship. The bumper signs announcing "make love, not
war" falsify. You can make war or make your bed, but you can't
make love. You cannot make another unless you reduce the self into
an instrument and the other into an object. You can make war
because war is an act of ultimate disrelationship. Love is an act of
ultimate relationship.

Making love will yield no compassionate feeling. You can have
"feeling" in the sense of experiencing sensations. You can feel
tumescence and detumescence. You can feel in the manner of
Tolstoy's nobleman, who sat himself heavily on the shoulders of his
servant while the servant carried the nobleman's obesity on his

shoulders, groaning under his burden. The nobleman "felt" compassion for him and, removing a large kerchief, mopped the sweat off the brow of the servant. The nobleman had "feeling," but he never got off his servant's back. This is the pseudo-feeling of sentimentality. Authentic feeling entails *mitleid,* compassion, a term literally meaning "to suffer." In an important sense there is no love without suffering. People are therefore often afraid to love because they would avoid suffering, escaping the vulnerability of loving. To love another is to know that the other has not only ears into which my concerns and rages may be poured, but also that the other has a mouth and may utter cries for help. To love is to be willing to suffer the hurt of another and open one's self to the possibilities of being hurt by the other. Who can hurt us more than someone we love?

Some, therefore, may turn to sexuality without love, not out of lust but out of fear. Behind much of the trivialization of sex, behind *Playboy* coolness, is the fear of authentic relationship, the fear to suffer, the fear to bear responsibility, and the fear to form community with an other. The issue then before us is not sexuality narrowly conceived. The issue is character, not the permissiveness of the new sexual morality but its implication for the moral character of human beings. The concern is over a heartless hedonism that demands instant joy, instant contact, here and now, and calls it love. The concern is over a defective character devoid of frustration tolerance, angry with any demand to postpone immediate gratification, impatient with the need to understand the needs of the other. Erotic action without any moral attachment, "without any strings attached," is not a rehearsal for marriage. It is a rehearsal for detachment and divorce.

MARRIAGE AND COMMUNITY

The Jewish wedding, the religious rite of passage, takes on its full significance when it is understood to express the sancta that a community ascribes to marital love. For Judaism marriage is not a private arrangement, a *mènage à deux.* Marriage celebrates the formation of moral community with a moral community. The vow that declares, "Be thou consecrated unto me," is not complete as it stands. It is followed by the statement that refers to community: ". . . in accordance with the community of Moses and Israel." When two persons are covenanted for the purpose of marriage, there is a third presence, and that presence is the Jewish community and its ideals of divinity. If willful celibacy is in some traditions a religious statement that transcends the needs of this world, marriage in Judaism is a political declaration in which two people in the presence of a *minyan* affirm the community and the world. So the ritual act wherein the groom breaks the glass dramatizes the fragmentation of life and the imperatives to respond to that condition. The broken vessel symbolizes war and poverty, sickness and hatred. *Shevirat ha-kelim,* the breaking of the glass, means that the bride and groom, as a Jew and a Jewess blessed with love, acknowledge the couple's task to enter the world, make whole that which is broken, and bind that which is bruised. Consecrated love has cosmic meaning. It is to salvage the sparks of divinity lodged in the husks of the world.

A Jewish myth (found in the Talmud, in the *Midrash,* and in the *Zohar Hadash*) tells us that the first human being created was androgynous. Adam, the first human being, was bisexual, male and female in one. Seeing the aloneness of Adam, God divided this bisexual being vertically into two, one side being male and the other female. The quest of each is to find the other without whom each remains *palgah gufah,* a half being. Originally, as an undifferentiated hermaphrodite, the first human being cannot know love. A self-sufficient Adam is tragically alone and ignorant. The self needs togetherness, and paradoxically union requires distance and separation. Separation means the recognition that there is an other who, though like me, is not me. There is an other whose inviolable uniqueness we come to respect through love. The ultimate task of life is to overcome separation without absorption of the other. Such a union respectful of the other requires wisdom. "Therefore shall a man leave the house of his father and mother and shall cleave unto his wife and they shall become as of one flesh." This new oneness refers to the union discovered through *da'at* or knowledge. *Da'at* in biblical Hebrew means both "to know" and "to love." To love is to know and to know is to love. Such a unified wisdom of love informs the Jewish attitude toward sexuality in its dialogue with the dualists of ancient and modern times.

Jewish

∧ **Marital Status**

☐ Single

☐ Not quite married

☑ Married

☐ Single again

　　☐ Widowed

　　☐ Abandoned

　　☐ Divorced

☐ Remarried

☐ Intermarried

☐ Gay or Lesbian

☐ Childless

13

Prelude to Marriage

Reuven P. Bulka

WHY MARRY?

For many in contemporary society, to be or not to be married is the question. Too many are opting out of traditional marriage and into new forms of relationship. We hear talk of trial marriage, open marriage, cohabitation without marriage, and other alternatives that steer clear of marriage pure and simple. Plainly, marriage pure and simple is neither pure nor simple. It is complex and complicated, with no guarantee of bliss. And, at the same time that we are preoccupied with the pursuit of happiness, indications are that society itself is far from being happy. Loneliness is a pervasive condition, mental hospitals are full, psychologists and psychiatrists are solidly booked, and we are hard pressed to see a segment of society that is reasonably happy.

In broad, communal terms, the answer to the question "Why marry?" is simply that without marriage, there is no prospect for a future Jewish community.

There is also a personal side to the question "Why marry?" The Talmud is very blunt on the matter. It asserts that anyone who is unmarried is incomplete. The unmarried person lives by the self, for the self, and knows only the self. According to the Rabbis, extending outward to embrace another is a fundamental component of being human.

The creation model, in the Bible, figures prominently in the matter of "Why marry?" The original human being, Adam, was of two forms, one male, the other female. These two components were separated by God's surgical procedure, and the two, male and female, in coming together, effectively return to the oneness that is their pristine state. Marriage, in the Bible, is thus projected as the natural human condition.

Marriage is an ideal that has no age limit. One should marry even in the twilight years, when childbearing might no longer be possible but value-sharing is still very much attainable. A good marriage, in which one partner cares deeply for the other, is the firmament for *hesed,* for kindness, concern, empathy, and warmth.

We do not worry that through concern for the other we may lose our individuality, our sense of who we are. Devotion to our partner in marriage is the way we emulate God and uncover our divine image. We achieve completeness not by turning inward, but by focusing outward.

HOW TO MARRY: DATING

The term "dating" is used to describe the male–female encounters that precede marriage. When marriage is the nub, dating takes on specific coloration. Rather than focusing merely on good times, dating becomes a serious time, so that future good times can be realized. But even before embarking on the process of completion by finding a marriage partner, it is vital to strive toward self-knowledge, the honest assessment of our strengths and weaknesses, for only then can we have a clear idea of which "other" will complement and complete us.

The process of getting to know "the other" is best achieved through conversation. It is obviously impossible to mandate precise guidelines for how often a couple should meet before deciding whether they might share the future together, but frequency is not a panacea. More important than the number of hours is the quality of time spent together.

Of utmost importance is that couples who are dating be absolutely honest with each other. Honesty here refers to more than not telling lies. Honesty here means telling the whole truth—not creating false impressions, or projecting false images. Dating couples must have an obvious picture of one another. It is hardly in anyone's interest to carry through a pretense when the future price might be disappointment, disillusionment, and even dissolution. It is incumbent on each of us to ensure that the other should never be able to say, "The person I was engaged to is not the person I married." This may seem simplistic, but the matter is of such consequence that it demands special attention.

Before marriage, we strive to "catch"; after marriage the other is "caught," or so our subconscious says. It is therefore advisable to view the dating period seriously, not as a time frame in which we behave differently, but as that time during which our postwedding behavior pattern is established. With due allowance for human frailty, it helps immeasurably to think in terms of trying continually to win over our mate, even after the mate is legally ours and we are legally theirs. Life contracts breed complacency and contempt.

However precise we try to be in our decision-making process, our decision to marry still involves a calculated risk. We may be sure of our present resolve, but we might not be sure of the future. Economic crisis or additional children may create problems that are difficult to anticipate. However, if we are unconditionally committed to one another, we can usually meet almost any crisis head on.

One more observation concerning the dating period. The first set of commandments, given to Israel on Mt. Sinai amidst great pomp and fanfare, did not endure. The second set, entrusted in a more sober setting, has remained with us for all eternity.

Similarly, exhilaration at finding the perfect partner may be thrilling but may not be indicative of an ideal partnership. Often the euphoria at having found someone who can do no wrong is a sign that we have placed passion before reason and have not approached marriage with the sobriety it warrants. Rather than to *fall* in love as a prelude to marriage, it is better to *rise* in love in the aftermath of marriage.

As with the commandments, not pomp and fanfare, but serious intent is conducent to an enduring union.

WHOM TO MARRY?

Ideally, we would like the right partner to fall into our lap, like manna from heaven, but it is always difficult to discern the heavenly gift from the human choice. We look for divine signals to confirm that this indeed will be a marriage made in heaven. But we do not really know; we hope, but we are not sure.

What is clear is that we usually mate with someone we deserve, because who we are impacts on the person we desire to marry. And how each spouse grows after marriage affects how the other will develop and how the marriage will grow.

Though it is generally true that we derive from marriage what we put into it, there are some basic features that increase the chances for a good marriage. Physical attractiveness is one such ingredient. Physical attraction is vital. We certainly should take this factor into account when choosing a mate. Misrepresentation concerning physical condition is prohibited. There is also the matter of physical compatibility; the prospective partner's height and age should be given serious consideration.

Important as the physical component may be, however, it is not primary. A physically beautiful partner who is not compatible in other ways is a poor marriage choice. Ultimately, a person's inner beauty is much more crucial to a marriage than external good looks.

Kindness, sensitivity, and responsibility are paramount in a marriage. Brazenness and arrogance are not noble traits, and we must avoid those who manifest them.

Should conceited and insolent people, then, remain single? If they persist in their aberrations, they really have no business marrying. Insistence upon marrying only those with decent character is a form of genetic engineering that seeks to weed out from the community those traits that are inconsistent with the ethos of Judaism. This should serve to establish communal and educational priorities and hopefully induce us toward improved behavior.

Since our families are the breeding ground for our values, much emphasis must be placed on the family from which our prospective mate comes. There is no guarantee that good parents have good children, but it is more likely. Family *yihus* (pedigree) is important, but only up to a point. A more determining factor is the stature of our potential spouse.

The Torah scholarship of a family is considered vital in Jewish tradition, but ultimately it is not intellectualism as much as character and lovingkindness that are crucial. Scholarship that does not translate into deeds is not scholarship. This is true not only of parents, but of our potential partner as well. High achievement in class is not a comment on one's character. And it is character more than learning that is basic to marriage.

There are times when parents may venture to express negative or positive feelings as to whom we should or should not marry. Our parents usually know better than most what is good for us, and their advice should not be underestimated. Imposing a choice upon us or vetoing our choice is another matter. We have the right to choose over parental objections, or to refuse our parents' choice. But it is equally absurd to reject parental opinion merely because it comes from our parents. Under normal circumstances, and there are exceptions, parents want what is best for us. The quest for autonomy should not come at the expense of those most committed to our welfare.

It is possible that even after a protracted search we may not find the, or a, right one. That is not a matter over which we have direct control. However, it helps at times to work on ourselves, to become the right one for someone who is also looking for the right one.

READINESS FOR MARRIAGE

For most commandments, obligation commences upon entry into *bar mitzvah* for males and *bat mitzvah* for females. This does not apply to marriage, where "eighteen years for entry into the nuptial canopy" obtains. Today, marriage obviously cannot take place that early; the eighteen-year concept is more to program readiness than to mandate obligation.

Given the proper conditions, there is reason to argue in favor of early marriage. Two mature individuals with the capacity to adapt may be better able to grow together at an early age than at a later age, when they are less likely to adjust and accommodate. Much care, however, must be exercised to prevent jumping into marriage prematurely. Parents should not push their children, for whatever self-serving reasons, before the children are ready, nor should children rush into marriage as an escape from predicaments they feel they are in. The end result may be even greater difficulties, from which escape is excruciatingly painful.

Maturity in marriage is essential. Maturity implies awareness that life is more than just pleasure and luxury, that it includes responsibility to our partner and to our children. Maturity, too, implies awareness that hard work is needed to ensure that a marriage develops properly and that crises of varying degrees will arise that must be faced together.

But maturity is more than abstract awareness. It is the capacity to translate this awareness into effective action. Maturity is often a function of age, but not necessarily. Some of us are mature in our teens, others are immature at thirty. To avoid future complications, it is vital that we be honest with ourselves and confront our own limitations before reaching out to others.

Finding the right one should not automatically translate into immediate marriage. Readiness to marry must perforce include the financial capacity to sustain the marriage adequately. It matters little which of the couple is to be the provider, or whether both together will provide. What matters is that a measure of financial stability should accompany the decision to marry. Marriage hardly ever solves our personal problems. Marriage is even more precarious if the actual event creates problems. Inadequate income is among the conditions most likely to threaten a marriage. To leave the matter of income to chance is irresponsible.

The obverse of minimizing financial needs is overemphasizing material considerations. Marrying merely for financial gain is contemptible. This does not mean that it is sinful to marry someone who is rich, only that wealth should not be the crucial factor when we make our decision.

When maturity is evident, there is little reason for us to delay marriage if our decision to marry has been made. However, the mature individual or couple may at times harbor doubts, even when everything seems right. Here maturity implies taking more time, or taking other steps to resolve our doubts. We should not be persuaded either subtly or openly. Relatives and friends should be careful to respect our doubts and patiently await our explication, however it may turn out.

Readiness for marriage is reflected in the priorities we set forth before the wedding. Too often we are bogged down by trivialities at the expense of essential considerations. It is preferable that we detach ourselves from the prewedding trauma and concentrate on our life goals and the values we cherish, and how we propose to implement these values and actualize these goals. Serious soul-searching by the bride and groom and study of Judaic tracts on ethical perfection are better ways to prepare for the marriage. Additionally, full knowledge of our responsibilities in marriage is essential and is spelled out in the Code of Jewish Law, the *Shulhan Arukh.*

Equipped with proper knowledge and attitudes, we are able, upon entering marriage, to become a joy to our partner, an inspiration to our community, and a force for Jewish continuity.

14

The Jewish Wedding Then and Now

Daniel B. Syme

BIBLICAL ROOTS

According to the Torah, the institution of marriage began with Adam and Eve. The Book of Genesis portrays God as saying: "It is not good that man should be alone. . . . Therefore shall a man leave his father and his mother and shall cleave unto his wife, and they shall be one flesh" (Genesis 2:18,24).

Most scholars agree that "marriages" originally constituted a man's "reserving" a particular woman or women as his property. This was accomplished simply by bringing a woman into his tent or cave (or palace) and having sexual relations with her. As such, it was referred to as "taking a wife."

In biblical times, fathers usually arranged marriages for their children. While romantic love was not unknown, it was not as central to marriage as it has become today. Accordingly, fathers—or their surrogates—sought out appropriate mates for their sons and daughters. Abraham's servant, Eliezer, for example, was dispatched to find a wife for Isaac (Genesis 24:1–4), and Laban had to give his permission for Jacob to marry Rachel (Genesis 29:15–19).

Since women were valuable workers in biblical households, any man wishing to marry paid money or property to the woman's father as a form of compensation, called the "bride price," or, alternatively, as in the case of Jacob, a prospective bridegroom worked for his father-in-law for a specified period of time. Over the centuries, the bride price often became a symbolic amount, usually used to help purchase the woman's trousseau.

Severe taboos were attached to a number of marriage categories; foremost among them were those involving blood relations. Incest was a capital crime in Judaism, long before more modern legal systems legislated against such unions. Marriage to cousins, however, was fairly frequent. Isaac and Rebekah were cousins, as were Jacob and Leah and Rachel. Biblical law strictly forbade marriage to the Canaanites, undying enemies of the Hebrews. It frowned as well on unions with men and women of six other nations (Deuteronomy 7:1–3). These Torah verses, root of the traditional Jewish position against intermarriage, resulted in the Hebrews being basically endogamous.

It is important to recognize, however, that the ban was motivated by religious rather than ethnic or racial considerations: "For they will turn away your children from following Me, that they may serve other gods" (Deuteronomy 7:4).

Accordingly, aside from the Canaanites, the ancient Hebrews were permitted to marry outside of their people if their mate embraced Judaism. According to rabbinic literature, Moses' wife Zipporah was a convert. Boaz married Ruth, born a Moabite, who chose Judaism and became the ancestor of King David. A number of Israelite kings married non-Jewish women of royal families in an attempt to forge alliances with foreign powers. In general, however, biblical society emphasized "in-group" marriage.

Special restrictions regarding marriage were placed on the *kohanim,* the priestly class. Owing to his special status, the *kohen* could not marry a divorcee, a nonvirgin, or a widow (in the case of the high priest). Other laws protected the dignity of a divorced woman. Once divorced, a man and wife could not remarry each other, if they had married and divorced twice. In addition, a man could not marry his divorced wife's sister during his ex-wife's lifetime.

Not all of the ancient Hebrews were monogamous. Abraham had three wives and Jacob two, whereas King Solomon had 700 wives and 300 concubines! Polygamy was permitted, but only men could have more than one mate.

Though polygamy was allowed, it was prevalent almost solely among the rich. Because of the rights of the bride as articulated in the Torah, only those of substance could afford more than one mate. Most of the prophets discouraged polygamy, pointing to the symbolic "marriage" of God and Israel as the ideal monogamous model for a man and a woman. The practice slowly disappeared among

Ashkenazic Jews, though it was not until the year 1040 c.e. that Rabbenu Gershom, a great Jewish scholar, issued a ruling that formally ended polygamy among the Ashkenazim. Among Sephardic and Oriental Jews, the practice continued until relatively recent times—and still is in evidence in countries such as Yemen.

Even as far back as the Torah, a married woman had rights. Exodus 21:10 clearly specifies that a husband cannot deny a wife food, clothing, and sex. The biblical institution of levirate marriage also served to protect a childless widow. In the event that a man died, leaving no heirs, the man's brother was legally obligated to marry the widow, care for her, and hopefully father children who would perpetuate the family name. A man who refused to perform this obligation had to endure public humiliation through a ceremony known as *halitzah* (release) (Deuteronomy 25:5–10). Such a ceremony is recorded in the Book of Ruth, chapter 3, and is still practiced today in Orthodox communities.

By the end of the biblical period, Jewish marriage was already sanctified and regulated by laws. It had begun to take on the shape, substance, and values of a religious and legal act.

MARRIAGE IN THE TALMUD

By talmudic times, the process of acquiring a spouse was far more formal and ceremonial than in the Bible. Basically, there were two parts to the ritual: *kiddushin/erusin* and *nissu'in*. The first, *kiddushin* (consecration) or *erusin* (betrothal), was equivalent to formalizing an engagement. *Kiddushin/erusin* was effected in one of three ways:

1. *Kesef* (literally, "money")—the formal exchange of an object of value, worth at least a *perutah,* the "penny" of antiquity. This practice, performed in the presence of two witnesses, eventually led to the modern custom of exchanging rings.
2. *Shetar* (literally, "document")—the signing of a legal document in the presence of two witnesses. This document, the *ketubah,* testified to the couple's intent to marry and specified the bride's rights in the event of a dissolution of the engagement or marriage, or in the event of her spouse's death.
3. *Biah* (literally, "intercourse")—while the Talmud is quite explicit in designating cohabitation as one means of betrothal, it was frowned upon and discouraged by the rabbis. They could not abolish it, as it had its origin in the Torah, and therefore had to be

treated as divinely commanded. Social pressures, however, as well as legal measures, sometimes as harsh as flogging, gradually eliminated this practice almost entirely.

Through *kiddushin/erusin,* a woman became *arusah,* betrothed. As such, neither she nor her fiance could contemplate marrying another person without a formal, legal Jewish divorce (*get*). The engagement lasted one year, during which time the bride assembled her trousseau. The marriage was then consummated through the ritual *nissu'in* (literally, "elevation"). The wife was escorted to her husband's house in a rite that later became ceremonialized as the *huppah* ("marriage canopy"). This ritual sealed the wedding pact.

In addition to the prohibitions delineated in the Torah that we have already studied, the Talmud explicitly forbids Jewish weddings involving certain individuals, among them:

1. Minors—boys under 13 years of age, girls under the age of 12;
2. Eunuchs—as they would be unable to fulfill the *mitzvah* of having children;
3. Deaf and dumb men and women—unless they could use sign language to make clear that they understood the legal and contractual obligations of marriage;
4. The incompetent—since they could not be assumed to comprehend and accept the legal obligations of marriage.

Furthermore, the Talmud forbids marriage between:

1. A man and his former wife (if she had been married to another man in the interim);
2. A woman and the man who represented her in her divorce proceedings;
3. A woman and the only witness to her husband's death;
4. A Jew and a *mamzer* (child of a forbidden marriage);
5. A Jew and a *shetuki* (person whose father is not known).

Special restrictions were placed on second or third marriages. A widower had to observe a thirty-day mourning period before marrying again. A widow or female divorcee had to wait ninety days after being widowed or divorced so that, if she was pregnant at the time, the paternity of the child could be determined. Also, if a widow or divorcee had an infant, she could not remarry until the baby reached two years of age. Finally, if a woman had two husbands who died from other than natural causes or accident, she was banned from ever remarrying.

Marriages were still arranged in talmudic times. While the institution of the *shadkhan* (matchmaker) had not yet come to full flower, parents busily sought to find the best prospective mate for their children. Where a *shadkhan* was involved, he/she received a fee and a percentage of the dowry. The rabbis offered guidance as to how to evaluate a possible "intended," directing their counsel to the male-dominated society in which they lived. Though clearly their advice is in large measure inappropriate today, it gives us a glimpse into the rabbinic mind:

1. Marry the daughter of a learned man.
2. Marry a woman of the same age, or about the same age.
3. Marry a woman of the same or lower social class.
4. Marry a woman of a different complexion, lest children be too pale or too dark.
5. Marry a woman of a different height, lest children be too tall or too short.
6. If possible, avoid marriage to a widow or divorcee.
7. Don't marry for money.

The Shadkhan

The *shadkhan,* the professional matchmaker, was for many centuries one of the most colorful Jewish figures, especially during the Middle Ages. The *shadkhan* sought to arrange marriages that would please the parents of both the prospective bride and groom. As early as possible in the children's lives, the *shadkhan* would approach both sets of parents with what seemed to him/her to be a "perfect match." The major goal for a match was compatibility; romantic love was viewed as a secondary consideration. A good match, it was assumed, would help to engender love some time later in life. During the late eighteenth and nineteenth centuries, romantic love became a major reason for marriage among the Ashkenazim. This shift in attitude spelled the decline of the Ashkenazic *shadkhan.* To this day, however, many Sephardic communities continue the practice of arranging marriages. Therefore, the *shadkhan* is still very much with us.

Once the *shadkhan* had proposed a match and elicited a tentative expression of interest from both sets of parents, all parties involved engaged in preliminary negotiations. Among the items discussed were the size of the dowry—the money and possessions that the bride would bring to the marriage, which set of parents would provide which household furnishings, and the date and place of the wedding. Also negotiated was the *mohar* or bride price, the value in money or services that the groom would pay to the bride's father for the privilege of marrying his daughter. In Eastern Europe it was customary for the bride's parents to pledge full board (*kest*) for the groom in their home, so that he might pursue his talmudic studies without the need to go out and earn a living. Also included was a provision for penalty fees should one side or the other fail to fulfill its promises, and, of course, the *shadkhan*'s fee.

When everyone agreed to all the conditions and stipulations, a document known as the *tena'im* was written.

Tena'im

The *tena'im* (literally, "conditions") date to the third century C.E., when betrothal became a legal act. The *tena'im* were preliminary to the actual betrothal. Once signed, they were as binding as a marriage contract, requiring divorce for abrogation. In ancient times, signing of the *tena'im* took place one year prior to the actual wedding ceremony.

Beginning in the twelfth century, when betrothal and marriage were joined, the signing of the *tena'im* was advanced to just before the wedding. The *tena'im,* having been negotiated in advance, were read aloud and signed in the presence of two witnesses. In a practice known as *kinyan* (acquisition), the groom was asked if he was prepared to accept the *tena'im.* To acknowledge his agreement, he grasped a handkerchief extended by the rabbi in the presence of two witnesses, who would later sign his marriage contract. A china dish was then broken by the mothers of the bride and groom as a reminder of the destruction of the Second Temple and also, undoubtedly, to ward off evil spirits. With the couple now formally engaged, everyone present shouted *mazal tov* and partook of refreshments.

Reform Jews rarely sign *tena'im* today, but the practice is followed among Orthodox and many Conservative families before the wedding begins.

Setting the Date

In times past, simply setting the date for a Jewish wedding was a challenge! First of all, there were (and are for traditional Jews) certain times of the year when marriage ceremonies were forbidden. These include: *Shabbat;* the festivals; fast days; the forty-nine days between the second night of Pesah and Shavuot, with the exception of Lag Ba'omer, the thirty-third day; the intermediate days of Pesah and Sukkot; the period between two somber fast days during summer months, the 17th of Tammuz and the 9th of Av.

After eliminating these dates, the couple then sought to schedule the ceremony on a day considered "lucky" in the context of their era and country. For example, German Jews liked to marry under a full moon, Spanish Jews under the new moon. Many Jewish communities favored a wedding during the first half of the month when the moon increases in size, seeing it as an omen of fortune, luck, and fertility.

Certain days of the week were considered particularly auspicious for marriages. Fridays were special favorites, in as much as they fell close to *Shabbat,* when having sexual relations with one's spouse was considered a double *mitzvah.* Virgins were most often wed on Friday, ideally immediately after Tishah B'av, Shavuot, or Yom Kippur. Tuesdays and Thursdays were commonly wedding days for widows or divorcees, while Mondays and Wednesdays generally came to be regarded as unlucky times, though the Talmud mentions Sundays and Wednesdays as good wedding days for virgins. Some modern Orthodox Jews opt to marry on Tuesday, since it corresponds to the biblical day of creation which God twice apparently pronounces to be good.

Whom to Invite?

Beginning in talmudic times, the rabbis required at least a *minyan* of ten male Jews, two of whom served as "witnesses." The custom derives from the Book of Ruth 4:2, which described Boaz assembling "ten men of the elders of the city" in preparation for his marriage to Ruth. In Reform Judaism, a *minyan* is desirable but not required. Reform Judaism counts women and men equally as members of the *minyan.*

The Aufruf

Aufruf (pronounced "owf-roof," or more colloquially "oof-roof") is a German word meaning "calling up" and refers to a special synagogue celebration on the *Shabbat* preceding the wedding. The custom is biblically based. According to the Talmud, King Solomon built a gate in the Jerusalem Temple, where Jews would sit on *Shabbat* and honor new grooms. When the Temple was destroyed in 70 c.e. and the institution of the synagogue gained strength, a form of the ancient Solomonic practice moved into the synagogue. Eventually, this custom became known as the *aufruf.*

On the *Shabbat* morning prior to the wedding, the groom is called to the Torah for an *aliyah* (honor of reciting the blessings before and after the reading of a section of the Torah). After he completes the concluding *berakhah,* the congregation showers him with raisins, nuts, and sometimes candy, indicative of their good wishes for a sweet and fulfilling marriage.

The Wedding Day

When the day of the wedding finally arrived, the bride had visited the *mikvah* (ritual bath). Many families provided a feast for the community's paupers a day or two before, thus fulfilling the *mitzvot* of *tzedakah* and hospitality.

The bride and groom would awaken in their respective parents' homes and begin a fast that would end only after the ceremony. Jewish tradition teaches that all past sins are forgiven on a wedding day. Therefore, the day gradually acquired the characteristics of a quasi-Yom Kippur afternoon service. Customarily, the wedding took place in the late afternoon, so as to enable as complete a fast as possible.

The Rabbis of the Talmud perceived the fast as a reenactment of Sinai, where Israel, by accepting the Torah, consummated a "marriage" with God. Just as the Israelites fasted in preparation for their betrothal, said the Rabbis, so it is fitting that a bride and groom do likewise.

In Yemenite homes, even today, each groom goes to his mother on his wedding day, asking her forgiveness for hurting her in the past. He kneels and kisses her knees, after which his mother gives him a coin to be used as a ring substitute in the wedding service.

JEWISH WEDDING SYMBOLS

The Huppah

The use of the *huppah,* or marriage canopy, is a ritualization of the ancient rite of *nissu'in.* Over time, the *huppah* came to refer to a special room where the couple retired after the wedding service for a period of seclusion, known as *yihud.*

By the Middle Ages, the *huppah* had evolved into a canopy— symbolizing the home. The *huppah* often was, and is, a plain *tallit;* the groom's *tallit* was, and is, sometimes drawn over the heads of both him and his bride. In France, the groom covered the bride's head with his *tallit* as a symbol of sheltering her. Modern Jews may use a *tallit,* a free-standing canopy, or some other portable *huppah* provided by the rabbi or synagogue.

The Ring

Both ancient and modern commentators have tried to explain the choice of rings as opposed to some other object. Some say that Jewish history is a chain of interlocking rings, and therefore the wedding ring symbolizes our link to the past and commitment to the future. Others look at the ring as a circle, having no beginning and no end. Similarly, they say, love never ends. Originally, only the bride received a ring. Today, of course, double-ring ceremonies are quite common.

The rabbis insisted that the wedding ring be a plain, solid gold band, lest there be any suspicion that the bride was marrying for the sake of a gift or lest the poor be embarrassed by their inability to "compete" with the rings of the wealthy. The ring was also to be plain to avoid the possibility of a fake ring, which could invalidate the marriage.

To this day, Sephardic Jews use a coin rather than a ring, usually the coin that mothers give their sons after the forgiveness ritual. In addition, more than one Jewish coin collector has used an actual *perutah* from antiquity as part of the wedding service in addition to the rings. This is a beautiful possibility, one that symbolically binds us to our ancestors.

The Ketubah

Ketubah literally means "written" and refers to the marriage contract signed and read at all Orthodox and Conservative weddings, and at a growing number of Reform ceremonies.

Most scholars assert that the *ketubah* first emerged during the Babylonian exile, following the destruction of the Temple in 586 B.C.E. The Talmud, however, states that King David gave *ketubot* to his wives, and Maimonides also assigns it an earlier date. Whenever it first came into use, the text was set about 200 B.C.E. and was composed in Aramaic, the Jewish community's most common language at that time.

Every bride received from her groom a *ketubah,* a legal document that protected her rights. The contract specified the groom's financial obligations, including a minimum divorce settlement and a minimum inheritance in case of the husband's death. In addition, the *ketubah* specified the woman's Torah-based right to food, clothing, and conjugal rights as well as the husband's responsibility to "care for her, provide for her, and cherish her."

The ancient *ketubah* represented a major step forward in women's rights. In a world in which women were often viewed as chattel, Judaism affirmed that every bride was to be accorded dignity and security in the marriage relationship.

The *ketubah* was also one of the great artistic "breakthroughs" of Jewish tradition. Usually on parchment, written by hand, and often illuminated in brilliant color, it manifested an artistic expression often stifled because of Judaism's prohibition against creating "graven images."

Today, we have the benefit of high-quality and high-speed printing techniques. Dozens of beautiful *ketubot,* some reproductions of original art, have thus been made available on a mass scale. Then, too, there has been a resurgence in use of hand-made *ketubot.* Fine Jewish artists throughout the world have begun to devote their talent to the creation of stunning marriage contracts.

More significant than the change in style, however, has been the change in substance of the *ketubah.* Sensitive to the male-oriented language of the ancient document and contemporary values, many modern texts are "equalized." That is to say, both bride and groom make the same commitments, one to the other.

In years past, while Reform couples sometimes chose to have a *ketubah,* most Reform weddings were commemorated by the signing of a marriage certificate. Today, however, in response to the express wishes of growing numbers of Reform Jews, the Reform movement has published its own *ketubot,* modern in style and language, but true to the spirit of our heritage. The Conservative movement, too, has modernized its *ketubot,* some of which are obtainable from the Rabbinical Assembly.

In ancient times, as today, the *ketubah* was signed just prior to the wedding ceremony. It required two male witnesses, unrelated to either the bride or groom. Today, especially in Reform congregations, both men and women are honored by being asked to certify the beginning of a new couple's life together. In addition, the bride and groom themselves often sign the document.

The *ketubah* is read under the *huppah* between the sections of the ceremony known as *erusin* and *nissu'in*.

The Modern Ceremony

We come at last to the actual wedding ceremony as it has emerged over the last several centuries. While many specifics of the Orthodox wedding have been changed and reinterpreted within the Reform, Conservative, and Reconstructionist movements, it will be helpful to begin with an outline of Orthodox practice of the eighteenth and nineteenth centuries, so as to better understand the thrust and rationale of subsequent reforms.

Scholars of the period tell us that in Eastern Europe the groom came to the courtyard of the synagogue at dawn, accompanied by his family, the rabbi, and his friends. Musicians, called *klezmorim,* led the way, sometimes in a torch-like procession, and usually playing a violin, bass, and clarinet. Shortly thereafter, the *klezmorim* department met the bride and led her and her family to the courtyard. There, she and her groom were showered with barley, a symbol of fertility, and all the assembled guests cried out *peru urevu*—"be fruitful and multiply"—three times.

The bride and groom then went into separate rooms. In one room, the groom and the other males signed the *tena'im* (conditions) and prepared and signed the *ketubah* (marriage contract). Then the men surrounded the groom and danced with him.

In the second room, the bride was seated on a beautiful, throne-like chair with her friends all around her. The chair was often covered with a white sheet and flowers. The *klezmorim* entered and cut off all the bride's hair, replacing it with a *sheitl,* or wig. Afterward, a singer called the *badhan* (jester) serenaded the bride with gloomy songs, allowing all present to give full expression to their feelings of nostalgia and sadness over the remarkable speed with which a child becomes an adult.

Badeken di kalah, or "veiling of the bride," was the next formalized step on the path to the *huppah.* The groom entered and looked at the bride. Then he covered her face with the veil, while the biblical blessing over the matriarch Rebekah was recited: "Our sister, may you be the mother of . . . tens of thousands" (Genesis 24:60). The groom departed, after which the bride's friends danced around her, gently showering her with raisins and nuts.

The practice of wearing a veil derived from the account in Genesis 24:65 of how Rebekah covered her face with a veil when she saw her husband-to-be Isaac approaching. Over the centuries, other commentators saw the veil as a protection from the "evil eye," as a safeguard against lustful leering by other men, and even as a means of insuring that the groom would not notice a pimple or scar on the bride's face and call off the wedding!

One beautiful interpretation asserts that just as one often covers one's eyes during the *Shema* as an expression of concentration upon and trust in God, so does a bride cover her eyes as a symbol of trust in her husband. Indeed, some Oriental Jews (who do not use a veil) and Hasidim to this day blindfold the bride during the wedding for just this reason.

The Book of Genesis records the beautiful story of Jacob's love for Rachel. Jacob worked for Rachel's father Laban for seven years in order to win Rachel's hand in marriage. But on their wedding night, Laban secretly substituted his elder daughter Leah for Rachel, later asserting that Jacob had to marry her before marrying Rachel. As a result of that undoubtedly traumatic experience, Jewish grooms to this day assure themselves before uttering their vows that the woman they are marrying is in fact their intended.

Immediately after *badeken di kalah*, the processional to the *huppah* began. First the *klezmorim* led the groom to the *huppah*, accompanied by his parents or by his father and father-in-law. Then they returned for the bride and her escorts: either her parents or her mother and mother-in-law. These escorts, or *shoshvinim*, carried candles and were often likened to a royal entourage, inasmuch as a bride and groom on their wedding day are truly like a king and queen.

With all the guests assembled, usually at least a *minyan* of ten, the wedding ceremony began. The traditional order of the service is as follows:

The groom enters first and stands under the huppah. Some interpreters state that just as God waited at Sinai for His bride (Israel), so does the groom wait for his bride to appear.

The bride arrives at the huppah with her escorts. In more recent times, this custom has been altered, with the father of the bride escorting his daughter down the aisle. The groom then walks to the father, shakes his hand, takes his bride's arm, and leads her to the *huppah*. This practice may have its origin in the way some primitive societies arranged marriages. A father would lead his daughter between two lines of unmarried tribal males. Whoever reached out and "claimed" her had thus selected a wife. A father's escorting his daughter, then, is a "borrowed" rather than uniquely Jewish custom.

The couple comes to the huppah, with the bride to the right of the groom. Psalm 45:10 reads, "The queen stands on your right hand in gold of Ophir." Since a bride on her wedding day is seen as a queen, she stands on the groom's right.

The rabbi reads or chants a section from Psalm 118 and/or Psalm 100 and then recites a medieval hymn. Psalm 118:26 contains a traditional Jewish blessing of welcome: "Blessed are you who come in the name of the Lord." Psalm 100 is a psalm of thanksgiving, expressing thanks to and praise for God. The words of the medieval hymn are: "May the One who is mighty and blessed above all bless the groom and the bride."

The bride, with an entourage, circles the groom three or seven times. While this custom is usually omitted from Reform ceremonies, it is part of many Conservative and all Orthodox weddings. The practice is based on Jeremiah 31:22: "A woman shall court a man." The rabbis interpreted this sentence to indicate that a woman should "go around" a man, hence the custom of circling. The more usual seven circles custom has been explained in a variety of ways:

1. There are seven days in a week.
2. There are seven *aliyot* on *Shabbat.*
3. In the Bible it says "when a man takes a wife" seven times.
4. There is a mystical teaching that the bride, in circling seven times, enters seven spheres of her husband's innermost being.
5. On Simhat Torah, the Torahs are carried around the synagogue seven times.

Explanations for the basis of circling three times include:

1. The three times in Hosea 2:21–22 when God, in reassuring Israel, says: "and I will betroth you unto Me."
2. A woman's three basic rights in marriage—food, clothing, sex.

Whether three or seven times, however, circling most probably reflected the structure of the family in times past. The custom implicitly made a statement that the bride's life revolved around her husband's. The bride's circling also grew out of a mystical belief that, by making a ring around the groom, the woman thereby protected him from evil spirits.

The rabbi or cantor reads or chants the Betrothal Blessing.

Kiddushin/erusin begins with a blessing over wine. The bride and groom drink from the same cup, symbolically affirming that throughout life they will experience both joy and sorrow, but always together. The *Birkat Erusin* (Betrothal Blessing) is then recited or chanted.

The groom places the bride's ring on her right index finger. Traditionally, the ring is placed on the index finger of the bride's right hand because it is the most prominent, and so that the two required witnesses can see the ring easily. Following the ceremony, the ring is moved to the more familiar third finger of the bride's left hand. This custom originated in about the fifteenth century and grew out of a belief that a vein in this finger runs directly to the heart. In many Reform ceremonies, the ring is placed directly on the third finger of the left hand. .

The groom recites the legal formula of betrothal. In the presence of the two witnesses the groom says: *Harei at mekudeshet li, betaba'at zu, kedat Moshe ve'Yisrael*—"Behold you are consecrated unto me with this ring, according to the law of Moses and Israel." In the Orthodox ritual, only the groom speaks, inasmuch as it is he who is "acquiring" a wife. In the more liberal wings of Judaism, the bride will frequently respond with the same or a similar formula as she places a ring on the groom's hand. With this single or joint recitation, the ceremony of betrothal concludes.

The ketubah is read. The rabbi, a friend, or a group of friends may read the *ketubah* aloud, after which the groom hands it to the bride. It is thereafter her property. Then, the marriage service (*nissu'in*) begins.

A second cup of wine is filled.

The rabbi, cantor, or friends read or chant the Sheva Berakhot. The *Sheva Berakhot* (literally "Seven Blessings") are the heart of the marriage ceremony itself. The first *berakhah* is the blessing over the wine, followed by blessings that praise God, extol the value of family life, and express hopes for the happiness of the bride and groom. The *Sheva Berakhot* are also sometimes called the *Birkat Nissu'in* or the *Birkat Hatanim* (Marriage Blessings). After the blessings are completed, the bride and groom drink from the cup of wine.

The groom breaks a glass. The custom of breaking a glass at the conclusion of the wedding began in talmudic times. Many scholars assert that the most primitive origins of the practice reflected a symbolic breaking of the hymen. Over the centuries, however, various interpreters have held that the breaking of the glass (1) reminds us of the destruction of the Second Temple in

Jerusalem in 70 c.e.; (2) teaches that, in times of joy, we must always be cognizant that life also brings sadness and sorrow; (3) is, like marriage, permanent; (4) drove away Satan and evil spirits, who, without this sudden noise, might have spoiled the occasion with some evil deed; and (5) warns us that love, like glass, is fragile and must be protected. Frequently, Reform and Conservative rabbis will bless the couple just prior to the breaking of the glass with the traditional three-fold benediction.

Everyone yells "mazal tov" or "siman tov." Mazal Tov and Siman Tov are both Hebrew phrases that convey a sense of "congratulations." Ashkenazic Jews usually yell *Mazal Tov,* while Sephardim yell *Siman Tov!* Interestingly, both phrases derive from astrology. *Mazal* literally means "planet"; *siman,* "omen." Thus, either exclamation amounts to wishing the new couple a "good horoscope" in addition to expressing a warm sentiment.

The couple spends a few moments alone before joining their friends and family. This practice, called *yihud,* or "privacy," is the traditional manner in which a man and wife symbolically recreate the third basic way in which couples married centuries ago. At one time, cohabitation constituted marriage. Today, traditional couples retire into a private room for a few minutes, break their wedding day fast, then emerge to join the celebration of this great occasion in their lives. A formal period of *yihud* is not observed in most Reform congregations.

The celebration begins. Extravagant wedding parties were never encouraged in Judaism. Indeed, a number of Jewish communities over the centuries (including modern Israel) actually passed legislation limiting their opulence. But, though Jewish custom frowns on ostentation, it is clear that a wedding banquet was and is cause for great joy and celebration, filled with music, dancing, and the fulfillment of the *mitzvah* to "make the bride and groom joyful." Beginning in talmudic times, traditional Judaism asserted that a marriage should be celebrated for seven days, with the *Sheva Berakhot* recited every day. Inasmuch as Jewish law requires a *minyan* in order to recite the blessings, the emphasis on a wedding as a major community event is clear.

Above all, the Jewish wedding is a celebration of the Jewish present and an affirmation of faith in a better tomorrow, a moment in Jewish time cherished by every Jewish family.

15

Why Observe *Niddah* and *Mikvah* in the 1990s?

Haskel Lookstein

This chapter is an attempt to explain the institution of *niddah* and *mikvah* from an Orthodox perspective.

In Leviticus 18:19, the Torah specifically prohibits sexual intercourse between a man and a woman when the woman has her menses. After the conclusion of the menstrual period, or a minimum of five days, the woman must then wait an additional seven full days, during which time there should be no further show of blood. After this interlude she goes to a *mikvah* and immerses herself in the water with no garment—or anything else separating her body from the water. Following that immersion normal marital relations may be resumed.

The Torah considers the prohibition of sex during the *niddah* period to be extremely important. It is of the same consequence as circumcising one's son, fasting on Yom Kippur, and avoiding the eating of *hametz* on Passover. The entire institution of *niddah* and *mikvah* is called *taharat ha-mishpahah*, the laws of family purity.

The gravity with which the Torah views this institution in Jewish life prompts one to ask why it is less observed than, let us say, *kashrut*, which, although important, is not placed by the Torah on the same level as *taharat ha-mishpahah*.

There are several reasons for the reduced observance of *niddah* and *mikvah* as compared with *kashrut*, although, it should be added, the number of people who practice these rules is growing significantly today. In my own thirty years in the rabbinate, I have seen a great increase in the number of people who keep these *mitzvot.* In my early years it was rare that I felt comfortable bringing up the subject of *taharat ha-mishpahah* in a premarital conference. Today, this discussion is a normal part of almost every such conference. Often, the bride and the groom desire specific instruction in the rules, and some even take classes to learn them more precisely. Nevertheless, there are still many people who keep kosher and who observe the *Shabbat* but who do not live by the principles of *taharat ha-mishpahah.* There are several reasons for this.

The first is that nobody talks about *niddah* and *mikvah.* How often have you heard a rabbi discuss this *mitzvah* from the pulpit? I suspect that rabbis of all branches of Judaism avoid this subject as too sensitive and too private. Mothers and fathers do not discuss this institution with their children. Mothers who do go to *mikvah* take great pains to avoid letting their children know when and where they are going. This is part of traditional *tzniyut* (modesty and privacy). But there is a price to be paid for such *tzniyut.* Young people often find out about the rules of *taharat ha-mishpahah* when they are least prepared to honor them—just before marriage. It is no wonder, therefore, that the rules are honored more in the breach than in the observance. What we do not see observed by our elders and what we know nothing about becomes strange, mysterious, perhaps archaic, but rarely compelling.

There is a second reason for *taharat ha-mishpahah* being observed less than many other *mitzvot* in Judaism, despite its import. It is a difficult *mitzvah* to keep. One of the great teachers of our day once said that it is the only institution in Jewish life that runs counter to a person's nature. *Kashrut, Shabbat,* even not eating on Yom Kippur, are all *mitzvot* that are relatively easy to keep. Abstaining from sexual activity, however, for a period of twelve to fourteen days a month is something that requires a great deal of restraint. It requires a greater sense of commitment and determination. But it certainly can be observed, and it does not diminish in any way the beauty and love that are experienced in marriage and in sexual life. It does, however, necessitate extra effort, which many people are not prepared to exert.

There is a third reason for lack of observance, and this one is entirely the fault of the Jewish community. For many years the *mikvah* was kept in very shabby condition. Somehow the community did not see fit to spend the money necessary to make the *mikvah* a beautiful and esthetically attractive place to which women would feel good about going. It was frequently dirty, rundown, and sometimes even located in bad neighborhoods. In most of America and the world this deficiency has been corrected, but the stigma attached to the *mikvah* remains with the older generation, and somehow it is transmitted to the younger generation. Although today's *mikva'ot* are usually beautifully equipped and furnished and immaculately kept, the image of a rundown *mikvah* still remains vivid in the minds of many.

Finally, there is a fourth reason that inhibits the observance of this *mitzvah.* Many women view the concept of *taharat ha-mishpahah* as an indignity. The usual translation of the biblical word *tameh,* which is associated with the state of *niddah,* is "unclean." This is an incorrect translation, but it has had its impact upon Jewish women nonetheless. Women do not want to be considered dirty or "defiled" for close to one half of each month. But, the fact is that there is nothing unclean about a woman during *niddah.* The word *tameh* is purely a ritual term and defines someone's fitness for a particular activity. For example: a kosher fowl is called *tahor* while an unkosher fowl is called *tameh.* Thus, a chicken is *tahor* and a peacock is *tameh,* although in terms of cleanliness one would imagine that a peacock would be a far cleaner bird than a chicken. One, however, is fit for Jewish consumption and the other is not. It has nothing to do with cleanliness.

Tameh actually has to do with the *kedushah* (holiness) of the Jewish people. Only Jews who have *kedushat Yisrael* are capable of being in a *tameh* state. As a matter of fact, the biblical prohibition of *niddah* does not apply to non-Jewish women. The rabbinic prohibition does apply but, fundamentally, this is a law that is associated with the *kedushah* of the Jewish people and, therefore, it is confined to Jews alone. Unfortunately, this is not appreciated widely and, therefore, women consider the institution to be one that disparages rather than ennobles them.

If we understand what *taharat ha-mishpahah* is and what some of the impediments to its observance may be, we are now in a position to comprehend its value. At the outset we must acknowledge that the *mitzvah* of *taharat ha-mishpahah* is known in Jewish law as a *hok*—a law whose reason is understood by God but not by us. In that sense, it is very much like *kashrut.* What we can try to do is understand the value of *taharat ha-mishpahah,* if not the actual reason for God having legislated it. I would like to enumerate four values.

THE PHILOSOPHICAL VALUE

Certain laws in Judaism are ways of mediating between the pagan and Christian approaches to physical pleasure. Classic paganism worshiped the physical world. The pagan attached divine value to the physical. He considered it intrinsically holy. This was his way of justifying submission to hunger, sensual desire, passion, and lust. The pagan orgy is a reflection of this worship of the physical. The "virgin goddess" who was the object of adoration during the harvest festival is a further manifestation of this. The pagans enjoyed the physical world to excess as a religious value.

In contrast to the pagan deification of the physical, and perhaps in reaction to it, Christianity repudiated the physical. Man's appetites lead him astray. His body is evil. Sex is sinful, at best a necessary evil. Food is a biological necessity that must be tolerated but not enjoyed. For the average person, physical pleasures are countenanced with some misgivings, but the ideal form of life is the monastic one. The monastic life is characterized by abstinence, a mild asceticism, and, above all, celibacy. The leaders of Christianity in ancient times, both male and female, were enjoined to live a life of celibacy even though that pattern might be too difficult and impractical for the laity.

Judaism rejects the extreme positions of paganism and Christianity. Physical pleasures are neither worshiped nor denied. They are enjoyed as God's gift; but this enjoyment is restrained through rules and limits. At the end of creation God sees all that He had made and behold "it was exceedingly good." This means that the physical world is objectively good and may be enjoyed, but Judaism adds, with limits.

Indulging the sex drive, therefore, is a *mitzvah,* endowed with holiness. It is good regardless of whether or not it leads, or even can lead, to procreation. However, there are strict limits on when one may enjoy sex and with whom one may enjoy it. These limits are articulated in the institution of *taharat ha-mishpahah.*

Through these regulations we raise the biological act to the level of the sacred. The blessing we recite at a wedding renders this explicit: "Blessed art Thou O Lord . . . who has sanctified us with His *mitzvot* and commanded us concerning prohibited sexual relations, forbidding relations during the engagement period, and permitting them during marriage. Blessed art Thou O Lord who sanctifies His people through the marriage canopy and the wedding ceremony."

This is the Jewish approach to the physical world: neither to worship nor to deny it, but to sanctify it by enjoying it with rules and limits. We sanctify the act of eating through *kashrut;* we hallow sex through marriage and family purity; we ennoble rest and relaxation, which the Protestant work ethic could never quite accept, through the Sabbath; and we render time sacred through the festivals.

THE PSYCHOLOGICAL VALUE

Judaism is interested in more than the sanctification of the physical and the ritual world. The Jewish religion is designed to sanctify *all* areas of life, the physical, the personal, the social, and the economic. In every phase of human activity one should feel the religious impulse, the divine imperative.

People are as much servants of God when at business as at prayer. People should experience their religious nature when closing a financial deal as when opening a Bible. Religion is not confined to the synagogue. It should exist in the marketplace. It is not something that we store in the holy ark from Sabbath to Sabbath. Religion sparks the holy life that we lead seven days a week.

The colonial Governor of Pennsylvania is reputed to have said once to a congregation of Quakers who were known to be pious worshipers on the one hand and shrewd business manipulators on the other: "I see that ye pray in the church on Sundays and that ye prey on the people the rest of the week."

How are we to avoid such hypocrisy that, regrettably, is not confined to eighteenth-century colonial America? How does Judaism try to infuse religion into every facet of life? It does so by touching the most temporal areas, sex and food. If one can make the most essential biological functions holy, this forms a psychological pattern that affects the rest of life.

It will be argued that there are some people who manage to observe *kashrut* and *taharat ha-mishpahah* and nevertheless conduct *treif* lives. There are people who are extraordinarily careful about what goes into their mouths but are rather careless about what comes out. There are those who would never consider violating the rule of *niddah* and *mikvah* but who have no difficulty engaging in sharp business practices or in filing false income tax returns. The fact that people can manage such hypocrisies is not a refutation of Judaism's sound psychology. Developing a religious pattern for the most basic human activities, sex and food, should lay the groundwork for adherence to the ethical norms of Judaism. The primary tenets of Judaism are abrogated if this does not occur.

When God gave Abraham the essential command: "Walk before Me in righteousness" (Genesis 17:1), we assume that the descendants of Abraham are required to walk in all places, at all times, and at all cost as Jews and as divine servants. "Know God in all your ways" (Proverbs 3:6). *Taharat ha-mishpahah* is psychologically an excellent point of departure for this unique journey of the *am kadosh*, a unique people.

THE SOCIOLOGICAL VALUE

Maimonides records these rules in his monumental work of Jewish law, *Mishneh Torah*. In the section entitled *Sefer Kedushah*—the Book of Holiness—he includes all the sexual ordinances and all of the dietary rules. These basic human needs can take on the uniqueness of *kedushah* and, if we follow them carefully, lead us to become a holy nation.

These rules help to set us apart socially from the people around us. That, too, is a measure of *kedushah*. The distinctive character of the Jewish people is not based upon racial differentiation. We have no unique physical, mental, or emotional characteristics. What makes us genuinely different is our way of life. The chosen people, it has been said, is a choosing people. Offered a pattern of living that is different, that has stringent rules and demanding strictures, we chose to accept this way of life. This alone is what makes us Jewish. When one keeps the rules of *taharat ha-mishpahah* carefully and confines one's sexual behavior to marriage and, then too, only to certain times during the month, one definitely sets himself or herself apart from the rest of society.

Young men and women who date and are not prepared to engage in casual sex run the risk, these days, of being considered strait-laced and Victorian. That is the price we pay for setting ourselves apart and remaining a unique people. The same is true in the area of *kashrut*. We do not eat in every restaurant. If we have a business lunch it either has to be at a kosher restaurant or we limit our menu. This distinguishes us and often raises inquiries from our acquaintances. So be it! This is fundamental to being an *am kadosh*—a unique and holy people.

Some consider this distinctiveness to be a weakness. They do not like to be cast in the role of outsiders in society. One might do well to consider whether particularity is indeed a weakness or not. The general view today tends to respect and to encourage "doing your own thing." In fact, being special these days is often the "in" thing to do, while trying to obscure or blur differences is "out." Moreover, when doing your own thing links you with the chain of Jewish tradition from Moses, to Akiba, to Maimonides, to your grandfather, it is all the more worth doing, especially since we believe that it is God's thing also, at least for the Jewish people.

THE RELIGIOUS VALUE

The modern individual likes to think that he or she is in control of life. We have the technology to exercise that control and the know-how to use it. The religious personality, however, understands that we control nothing. Our health, our well-being, our happiness are all in God's hands. We pray to God to help us control our lives; we do not expect to be able to control life ourselves.

The Torah teaches us that in the most fundamental areas of life—sex and food—we cannot simply have things our own way. Adam had to learn this in Paradise when he was given one commandment, not to eat from a specific tree. The purpose of that commandment was to teach him that he was not in control, even though the entire world, as it were, was his to enjoy.

When we engage in sexual activity within a proper Jewish framework, we affirm that it is God who has ultimate control over our lives rather than we. When we avoid certain foods because they are prohibited, this is a further affirmation that we do not exercise full control over our lives and that we submit to the will of God.

In our freewheeling society, where people do as they please, this message is difficult to transmit and perhaps even harder to accept. But it is an important part of one's religious consciousness. The world is God's. He gives it to us to enjoy, but there are limits. Those limits remind us of our humanness and of God's divinity.

These are the values of *taharat ha-mishpahah.* It is not an easy *mitzvah* to keep, but it is a most important thread in the fabric of a Jewish life. It is a *mitzvah* about which very few people speak because of their natural modesty; but its significance should not be underestimated because we fail to promote it. It is an institution that fell into disrepute in America during the immigrant and first-generation periods, but is growing in acceptance among young people who appreciate a life of Torah and *mitzvot* and who are ready to make sacrifices in order to live such a life. *Taharat ha-mishpahah* distinguishes us from both pagans and Christians in our approach to the physical world. It reminds us that God and Torah should touch every facet of our lives. It helps to set us apart and maintain us as a holy people, and it reminds us that although we feel that we can fully control our own lives, we are ready to submit to the will of God as set down by our sages. In so doing we give added meaning, not alone to our sexual life, but to every facet of human existence, as a "kingdom of Priests and a holy people."

16

Mikvah Blessings

Barbara Goldstein

"Blessed are You O Lord who has kept me in life, has sustained me and enabled me to reach this moment."

Many times, in the course of my life, I have had the pleasure and the privilege of reciting *she-heheyanu*. I never take this blessing for granted—even when I light *yom tov* candles. I feel its meaning in the power of a particular moment. But this day, the 12th of Elul 5748, the *she-heheyanu* was different, even if only for a brief glimmer of time.

My second daughter was about to be married. It was Thursday and Devra's wedding was Sunday. The wedding and the *mikvah* visit were timed to her cycle. "Going to the *mikvah*?" her friends and many of mine queried. The bemused expressions on their faces spoke more than volumes.

I too once had, and still have, many negative feelings about the entire concept of *mikvah*. The idea that, as women, we are physically impure and require ritual purification is abhorrent to me. From the time of marriage through all of our childbearing years, we are "defiled" for half of our lives. Leviticus 18:19 prohibits conjugal relations for seven days during a woman's period of uncleanness. The Torah restriction of seven days was then extended by the rabbis for another seven days—"*niddah*." Why *mikvah* at all? Since the destruction of the Temple, none of the other ritual purifications are necessary. Why single out women? Is it because we can't find any

more "red heifers"?[1] Nevertheless, despite my ambivalence, I advocate *mikvah* because I know from my own experience that it can be
spiritually transcending. Furthermore, it is exclusively a woman's
mitzvah, only one of three, and is, therefore, mine. It ties me to
generations of Jewish women who went to *mikvah* before me. Nor do
I choose to allow it to become solely the property of Orthodox
women.

The first thing I had to do, then, was to find out where the
mikvah was located. I knew there was one in Highland Park, a town
five minutes from mine. Whom should I ask? The thought occurred
to me to call the kosher pizza place. I did, and they gave me the
telephone number and address. I telephoned and made an appointment for Thursday morning. I told Devra that going during the day
is a privilege granted only to brides. We entered a World War II
suburban house and were escorted by two children into the waiting
room of the "ritualarium." I had forgotten the English word for
mikvah. That is why I couldn't find the number in the phone book.

We sat for a few moments when Sara, the *"mikvah* lady,"
appeared and greeted us. Radiant, a young *ba'alat teshuvah,* she
told us of her encounter with the Chabad *Hasidim* at the University
of Buffalo while she and her husband were shelling shrimp in a
nearby restaurant. She showed us around the building and then
asked if Devra had prepared herself at home. We said "no," and
Devra went into the washroom with Shira, her older sister, who
accompanied us. Shira had been married several months earlier in
Jerusalem, where she, too, had gone to the *mikvah.* In Israel, the
spirituality we so eagerly sought was totally destroyed, because a
bride must present proof of her immersion to the *Rabbanut* before a
ketubah can be issued. In our people's history, an act of faith was
never meant to be legislated.

Now Shira was here for the wedding and was anxious to assist
her sister, Devra, with her first *mikvah* visit. My own mind raced
back twenty-seven years to my first *mikvah* experience. I was then
the bride and my mother thought I was "crazy" to want to go to
"that place," as she filled me with bizarre stories of her own
unpleasant *mikvah* reception before her wedding.

In considering the time frame of our grandmothers' and mothers' generations, many *mikva'ot* in poor immigrant neighborhoods

---

[1]The red heifer (*parah adumah*) was the animal whose ashes were used in
the ritual purification of persons and objects defiled by a corpse (Numbers
19).

were indeed dingy and dark. My mother feared going to the *mikvah*. In ominous tones she warned me that they would cut my hair and nails to the quick. How sad, I thought, that my mother had refused to share this special moment with me, as I was about to do with my own daughter.

I walked into the washroom and saw my two "little girls" playing. Shira was washing Devra's hair, using a cup, as I used to. "Put your head back so that the soap doesn't run into your eyes." It would be the last time the two sisters would have this moment together, as one was already married and the other was on the threshold of *huppah*. "Okay," they said, "we're ready." Having gone through the checklist, removing nail polish, toenail polish, etc., we called for Sara.

From the washroom a door led into the actual *mikvah*. Devra descended the stairs and was ready for the immersion. "All the way under," Sara said softly. Devra immersed herself, and as she did, I heard the sounds of *tekiah-teru'ah*. I realized that Sara's husband was upstairs reciting his morning prayers which were followed by his blowing of the *shofar*, as is customary in the month of Elul. The piercing sound of the *shofar* heralded the occasion appropriately. "Kosher," Sara exclaimed as Devra recited the blessing. Shira and I answered, "amen"; our eyes filled with tears of joy. Shira's younger sister, my daughter, Devra, was now indeed a *kallah*. She emerged, nymph-like, from the water and ascended the stairs glistening from the softness of the rain water. Sara wrapped her in a sheet and wished her *mazal tov!* Devra radiated beauty and sanctity, the kind of glow that comes from within as the *Shekhinah* shines through.

She got dressed. I inquired what the fee was. Sara waved her hand, "Brides are free," she said. I thanked her and gave her *hai*.[2] She asked Devra where she was going to live. When she heard Puerto Rico, she said, "Shh—just go right into the ocean!"

Sara's last words to us were, "Remember, a child born of *mikvah* carries a special blessing." And so I thought: My blessings were not all luck, for my three children were conceived after *mikvah*.

As we drove away, the conversation turned to Masada. Devra reminisced about our trips to Masada and explanations of the ancient *mikvah* there. Suddenly she felt connected to 2,000 years of her people's history. She was at one with the past—even as she was about to create a new link to the future.

It was hard to explain to everyone what had happened. One

---

[2]$18.00.

rabbi asked if *mikvah* wasn't superfluous, considering that most brides aren't virgins. I answered, "All the more reason, a bride and groom enter the *huppah* with their sins washed away." The *huppah* and *kiddushin* create a new beginning. What better way than for the bride through *mikvah*—"*mayim hayim*," "living waters"—to prepare herself for the groom and the life they are about to begin.

I spent the rest of the day suffused with joy. The unique action bonded the three of us. I prayed that each of my daughters would one day have the same privilege with their daughters. A new Jewish home was about to be consecrated. My husband and I had given our all to make this happen. We are grateful to God that we have reached this season.

17

Reading the Jewish Tradition on Marital Sexuality

Eugene B. Borowitz

We begin, first, with the fundamental premise of the discussion. For Judaism, marriage is an overwhelmingly important human duty, and spousal sexual intercourse is intimately bound up with its fulfillment. Though the *halakhah* occasionally provides for celibate marriages (as contrasted to nonprocreative ones), as in the case of continual menstrual bleeding, it is diametrically opposed to those tendencies in Christianity, Hinduism, and elsewhere that seek to spiritualize marriage by eliminating intercourse. Our sages so oppose such a practice of celibacy that their occurrence qualifies women as well as men to demand that the Jewish court effectuate their divorce.

Yet, as the personalist perspective makes plain, the Rabbis, for all their concern about sexual intercourse, give us relatively little instruction as to how we might best engage in it so as to reach its Jewish goals. They do provide us with voluminous, detailed instructions about various sexual prohibitions, most particularly when the wife is halakhically a menstruant. By contrast, their positive interpersonal guidance is minimal and marginal. They seem rather inhibited about direct sex education, fearing *nibul peh* (filthy speech) and immodesty so much that they prefer to err on the side of saying little. And when they do speak, their meaning is somewhat clouded by their addiction to euphemism. Modernity has taught us that we have a better chance of accomplishing our Jewish goals by being less covert about what is so important in our lives. To be better

Jews, we need to learn directly about human sexuality and to discuss it openly with our spouse so that we can recognize and respond to our individual and mutual needs. We also will benefit by learning how to educate one another about our sexuality as we face the personal and biological changes that continually reshape our marital relationships over the years.

Second, our tradition connects the act of marital intercourse with the highest expressions of holiness of which people are capable. That follows from our having a covenant with the Most High and has nothing to do with soil or blood or national destiny. But I do not see much of this tone of sacred sexuality in our early Jewish books. The *halakhah,* precisely as law, is concerned with the legal entailments of betrothal and marriage. *Kiddushin,* despite all our homiletics, is essentially the setting apart of this woman for this man exclusively, just as a sanctuary is set aside from all other places and must not be defiled. Without doubt, elements of spiritual sanctification do enter the relationship, as the blessings under the *huppah* indicate.

However, when the mystics employed a near-pagan symbolism for God to suggest a mythology of divine fragmentation and reintegration through human religious behavior—only then did sexual intercourse become directly endowed with sacred overtones. If further evidence is required of the congeniality of this attitude to rabbinic Judaism, we need not look far. The talmudic *halakhah* makes a wife utterly subject to her husband's sexual whims, but by the Middle Ages, the Rabbis insist that he has no right to have intercourse with her without her free consent.

Yet, dialectically, by modern standards, the specific rules by which the Rabbis safeguard the sacredness of human sexuality often seem no longer appropriate. The sages seem frightened of our having fleeting thoughts or images of sexual pleasure (*hirhurim*). They warn us against these dangerous mental intrusions and suggest strategies by which to avoid them. These not succeeding, we should discipline ourselves to repress our sexual imagination. As a result, what might be one of our greatest human fulfillments is associated with what is dirty and defiling. Thus, they instruct us to have intercourse only in the dark and regardless of our window shades, never during the daytime.

By contrast, the modern notion of sexuality as being natural to people seems far more likely to sanctify this drive. Our sexual fantasies usually testify to nothing more than our continuing vitality. How we allow our imaginations to influence our acts, not our daydreams, is the truer indication of our character. Being creatures of whim and fancy, if we turn to one another in love by day, or enjoy seeing one another as we reach out by night, then surely these acts will only enhance the personal and, potentially, the sacred aspects of our sexual union.

Third, for all its insistence upon sexuality, rabbinic tradition felt it had only a limited place in marriage. The covenant is for all of life, not merely to express our sexuality. In Judaism, the marital relationship encompasses far more than sexual satisfaction, because the sex act symbolizes the unique bond between the spouses. So much has been said about rabbinic Judaism being a worldly religion and having a positive attitude toward sex that we forget its countervailing tendency to sexual self-denial. The laws concerning marital separation during menstruation, most notably the insistence of seven clean days beyond the four-plus days of actual flow, and the heavy condemnation of adultery, radically subordinate the sexual drive to a great purpose.

Moreover, males are often cautioned to limit their sexual activity to rather modest rates of intercourse. The modern world, by contrast, seems obsessed with sexuality and compulsive about better and more frequent sexual performance. It tends to subordinate the personal to the biological, and the relationship turns into an idolatry of sensuality and orgasm. Restoring a covenantal context to our sex lives would give us a more human sense of its virtues and limits.

Yet it must also be acknowledged that the contemporary preoccupation with sex arose in reaction to the heavy repression that all the religious traditions directed toward it. Thus, modern Hebrew writers of the turn of the century (such as Tchernichovsky and Berdichevsky) welcomed the modern understanding of life, for they felt their people had long been deprived of adequate love and sexuality. We may well attribute the morbidity with which much of ghetto Judaism invested sex to the stark dualism of body and spirit that medieval Jewish thought brought into our tradition.

Nonetheless, we cannot deny that a similar negative note appears early on in Judaism. The Bible declares a man ritually impure until evening, after he has had an ejaculation, and the Rabbis regularly use repressive terms like *kof et yitzreinu* and *kovesh et yitzro* to describe how we should deal with our sexual urges. The Rabbis' rules and attitudes seem unduly restrictive when we view sexuality as central to human personality. Less fear of our libido and more ease with the free flowing nature of the personal life need to be infused into our contemporary Jewish sexual style.

Fourth, the Jewish writings consider the goals of intercourse to be far broader than sensual satisfaction. The covenant between the partners is not founded on their facility in giving each other pleasure but in living together in sanctity. By contrast, Americans have come to value highly their technical know-how in producing and varying sexual pleasure. Often, then, what was once touted as an act of love becomes another test of our capacity to produce results. Not only does the relationship wither in the objectification, but the sex itself finally cannot live up to the anticipated ideal. The hedonistic paradox reasserts itself—directly pursuing happiness only makes it more elusive.

Although they occasionally acknowledged the human playfulness we so easily associate with personal sexual activity, the Rabbis did not give it very much scope or recognition. Some silliness and foolishness is often a most delightful accompaniment to our sexuality. To deny it in the name of human dignity is to miss much of the positive reality of what it is to be a person.

Fifth, our tradition proclaims procreation to be the primary, although not the exclusive, goal of marriage. The covenant is made not only between the present partners but with the generations that were and with the generations yet to come. Infertility is thus a terrible calamity to a loving Jewish couple. We gladly summon every resource of medical science to make it possible for the spouses to have a child. And our community rejoices with happiness when we hear of a new pregnancy or the birth of a new child. Surely some special wisdom was attached to propagation since it was the first commandment recorded in the Torah, and it is one in whose fulfillment Jews have regularly known the *simhah shel mitzvah.*

Yet here, too, Jewish tradition interpreted a worthy value to the extent that the personal welfare of the partners was subordinated to the law and its communal–historical ends. Should the mother's life be threatened, contraception might or must be used. But severe economic hardship or human deterioration as a result of bearing many children were not halakhically acceptable reasons for thwarting conception. Rabbinic literature has many discussions of the evils of wasting male seed and strategies to avoid this abominable occurrence. The modern mind is far more concerned with the human waste produced in the lives of the parents, the infant, and the siblings by insisting that mothers bear children even when the parents responsibly determine it is not to their or their family's best interest to do so. For moderns, companionship is a more significant goal than procreation—though one wondrous aim of a true Jewish marital friendship is the genetic blending of persons to produce a totally new individual.

Sixth, from its earliest days, Judaism taught that marriage was the only acceptable social setting for the sexual relationship. It required some advancement beyond the common conventions of the ancient Middle East to reach the monogamous marriage. The logic of the covenant, as exemplified in this most intimate of human relationships, led Judaism to insist that it involve but two partners. In marriage, the spouses undertook ultimate responsibility for one another, and for the possibility of producing a new life together and nurturing it to maturity. In the divine model, God occasionally threatens the wayward covenant partner, Israel, with a divorce, but their relationship was established for all time. Human beings, in all their fallibility, ought to strive for permanence as the ideal of covenant life. Should they not be able to manage it, our tradition accepts the necessity of divorce, though it considers the dissolution of a marriage a tragedy.

But the stability of the Jewish marriage was procured at the cost of subordinating a woman's life to that of her husband. The idea of a wife as a full personality in her own right, entitled to pursue her individual goals as her husband pursues his, is a recent possibility. Yet can we call the covenant life between husband and wife humanly complete unless two equal partners bring it into being and maintain it? And that must hold true for the wife's sexual drives and aspirations as well as for her husband's. The flow of initiation, action, and reaction needs to be as open to the wife as to the husband, allowing her to act in ways previously considered unseemly for a Jew. What the ideal of equality will eventually do to transform the Jewish covenant of marriage, I do not think anyone can now know.

Seventh, sexual faithfulness is a cardinal sign of a good Jewish marriage, and adultery is a most heinous sin. The covenant bespeaks a unique relationship. Performing its unique marital privilege with other partners seriously damages the ties that once existed between the spouses when the intimacy they shared was unique to one another. On the divine level, the prophets frequently denounce the people of Israel for its marital unfaithfulness. So, too, though sexual loyalty requires abstention from other exciting sexual relationships and is a species of Jewish asceticism, nothing can take its place in a Jewish marriage. Our pledge to each other carries special weight when you and I know only each other as sexual partners. Should one of us break that vow of exclusivity, particularly if we do so willfully and self-consciously, we will damage our relationship most seriously. Indeed, even if we find a way to restore it, what we mean to each other cannot ever be quite the same. Some Jews today, fearing this disappointment, agree in advance to allow for occasional acts of adultery. In so deciding, they practically invite the evil *yetzer* to live with them and never can savor the hope and fulfillment of true covenant. Their "open marriage" testifies to the diminished standards of human integrity common in our time.

Yet it is also true that the rabbinic laws of adultery are notoriously one-sided. Classic *halakhah* does not apply them in the same way to men as to women. Moreover, in the so-called "laws of jealousy," it gives husbands preemptive rights over their wives' acts so that mere suspicion of misbehavior becomes grounds for divorce. And shall we agree to the law that after adultery a husband may never take his wife back, ignoring every human consideration as to what brought the act about? Here the law speaks with implacable, impersonal rigor. In the name of community standards of sanctity, it calls for depriving the people in the relationship of the right to a positive decision as to what might now best become of it. I do not see that it is a fatal mitigation of the seriousness of adultery to suggest that our modern understanding of persons requires us to introduce more compassion in dealing with a transgressor in this area than the *halakhah* did.

Eighth, incest is a major violation of Jewish marriage. The generations each have their place in the historical progression from creation to the Messiah. We do not mix our obligations to our generation with those that apply to the generations that came before us or the ones that follow us in turn. And the betrayal of exclusiveness found in adultery takes on special pain when we confuse those who are close enough to be loved uniquely with the one we love so dearly in a bond of sexual sharing. The infidelity of incest not only breaches our special tie with them but does not allow our family relationships to function in that unparalleled covenantal mix of high intimacy without genitality.

Here, too, by personalist standards, the *halakhah*'s impersonal specification of forbidden partners seems unduly extended. It specifies in great detail those whom we may not marry and does so without regard for age, needs, or other personal considerations. Incest may require a definition in largely impersonal terms so as to place an objective limit to our polymorphous sexual cravings. Nonetheless, the rabbinic extensions of the prohibited list of marriage partners (and perhaps even the far reaches of the biblical list) might, depending on the personal circumstances, warrant suspension of our ethics of marital sexuality.

Ninth, Judaism insists upon the communal context of our private sexual activity. What we do does not merely affect us alone but is an important part of the way the covenant people seeks to live out its responsibilities to God. Being concerned with modesty, the sages directed that intercourse be quite a private matter. They not only barred the presence of all other adults and insisted on the seclusion of the spouses; they were also concerned about the possible presence of their children. At the same time, they did not consider Jews who, when away from others, may conduct themselves in whatever fashion they might agree to. Being Jews, they should share in the high human standards and messianic aspirations of their people's covenant wherever they are and whatever they do. Without its members living up to Israel's historic hopes, how can our people ever fulfill its responsibilities for bringing the Messiah? And the evil *yetzer* being so strong and human will being so frail, are we long likely to remember the sanctity of our sexuality without keeping in mind the communal dimension of our private sexual life?

This social aspect of our sexuality can be conceded without vitiating the counterbalancing criticism, i.e., though the Jewish tradition richly informs us about our common human and covenantal Jewish sexual goals, it offers us little help in learning how to express sexually just what two people mean to one another. Consider a problem that has grown with our new knowledge and openness toward sex. How shall we continually transform the exclusivity of the Jewish marital pact in relation to the differing rates and paths of the partners' personal sexual development over the many years of an enduring marriage? Our sages have had little to say about keeping our sexual life fresh over the years. They either did not know about this problem or did not consider it worthy of their attention. Caring more directly about persons, we have a greater range of spiritual needs. Therefore, alongside static communal standards we need a sense of what enriches a modern Jewish marriage as the spouses age.

I realize that in this presentation of nine Jewish theses and my personal counterpoises, I have sacrificed depth analysis to comprehensive sweep. I am also conscious of not having touched on many other vital matters and of possibly suggesting that I have formed a focused judgment on all other issues. Permit me to remedy at least the latter failing by testifying to my—and perhaps our—continuing confusion in this area by saying a word about two perplexing matters, one raised by the *halakhah*, the other by personalism.

I doubt that any category of Jewish law more seriously affects marital sexual life than the regulations concerning menstruation and separation. If we take our tradition seriously, we must acknowledge that these meticulously elaborated rules and their high emotional overtones cannot be censored out of the Rabbis' understanding of how to consecrate a Jewish marriage. But what shall we liberal Jews make of them? Perhaps we can all agree on one step: the sexually proscribed seven clean days after the cessation of menstruation and the high fastidiousness of the sages about any later show of blood seem obsessive and ought summarily to be abandoned for a more humanistic, interpersonal evaluation of what sexual activity is fitting.

But we are still left with endless, detailed regulations about the onset of the period, taboos during the flow, and what constitutes its proper conclusion. Does all this say anything to us? Here we must certainly need the help of our female colleagues and of Jewish women generally. They need to take the leadership in helping us rethink our old, often archaic feelings about blood and menstruation. Perhaps then we can find an appropriately personalized way for modern Jews to sanctify this significant aspect of female sexuality and thus of Jewish marriage.

The other problem arises from our contemporary culture. We liberal Jews have welcomed women's liberation and have taken some few but important steps toward making it a reality. But how will the presence of a fully self-determining, demanding, as well as acquiescent wife change the old tacit arrangements of Jewish marriage under which most Jews still operate? Consider, as one aspect of the problem, what the modern world has done to damage the male libido by harnessing it to economic or career-oriented ends. Our home lives have suffered and the marketplace has become foul with our displaced sexuality. If women should now similarly channel much of their sexual drive into the pursuit of success and power, what will become of the sexual primacy of the marital bed? How, we must now wonder, can liberal Judaism today combat the destructive power of a society bent on exploiting the new sexual freedom for women?

In sum, the Jewish teaching on sexuality continues to express with compelling power the mandates of existence under the covenant. It provides us with a ground of value, standards of practice, and ideals to which to aspire. It directs us to structure our existence so that our lives are not a random sequence of events or experiences. It puts us in a historic context so that the present moment takes its place not only within our personal history but that of our family, our people, and thus of humankind slowly moving toward God's kingdom. It invests our sexual lives with sanctity, raising our animality beyond the human to where something of the divine image may be seen in us.

Despite this incomparable service, Judaism's sexual teaching shows three major areas in need of reform. First, its historical–communal–institutional objectivity causes it to be relatively impersonal. We need to balance Judaism's preoccupation with abstract standards by a strong commitment to the individual, which we consider basic to our mature existence. Second, its fearful understanding of the relationship between God and our genital activity can easily enshroud sexual activity with a heavy cloak of shame. We now recognize that exacerbating sexual fears and anxieties can cripple our humanity. We need to connect our sex life with the transcendent without making our sexual guidance damagingly repressive, but rather therapeutically liberating. Third, and most obvious these days, classic Jewish texts are almost entirely concerned with male sexuality and male religious responsibility. A complete reworking of all these materials in terms of women's equality must now be undertaken. That cannot be done by males alone. The equal partner must have an equal voice. Indeed, considering the continuing prejudice of most of us men, leadership in this, as in many other areas, should be in the hands of women.

18

Happy Marriages

Francine Klagsbrun

What are the characteristics of long, satisfying, happy marriages? There is no formula, no single recipe that will produce the perfect marriage, or even a working one. Rather, there are certain abilities and outlooks that couples in strong marriages have, not all of them at all times, but a large proportion a good part of the time. They fall, it seems to me, into eight categories.

AN ABILITY TO CHANGE AND TOLERATE CHANGE

Change is inevitable in marriage as in life. Partners become involved in work and pull back from work; children are born, go to school, leave home; spouses age, get sick, drop old interests, take on new ones, make new friends, live through the sorrows of old ones; parents get old and die; couples move from apartments to houses and back to apartments, from one town to another. Changes bring anxieties and disequilibrium. Yet in the strongest marriages, each partner is able to make "midcourse corrections, almost like astronauts," as one psychiatrist put it. That is, they are able both to adapt to the change that is happening in the marriage or in the other partner and, when called for, to change themselves.

Couples whose marriages have lasted fifteen years or more have lived through some of the most rapid and overwhelming social change in modern history. These people married at a time when marriage had a set form, when husbands knew that their work was to provide for the family and wives knew that theirs was to care for the home and children. During the course of these marriages, the world turned upside down. Marriage was ridiculed as a dying if not dead institution. Husbands who played out the traditional roles they had been taught as children were now seen as "insensitive," dictatorial "patriarchs," while wives were "oppressed" in "stifling" marriages. Along with the rhetoric came real change, a new emphasis on a woman's right to seek her own work outside her home and on a man's responsibility—and right—to shift some of his energies and time away from the outside to his home and to his family. The changes brought chaos to many marriages that found all the premises on which they had been built cut out from under them.

In the marriages that have remained strong and viable, partners have had the flexibility to change their marriages to incorporate new ideals.

Great changes have taken place in couples who have shifted their life patterns as social values have shifted. The women who have gone to work or back to school years into their marriages have come to see themselves as different beings than they were in their earlier days, and in doing so they have changed their marriages. Their husbands have accommodated to those changes—some more willingly than others—and many have changed themselves. They have changed by taking on household tasks they would not have dreamed of when they first married and by rearranging their schedules to make room for their wives' schedules. More important, they have changed inwardly, many of them acknowledging their wives' ambitions and accomplishments outside their homes. One tiny manifestation of these changes in long marriages are the numbers of no-longer-young men I see at dinner parties automatically getting up to clear the table or serve a course, while their wives sit and chat with guests. Such acts are not merely gestures; they represent an inner change.

But there is an attitude toward change in long marriages that goes far beyond the social issues. There is this: People who stay happily married see themselves not as victims of fate, but as free agents who make choices in life. Although, like everyone else, they are influenced by their own family backgrounds, for the most part they do not allow their lives together to be dominated by their earlier family lives apart. Because they choose to be married to each other, a choice they make again and again, they are open to changing themselves, pulling away from what *was* in order to make what *is* alive and vital. In other words, as much as they are able to, they try to control their lives, rather than drifting along as the patsies of destiny.

In the best of marriages, change takes place in a context. It is contained within the boundaries of the marriage. Within those boundaries each partner acts and reacts, bending to the changes in the other and in the world outside. And even while they change, couples recognize that some things cannot change and should not change—and that leads to the second characteristic of long-term marriages, and its major paradox.

AN ABILITY TO LIVE WITH THE UNCHANGEABLE

This means to live with unresolved conflict when necessary. The simultaneous acceptance of change and of lack of change in long marriages is summed up by the words of a shopkeeper, married thirty-eight years: "You have to know when to holler and you have to know when to look away."

A statement made by many couples when asked about the "secrets" of their happy marriage was, "We don't expect perfection," or some variation thereof. They would go on to explain that their marriage had areas that were far from perfect, qualities in one another that they wish could have changed but they have come to recognize as qualities that will never change. Still, they live with those unchangeable, and sometimes disturbing, qualities, because, as one woman said, "The payoff is so great in other areas."

Long-married couples accept the knowledge that there are some deep-seated conflicts—about personality differences, habits, styles of dealing with things—that will never be solved. In the best of situations, they stop fighting about those issues and go about their lives instead of wasting their energies on a constant, fruitless struggle to settle differences "once and for all."

Couples who get pleasure from their marriages often say that they do so because they focus on the strengths of the marriage, not its weaknesses, on compatibilities rather than dissonances. With that outlook they are able to enhance what is good so that it becomes the core of the marriage while the negatives cling only to the periphery.

The point is not that we must all sit back and let life wash over us without trying to shape and control what happens to us. The point is that we can best control our lives—and our marriages—by acknowledging that some things will never be perfect and some things cannot be turned around, and apply our strengths where they can make a difference.

AN ASSUMPTION OF PERMANENCE

Most marriages, first, second, or later, begin with the hope and expectation that they will last forever. In the marriages that do last, "forever" is not only a hope, but an ongoing philosophy. The mates do not seriously think about divorce as a viable option. Certainly there are "divorce periods," times of distancing and anger, but even if divorce itself crosses the minds of the couple, it is not held out as an escape from difficulties. This attitude that a marriage will last, *must* last (not because some religious authority or family member says so, but because the marriage is that important to the couple), tempers a husband's and a wife's approach to conflicts and imperfections. They see the marriage as an entity in itself that must be protected. In today's terminology, they are committed to the marriage as well as to each other.

The commitment, however, is *not necessarily equal* at all times. In marriage after marriage, I had the impression that one partner more than the other was the "keeper of the commitment." One usually seemed more willing to give in after a fight or more prone to compromise to avoid the fight altogether and hold the marriage on a steady keel. That partner may have been the more dependent one, but was just as likely to be the stronger and more mature one, the one more able to swallow pride, break stalemates, and see the other's point of view. Caring and dedication to the marriage, however, must be strong enough on the part of both partners so that when the "commitment keeper" pulled back, or refused to be the conciliator on some issue, the other moved in and took over that role. The commitment to marriage is not always top priority in both partners' lives at the same time, but it is usually top priority for one or the other at different times.

It should be pointed out that the commitment to marriage by long-married couples is usually a commitment not only to a relationship, but also to marriage as an institution. Mae West's famous remark that "marriage is an institution, and who wants to live in an institution" makes sense when the institution is seen as a static, stifling edifice. But to couples who value marriage, it is regarded as an institution that adds stability and order to life, transmits ideals from one generation to the next, and provides a structure within which a woman and a man can entrust their souls to each other, knowing that they will be sheltered and protected by its permanence.

TRUST

This is a word used again and again by couples, and it means many things. It means love, although people tend to use the word "trust" more often than they use "love." In part this is because "love" is an overused word, and one whose romantic meanings have overshadowed the deeper, more profound meaning of the love that binds married people. In larger part it is because feelings of love may wax and wane in the course of a marriage—in times of anger, for example, few people can keep in touch with those feelings—but trust is a constant; without it there is no true marriage. Trust also implies intimacy, or, rather, it forms the base for the closeness that couples in good marriages have established.

Once that trust exists, there is no set form intimacy must assume. Not every couple in a strong marriage communicates as openly as the much-publicized communication ideals of our society would have them. Some do. Some are open and loose with each other, ventilating feelings and sensations freely. In other families, one partner, or both, may be more closed off, less able or willing to pour out heartsounds. But these marriages have their own ways of being intimate, which grow from the trust between partners. It may be that one partner is the expansive one while the second is more silent, relying on the other for emotional expressiveness. Or it may be that both are somewhat restrained in revealing sensitivities, yet they understand each other and feel comfortable with the more limited interchanges they have. There are many styles of relating among long-married couples, and no one seems better than another as long as each couple was satisfied with its own style.

The trust that lies at the heart of happy marriages is also the foundation for sexual enjoyment among partners. When mates speak about sexual loving, they almost always speak about trusting feelings that had expanded over the years. "Sex is richer and deeper for us," said one woman. "We trust each other and we're not ashamed to get pleasure." Trust is also the reason invariably given for a commitment to monogamy, as in "I may be tempted, but I wouldn't want to violate our trust." When a partner has had a fling or brief affair, trust is the reason most often offered for having ended it or for avoiding further extramarital involvements. In short, trust is regarded by many couples as the linchpin of their marriage.

A BALANCE OF DEPENDENCIES

This is another way of saying a balance of power. "Dependency" is preferable, even though "power" is a sexier word, with its implied comparison between marriage and politics; it better conveys the way couples see and regard one another. They speak of needing each other and depending on each other, and in doing so, they are not speaking about the weaknesses of marriage, but about its strengths. In the best of marriages, partners are mutually dependent; interdependent is another way of saying that. They are aware of their dependencies and not ashamed to cater to them, acknowledging openly their debt to one another.

There has been a great emphasis on egalitarian marriages in recent years, marriages in which both spouses share economic earnings and power and both share household duties. Let us hope these marriages increase in number. However, an impression that grows out of this emphasis on economic egalitarianism is that emotional egalitarianism automatically follows and that, by contrast, in traditional marriages the dependencies are all one-sided: the woman depends totally on the man. This has not been borne out among couples in solid, long marriages. Mates in nontraditional marriages as well as those in more traditional ones share emotional dependencies. Rarely are husband and wife equally dependent on each other at any particular point. Rather, the dependencies tip back and forth during the course of a marriage, each spouse nurturing the other as needed, so that over time, a balance is established, and that balance keeps the marriage strong and stable.

Dependency, it needs to be added quickly, does not mean an obliteration of self. No matter how close or how interdependent a couple, each spouse must retain an individuality, a sense of self. If one or the other loses that individuality and becomes completely submerged or exploited by the other, one or both partners usually become deeply unhappy in the marriage. Again, even in the most traditional marriages, where a women's social identity may be tied to her husband's occupation or profession, the women who speak most convincingly about the satisfactions of their marriages are women who view themselves as individuals and who do not rely on their husbands to make them feel worthy.

AN ENJOYMENT OF EACH OTHER

Wives and husbands in satisfying long marriages like each other, enjoy being together, and enjoy talking to each other. Although they may spend evenings quietly together in a room, the silence that surrounds them is the comfortable silence of two people who know they do not *have* to talk to feel close. But mostly they do talk. For many couples conversations go on continually, whether the gossip of everyday living or discussions of broader events. And they listen to each other. I watch the faces of people I interview and watch each listening while the other speaks. They might argue, become irritated, or jump in to correct each other, but they are engaged and are rarely bored.

They enjoy each other physically also, and sexual pleasures infuse many marriages for years and years. Sexual electricity can be sensed between some partners. A different kind of warmth emanates from others, a feeling of closeness and affection. They hold hands, they touch, they smile, and they speak of sex as "warm and loving," as one woman said, "maybe not the wildness of our early marriage, but very pleasing."

They laugh at each other's jokes. Humor is the universal salve and salvation, easing tensions and marriage fatigue. "If you can laugh about it," many say, "you know it will be all right." And for them it is.

They find each other interesting, but they do not necessarily have the same interests. And that is a surprise. Far fewer couples than would be expected speak about sharing interests or hobbies.

Some make fewer concessions than others to their spouses's interests. They might take separate vacations or go to movies or lectures with friends rather than with each other, and they find that for them that separation works better than forcing themselves to put in time at activities that one or the other hates. And for some married people, having separate interests makes each more interesting to the other. The only danger in this kind of separateness, especially for new marriages, is in its extreme. Spending a great deal of time apart is bound to cut into the closeness a husband and a wife build up. It also shuts off opportunities for them to get to know each other and, if not enjoy, at least appreciate and learn from the other's interests and obsessions. As in so many areas, couples in strong marriages try to find a balance between participating in each other's activities and going their own ways.

But if sharing interests is not a prerequisite for a rewarding marriage, sharing *values* is. Values refer to the things people believe in, the things they hold dear and worthy. The philosopher Bertrand Russell explained their importance in marriage well when he wrote, "It is fatal . . . if one values only money and the other values only good works." Such a couple will have trouble getting along, let alone enjoying each other's interests or ideas.

Mates who feel well matched share a common base of values even when they disagree about other things. One couple describes having their biggest arguments about money. He loves to spend whatever they have on clothes, records, and the theater; she watches every cent, wearing the same dress again and again. Yet they had an instant meeting of minds when it came time to buy a cello for their musically gifted daughter. They bought the best they could afford, even using a good part of their savings, because they both value their child's music education above anything else money can buy.

For some couples, religion is the value that informs everything else in life. These couples are a minority in our secular society. But those who do value religion consider it the strongest bond in their lives, and many attribute the happiness and stability of their marriages to that bond. I have found that marriages in which both partners value religion, even if the partners are of different faiths, have fewer conflicts over religious issues than same-faith marriages in which only one feels a religious commitment, especially if the other partner is disdainful of religion.

For all marriages, sharing values enhances the intimacy and mutual respect spouses feel, adding to their enjoyment of each other.

A SHARED HISTORY THAT IS CHERISHED

Every couple has a story, and couples in long marriages respect their own stories. They are connected to each other through these stories, and even the sadnesses they share are a valued part of their history. "Our life is like a patchwork," one woman said. "We pull in red threads from here and blue threads from there and make them into one piece. Sometimes the threads barely hold, but you pull hard at them and they come together, and the patchwork remains whole."

For the past two decades and more, educators have complained that young people are ahistorical. They have little sense of history and less interest in trying to learn about the past. They live in the present and they live without memory, a collective memory, of World War II, of the Holocaust, of Watergate or Vietnam, of McCarthyism or the Great Depression. That absence of history, that amnesia, as it were, for all that came earlier, adds to the rootlessness that many of the young feel. To exist without a past, without a framework of history, makes life in the present that much more difficult. And while many factors are involved in the high divorce rate among young couples today, their indifference to history is one more contributor. It's easier to end a marriage because of immediate problems when you don't see it as part of a larger fabric that stretches backward and forward, an entity that has a reality and history of its own.

People in long marriages value their joint history. When their ties in the present get raggedy, they are able to look to the past to find the good that they shared, rather than give in to the disillusionments of the moment. Their sense of history also gives them a respect for time. They know, by looking backward, that changes take time and that angers vanish with time, and they know that there is time ahead for new understandings and new adventures.

LUCK

It has to be said, because everyone said it. With it all, the history and the trust, the willingness to change and to live without change, people need a little bit of luck to keep a marriage going.

You need luck, first of all, in choosing a partner who has the capacity to change and trust and love. In their book *Marriage and Personal Development,* psychiatrists Rubin Blanck and Gertrude Blanck make the case that marriages work best when both partners have reached a level of maturity before marriage that makes them ready for marriage. They are quite right. The only difficulty with their case is that few people are terribly mature when they marry, certainly not people in first marriages who marry young, and not even many people in second marriages. Yet many marriages work because partners mature together, over the years of matrimony. So, you need a little luck in choosing someone who will mature and grow while you, too, mature.

And you need a little luck in the family you come from and the friends you have. A horrendous family background in which parents abuse their children or offer no love can set up almost insurmountable obstacles to the ability to sustain a marital relationship. Yet there are couples in long, happy marriages who did have devastating backgrounds. Often they were able to break the patterns they had known because of the encouragement of an aunt or an uncle, a grandparent, a teacher, a friend. They were lucky in finding the support they needed.

Then, you need a little luck with life. A marriage might move along happily and smoothly enough until a series of unexpected events rains down on it. A combination of illnesses or job losses, family feuds or personal failures might push the marriage off-course, when without these blows, it could have succeeded. Every marriage needs some luck in holding back forces that could crush it.

These aspects of luck may be out of our power to control. But the good thing about luck is that it is not all out of control. Many people who consider themselves happy in marriage speak about themselves as being lucky. Since they seem to have the same share of problems and difficulties as anyone else, sometimes even more than their share, luck in marriage, as in life, seems to be as much a matter of attitude as of chance. Couples who regard themselves as lucky are the ones who seize luck where they are able to. Instead of looking outside their marriage and assuming the luck is all there, in other people's homes, they look inside their marriage and find the blessings there. They are not blind to the soft spots of their marriages—nobody denies difficulties; they just consider the positives more important. So they say they are lucky. And they are. They have grabbed luck by the tail and have twisted it to their own purposes.

Jewish
∧ **Marital Status**

- ☐ Single
- ☐ Not quite married
- ☐ Married
- ☑ Single again
  - ☑ Widowed
  - ☐ Abandoned
  - ☐ Divorced
- ☐ Remarried
- ☐ Intermarried
- ☐ Gay or Lesbian
- ☐ Childless

19

A Time to Mourn, A Time to Dance: An Unfinished Work in Progress

Gail Katz

YOUNG WIDOW IN THE ORTHODOX WORLD

Pushing my way through an unpacked moving box, I smiled. The hubbub of moving, painting, starting kids off at yeshivah and bus stops had quieted down; the *yom tov* marathon of cooking and hosting had subsided; the children, 1 through 11 years old, were finally all sleeping through the night. On my birthday that week I would be 31. We were at peace in our new house, and I thought of Stan and smiled. Now there would be time for us.

What does it mean? What do we learn from this when one week later this life of peace and love is finished?

It is five days after my thirty-first birthday. Stan is dying in an emergency room of myocardial infarction. But he was so healthy—a biker, nonsmoker—he had no heart problems, no blood pressure history, no familial health problems.

A young Israeli resident with a pained face is trying to explain to me, but he keeps shrugging his shoulders and few of his words make sense.

"We're going to keep trying, though, but it's really bad."

A heavyset nurse with bushy knit eyebrows shakes her head silently as she waddles toward my open hands with a heavy paper bag. Deadweight, it pulls at me. Through a fog of sirens deep inside my skull, I open it to find Stan's pants, shoes, cut open *tzitzit*, and shirt. Dry mouthed, I look up as the sad resident slowly moves toward me. My ears are ringing, but I can hear what he is telling me almost before he says it.

"I'm sorry. We. . . . He. . . ." He is dead. My whole life, as I knew it, is dead.

"I need a phone."

"What?"

"I need a phone."

And in five minutes I call my rabbi, the rabbi who will deal with the medical examiner, the funeral chapel, the baby sitter, his parents, my two friends.

And yet. . . .

But who will take care of me? Who? What about me? Who will hold me?

At dawn I wait for my children to awaken.

"*Ima?*"

"*Leezie*, there is a story. . . ."

"*Ima*, what's wrong?"

"There is a story of a man who came home to see his wife and two sons, and his wife said, 'If a king lent you two jewels to enjoy, and then, after a time, he took them back. . . .' "

"Oh, *Ima*, oh . . . but I know that story," she wept, her head trembling in my lap.

"My son, *Abba* has died."

"But people go to the hospital to get better."

"He has died. The doctors couldn't make him better this time."

"But that doesn't happen, does it?"

"I'll hold you."

"No! No . . . oh."

"My father's dead," the 4-year-old announced at *shivah*. Then, "Listen, we're going to be big when we sit *shivah* for you, *Ima*, right? Right?"

For how can a boy so small survive without the father of his life—

Trying hats and zipping flies . . .
Flying kites and dreams . . .
And, ah, littlest one, there is no milk left to nurse you.

Late into the night the *shivah* candle dances shadows around my cold walls. Sleep? As if I might ever sleep again as I once did. As if life would ever be safe as it once was. I creep upstairs in the dark, still house as a scream swells in my throat. My mouth is completely closed, yet my lungs scream raw anguish into the emptiness.

It's like falling with your eyes open
Into a bottomless
Endless
blackness
only to fall still more.
My hands numb
I pull at the icy blankets
And edge stiffly between them
Biting my cheek to keep back
The
Scream.

I clutch my shoulders
And nod and rock
Aye . . .

It's all a mistake . . .
They meant to come get me . . .
They got the wrong guy—
He'll be back—
It's a dream
What if—
I should have—

I should have
But
but
How can I raise four children alone?
I am 31 years old
And a widow with four children
Who will take care of me?
Who will hold me?

Father and Mother and More

  The nightmare has only just begun.
There is business to be taken care of.
The banks close the accounts and the vault is sealed.
Social Security needs me for an interview.
His employer requests I come over to finish signing paperwork
    and clear out his office
The life-insurance policy—
Is there one? Is there? If there is, where is it? Where?
And how did he pay bills? Master and VISA from every bank
    downtown?

Why didn't we practice my paying bills and managing the bookkeeping? Because. That's why.

Because we never thought this would happen.

Not to us.

So I never handled billing. Not once. And as I sit down to pay mortgage, utility, insurance, yeshivah tuition, car loan and funeral bills that second week, I vomit all over the desk.

Hey, Stan!! Hey!

And as I try to load the car to take the children away for *Shabbat,* I can't get the clothing, pampers, and portacrib in the way they had always fit; the trunk will not close!

Hey, Stan!

And the furnace needs water, and the bricks need pointing; and the garage door doesn't close; and we have squirrels, and I get weird phone calls, Stan! Stan!

And your health insurance dropped us

—and Ethan needs hernia surgery! And I need you! I need you! Oh! Stan!

And Shana has begun to walk

And Dovie takes his guns to school

And Ethan is so very quiet

And Leezie tries to smile. Sometimes.

And I drive Ethan to *maariv* every night to say *kaddish.* An 8-year-old *kaddish,* Stan.

And I move with the screaming

Inside my head

Stan!

Stan!

THE EARLY YEARS

Think of the Children

"You must be strong for your children,
You must—"
"There are the children to think of;
Remember the children,
Remember—"
"Think of the children."

They half wince when they see me
"You should only have *nahas* from the children."
Only? Only? I should only have?
May God not punish me, is that all

There is to hope for? Is that to be my only blessing?
What will restore the well of strength
That I may give to their need
What about me?
Hey Stan!
Hey God!
What about me?

"But all the parents are coming. You'll come to school, won't you?"

So I sit in the back with women who wave to their sons and husbands at the front tables of the yeshivah dining room. The fathers snap pictures as the awards are presented. Stan's camera is a dead weight in my hand.

A restless baby cries out in the women's section; his mother stands to take him out. From across the room, the father runs to the cry. Soothed in his father's arms, the child coos and nestles as the man returns to his seat.

So that's why a kid has two parents.
When one is tired, the other is there.
    Broken, I run from the room.

Losing the ability to swallow life
I have lost twenty pounds
And my sense of wholeness and safety in the world.
I move cautiously
Waiting for the trap door to spring open
Beneath my feet
Or for the *other* shoe to fall

"But you cannot live like this
The children need you."

Shhh . . . there is a secret I cannot tell you.
There isn't enough me to give to them. Sh . . . I'm all used up.
    used out
    used.
I'm sorry.
I'm sorry I'm not
Nobler
Better

I'm sorry *Abba* is dead
Maybe they came for *me* and he said,

"No! Take Me!" and they said, "Okay."
Maybe if they took me he would know
How to take care of everything
And organize
and fix
and mobilize
and remarry
And help you live.

Home

My house is darkness
And I
Have to be the light.
It is hollow.

Visionless

And I must find
The molecules of dreams
to light the lights
and I have no strength
left
to me.
My shoulders sigh
and I plod on.

But my children need light
to live
And I must gather the will
to make
the light
to kindle
to nurture the light
that they may live

Such, such pain
to light their lights
unrestored
alone.

Once
Once I knew who I was.
Once I was soft

And young
And warm
And knew that God was good
And life was good

And now
Now I am lost
And running
because I can no longer pretend
to stay in a world
I once lived in.

Widowspeak

Yes, dear world, I am married
I am married to a man who died,
I am married to a life that died
Our life
My life as I knew me
Who I was—

Life ahead—
        Dead.
All.
Each.
We—
I—
me—
Dead.

My ring—
His ring—
Our ring is in the bank vault,
Cool steel keeps it in its place below ground.

But I was his. I have his name to prove it.
And now that he is not
I am not.

Don't you see? You shake your head no,
but can't you see?
I was his
And now that he no longer lives
I am—

Nobody's.
I belong to a memory.
I belong with a memory.
I am a memory.

Then who is this person
who leaves for work daily
shielding the kids from the world?
Who is this woman who stretches and reaches
to make time and life go on?
Through nights—
and homemade soups—
Granola / dried flowers / sightseeing day trips—
taxes—
children frightened of the dark—
carburetors—
gravestones—
not-quite-broken arms / appendicitis
field mice / water bugs—
gland lumps—
insurances that won't renew—
twenty-one undone homeworks—
camp trunks / name tapes—
fever—
school bus accidents

And they say I should only have *simhahs.*

I remember I opened his closet
Three months after he was gone
And placed my hand on the shoulder
of his herringbone brown tweed suit
and slowly embraced the jacket
where his back once used to be—
Fingers moving slowly—
My head pressed to the lapel—
And a moan escaped
From somewhere
Locked deep beneath the pose
of
sanity.
And I stood inhaling his scent
A light warm softness that was him.
Solid.
There with me.
There for me
Of me.

And my hand stroked the empty shoulder
slowly as I wept
until I sank
to the floor
Drained
Lost.

And later
when the wave of sorrow
passed
once again into silence,
I thought of at least three
things I should be doing.
Right away. Right away,
Up, up and away

Still at midnight
I look through the *Times*
How often I have fallen asleep
in this chair
Awake
so tired—
but sitting downstairs
still
unable
to get myself
to
go
up
to my room.
Sleeping alone is impossible
After the years of peace
as one.

He is dead.
Very.
I have stopped
touching
the spot where my ring once was
You know, with my thumb?
Only sometimes
I reach for
what was.

What was
Is not.
Yet I am quite married.
I am married to a life that died.

THE MIDDLE YEARS

Best Foot Forward: The Widow Dates

What shall I wear
That will help him decide
    to call back?
How can I capture his eye
That he will skim the list of one hundred names
    given him
Till he spots mine.
    Me!
Oh, me!
I'm over here!
    Yoo hoo!
I'm different from the others
Choose me
Oh, me
Choose
Oh choose
    me.

And don't wear those awful shoes
so frumpy, ich—
Buy a boot, for heaven's sake.
And no skirt and blouse
That's date dress for kids
Not
Adults
And his wife was
An adult,
dear,
So it's an adult he's looking for.
A dress or a suit. That's it. A dress
    or a suit.

But—he may come in a sweater, you know.
    It's happened that way before.
No.
You don't know, do you? How could
    you know?
No.
Sooo
A skirt, blouse and blazer
will juggle me through.
And it should be a blouse

that drapes beautifully.
And I guess I'd better
have my nails done.
Simply.
Colorless
but shining
would be best, yes?
And the right bag.
I'll need a new coat—mine is dead.
It's from another life
That no longer is who I am.
A new coat, yes.
Young—
with the times . . .
Pretend.

Pretend this first date
Is simply to have
A lovely evening
Yes.
That this best behavior careful smiling
neat, supportive, quiet, genteel woman
Is really
me.

Putting my best foot forward
Trying not to let it end up in my mouth.

AND LAST YEAR

Phoenix

Moving
Shaking her feet slowly
    in disbelief
The Phoenix stretched
Her long legs.
First one
Then the other
Shaking off the ashes of yesterday.

Strange, she thought,
Hm—
I would have sworn
    life was over—

I remember
I wanted to jump into the flames
   of yesterday's end
That I
  would
  be
  no
  more. That I would ache
  no more.
That I might die
if not instead of
  then
At least
  with
yesterday.

But—
but
I am
here.

Changed
yes, surely changed
But
yes,
yes
I am here.

She leaned back
and reached out
her neck
Her face
up
beyond the
  ruin.
The sun shone
  above her.
The soft wind
stroked her cheek
  calling her soul,
"Arise!"

Lifting her wings so slowly
she inhaled,
Then sighed—

Then breathed in again
Reaching higher
and higher
To embrace the day.

Oh, dear God—
    there *is* day!
There is *still*
    beautiful new day
beyond here—
Oh, look at the day!

A small movement in the
    clouds above
Held her a moment.
Drawn, she watched an arrow pierce
    the open space.

The geese followed the leader.

        Did you know that geese
        Mate for life?
        For life.
        But . . .
        Well, but he can lead.
        And take care of
        And do things well—

        But is that enough for a goose?
        Silly goose.
        It needn't be so—
        Silly goose. If you let it be so
            It will be so.

And the Phoenix
stood
And looked at the ashes
    of yesterday.
And kissed them sadly
    with her soul

And,
    turning her face to
        the sun
Arose
    took flight
        to join
            tomorrow.

20

Acting Like a Widow

by Rhoda Tagliacozzo

I know a woman who last year celebrated a happy golden anniversary: her marriage exists on borrowed time. At her twenty-fifth anniversary, less than 10 percent of her contemporaries were widowed, yet with each passing decade the figure has more than doubled. Now she is in her late 70s; over two-thirds of her friends are alone.

This woman cares a lot about her friends. She is fully committed to supporting others; she believes in the Jewish tenets of faith and charity. She knows that although death is inevitable, life is sacred; therefore, she helps her widowed friends preserve and better their lives. But even if she is experienced and wise and naturally empathetic, there will always be gaps in her perspective toward these women. For she is part of a couple; she is married, single. She finds much of her status and some of her identity in wedlock; she participates often in joint pursuits. No matter how much she tries, she will never fully understand a widow's point of view. She is still a wife.

Lately, I have been speaking to older widows and have been startled at what some of them are hiding: many of these women—especially those whose husbands died recently—see themselves no differently than the married woman I first described. Secretly, they, too, are still wives, astonished to find they are trapped in the body of this strange, new creature—widow. They each suffer from their husband's disappearance as if a well-worn, taken-for-granted limb had been excised, and at the point of contact where the severance took place, they ache as well.

"My husband was sick and he tried to prepare me," one recent widow told me, "but when he died, the reality of my daily life was so much worse. I miss his physical presence terribly. He would always call out to me—'Come read this in the newspaper! Come, see this program on television.' He was my pipeline to the world. Yet even when he said nothing, I knew he was there."

How many women pace through the rooms of their suburban homes or their urban apartments surrounded by more than silence; they manufacture a scenario that only days ago, months ago, years ago had two real participants and thus the simple choice of whether or not to have a conversation.

"Even now, I ask him questions and often he answers me," one widow said. "We still have an uncanny closeness."

"I talk to his picture," another told me. "I ask for his advice. I try to share with him the sunset and news about our grandchildren. I want his opinion about the little trials in my life." She paused. "And the big ones, like getting older."

Yet from someone widowed longer: "If only I could discuss things with him! I can't anymore. But he's never left my mind."

Listening to these women, I wonder about their "grief work." I think, what a busy sociological term that is for what must be such a lonely occupation. How did these women move from the initial raw agony of a spouse's death to some kind of acceptance? Which women succeeded at this and which did not? Who helped them travel from wifehood to widowhood without a loss of self?

What I see is that it could not have been easy for any of them. We live in a society where just talking about death can be awkward, where even friends and family might withdraw from discussing the widow's "loved one," where neighbors and colleagues try to speak of "happier things," where not only her spouse can become taboo but so can she.

Only a century ago—not very long in the history of the world—death was a more familiar part of life. Infants lucky enough to grow up and grow old expired among their families or died from what were often seen as acts of God. Perhaps then there were fewer expectations to cure the world, and because death was accepted, so, too, was the widow. She had her family, usually large and extended; her village or town, where people had known her all her life; and her religion and its institutions, which guided the community with its moral force.

Today these traditional supports have lost their potency. Sometimes they have disappeared and have not been replaced. Older widows may live far from their families, their sons and daughters scattered across America in jobs that distance not only them but precious grandchildren as well.

"I miss those babies so much," one widow told me sadly. "But I keep quiet. I'm a good sport."

"I tried to show everyone how independent I was," another told me. "I guess I should have reached out more to be with my family. To cuddle my granddaughter. To come to her school play. To hug her."

What I heard was not only the nurturing these women longed to give but the nurturing *they* needed too. Who was hugging these older women? A wife who for decades has lived happily with her husband must ache merely to be touched; if she can no longer feel his kiss on her cheek or his hand pat her back, she should be able to connect in other ways.

Grandchildren are a "legitimate" form of physical connection; so are pets. But can they be a woman's sole emotional and spiritual support? Not one of the widows with whom I spoke felt any deep commitment from her local synagogue or Jewish center.

One told me wistfully, "My Catholic neighbor seems to get more comfort from her church than I do from the synagogue. The women's church groups follow up on those who are bereaved. They have a better rate of success at persuading women to leave their homes and go out in the world."

This was said to me by a suburban widow. Among women with few financial worries, isolation can be an unexpectedly impoverishing factor. Many of these women do not have to earn money; yet despite its rigors, work can be a stimulating social activity. Widows often live on their husbands' pensions or social security and investments, and as they grow older, their assets may grow but their own capabilities may lessen; many cannot, or should not, drive anymore, and so they are forced into loneliness.

In the city, older widows suffer from different problems. Walking to subways or buses can be dangerous, especially at night or if the women live in decaying neighborhoods. An apartment can become a prison, with the television set as one's only companion, another form of entrapment.

The women who seem to do best are the ones who sooner or later, and despite everything, reach out, who find the world outside themselves even if the world does not find them.

One urban widow eats lunch every day at a local coffee shop. "I wake up tired and sad," she told me, "but I make myself leave my apartment."

She takes two buses to get to the coffee shop and lunches as she talks to her countermates. She has a lovely appearance and gets her hair "done" regularly; her quick welcoming smile is an integral part of her outfit. Yet she told me that she would never marry again, that her need to "socialize" extended only so far.

Another woman, a suburban widow, finds any socializing difficult. She cannot drive and verges on agoraphobia. She feels that her husband babied her; I hear anger in her voice when she says that he made her too dependent. "It's harder to cope with everything widowhood entails when you've never paid a bill or taken care of finances," she told me.

She moves from her bedroom to the kitchen to the garden, and is clearly fearful as well as miserable. "I watched my husband go from a strong healthy man to a weak pathetic shell of himself. Fifty-five years ago he was my beau. At the end, he didn't even recognize me."

The implication was evident; if it could happen to him, it could happen to her or to anyone she cared about. When someone suggested that she get a pet to keep her company, she refused. Right now, I don't think she can bear to love anything.

Perhaps this is a temporary state in her case; perhaps it is not. What strikes me listening to these women is how closely love and need are entwined. Those widows who felt needed seemed to have retained the capacity to love.

One told me about a cruise that she had taken: "When I entered the dining room, even with good friends, I still felt alone, like a third wheel. The couple I was with could always rely on each other for company, even if I wasn't there. I just didn't feel important anymore."

Yet when she speaks about her troubled adult son, her voice grows stronger, even younger. "I want to stick around for his sake," she said. "He needs me to be strong. To listen; to be there for him."

Another woman spoke about giving up her isolation to become the mainstay of her apartment building: nursing the sick, running errands for those older than herself, helping new mothers. Some women formalize this into volunteer work, although many American Jewish women already are accustomed to donating their efforts to worthy causes. They have often been the mainstays of social service organizations, whether secular or religious. These organizations in turn can be helpful to them when they become widowed, providing a necessary structure for their days and a possible outlet for their emotions.

"When my husband died," one Hadassah woman told me, "my volunteer work gave me a reason to go on. I could put myself in another world for a while and shed my problems. It was and is an integral part of my life. It's like an extended family. It helped me refuse to feel sorry for myself and gave me a place to go."

"Living alone at first was a trauma," one widow told me. "I felt angry all the time at God. But who are we to question Him? My husband was very sick and I was his nurse. Running all day. Now, to be honest, I'm appreciating making my own schedule. I'm more competent, too. There's a strange kind of freedom," she told me shyly, "and I've made some kind of peace with myself."

I hear in her voice an acknowledgment of the changes she has been through, an understanding that she is not the same person she was before. I do not hear her saying that she is a better person or a worse person, only that she is a different one. Her husband has been dead for ten years.

She is much removed from another woman whose husband died recently. "People tell me to do things with other widows, but I'm sure that I wouldn't enjoy it," she told me angrily. "Then I resent it when they say that I'm not acting like a widow."

Why should she? Inside her, she is still a wife.

I imagine that some women may never leave this ghostly married state. It is a worrisome possibility that they will remain static for the rest of their lives, unable to move in any direction. It makes me think how brave the ones who try to change are, these older widows who keep taking chances and reach out toward the world. I hope that our society can find ways to reach back, instead of leaving them alone.

Jewish

∧ **Marital Status**

☐ Single
☐ Not quite married
☐ Married
☑ Single again
    ☐ Widowed
    ☑ Abandoned
    ☐ Divorced
☐ Remarried
☐ Intermarried
☐ Gay or Lesbian
☐ Childless

21

A Different Kind of Hostage

Robert Gordis

The most agonizing moral challenge confronting Jewish law in modern times is nearly 2,000 years old. It is the plight of the *agunah*, "the chained wife," which has troubled Jews through the centuries. No one who has read Chaim Grade's powerful novel *The Agunah* will soon forget its tragic heroine, whose husband has left her and refuses to give her a *get* (Jewish divorce), so that she can never remarry.

Actually, the novel describes only one of several categories of *agunah*. Fundamentally, the pathetic situation of these women stems from the fact that the rabbinic interpretation of Deuteronomy 24:1-4 places the initiative for the issuance of a *get* solely in the hands of the husband. The tragedy has been immeasurably compounded in modern times by the erosion of authority in the Jewish community, so that the community itself is now powerless to compel the husband's obedience.

The problem has a long and painful history. The ancient and medieval rabbis were highly sensitive to the woman's undeserved suffering and sought every conceivable method of freeing the *agunah* from her chains. Thus, the Talmud went so far as to rule that if the woman herself had evidence that her husband had died, her unsubstantiated testimony would be acceptable, and she would be declared a widow, free to remarry. The radical character of this decision becomes clear if it is recalled that this ruling sets aside three fundamental principles of *halakhah*—first, the rabbinic rule that a woman is ineligible to testify as a witness; second, the biblical law that two witnesses are required to establish valid evidence; third, the rabbinic principle *"adam karov etzel atzmo"*—"every person is close and partial to himself"—and, therefore, his testimony on a case in which he is involved is invalid. Nonetheless, the rabbis accepted the woman's sole testimony as a witness.

Furthermore, the rabbis in medieval and modern times left no stone unturned in searching for the missing husband and in the effort to persuade him to issue a Jewish divorce to his abandoned wife.

It is clear from the sources that customary law, as practiced over a period of ten centuries in Egypt and Palestine, employed far-reaching procedures to compensate for the women's legal inability to dissolve a marriage. These provisions dealt not only with the problem of abandonment; they also made it possible for the woman to demand and receive a divorce when she found her marriage intolerable. In fact, documents have survived that indicate that in some cases it was sufficient for the wife to come to the court and declare, *"Lo erhemeh"*—"I do not love him"—in order for the judges to compel the husband to issue a divorce.

The problem of the *agunah* was relatively soluble as long as Jewish tradition retained its authority and the Jewish community had the power to enforce its decisions. This condition prevailed everywhere during the Middle Ages and, until our own century, in Eastern Europe. And because it did, there were extralegal procedures, such as public opinion and social ostracism, that could be used to secure the husband's compliance. In addition, the court could impose a *herem* (excommunication), which meant total isolation for the offender. Generally, the threat sufficed to bring the husband into line.

Nevertheless, the *Responsa*, the legal decisions of the great rabbinic authorities of the Middle Ages, include many cases of unfortunate women chained to a recalcitrant or nonexistent spouse.

The breakdown of the Babylonian center about the year 1000 C.E., and its replacement by a multiplicity of independent communities in North Africa, Spain, France, Germany, Italy, and Eastern Europe, led to a general fragmentation of authority that created many areas of local jurisdiction. The power of individual rabbinic leaders to compel obedience was now correspondingly reduced. The frequent uprooting of Jewish communities, the mass migrations and the transplantation of individuals, accompanied by the deaths of countless individuals through natural disaster, famine, or massacre, substantially increased the number of *agunot*. In spite of all ameliorative efforts, the lot of the *agunah* remained an unhappy one.

Beginning with the second half of the eighteenth century, the Enlightenment and the Emancipation wrought havoc with the traditional pattern of Jewish life. The admission of Jews into political citizenship, civic equality, and economic opportunity was directly and explicitly linked to the surrender of the authority of Jewish traditional law and to the loss of the legal status of the Jewish community, which now became in effect a voluntary association with no coercive power.

In some quarters today, both the Emancipation and the Enlightenment are decried as totally evil, though one sees little evidence of a wholesale stampede to turn in citizenship papers and return to the ghetto. (The only possible exceptions are some hasidic groups that have never left it.) The fact is that both modern movements brought substantial benefits to Jews and Judaism—but they exacted a heavy price, in the form of assimilation and alienation.

The rapid growth of secularism and the establishment of civil marriage and divorce in nearly all Western countries coincided with the mass migration of millions of individuals from one country to another. These factors gave rise to a large increase in the number of *agunot.* Women loyal to Jewish tradition were, of course, the chief victims.

In sum, four principal categories of the *agunah* have emerged in modern times and are on the increase:

1. A man divorces his wife in the civil courts and possibly even remarries, but refuses to give his wife a *get,* either because of malice or greed. All too often the husband tries to extort money from his wife in exchange for the *get.*
2. A man disappears without leaving a trace, so that he is not available to issue the divorce that *halakhah* demands. During the early decades of the twentieth century, when mass Jewish immigration to the United States from Eastern Europe reached its height, Yiddish newspapers published a regular feature, "The Gallery of Missing Husbands," asking readers to help locate the errant spouses. Together with photographs, there would appear pathetic pleas for help from the deserted wives.
3. The man is lost in military action or dies in a mass explosion. In modern war, combatants are often blown to bits. Where there is no hard evidence that the soldier is dead, the wife becomes an *agunah,* since *halakhah* has no such category as "declared or legally dead."

During the Russo-Japanese war of 1905, some great Russian rabbis visited the troops before they left for the front and persuaded the Jewish soldiers to issue a *get al tenai*, a "conditional divorce," so as to free their wives from the status of *agunah* should the men fail to return. But obviously this temporary procedure, however helpful in individual cases, did not meet the growing dimensions of the problem.

4. Not strictly a case of "desertion" but similar to it is the rarer case of a childless widow who, according to *halakhah*, requires *halitzah* (release) from her husband's brother before she can remarry. This situation has also served as an occasion for extortion.

The agonizing dilemma facing the chained wife is clear. If she remains obedient to Jewish law, she can never remarry. If she does remarry without a *get*, she is committing adultery in the eyes of Jewish law, and her children carry the taint of illegitimacy.

In the face of these burdens, the temptation to cast off halakhic restraint has been great. Many women, both young and old, resent a law they perceive as unjust. And many *agunot* who have remained loyal to Jewish tradition spend lonely lives in quiet desperation.

The problem in our time is further compounded by the fact that the Reform movement has abolished the whole concept of Jewish divorce. The Reform have declared that marriage is a religious rite requiring a rabbi, but that divorce is simply a civil act, needing only the decision of a secular judge to dissolve the marriage. The obvious inconsistencies of this position are not my present concern. Increasingly, voices in Reform circles are calling for a reinstatement of some form of Jewish divorce.

The Orthodox rabbinate has been aware of the problem and has been deeply sympathetic. But by and large it has done little to improve the situation. A few scholars, including some Sephardic authorities, have proposed solutions to the tragedy that are compatible with Jewish law, but theirs have been voices crying in the wilderness. No irreverence is intended, but the failure of sympathetic rabbis to act reminds one of the shopworn tale of the father spanking his son and telling him, "Son, this hurts me more than it hurts you." To this the lad replies, "Yes, Dad, but not in the same place."

Only the Conservative rabbinate has sought to translate its concern into action, through a variety of approaches.

In 1930, Rabbi Louis M. Epstein of Boston presented a plan for dealing with the problem. Leading rabbinic scholars, including the saintly Rabbi Abraham Isaac Kook, agreed that it was in total conformity with *halakhah*. Rabbi Epstein proposed that a groom, before his marriage, designate individuals to serve as his agents for the issuance of a *get* (*minnui shelihu*) if, at some future date, (1) a civil divorce were to be issued, or (2) the husband were to disappear, or (3) he were to be lost in an accident or in military action, with no witnesses, or (4) he were to remarry. The Epstein plan was adopted by the (Conservative) Rabbinical Assembly in 1935, which proceeded to implement it.

Subjected to a barrage of misrepresentation and proving unwieldy in operation, the Epstein plan, after being used in many cases by the Rabbinical Assembly with soldiers going into action, fell into disuse. Ironically, virtually the same procedure was adopted by the Orthodox Rabbinical Council.

A more comprehensive approach to the problem was imperative. That step was taken in 1953, when the Rabbinical Assembly's Committee on Law adopted the "Lieberman *Ketubah.*" The text was the work of one of the most eminent modern rabbinic scholars, Prof. Saul Lieberman. He was universally recognized as a *gaon*, a luminary of the Torah, whose credentials in piety and learning could not be challenged.

In essence, Rabbi Lieberman added a clause to the traditional marriage contract, in which the husband and wife agreed that they would be governed in their life together by the provisions of Jewish law. Hence, if the marriage was subsequently dissolved, and the husband refused to issue a *get*, the wife could turn to the civil courts and request them to order his compliance with the terms of the contract, which called for obedience to Jewish law, including the issuance of a *get*.

The theory behind the Lieberman *Ketubah* is that the courts would not be intervening in a religious issue. They would merely be called on to require "specific performance"—a matter of contract law—as promised in the original marriage agreement.

Only one such case has thus far come to trial. In that instance, the New York Court of Appeals—the highest tribunal in the state—ruled on a case involving the Lieberman *Ketubah*. The woman's suit requested the court to order the husband to issue the *get* he had originally promised. Her suit was supported by several organizations, including Orthodox as well as Conservative legal groups. By a vote of 4 to 3, the court upheld the woman's suit. The majority of the justices declared that church–state relations were not involved; the issue was the husband's failure to perform an act that had been stipulated at the time of the marriage. Accordingly, the court returned the case for retrial in the lower court.

Unquestionably, this decision is a gratifying development. It offers hope that women, civilly divorced by their husbands, will not be easy victims to malice and greed. The ruling is to be welcomed as an important step in the right direction.

It is doubtful, however, that it represents a total or even a major solution to the problem of *agunah*, either on pragmatic or theoretical grounds.

Not only was the decision in the Court of Appeals very close, but there is no assurance that it will be followed by other courts. In other states, judges are famous for preferring to settle cases before them on the narrowest possible legal basis. It is very likely that many other judges would view such a suit as an example of the state intervening in religious issues, and they might well declare it outside their jurisdiction.

Even in this case, there conceivably could be a long road ahead before the *get* is issued. Certainly not every *agunah* would be in a position to undertake extended and costly litigation with no assurance of success.

A variant of the Lieberman plan has been proposed by some individual Orthodox rabbis in the form of a prenuptial agreement. The husband would stipulate that in the event of a civil divorce, he would issue a *get* to his wife. Should he fail to fulfill his obligation, she could sue for "specific performance," as in the Lieberman plan. It is possible that some individual rabbis have actually put the plan into operation, but there has been no public announcement, and surely no collective action by any Orthodox rabbinic body. Indeed, the Rabbinical Council of America has announced that all research on this approach has been terminated.

Unable or unwilling to deal creatively with the rabbinic law of divorce, Orthodox Jewish leaders, both lay and rabbinic, came up with another proposal. They succeeded in having the New York State legislature adopt a law that no civil divorce would be issued if "there were any impediment to the remarriage of either partner." The euphemism was designed to avoid the obvious objection that the law represented the interference of the state in religion.

Governor Mario Cuomo of New York State, facing the same kind of pressures as did the legislators, signed the bill but expressed his grave doubts as to its constitutionality. It has not yet been tested in the courts. Attempts to pass similar legislation in Connecticut and Pennsylvania have failed.

To justify the involvement of the civil courts with the issuance of *gittin*, the argument has been advanced that the issuance of a *get* is not a religious act, but rather a civil procedure. Many experts, both in the civil law and in *halakhah,* would maintain that issuance of a *get* is definitely a religious act.

The issue here touches us both as Jews and as Americans. These days, when the basic principle of church–state separation is under assault, we need to be particularly zealous in guarding it—for upon it our sense of at-homeness in America is grounded. And that principle also helps preserve *halakhah,* which depends on its insulation from the civic realm.

Finally, to rely upon secular government to right the wrongs that arise from the observance of *halakhah* is—or should be—intolerable on religious grounds. It would be a confession that *halakhah,* which derives its authority from God on Sinai and is intended for all times and places, lacks the resources to do justice, enforce equity, and relieve human misery. For this writer, the major practical difficulties involved in implementing the unholy marriage between *halakhah* and the secular state are less important than the affront to the dignity and honor of Jewish law.

Clearly, another approach, universal in applicability and ethically unobjectionable, is required. Such a procedure was adopted in the late 1960s by the Rabbinical Assembly, which authorized its *Bet Din* (rabbinical court) in New York and other cities to deal with cases of the *agunah.* The *Bet Din* utilized a far-reaching talmudic doctrine that had been invoked earlier by some individual rabbis (primarily Sephardic) as pointing the way to a solution of the *agunah* problem.

The doctrine is referred to in the Talmud frequently (*Yevamot* 19a, 110a; *Ketubot* 3a; *Gittin* 33a, 73a; *Baba Batra* 48b). It declares that "whoever enters into Jewish marriage does so by the authority of the Rabbis" (*'ada 'ata d'rabbanan*). Hence, if the need arises, "the rabbis have the power to annul the marriage retroactively (*'afkinho rabbanan lekiddushei minneh*)," so that no divorce by the husband would be necessary. It should be understood that though the marriage may be annulled, the legitimacy of the children of the marriage is not in question. In other words, since Jewish marriage is an institution established in Jewish law, the rabbis have the authority to annul a given marriage when necessary. As a creation of the Jewish community, Jewish marriage is subject to its jurisdiction.

Actually, in New York, the Rabbinical Assembly's *Bet Din,* headed by Rabbi Edward Gershfield, professor of Talmud at the Jewish Theological Seminary, and similar rabbinical courts elsewhere have found it necessary to invoke this principle of annulment (*hafka' at kiddushin*) in only a very limited number of cases. When a woman has been civilly divorced, but finds it impossible to secure a *get,* the *Bet Din* uses everything in its power to persuade or convince her recalcitrant husband to act ethically and to dissolve the marriage by issuing a *get.* If he remains obdurate, he is reminded that he will no longer be able to vent his anger or indulge his greed by refusing the *get,* since the *Bet Din* stands ready to annul the marriage legally and to free his wife. Rabbi Gershfield informs me that the annulment procedure has had to be used in only some fifty to seventy-five cases in over a decade.

The all-encompassing authority of the rabbis in the area of marriage and divorce is a far-reaching principle. Unlike other, more limited techniques, the procedure of *hafka' at kiddushin* solves the problem for all categories of *agunah:* the unyielding husband who refuses to give a *get,* the spouse who has disappeared and cannot be located, and the husband who has been lost in military action or in some other disaster.

It also solves two additional problems. The first is the childless widow, who, according to Jewish law, needs *halitzah* from her dead husband's brother. The second is that of a husband who becomes insane and is therefore not legally competent to issue a *get.*

In addition to all these practical advantages, it has one important theoretical virtue. It underscores the power of the community and places the authority once more where it belongs—in the collective rabbinate, which is the representative of the Jewish community. It thus points the way to the ideal solution of the *agunah* problem, which still lies in the future: the transfer of the power to issue a divorce from the individual to the duly constituted authorities serving on a community *Bet Din* or court.

But even at present, and at long last, the resources of *halakhah* can be and are being utilized to relieve the suffering of the *agunah.* It is important that this procedure be more widely known and more generally adopted. It offers a workable plan for healing an ancient wound, indeed righting an ancient wrong. If, in the future, the problem of *agunah* is not solved, it will be the fault not of Jewish law, but of its latter-day defenders, who invoke the memory of the great sages of the past, but lack the courage to follow their example.

Jewish

∧ **Marital Status**

- ☐ Single
- ☐ Not quite married
- ☐ Married
- ☑ Single again
    - ☐ Widowed
    - ☐ Abandoned
    - ☑ Divorced
- ☐ Remarried
- ☐ Intermarried
- ☐ Gay or Lesbian
- ☐ Childless

22

Jewish Divorce Law: If We Must Part, Let's Part as Equals

Blu Greenberg

A year ago, while on a sabbatical in Israel with my husband and children, we employed a Yemenite woman of 33 as an *ozeret* (housekeeper). During the course of the year, she went through a costly divorce. While both Tikvah and Shmuel wanted the divorce, as he got closer to the rabbinic courts he began to sense what he did not know before—that he had great power over her.

What had started out as a fairly just settlement turned ugly. Little by little, his demands accelerated. Finally, Tikvah's lawyer told her to sign over to him her half of the apartment's eventual resale rights and be through with him; otherwise, the case would drag through the rabbinic courts for years. And that is what she did. Despite some flashes of resentment, she considered herself lucky.

Traditional Jewish divorce law points up two things: how much change has taken place during the evolution of this *halakhah* (Jewish legal system) and how much further development it needs to serve women more equitably and indiscriminately.

According to biblical law, a man is permitted to divorce his wife at will and send her away from his home. The second aspect highlights biblical women's vulnerability: economic, physical, and psychological uprooting faced the woman who displeased her husband sufficiently to cause him to divorce her. She had no leverage to prevent or refuse the divorce. Neither could she divorce him.

> When a man takes a wife and marries her, if she finds no favor in his eyes because of *ervat davar* (some fault or indecency) and he writes her a bill of divorce and puts it in her hand and sends her out of his house—and she marries another man, and the latter . . . writes her a bill of divorce . . . or dies—then her former husband cannot marry her again because she has been defiled . . . (Deuteronomy 24:1–4).

Yet there were qualifications, important because the rabbis who interpreted biblical law for later generations built the legal structure on them.

The husband had to write a bill of divorce and present it to his wife before sending her away (Deuteronomy 24:1–3; Isaiah 50:1; Jeremiah 3:8). This served as protection for her, as a delaying mechanism so that in a fit of anger a husband could not simply pronounce a declaration of divorce and be done with her. Second, it was deduced from the biblical law on the accusation of premarital sexual experience that a husband was required to pay some kind of alimony settlement upon divorce. (It was this payment that the accusing husband sought to get out of; he had nothing else to gain from the procedure as he could divorce his wife at will.) Third, there were two specific instances recorded in the Bible in which a man could never divorce his wife: if he had falsely accused her of premarital sex or if she was a virgin he had raped and was forced to marry. (This law, which appears to us crude, was designed for the protection of the woman who, having lost her virginity through no fault of her own, would be otherwise unmarriageable.)

> If a man takes a wife and . . . hates her and . . . spreads an evil name about her saying . . . "I found no signs of virginity in her," then her father and mother must bring forth the signs of the wife's virginity to the elders of the city. . . . They shall chastise that man and penalize him 100 shekels of silver and give them to the father of the wife because the husband spread an evil name upon a virgin of Israel. She shall remain his wife and he shall not be free to divorce her (Deuteronomy 22:13–21).

Though in themselves these limits represented very minor safeguards for women, they must be understood as the first breakthrough in establishing a crucial principle: the right of a community to set limits on a man's absolute and private right of divorce.

Moreover, it appears from biblical narrative that the social sanctions against divorce were quite powerful and that it occurred rarely. In the isolated instances where a woman was sent away (e.g., Genesis 21:11–12; I Samuel 3:14–16), it was a great trauma for her husband as well. The fact that the divorce law appears as an aside (in the context of a law forbidding a man to remarry his ex-wife) can be understood both as a limitation of a man's absolute control over divorce and as an indication of the general inappropriateness of his divorcing his wife.

The rabbis were not insensitive to the inequities in biblical divorce law. In talmudic and post-talmudic literature, they articulated many elaborations and emendations of this law (as they did with biblical law touching all areas of life), which gave women greater protection. Little by little, the imbalance of biblical law was tempered by numerous restrictive rabbinic measures. Thus, the theoretical basis of the law—that divorce was a man's God-given right—remained intact: it was not challenged but rather modified in many practical ways to neutralize its force.

We can see this pattern, which characterizes much of rabbinic action, or nonaction, for many ensuing centuries, begin to emerge in an early rabbinic dispute between the schools of Hillel and Shammai (first century B.C.E.). Shammai, the strict constructionist of biblical law, maintained that the scriptural words *ervat davar* meant, literally and exclusively, "adultery." Thus, a woman's infidelity was the only legitimate grounds for divorce. Hillel, known as a liberal because he generally interpreted Scripture more broadly, interpreted *ervat davar* as anything that was offensive to the husband. As in most disputes, rabbinic law followed Hillel.

For the next few centuries, major Talmudists reiterated the principle of the unrestricted right of the husband to divorce his wife. The opposing view restricting this right made itself felt in the many critical moral judgments against divorce (such as Rabbi Yohanan's statement that "He who divorces his wife is hated by God") and in the growing number of curbs on a man's absolute right.

Throughout much of rabbinic history, three interacting forces were adjusted in each decision concerning divorce law: (1) the theory of man's absolute right; (2) the biblical precedents establishing some qualifications of this right; and (3) the earliest rabbinic sources, which construed the biblical laws strictly or broadly. These three variables could be juggled, depending on one's teacher's views, the climate of the times, one's inclinations in these matters, and the particular divorce case at hand.

The rabbinic qualifications took several different forms: enlarging the number of cases in which there is an absolute prohibition against divorce; embellishing and making more complex the formalities in the actual divorce proceedings; placing greater financial responsibilities toward a divorced woman; and finally, enlarging the wife's role in assent or dissent—and in assuming some mastery over her own fate as a married woman.

Enlarging cases of prohibition of divorce: One example of the absolute prohibition of divorce involved the wife who had become insane and would thus be unable to take care of herself. Another was of a wife taken captive: the Rabbis obligated him to send even the dowry money to ransom her. A third example was a child-bride.

Embellishing the formalities: A Jewish divorce goes something like this: After all attempts at reconciliation have failed, and the husband and wife have either been granted a civil divorce or have mutually agreed to seek one, they arrange to appear before a *Bet Din,* a Jewish court of law. The *Bet Din* consists of three rabbis, each of whom is an expert in the intricate laws of *gittin,* Jewish divorce. Since Jewish divorce is not a decree of the court but rather a transaction between two parties, various authorities maintain that a single expert suffices. (The prevalent custom in America is to require only one rabbi.) In either case, a *sofer* (scribe) and two male witnesses must also be present. The wife will often bring along a friend to help her get through the trying time; so will the husband. The appointment with the *Bet Din* or officiating rabbi can be scheduled by one's own rabbi, lawyer, or by the parties themselves.

First the scribe must write the writ of divorce. Before he begins the actual writing, however, he makes a formal gift of his materials to the husband, who must authorize the writing of the *get* on his behalf. The husband lifts the writing materials and offers them back to the *sofer,* saying, "I give you this paper, ink, and pen and all the writing material, and I instruct you to write for me a *get* to divorce my wife." The *sofer* hand-letters the *get,* filling in the details such as the names of the two parties, the city, the time, and the standard text of the writ of divorce in which the husband attests to divorcing his wife and setting her free to marry any other man. It generally takes an hour for the scribe to write the *get* in Hebrew lettering, during which time the man and woman to be divorced usually wait in separate rooms.

After the *sofer* finishes his writing task, he and the witnesses make a distinguishing mark on the *get.* The witnesses read the document and affix their signatures to it. One of the three rabbis of the *Bet Din* will then ask the following questions:

To the *sofer:* "Is this the *get* you have written?" "Is there any special mark by which you can identify it?" "Did the husband tell you to write the *get?*" "Were the witnesses present, at least during the time you wrote the first line?"

To the witnesses: "Did you hear the husband order the *sofer* to write a *get* for his wife?" "Is this your signature?" "Did the husband tell you to sign it?" Then the *get* is read again.

To the husband: "Do you give this *get* of your own free will?" "Did you perhaps make a statement you may have forgotten that might cancel all other statements you made?"

To the wife: "Do you accept this *get* of your own free will?" "Have you made any statement or vow that would compel you to accept this *get* against your will?" "Have you made any statement that would nullify the *get?*"

To those present: "If there is anyone who wishes to protest, let him do so now."

The husband then calls upon the witnesses to witness the delivery of the *get.* The rabbi tells the wife to remove all the jewelry from her hands, and to hold her hands together with the palms open, facing upward, so as to receive the *get.* The *sofer* folds the *get* and hands it to the rabbi. The rabbi hands it to the husband who, with both hands, drops it into the palms of his wife. He says, "This is your *get,* and with it you are divorced from me from this time henceforth, so that you are free to become the wife of any man." The wife holds up her hands with the *get* in them, walks a few paces, and returns. She hands the *get* to the rabbi, who reads it again with the witnesses who are asked once more to identify the *get* and signatures. The rabbi pronounces an ancient ban against those who try to invalidate a *get* after it has been transferred. Then the four corners of the *get* are torn, so that it cannot be used again. It is placed in the files of the *Bet Din* for safekeeping, and the rabbis give each party a *shetar piturin,* a document of release, stating that the *get* from X to Y is effective, and each is now free to remarry.

If either of the parties cannot, or desires not, to be present, he/she can appoint an agent to stand in. The husband must place the *get* that he authorized and was written for him by the *sofer* in the hands of the agent, who proceeds to deliver the *get* to the woman or her agent on a day that is specified in the *get.* The laws of agency are quite complex, which is why the rabbis of the *Bet Din* prefer both parties to be present. Nevertheless, agents for the principals are used whenever necessary.

The standard process of divorce was so exact and so detailed that those in attendance had to be experts at it. The real purpose of the complexity was to bring the couple into contact with the rabbinic court whose members understood their function as extending far beyond that of interpreting the law; they used their offices to try to effect a reconciliation. Furthermore, a significant effect of this procedural change was ultimately to undermine the notion of absolute right. In practice as well as in the popular mind, the husband now had to look to the rabbinic court for sanction.

Enlarging the husband's financial responsibilities: These responsibilities, incorporated into the *ketubah* (marriage contract), entitled the wife to a return of her dowry and any property she had brought with her into marriage, plus support until she remarried. The *ketubah* protected her interests during the marriage as well; the husband was obligated to provide for her according to her station in life, to pay her medical and dental bills, to ransom her from captivity, and to provide her proper burial (*Ketubot* 4:4–9).

The Talmud did not formalize the standard *ketubah* text. It did establish a minimum level of recompense; beyond that, it allowed many variations. Throughout the ages, there have been examples of tailor-made *ketubot.* In several recently discovered *ketubot* that are more than 1,000 years old, the wife stipulated that her husband must grant her a divorce if he takes a concubine. It is clear that some women negotiated their own conditions for a viable marriage.

Wife's rights of consent: The theoretical right of the husband to "put away" his wife, continually eroded throughout rabbinic times, was formally limited by the halakhic decree of Rabbenu Gershom of Mayence early in the eleventh century. From that point on, a woman could not be divorced except by her consent. The woman's will now carried legal force.

Although the rabbis did not have the will or the strength to make a *takkanah* (a formal rabbinic decree) that would have granted the woman greater equality in divorce matters, nevertheless they did try to protect her and to limit the situations in which she was vulnerable to abuse. Some grounds entitling the wife to sue for a divorce were quite sensitive to her needs, among them her sexual satisfaction. In the case of the husband's refusal to meet her conjugal rights, if she did not want to exercise her option for divorce, he could be fined, week by week (*Ketubot* 61b–62b). Impotence was also legitimate grounds for divorce, with the burden of proof upon the man (*Yevamot* 65b).

A woman was also entitled to a divorce for the following: (1) if her husband had a serious disease or a continual bad odor from his occupation (like gathering dung or tanning hides) (*Ketubot* 7:9); (2) if he did not support her in the style to which she had been accustomed or, if wealthy, in the proper manner for a man of his means (*Ketubot*

5:8,9); (3) if he beat her (*Rama Even ha-Ezer* 154:3); (4) if she wanted to live in the Holy Land or move from one city in *Eretz Yisrael* to Jerusalem and he refused to follow her or to remain there with her (*Ketubot* 110b); or (5) if he behaved licentiously, i.e., frequented prostitutes (*Rama Even ha-Ezer* 154:1).

What about the right of a wife to sue for divorce? The germ of such notion existed in the biblical law regarding a bondwoman-cum-wife whose husband marries another.

> If a man sells his daughter to be a maidservant . . . if her master takes another wife, he shall not diminish the food, clothing, and conjugal rights due (his first wife). And if he does not provide these, then she shall go free, without money (Exodus 21:7–11).

If he didn't continue to provide her with food, clothing, and sexual satisfaction, then she had the right to go out free from debt without a financial settlement, but with a divorce. This bill of divorce was assumed to have been mandated by a court or by the elders because a bondwoman obviously had no power in her own right. It was assumed that if a bondwoman had the *right* to a divorce under such conditions, how much more so did a wife who came into the marriage as a free woman.

The notion that marriage placed the husband under contractual obligations was further expanded in rabbinic times. If a man did not fulfill certain conditions that made the marriage viable, he was liable to a divorce suit from his wife. She could go to a *Bet Din,* present her case, and obtain a court decree compelling him to appear to answer the charges. If the charges were justified, the court intervened to compel him to fulfill his obligations toward his wife. If he failed to do so, then the court could resort to various economic or social sanctions to coerce him to grant a divorce. The law still maintained, however, that he was doing this "of his own free will." By such legal fiction, the old theory of man's right remained intact, whereas the wife's real power increased.

Thus, a pattern emerges. In the case of the husband, the original right was open-ended and absolutely private, but the historical development of the law served to continually limit it. In the case of the wife, there was but an initial hint of some sort of rights. As *halakhah* developed through the post-biblical generations, wider powers accrued to her. This unmistakable pattern is sufficient to refute the simple-minded charges that the rabbis seized every opportunity to keep women powerless. Quite the reverse is true; considering all the power the rabbis had—what with the biblical guidelines and their own transfer of male authority from one generation to another—there is an impressive degree of sensitivity and benevolence in the unfolding of the law. The growing set of obligations of the husband to his wife and the increasing formalization of her rights to redress through the *Bet Din* are clear indicators of an attitude of concern for the women.

Still, we are left with some large and serious problems. First, instead of grappling directly with the sexist principle that only a man had the right to divorce, the rabbis used various legal fictions to subvert its original intent. The exclusive right as derived from the Bible was never challenged or abolished; it was simply chiseled away bit by bit. As a result, the rabbinic authorities in any given generation could revert back to the original notion of the husband's power over the wife.

A perfect example can be found in a qualification recorded in Rabbenu Gershom's decree that a man could not divorce his wife against her free will: if a recalcitrant wife refused a divorce or was physically unable to accept it, a husband had only to deposit the writ with the rabbinic court, announce his intention to divorce widely, and thus receive approval of one hundred rabbis (*Even ha-Ezer* 1:10). Thus, here as in other instances, some of the more positive decisions concerning women could be withdrawn or tempered on the principle that the ancient legal right of the husband could not be abrogated (Maimonides, *Laws of Divorce* 10:23). Somehow, the *halakhah* managed to find a way to get around the biblical and talmudic requirement that the husband hand the wife a bill of divorce; one need not wonder too long why the *halakhah* did not find a parallel loophole to allow a wife's release from a similar situation.

That brings us the second problem: that a woman is not empowered to present a *get* to her husband and thereby divorce *him*. A legal theory supporting this is that since he is the one who creates the marriage bond, he must also be the one to sever it. There is no proceeding in Jewish law whereby a divorce is granted by a court in the absence or without the consent of the husband. Thus, there is great potential for abuse built into this law—and there have been, in each generation, countless sinister tales of resistant husbands' extortion and delay.

Moreover, this aspect of the law has led to the tragic situation of the *agunah* ("anchored wife"), a woman whose husband has deserted her, or is insane, missing, or presumed dead (though his death has not been verified by the requisite two witnesses). In every generation, the rabbis tried to alleviate the plight of the *agunah*. Even today, many individual cases remain in Jewish communities all over the world. And despite the compassion and gentleness of the man and of rabbis who resolve individual cases, women testify to a certain humiliating quality inherent in the notion of *agunah* and in the very process of release from this status.

Finally, in certain ways, the modern, open society has worked to woman's disadvantage. In the closed, relatively autonomous Jewish communities of the past, the religious authorities and lay leaders could coerce and level sanctions against a man whose wife brought a legitimate suit of divorce; in modern societies outside Israel, however, a rabbinic court has authority only over those who voluntarily place themselves under its jurisdiction. Even in Israel, there are men who have chosen to remain in the jail to which the *Bet Din* sentenced them for refusing to grant a divorce, rather than free their wives.

Thus, in an attempt to close the gap between men's power and women's powerlessness in the divorce issue, the rabbis tried hard, but not hard enough. It would have taken little more collective maturity to close the gap altogether, to create a situation of real equality under the law. The rabbis assumed wide powers of interpretation—and even of innovation—in situations where the general needs of the community called for accommodation rather than rationalization of an unwieldly situation. Failure of contemporary rabbis to acknowledge that past improvements in divorce law are but part of a continuous process—"on the way to becoming"—leads one to conclude that, in their heart of hearts, many would like the gap to exist, apologetics notwithstanding.

Several solutions have evolved in modern times. Reform Judaism approves of civil divorce. But the Orthodox consider a woman divorced according to Reform practices an *ayshet ish,* another man's wife (since she has no "proper" *get*), and she is forbidden to marry an Orthodox or Conservative Jew. Moreover, the children of her second marriage are considered *mamzerim* (bastards, born of an adulterous union) and are forbidden to marry into a halakhic community. Conservative Judaism has added a clause to its *ketubah* giving the *Bet Din* powers to end the marriage, with the additional provision that the secular courts can be turned to for enforcement should the husband not live up to the agreement. In the Orthodox community, Rabbi Zev Falk has set forth many precedents that traditional halakhists can follow today. Rabbi Eliezer Berkovits's proposed solution rests basically on a conditional clause inserted in the marriage contract, which allows for the dissolution of the relationship (rather than the couple's divorce) if the spouses have been living apart for a specified length of time.

There has been great resistance in the Orthodox community to these and any other proposals for change. Therefore, we have today a situation unprecedented in the history of Jewry—we have four sets of divorce law, as if we were several different religious communities.

What remains to be done is to formulate a rabbinic decree or firm qualifications of the existing *halakhah* that will both eliminate any potential for abuse of women and will be acceptable to and unite all branches of Judaism. Achieving both goals means that all Jews will have to accept that there is something distinctive about being a Jew and living under Jewish law. It means that we all have a heightened sense of awareness that marriage and divorce and every other event in our lives should be properly articulated as Jewish events, experiences within the framework of a holy community. It means that the branches of Judaism will have to sit down together to work out a mutually acceptable solution, each reconciling the other as part of *Klal Yisrael* (the people of Israel). It also means that, given the institutional status quo and entrenched interest, Jewish women of every political and religious shade will have to pressure and politicize until the entire community accepts a unifying and equitable law.

It is hard to project what would be the optimal form of revision. Perhaps it will be along the lines of Berkovits's conditional clause in the marriage contract; perhaps it will empower the wife to write and deliver the *get*. It would be dishonest of me not to admit to a sense of ambivalence, a hesitation—even a fear (trembling)—as I speak of fundamental change from the biblical principle. For I am emotionally and theologically rooted in this community that, at most, allows itself to speak in hushed tones about gradual change over a period of two millennia.

On the one hand, I feel a preference to call for a revision that would serve the two functions yet involve the least change in the basic structure of *halakhah*. On the other hand, I must ask whether this halfway step would be doing a disservice to women two or three generations from now. Then again, I am not unmindful of the fact that the divinity of the Torah has remained so strong throughout our history precisely because the rabbis were so careful not to "forbid what was permitted or permit what was forbidden" in the Torah. However, still another part of me feels compelled to press, to politicize, to call for change with absolute certainty. The strongest motivating force is bound up with Jewish tradition itself.

Recently I addressed a traditional community on the subject of which areas of the *halakhah* could incorporate the new needs and expectations of women. After I had finished, an old friend, a former pulpit rabbi turned businessman, got up and said, "Not everyone's needs will be met by every law. Some people will have to suffer under some laws. That's *halakhah!* That's it!"

Leaving aside that inaccurate perception of *halakhah,* men can no longer decide that it's all right for women to suffer indiscriminately. It is inevitable that there will always be inequities, injustices, imbalances in every divorce situation; that is the nature of the dissolution of a human relationship. But the law itself should not discriminate against one sex. If there is one woman in each generation who suffers unnecessarily as a result of the law, then the law is biased against all women. To one who believes that Judaism is the most ethical and sensitive of religions, to one who believes that from Revelation on, Judaism has continually moved toward its own best values, a change that would bring about a greater equality should be articulated not in categories of change, but rather as part of the organic growth of a holy community as it moves through history.

23

One Single Jew

Sheila Peltz Weinberg

My husband of eleven years and I were divorced five years ago. My son was 2 then, and my daughter was 6 years old. When I was 19, I left my father's house to enter my husband's house. Now at 30 I was facing adult life for the first time. It was a decision filled with terror of the unknown, with burning emotional convictions and immense pain.

I asked my rabbi if there was some ritual like the gradual mourning rehabilitation process to help people deal with the trauma I was experiencing. He told me that the *shivah*, seven days of mourning, corresponds to the *sheva berakhot*—the seven blessings and days of marriage celebration. These were the ultimate ritual poles—separation and union.

"Divorce," he told me, "is bittersweet." One experiences the death of collective life and the birth of a discrete human being. Hence, there is no ritual, no clear practice. This was a constructive context in which to view the journey facing me.

In those days I felt guided, as if the cloud of the Presence were in front of me by day. I made rapid and focused decisions that led me to a new city, a new job, a new home, schools for my children, and a new Jewish community. All of the pieces fell together rapidly. I felt as if I were jumping off a cliff and landing miraculously in a soft meadow—warmer and more receptive than I had known in my life before.

But I am still in the midst of struggle. It is over how to clarify what is internal and what external.

GIVING AND RECEIVING IN A RELIGIOUS COMMUNITY

A vibrant *havurah* community was in existence in my new neighborhood. I started to attend *Shabbat* services regularly with my children and quickly assumed responsibilities for leadership as well. I found healing in the rhythm of *Shabbat* among faces becoming familiar, in the joint adventure of cycling through the Torah and holidays, singing together the ancient poems, and the hugs and handshakes after services. The stringent commitment to equal participation of men and women for the first time in my own Jewish experience was essential to making me feel comfortable. I was encouraged to give as well as receive and was acknowledged in this community as a full human being. My entry into the community was greatly facilitated by joining a smaller Thursday evening women's group composed of some of the longer standing *havurah* members. Without *Shabbat* or *siddurim,* we were free to articulate our deeper fears and hopes in an intimate atmosphere. The bonds carried into the *davening.*

When the initial glow began to dim, I became aware that some of the intimacy and devotion evident on *Shabbat* was illusory. How much support is really available from others, each of whom is scrounging for his own nurturance? I often heard the bitter tones of disappointed expectations. I looked around sometimes on *Shabbat* and saw mechanical stares, mumbling, emptiness, and pain—and knew that on this day I would neither give nor receive.

Friendships within our little sect, as elsewhere, develop slowly. The divorced woman with children does not quite fit in with the couples or the child-free singles. My agendas are different from the first (I am somewhat of a threat, even here), and my energy does not mesh with the others. I fall into self-pity and spiral downward. The community at its best and healthiest does not tolerate self-pity—and this above all is its healing power.

Despite a "good" Jewish education and upbringing, I had not felt comfortable since adolescence in a regular congregation. The *havurah* is plagued by the absence of what the synagogue has in excess. The rigidity of the pews, the sterility of audience-style "worship," the condescension of professional leadership, and the typical guilt-battering of preaching to the converted makes me wary of most synagogues. The *havurah* suffers from a lack of spiritual focus, the vagaries of communal decision making, and the absence of consistent quality and able leadership.

I crave what may be the impossible for my Jewish community, both stability and stimulation (*keva* and *kavanah*), consistent structure and inspiration. I know, however, that my task is to bring both aspects to the community, as well as to receive them. I am grateful for the opening offered in my current setting. Meanwhile, the dance goes on in a halting rhythm.

A JEWISH HOME WITH FLEXIBLE ROLE MODELS

I acknowledge the fact that my life is a maze of contradictions, colliding and birthing changes. What can we transmit to our children besides the flexibility to live with change? Perhaps we can give them the most beautiful elastic inspiring symbols to which we have access. I have chosen to enroll my children in a Hebrew day school. The symbols are presented in school and at home. The teachers are warm and supportive. There is a music to their lives. Despite the high cost of tuition and the dangers of parochialism and chauvinism, I still feel this is a more viable alternative than the frustrating imposition and auxiliary nature of afternoon Hebrew schools. A friend told me recently that there is not one *mitzvah* that I keep according to the book. I guess this is true. Nonetheless, our home is full of the sacred words and objects of the Jewish People. I am outraged and delighted, brought close to and confounded by our history. But all human history is outrageous; how can ours be any different? My children have myriad responses to their Jewish identity and education. They, too, are often delighted and sometimes annoyed. I asked my daughter to complete several sentences:

I am proud to be Jewish because . . . "That's what I am," she said quickly.

If I had one wish for the Jewish People it would be that . . . "God sends the Messiah today," she rejoined with scarcely a second thought.

Some Jewish customs I would like to change are. . . . To this she replied: "First of all, I think we should be able to watch TV on *Shabbat.* Also I think it would be good to change 'kosherism' because I really would like to be able to eat all those good things. But if we changed 'kosherism,' then we would need something else to make us different," she paused and pondered for a moment. "I know," she exclaimed, "let's have another *Shabbat* on Wednesday."

Unlike her mother at ten, Abby is quite uninhibited in her aspirations for herself. She doesn't feel restricted by being a female. She reads Torah and recites *kiddush*. A few years ago, when asked what she wanted to be when she grows up, she said, "A rabbi, a doctor, or an astronaut." How well I remember the overwhelming shock I experienced in my late 20s when I heard that a woman could be a rabbi.

My son appears to have picked up the patriarchal stereotypes floating around society with much greater eagerness. During our first year without a live-in father, I felt strange about making *kiddush* in mixed company. If we had a male guest, I would quickly defer. Eventually, I assumed the role of householder and play it now with more ease. Ezra, however, never fails to encourage me to relinquish the job of *kiddush* to a surrogate *abba*. He has either played or observed little boys playing *abba* in nursery school. He wants an *abba*. He challenges my complacency with our Jewish family. To find the strength to feel comfortable with the present is not a simple task, particularly in a milieu, the Jewish community, that does not and perhaps cannot acknowledge the reality we are living.

OUR PRESSURED URBAN EXISTENCE

Shortly after my father died (two years after my divorce), I found myself at a conference of rabbis and Jewish professionals. I woke up early for the *minyan* and found that I was permitted to *daven* only behind a high *mehitzah*. I went to an adjoining room to pray alone. The only words I could see or hear were *yatom* and *almanah*— widow and orphan. . . . Protect the widow and orphan . . . remember the widow and orphan. I felt like a widow and an orphan, mother of orphans. Not only was I lacking protection—I didn't even count.

Again the downward spiral of self-pity and anger. The tears flowed, burned, and then passed.

The needs of a single mother—the need for more money, more time, the need for help with housework, home and car repairs, child care, the need for some respite from the lonely burden—are the crying needs of most families living in the urban machine. They are often exacerbated by vengeful ex-husbands, and money and energy soaking legal embroilments. The logical approach of organizing

support networks and championing institutional innovations requires a devotion of time and energy that the people most in need are
sorely lacking. There is within the Jewish communal structure an
apparent reluctance to develop outreach assistance to single parents. This stems, in my opinion, from the fear that if we support
them, we are validating them. They are, after all, unlike traditional
widows and orphans, self-inflicted pariahs. Ultimately, they represent a threat to the Jewish way of life. One detects some changes in
this attitude, although response lags abysmally behind need.

Meanwhile, there is the personal internal struggle to live a
human-paced existence—to stop proving that one is superwoman.
Frantic filling of time can also be an escape from feelings of anxiety,
loneliness, lack of self-acceptance. The pace of society around us
helps keep us frantic. But there is a devilish pleasure in having
someone say, "Wow—how do you do it all?" that compensates in
a false way for the lack of internal confidence and the absence of
a fulfilling love relationship. The need to prove oneself—the obsti-
nate side of cultivating independence—prevents one from saying,
"Help me." The learning of when and how to ask for help from
the wellsprings within and resources without is difficult for many
of us.

PARENTING CHILDREN

The greatest deterrent to my divorce was the fear of causing damage
to my children. My sister, a wise and helpful counselor, gave me the
courage to realize that I indeed was damaging my children as a
parent involved in a relationship that was sapping my strength and
defiling my self-worth. In the early days of our divorce, I acted
toward my son and daughter with great ambivalence emerging from
the guilt I felt from my own actions. My daughter was depressed,
subdued, my son difficult to control.

With the passing of time and the help of friends and counselors,
I realized the distinction between guilt and remorse. The more guilt
I dropped, the clearer I became. I had indeed acted responsibly, for I
acted for my own psychic survival and, therefore, for that of my
children. Our relationships improved correspondingly. We started to
become healthier. The remorse, however, exists on a deeper level.
The remorse stems from the error, the *het*, of making an adult
commitment of infinite responsibility—marriage and the creation of
new life—when I was unformed, unaware, unprepared for the consequences. Herein lies an element of deep tragedy.

With this understanding, I am struggling to be a multifaceted person. I need to in order to nurture and give an unbounded love, comfort, and support to my children, while simultaneously proclaiming limits and setting demands for cooperation and quality.

Parenting requires both closeness and distance. In two-parent patriarchal families, mommy is all closeness, father all distance. This produces the typical neurotic excesses exposed by psychological theory and refined by contemporary feminist authors (Esther Harding, *Women's Mysteries;* Dorothy Dinerstein, *Mermaid and Minotaur*). The son is stamped with the mold of his distant father; he looks for a wife to be his mommy, to continue indulging the greedy little boy. And the daughter grows to self-sacrifice; all the while she is ravaged by an absence of self-esteem and doesn't really feel she can find approval in the eyes of man or God above her.

I am not proposing that the single-parent family is the solution to neurosis. I do suspect that the task of integrating nurturer and executive—of becoming a whole person in relationship to one's children—is a model for parental and therefore human development. A model for raising boys who can cry and show affection and girls who can have a sense of their independence and strength.

A pitfall of single parenting (endemic to two-parent families as well) is exploiting our children to fill our own emotional voids. The temptation is great, particularly if one does not have satisfying adult companionship. I find myself unloading on my children, turning to them for the support that their tender shoulders cannot bear. It is important to catch myself.

One of the joys of a Jewish community that celebrates together is the opportunity for children to develop independent relationships with other adults. I am surprised and delighted to observe this happening. Occasionally, my children connect with people that I don't particularly find appealing, but who have a quality that meets the children in their world. This is a blessing, especially for a single parent, and should be articulated as a value by the community.

I recently passed a very painful struggle for the custody of my children, which led me to explore another dimension underlying both our religious understanding and our relationship with children. I asked myself, whose children are they? Ultimately, while I birthed them and care for their growth, I do not own my children. They belong to no one, but themselves—and God. This dawning recognition leads to the ability to accept their uniqueness and independence. This is a fundamental spiritual value, reinforced by the symbols and celebrations of our People, a consciousness underlying *brit, bar/bat mitzvah* and study of Torah.

DEVELOPING NEW RELATIONSHIPS
WITH MEN

I saved this issue for last. Perhaps it is the most difficult. As a single mother, I share the questions common to all single women; to look or not to look, where to look, how to look like you're not looking when you're looking, how to begin, what to look for, leftover anger from the past, lack of trust, bitterness, vulnerability, fear of mistakes, "If it's magic why can't it be everlasting," saying yes, saying no, making space and time, sex and again sex, ad infinitum, ad nauseam.

There are a few extra issues that specifically affect a woman with children. First is the benefit in not being desperate to have children, a desperation that afflicts so many single women. This is clearly a great boon. The other side of the coin, however, is less available time and energy to devote to meeting men and developing relationships.

I am perplexed, too, by the problem of my children's attachment to men friends who may be passing through my life. Conversely, how do I and my children relate to the families of my men friends? How will all this affect them? How much flexibility can I demand of them? To what extent should men be evaluated on the basis of their interaction with my children? I am, after all, a "package deal." My son used to ask, "What ever happened to so and so?" Suddenly this major figure in our lives is no longer on the scene. Ezra is anxious for me to remarry. He says, "You can marry so and so if you like and he wants to marry you. If not, then you can marry the next one, or the one after that. . . ." These statements are difficult for me to integrate. Perhaps my anxiety about the children is a camouflage for my own. In many ways they seem more readily able to cope with the uncertainty than their mother.

And that is the ultimate reality—experimentation and uncertainty. I have a real longing for an *ezer k'negdo*—a mate opposite— equal, unique, and independent. It is not a vision of a perfect man. It is a vision of a friend who is willing and able to share the journey with me. I don't harbor the fantasy that a man will solve my problems, as I did when I was 19. I do believe that the blessings of this life hover around us and our task is to ready the vessel.

My Jewish connection to people and tradition has helped coax out some understanding. Sometimes it has offered obstacles to be overcome, a fierce night angel to wrestle. Sometimes it has offered the solace of continuity amidst the dizzying change. My hope is to continue to look at the ancient words, symbols, and holy moments through ever wiser eyes, allowing the understanding growing within me to interact with the timeless mysteries.

I feel the deepest connections to the women of our collective dream. I know that their stories are much richer than what has been left to us in the fragments. We ourselves, I myself, will help to write their stories and give voice to their silent songs. We will do this, I will do it, by finding in our new lives the courage and strength to live in new ways and to form understanding.

24

The Divorced-Parent Family and the Synagogue Community

Barbara Kalin Bundt

One of the most alarming aspects of adults experiencing divorce is their newly developed negative attitudes toward the rabbi and the synagogue. These feelings are generally characterized by two stages: hostility and self-exile. Open hostility, with escalating vindictiveness, is often aimed at the rabbi and is frequently followed by withdrawal from Judaism and experimentation with non-Judaist and even non-Jewish lifestyles.[1]

At first glance, this behavior appears to be irrational. As more or less observant Jews, we were taught that the synagogue is our source of strength, a place to turn to in times of personal crisis. However, it becomes understandable when we remember that many single parents were raised with traditional attitudes toward the Jewish family. They feel that the collapse of their own marriage violates their Jewish adulthood. The Jewish mother—"The Woman of Valor"—is particularly embittered. Judaism implies that she is responsible for keeping the family together. For members of a family experiencing a divorce, Judaism may seem inconsistent with, even antithetical to, the realities of their own lives. The ceremonies of the home and the synagogue are visibly focused on the traditional

---

[1] A Judaist is a Jew who practices Judaism. A Jew is a person who by birth or conversion identifies with the Jewish people but who is not necessarily a Judaist.

196

family. The mother blesses the candles; the father chants the *kiddush.* Couples are called to open the Ark. Babies are named; anniversaries are celebrated. This pageantry of the Jewish lifecycle is painfully family centered.

Attempts by the single parent to adopt a non-Judaist lifestyle are often used to provide a healing distance from the pain created by this omnipresent coupledness.

Regardless of the real facts of the marital collapse and the following lifestyle, most divorced parents carry a heavy burden of religious guilt. Dealing with this guilt is the continuous task upon which the relationship of the single-parent family and the synagogue is rebuilt.

The major task of the congregation during these early stages of divorce should be to maintain contact with the adults although their anger may be discouraging. How often the rabbi has heard: "The rabbi was absolutely useless during my divorce"; "Every time he sees me, he turns the other way"; "I feel like a second-class citizen."

The rabbi needs to step beyond these statements and understand that the congregant, who really is feeling guilt and shame, is unconsciously using the rabbi as a scapegoat. By being aware of the source of this verbal rejection, the rabbi and the congregation may be more willing to extend the initial invitation of reconciliation that can ease the single parent's return to the synagogue.

In a recent marketing study of a local Jewish community center, the polled group composed of divorced parents felt that Jewish institutions, *especially the synagogues,* should initiate contact with its members upon hearing of a marital separation. Synagogues should not remain aloof, afraid of interfering. Letting the parties know that the rabbi is available as a willing, nonjudgmental friend can result in the much-desired and needed *nontherapeutic* "someone to talk to." In this early period of separation, an invitation to a *Shabbat* or holiday dinner might be appreciated.

The study's participants also stressed the financial panic that accompanies every divorce. Rare is the family that can continue to pay the same synagogue dues. Rarer yet is the person who can ask for a dues reduction without directing anger at the synagogue. A call from a thoughtful business manager or dues chairman suggesting a temporary reduction of dues can help maintain membership.

Rabbis have an essential role in educating psychotherapists, lawyers, and accountants about the importance of including provisions for the *get,* Jewish education, Jewish summer camps, holiday observance, and lifecycle celebrations in civil divorce decrees. These inclusions help prevent such issues from becoming future arenas for prolonged warfare. Members going through divorce should be given a checklist of these items important to future Jewish living.

Special divorced-parent family activities within the synagogue are of dubious benefit. If their synagogue socializing is limited mainly to "singles," neither the parent nor the children learn to deal with their own feelings of being "different" from other synagogue families. Preferring to be "just like the other kids," children of divorced families particularly object to being placed in single-parent family programs. Most important, by isolating the divorced-parent families into a separate subgroup, the rest of the congregation does not learn to relate comfortably to them.

Instead of putting effort into single-parent family programs, a congregation might examine existing programs that would allow these families to be re-introduced rapidly into the total synagogue structure. *Havurot* present an excellent opportunity to involve such families. Single adults should be invited *repeatedly* to work on the various synagogue committees. Study groups and other special interest groups are excellent means of recreating social circles without creating an isolated "singles" world.

Regardless of the sensitivity of the synagogue toward the single parent, the most important issue is the rebuilding of the adult's personal relationship with his or her own Judaism. In this area, a pragmatic shopping list of congregational "do's" cannot be presented: the resolution lies completely within the individual.

Personally, there were two major turning points in my own return. The most dramatic event was the presentation of my long sought-after *get.* Not only was I now freed from my civilly dissolved marriage, but also I felt "cleansed" and ready to reenter synagogue life. This dramatic reaction, which was extremely pivotal to my own Judaist observance, underscores the importance of the *get* both for Jewish legal reasons and for psychological self-absolution.

The other turning point was the gradual realization that, although the marriage was gone, the family still remained. Within the context of Judaism, the protection and companionship of coupledness was gone, but the privilege and *nahas* of rearing Jewish children still remained. As I learned to accept and enjoy my aloneness, I was able to focus on the need to reestablish stability and order within the family.

If Judaism presents a problem to single-parent families, it also presents a much-needed structure. Through the observance of *Shabbat* and *kashrut,* for example, families can reestablish the time and space needed to delineate the bounds of the present unit. Being together every *Shabbat*, regardless of external enticements, strengthens family bonding and, by example, increases the concept of the importance of primary familial obligations.

As a family unit, the duties and privileges of Jewish home rituals remain to be filled. The single parent must learn new religious skills once performed by the other adult in the former marriage. For this reason, both men and women should be familiar with all home rituals.

Another problem of single parenting is the lack of support from another adult who has similar values. The single parent is burdened with being the sole judge and model, but synagogue-focused Judaism can offer an alternative to this situation.

In many ways, the synagogue community can become the other parent. Through the pageantry of *mitzvot* and holidays shared with the synagogue community, the single-parent family gains a greater insight into the essential similarities of all families' behavior— "singled" and "paired."

As friends who share the same Judaic value structure, the rabbi and members of the congregation are available to "check things out" and provide much-needed reenforcement.

Despite the initiative of the rabbi and the synagogue and despite the soundness of the single-parent family's relationship to Judaism, one fact still remains: the single adult and the single-parent family exist outside the norms of Judaism. For the sake of Jewish survival, the traditional model of marriage and family life must continue to be stressed; therefore, adults who are single either by choice or circumstance and members of single-parent families face the continual, guilt-producing conflict between their own lifestyle and traditional Judaism. The congregation and the rabbi must recognize and understand this struggle. Only through sincere acknowledgment and sensitivity can synagogues hope to maintain and even increase the participation and affiliation of single Judaist adults and families.

POSTSCRIPT

This article was originally written over ten years ago at the request of Rabbi Bernard Raskas at Temple of Aaron, St. Paul, Minnesota. At that time the Conservative Movement was beginning to explore the challenge of atraditional "families" and the synagogue. Today, at least at my own congregation, Adath Jeshurun in Minneapolis, I feel progress has been made.

I can look at my own family and see the results of this progress through our accomplishments. I completed a Ph.D./M.B.A. and wrote a dissertation based on a market study of Shabbat observance in the Twin Cities. This unusual dissertation topic was stimulated by our family bonding experiences through Shabbat observance, which we learned at the synagogue. The study was partially funded by the synagogues.

All four children, now grown, attended Camp Ramah for many summers and returned as staff members also for many summers. The synagogue provided generous scholarships.

Three of the children are living in Israel. The oldest has made aliyah and has served in the army. The next child is a practicing artist, and the youngest is at Hebrew University for the year. Their initial exposure to Israel came from Ramah Israel, but their comfort in living in a Jewish environment came originally from the Adath Jeshurun community.

What did Adath Jeshurun do? They invited, they welcomed, and they underwrote at an appropriate financial level. What did we, a single-parent family, do?

We participated. We accepted the fact that we were different from the mainstream but that our goals and aspirations and Jewishness were NOT different. In other words, the physical structure of our family was different but the substance of our lives was not.

Who benefited? We all did—the children and I, the synagogue, and the Jewish community and Israel.

My status is now that of a single parent whose children have left home physically. This is quite different from a single parent who has primary care responsibilities for her/his children. My own career has been very successfully launched. I direct the market research and information function of a major company. I have chosen for now to remain single. I am at a stage in my own life when, as Marshall Sklare pointed out, Jewish institutional contact decreases. I am not involved enough to evaluate the quality of the relationship between single families and the Jewish community; but, at least in the Twin Cities, I see a wide variety of programs. How different this is from the time when I originally wrote this article.

25

New-Style Father

Shaye J. D. Cohen

I'm very good at pigtails and pony tails, but I'm afraid that braids are beyond me. What does a 38-year-old man know about braids—regular braids, French braids, Pocahontas braids? But on those mornings when my daughter turns to me and says, "I think I want a braid in my hair today," I have no choice. I braid her hair as best I can. Once I get the braid started, I'm home free, but the hard part is to get it started. To divide the hair in three reasonably equal parts and to do the initial weave in such a way that the hair lies flat and smooth are not easy tasks in the best of circumstances, and when the subject is an 8-year-old girl who cannot hold her head still for more than ten seconds, the circumstances are far from the best. Although I've produced some passable braids, and even one or two really excellent ones, I still tense when my daughter declares that the preferred hair style for the day is braids. Why can't she ask for something easy, I say to myself, like pigtails or a pony tail or—even easier—a head band or a few barrettes?

For a long time I did not have to concern myself with my daughter's hair style. From the beginning my wife and I shared parental responsibilities for our daughter. I did my share of diaper changes, baths, and cradle rocking. As often as not, I was the one to go to the store to purchase the clothes for our daughter, or to exchange the outfits we received as gifts. All of this seemed quite natural for me, even if my father had never done any of it.

I am a very Jewish person, a "professional Jew." I make a living

201

by teaching Jewish history to Jews in a Jewish institution. When I am not teaching Jewish history I am studying it. In the Jewish tradition, it is the father who raises the sons, and the mother who raises the daughters. The proverb "Like mother, like daughter" is at least as old as the sixth century B.C.E. (see Ezekiel 16:44). As a child and young adult I heard from my mother many times that a special relationship exists, or ought to exist, between a mother and her daughters, a relationship that could not exist between a mother and her sons or a father and his daughters. I was brought up believing that girls belong with their mothers.

Regardless, I became a "new-style" father to my child. I do not see why a man cannot change a diaper as well as a woman, or why a man, who has to assemble his own clothes every morning, cannot select attractive clothing for his child as well. But when my daughter became old enough to insist that she wanted her hair *long*, I sensed that this was a matter that should be left to my wife. Similarly, when my daughter decided that she wanted to have her ears pierced like her mother's, it was my wife who took her for the procedure and helped her to select the earrings she would wear. Nail polish was another area where I had no involvement. On those special occasions when all of us wanted our daughter to look extra special, it was my wife who selected and applied the nail polish. When my daughter braids her hair, puts on earrings, or polishes her nails, she is performing rituals that declare her to be not just a child but a *girl*, a youthful member of the tribe of women. These rituals are mysteries from which men are excluded. My wife sensed this as well; all other areas of child care were divided equally between us, but these three were reserved for her alone. I never had to learn how to do braids.

A year ago, after two or three years of increasing tension between us and endless discussions about the state of our marriage, my wife and I separated; we are now divorced. Our parting was amiable, as far as these things go, and we did our best to protect our daughter from psychic harm. When I realized that divorce was inevitable, I first imagined that our daughter would live with her mother and that I would visit my daughter on weekends, holidays, and other regularly scheduled times. After all, I reasoned, don't girls belong with their mothers? But I quickly convinced myself that this arrangement was not in the best interests of either parent or child.

The Jewish tradition that regards the father as responsible for the education and training of the sons and the mother as responsible for the daughters derives from a time when the man's sphere of activity was the synagogue and the school and the woman's was the household. But in all varieties of non-Orthodox Judaism, the synagogue and school are no longer the exclusive preserves of men, and in many families domestic responsibilities are no longer the exclusive preserve of women.

Thus, I realized that I should not depart from the role of active caretaker/nurturer/parent merely because my daughter's mother and I could no longer live together. I discovered that virtually all my colleagues who had been divorced had obtained joint custody of their children, and I decided to do likewise. My wife quickly agreed; I suspect very strongly that she had no desire to become the sole custodial parent. Three months before I moved out we announced to our daughter the sad news that we were separating, but we reassured her that she would still have two active, loving parents and that she would divide her time equally between us.

Thus, for a week at a time every other week, I am Daddy and Mommy rolled into one. When my daughter is with me I kiss her good morning and help her get dressed. We eat breakfast and brush our teeth together. I pack her lunch box and see her off to school on the bus. I greet her at the bus stop in the afternoons and arrange play time for her with her friends. We play games, watch television, and do the laundry together. I celebrate *Shabbat* and the Jewish holidays with her and aid her development as a Jew. Even with all my advanced planning and research, I did not know what to expect from a joint custody arrangement. I did not anticipate either its tremendous emotional rewards or its tremendous drain on my emotional and physical energies. I also did not anticipate the fact that I was not completely familiar with the rites of young girls. I have not yet tried to polish my daughter's nails, but I am not frightened at the prospect. I have learned how to help her with her earrings. When she gets older and hormones start to course through her system, no doubt she will need her mother for guidance and instruction in the ways of women. However, when my daughter becomes an adult and has children of her own, I hope she will tell them that a daughter can have a special relationship not only with her mother but also with her father. In the meanwhile, I do not feel at any disadvantage. There's just one nagging problem . . . braids.

26

Toward a Strategy for Integrating Single-Parent Families within the Organized Jewish Community

Chaim I. Waxman

Outlined below are the elements of a possible action program, based for the most part on conversations with members of single-parent families and with social workers—both professionals and students—speaking from their practice in the field.

Some of the recommendations have to do with institutional reappraisal. Others are political in the sense that they bear on the position of single-parent families in the decision-making structure. Still others are economic, having to do with the cost of services to the persons being served. The majority focus on particular programs or procedures designed to reach out to and serve families as a whole, the parents, or the children.

The strategy set forth here claims no finality or comprehensiveness, for the issues are so complex that no one individual could account for, let alone resolve, all their intricacies. Only a few suggestions will be considered—in keeping with the talmudic adage: "If you grasp a lot, you cannot hold it; if you grasp a little, you can hold it" (*Rosh Hashanah* 4b).

The steps advocated should accomplish two things: They should highlight the great variety of needs (including the differential needs of different family segments), and they should spark an initial attack on the most pressing needs (which may, in turn, generate momentum for a broader attack).

INSTITUTIONAL SELF-EXAMINATION

Many of the operating procedures of Jewish communal institutions today seem to persist simply from force of habit. Followed unquestioningly for a long time, they have come to be taken for granted, even after changed circumstances may have made them inappropriate. Each Jewish communal institution, organization, and agency should appoint an internal review board to evaluate current policies, programs, and procedures and recommend changes in those practices that hurt, or fail to help, single-parent families—for example, unsatisfactory scheduling (see below).

CLIENT REPRESENTATION IN DECISION
   MAKING

Synagogues, schools, and other communal institutions have not been sufficiently aware of the distinctive needs, perspectives, and sensitivities of the single-parent family. If they are to serve such families (as well as dual-career families) effectively, they must see to it that the intended clients are represented on their advisory and policy-making boards.

Without such representation, programs tend to be planned paternalistically, with no input from those to be served. If single parents had a hand in decision making, they probably could suggest programs that would integrate them instead of possibly isolating them further.

ACCESS TO SERVICES

Like others in need of assistance, single parents often fail to make use of available services, either because it does not occur to them that such services exist or because they do not know how to find out about them. A local referral mechanism, possibly in the form of one or several neighborhood storefront centers, and a hot line for quick action, would help.

Beside serving as transmission belts to formal Jewish social service agencies, these referral offices could provide informally for some kinds of services. (For example, the hot line office might maintain a list of reliable baby sitters available at short notice.) In addition, they could function as outreach centers for persons not yet looking for a specific service, and as cultural centers, providing information on existing Jewish activities in the area and helping organize new ones as needed. Offices might even include a lending library on Jewish subjects—a service that might be welcomed not only by single parents, but by many others among the unaffiliated 50 percent of American Jewry.

Jewish family agencies can play a major role in outreach, because they have the most frequent contacts with single-parent families. Although the old, complicated question, "How Jewish should a Jewish family service be?" is still unresolved, such agencies are in a unique position to provide information about the Jewish community. They can do so without compromising their professional standards by what might be deemed "missionizing," if they leave clients free to act on the information if they so desire.

DUES AND OTHER CHARGES

Active membership in the American Jewish community is expensive. The synagogue, the Jewish school, and just about every other institution asks for annual dues, tuition, contributions, admissions, and so on. These demands are probably heavy enough to frighten away some two-parent families; they certainly are too heavy for single-parent families in their frequently straitened circumstances.

Communal institutions would do well to reorganize their dues and rate structures accordingly. In some cases, they might offer special half-price memberships; or, as some synagogues do, they might provide two-for-one memberships covering both the head of a single-parent family and the other parent, just as a regular membership covers both parents of an intact family.

Educational institutions, especially day schools, might consider free tuition for single-parent family members. Recent studies suggest that Jewish education, if intensive enough, is second only to the family in forming Jewish identity—which has prompted Arthur Hertzberg to propose that Jewish education be made tuition-free for all. No doubt Hertzberg's suggestion is too far-reaching for the Jewish community just now; but free tuition just for single-parent family members may not be too radical an idea.

MONEY AND JOBS

Jewish vocational service agencies should make particular efforts to reach single parents with financial and job counseling. Where no such agency exists, a special office should be set up for the purpose. Ideally, this office should be run by professionals, but where that is not immediately feasible, it can be staffed by well-informed nonprofessional volunteers. Such a service, offering an immediate response to a particularly pressing need, would be especially suited for keeping clients in contact with the Jewish community.

THE LOGISTICS OF LIVING

Some Jewish community centers and Ys have begun to reach out to working single parents (and dual-career parents) by providing day care for their children. Such efforts to help deal with the logistics of living should be expanded and diversified. Virtually every Jewish organization and institution could offer simple, inexpensive, and potentially important aid in managing daily life—as well as in keeping up religious ties and marking special occasions.

For example, parents of children in Hebrew school can be offered participation in a car pool, so that the complications of bringing and fetching will not force the child to drop out. Synagogue members can approach single parents whose children are due for *bar* or *bat mitzvah*, or are about to be married, and offer to help with the preparations. In particular, a single parent involved with the synagogue can effectively advise and counsel other separated or divorced parents who are uneasy about meeting their former spouses at occasions like these.

IMPROVED SCHEDULING

Many institutions habitually schedule all or most of their activities and functions—for example, parent–teacher conferences, counseling sessions, courses—for daytime hours on weekdays, as if every family still included a mother who stays home. The hardships this creates for working single parents (and parents in dual-career families) are overlooked, evidently because institutions have not stopped to determine how many families are thus affected. It would be in the agencies' own interest to make the needed adjustments, because that would enable more people to become involved in community activities.

COMBATING LONELINESS

One besetting hardship of single parents is loneliness. In particular, weekends, like holidays, are often difficult times for them, especially if they do not have custody of their children. So far, however, the

Jewish community has provided few or no settings in which to meet people and find companionship—with the result that predominantly or wholly Jewish groups of single parents often gather in churches or other non-Jewish premises. Community centers and Ys, as well as synagogues and other Jewish communal organizations, should make it their business to provide places and sponsorship for inexpensive, meaningful weekend activities in group settings.

A more fundamental way to minimize loneliness, as well as to meet other needs, might be to organize residential communes, on the *havurah* model. Although communal living clearly is not for everyone, quite a few single-parent families might welcome it because of the opportunities it provides for mutual moral support and practical help. At the same time, a commune that is definitely Jewish in character would help preserve and sustain the participating families as Jewish families.

Since lifestyles and housing codes vary from city to city, each community would have to explore whether communal living centers would fill a local need, whether they would be feasible, and what form they might take. The idea may or may not prove appropriate in a given locality; but even if it is not, discussing it may suggest more suitable solutions.

DIVORCE COUNSELING

The community can help mitigate what is, at best, a painful and difficult situation by providing counseling for families in the throes of breaking up. Until now, only a few Jewish communities have offered divorce workshops to help spouses and their children weather the unavoidable emotional conflicts. The service should be made more widely available. The rabbinate could play an important role in doing so, because many Jewish couples facing divorce call on a rabbi, if only to obtain a *get* (religious divorce decree) in addition to the civil one. (Reform rabbis differ on the need for a *get,* from both ideological and pragmatic perspectives, but in the Conservative and Orthodox denominations it is almost uniformly considered necessary.)

Rabbinic organizations should urge their member rabbis to involve social workers in divorce counseling. Programs could be set up with relative ease; the services of Jewish family agencies and those of the rabbinate (if not the synagogue) in this field would be wholly compatible, especially since many social workers have become increasingly attentive to their clients' religious needs and sensitivities, while many rabbis now value social-work skills, and some of them even pursue graduate studies in the field. If divorce workshops became a standard part of rabbinical divorces, they would not only fill an important need for the persons served, but they would also anchor them more firmly in the Jewish community.

SUSTAINING THE CHILDREN

To help children cope with anxieties inflicted by their parents' marital breakup, the Jewish community should arrange with some appropriate agency to provide in-school or after-school counseling sessions. Many of the children would benefit from group raps to explore and deal with their fear, guilt, or loneliness; others, who may not yet be ready to reveal such feelings before a group, could be helped by individual sessions. Either procedure will help awaken or reinforce the children's Jewish identity and their identification with the Jewish community.

In addition to formal counseling, the Jewish Big Brothers–Big Sisters movement, so important at one time in Jewish social services, should perhaps be revived under professional auspices. There were reasons for the movement's decline, but the growth in single-parent families would seem to be giving it a new *raison d'etre*.

REMARRIAGE

Though single parents have many problems in common, they are not a homogeneous group in certain important respects. For example, some are not at all interested in marrying again and probably would resent "matchmaking" efforts, while others might welcome sensitively conducted activities through which they could enter new relationships. Though it may sound old-fashioned to some, the remarriage statistics prove that there always are many people on the lookout for new mates. Therefore, Jewish institutions should not be too quick to reject the function of matchmaker (*shadkhan*). Enough single parents may be interested to restore the *shadkhan*'s role to its former respectability in the Jewish community.

A MATTER OF CREDIBILITY

There is no simple or magical way of coping with the needs of single-parent families, nor with the contradictions their existence poses for us. We must overcome our own negativism, lest it keep us from responding constructively to them. We must prove to them—especially to those whose Jewish commitments are weak—that the Jewish community welcomes them and wants to help them. And we must remember that there is a symbolic as well as a pragmatic dimension to whatever we do, or do not do. By failing to reach out to single parents, we will convince them that we reject them as "deviants," and kindle their resentment against our neglect and indifference; by rendering tangible aid, we will give credibility to our compassion and concern.

Jewish

∧ *Marital Status*

- ☐ Single
- ☐ Not quite married
- ☐ Married
- ☐ Single again
    - ☐ Widowed
    - ☐ Abandoned
    - ☐ Divorced
- ☑ Remarried
- ☐ Intermarried
- ☐ Gay or Lesbian
- ☐ Childless

27

Elastic Boundaries: The Remarried Jewish Family

Vicki Rosenstreich and
Susan Weidman Schneider

The scene is the synagogue chapel, the music is Israeli melodies, the mood is joyous, and the wedding begins. Though the trappings are familiar, this particular scene is remarkable for the fact that the poles of the *huppah* (symbol of the new home the couple is creating) are held up by the teenage children of the bride and groom. The presence of the children tells us that this marriage differs in significant ways from the one that was first for both parties.

Remarriage is an old story in Jewish life. Our history and fiction are replete with tales of families shaping and reshaping themselves after the dissolution of a primary family because of death, divorce, or tragic separations. Is anything different for Jewish families? First, Judaism has a strong tropism toward marriage and childbearing, which encourages remarriage as well—there is no "state of single blessedness" for Jews. A person is considered incomplete until married, according to the Talmud, to Jewish mystics, and to the parents of most Jewish singles. A second consideration for Jewish remarried families are the messages about civilized behavior that the traditions bring: honoring father and mother can be extended to include honoring those who were once parents-in-law; the injunction against speaking ill of someone (*lashon ha-ra*) provides a model for ex-spouses to follow in not denigrating one another, especially in front of the children.

Currently, the majority of remarriages take place within five years after a divorce, and at least one of the adults is likely to have a child from a previous relationship. The supporting cast (literally, one hopes) can include former spouses, biological parents of the children, grandparents, and assorted other relatives who de facto become part of the remarried family. Indeed, one characteristic of a remarried family is that the primary unit is a whole web of relationships, not just the couple itself. The Miami Beach remarriage—of older people with grown children marrying after the death of a first spouse—still happens, but more common now are second marriages of younger people with younger families, with all the complexities that situation calls forth.

Characteristic of every second marriage are residual feelings that include loss of a significant family member and loss of community and friends to some extent (at the least because of a household move, at worst because of a fractious divorce). While the common wisdom has it that all Jews value family stability and continuity, recent research substantiating this shows that Jews suffer considerable loss of self-esteem when a marriage dissolves. These feelings obviously do not exist in the same way for a first marriage.

The couple mentioned at the beginning of this chapter included each of their children when they decided to marry and blend their families. This dose of reality helped counter the children's not-so-uncommon fantasy for a reunion of the old family. The *huppah* (wedding canopy) at the "remarriage" provided the symbolic manifestation of their children's participation.

The comfortable feelings that these family members may develop in the future will not blossom spontaneously as they walk back down the aisle after the ceremony. The adults and children may yearn for "instant family bonding" or "instant love." This unrealistic expectation—often on the part of women, who assume the lion's share of responsibility for the peaceful coexistence of the new family—may disappoint and may add to the tensions. The classic "Brady bunch" harmony of the television sitcom does not reflect reality. A real-life mother, living in a household with two children from her first marriage and one from her spouse's first marriage, says with what could be described as a wry smile, "You have to look away a lot." The Jewish ideal of *shalom bayit*—peace in the house—certainly supports a nonconfrontational mode, especially useful in stepfamilies.

The issues for a stepmother appear to revolve around love and acceptance; for a stepfather, the difficult issue is more likely to be discipline; for the children, the big issue is how to make sense of all this: his kids, her kids, their kids. In a remarriage, the bond between parent and child obviously predates the bond between the new partners. The task of a remarrying couple is to forge a bond between themselves so as to become happily married.

Children and adults face "boundary issues" that arise from being linked to more than one basic family unit, with the possibility of different rules, roles, and expectations. Some blended families wrestle with resolving differing standards that had prevailed in their earlier households. What kind of Jewish education will the children receive? Who will pay for this? Should the children be permitted to date non-Jews? Values and expectations may be different both between the new partners and between the households of the two biological parents—different attitudes toward food, space, money, and privacy.

These "boundary" issues, which the couple has to negotiate, may be critical in a Jewish family. In Jewish life—for all Jews—there is much diversity in practice: how holidays are to be celebrated, rituals observed, landmark events noted. The family may become the focus for a good deal of negotiation about religious and family lifestyles. A remarried family, in this context, may have greater "choices" but also fewer guidelines toward resolution.

How observant will the household be? Will the woman light *Shabbat* candles before sundown, or will she wait until the family joins her at the dinner table later? Will men and women say *kiddush* together on Friday evening? How much will the children participate? Will only one partner expect them to stay at home with the family on Friday evening? Who conducts the Passover *seder:* the man, accustomed to making all the decisions, from apportioning readings from the *haggadah* to setting the pace for the songs, or the woman, divorced for many years, accustomed to doing all the traditional *Pesah* preparations in the kitchen and then leading the entire *seder* for a group of her friends and family members? Some of these negotiations take place in every marriage, but in a remarriage there are two important differences: one, children are usually involved, and two, previous patterns are reinforced because the partners have been "doing it this way" as adults.

A remarried family creates its own history, even by such simple things as the jokes they share. When all the members learn to laugh at the *matzoh* balls that turn out to be the consistency of hockey pucks, these family jokes and "new" traditions are grafted on to those from previous families. The goal here is to respect and value one's own past and not disparage it (no *lashon ha-ra,* remember).

The familiarity of holiday observances, for example, even with their potential for evoking painful memories of other times and places, links that past to the present.

The very specific and regular events on the Jewish holiday calendar mean that the inchoate quality of the remarried family's complex relationships demands clarification several times a year. This "working through" can be very helpful in shaping the blended family's new reality; the holidays provide the chance to rehearse and perform various new family roles.

Concrete events such as *Shabbat,* Hanukkah, Purim, even a child's model *seder* in Hebrew school, are dynamic opportunities for concrete family negotiations, decisions, and *action* (whom to invite . . .) that can help the family forge its new identity. It is not just what you *feel* that matters as much as what you *do*—a very Jewish view. Deciding which grandparents should attend what events or how the biological parents will celebrate Jewish milestones with their child(ren) can highlight the allegiances and redefine the boundaries in ways that may be taken for granted in nuclear families. Some remarried families find that they expand their Jewish calendar in order to incorporate relatives on all sides: celebrating Sukkot and Shavuot with family gatherings, for example, whereas before these holidays had gone unmarked.

Such occasions, which some people understandably see at first as events that stir pain, conflicts, and hurts, also have within them the seeds of healing. For example, in the spirit of liberation and rebirth that the holiday brings, the Passover table provides an opportunity for a remarried family to include relatives from the "other side," get over past grudges, and reweave frayed kinship ties. The in-laws—cousins or grandparents—might be invited to the *seder.*

Of course, there are many "special cases" in any generalization one might make about family life. In remarriages, the pain over potential loss that many grandparents feel when grandchildren go to live in a "new" home is one example; another is the feeling of a single woman who gives up hopes of having her own biological children in order to be a stepmother to her husband's children.

These concerns do have potential resolutions: Many women who do not bear their own children enjoy the nurturing of stepchildren, when this is permitted and encouraged by the children's father and biological mother. Grandparents, for example, can see as their task the building of bridges, not walls. One sensitive grandmother would bring at Hanukkah time eight days of presents not just for her biological grandchildren but for all the stepsiblings. "It was time-consuming and expensive, but definitely worth it. The kids didn't feel so separate from each other," was her conclusion. Another woman decided, when her son and daughter-in-law divorced and each remarried, to construct a family schedule around the new realities, alternating *Shabbat* invitations, including at her table even her ex-*mehutanim.*

These issues are even more complex in cases where the second marriage is an intermarriage, as is frequently the case. Several studies show that a remarriage following divorce is, as likely as not, going to be an interfaith marriage. Raising children of two different religious backgrounds in one household is complicated indeed, more so if the partners have not decided on one religion for the home. In a nonconversionary intermarriage (more probable if both partners have children), the Jewish partner often has a very difficult time asserting what Jewish observances are important to her or him.

An interfaith remarriage requires that the Jewish partner be assertive about maintaining whatever Jewish aspects of life are important for the Jewish family members. Christian observances, because they are part of American culture, need no special pleading in many cases. These families have, obviously, even more need for negotiation over religious lifestyles, more need for careful communication, more feelings of guilt concerning betrayal of family and ancestry. Power issues are very confusing here—some interfaith couples use their religious differences as a convenient file into which they can lump all disagreements. The complexities here are legal as well as religious—for example, if the remarried couple should divorce, what will be the religious identity of the children they share in common?

People do not have to answer these questions and meet these challenges alone in their tidy nuclear families. Building kinship networks can provide new energy and new resources for people living in blended families. The family does not have to carry the whole burden of the children's Jewish identity, which it certainly did not in earlier times in Jewish history, when the synagogue and the study hall served as a second home to Jewish children. Returning to a more collective model may mean that, for example, a remarried family might invite indigent or homeless people to a communal *seder* rather than opting for a somewhat uneasy Passover celebration at home. Or it may mean that the couple tries to become involved jointly in synagogue committees as a way of building something together that has transcendent value outside of their relationship and their family, in order to create a shared history.

Atypical families of any sort—divorced or single-parent as well as remarried families—often feel isolated. Authentic connections with the Jewish community such as *bar* and *bat mitzvah* celebrations, weddings, naming ceremonies, and the *shivah* ritual keep the remarried family connected to a larger community and can buttress and stabilize the new family, especially when the older generation—the potentially healing grandparents—live far away.

What are some specific solutions in a Jewish context that can help the blended family? Starting from the beginning, with the post-divorce issues that predate any remarriage, the ideal is to work toward a "real" ending: legal divorce and psychological disentanglement, without a cutting-off, which would hurt any shared children. Arranging a *get* (traditional Jewish writ of divorce) provides a ritual disengagement to the marriage and is critical to ensure the legitimacy under Jewish law of future offspring of the new marriage. This formal separation is especially important when one realizes that more than 80 percent of divorced people remarry within three to five years. This means that the residue from the earlier marital experience is still quite fresh. The *get* treats the previous marriage respectfully in recognizing that it is worthy of a ritual closure.

Once the previous marriage has ended, the state of single parenthood provides a chance to build emotional independence and readies individuals for new involvements. The Jewish community can play a role in making remarried families more visible and more welcome. Consideration can be shown even in so simple a project as the construction of a family tree for Hebrew school. Asking young children to bring in pictures of all the members of their extended family shows caring and sensitivity. Such exercises help the children, and even the adults, to disengage from some idealized, unrealistic model of "the" Jewish family and enable them to see the true diversity that exists. A simple enough system, such as rearranging Hebrew school schedules for children who cannot attend on Sundays because of parental visitation patterns, goes a long way in reducing the dropout rate for these children.

These sensitivities benefit not only the individual families but also go a long way toward ensuring that they will want to stay connected to the Jewish community. Marginality comes in clusters. People in remarried families may already feel estranged or marginal to the community, somewhat isolated because of their disjointed histories. The community should feel a special urgency to embrace them and help them feel comfortable and welcome.

Rabbis can provide a model here if they officiate at remarriages, or at *bar/bat mitzvahs* and other public ceremonies, even funerals, *acknowledging* both the past and present realities. When planning even so routine a matter as a discussion with family members before a *bar/bat mitzvah,* the rabbi can play a very helpful role by encouraging cooperation between the biological parents and the stepparents to participate wherever possible in the planning, if not in the ceremony.

The Jewish tradition expects a transcendence of one's own concerns for the good of others, especially at holiday times and other celebrations. For example, one is commanded to invite the hungry to a Passover *seder,* to give charity at Purim time, to invite others outside the immediate family to a festive meal accompanying a *mitzvah* celebration. This principle of transcendence of the self can be applied to situations where all—the remarried couple, the ex-spouse, and the grandparents, as well as the cousins—need to keep others in mind.

The Jewish community can provide a nonthreatening context for acknowledging common pitfalls. The burgeoning numbers of discussion groups for remarried couples, through Jewish community centers, Ys, and other Jewish institutions, provide support not only for the adults but for children, too. One group, for example, sponsors panel discussions for teenagers in stepfamilies so that they can air their concerns—and their creative solutions.

Jewish life has managed to transcend national boundaries and language boundaries and even, sometimes, ideological boundaries. In remarriage some of this history of vaulting over boundaries can be applied to transcending the structure of the original family unit, moving beyond the nuclear family to create something more diverse. Jewish life provides many examples of kinship ties; one, the "cousins' club" that was formed in America to integrate newcomers in the early part of this century, lived on into the 1950s and 1960s as a net for holding family members together. Can blended families make use of this model? If the adults can get beyond past angers for the sake of the children, and for the sake of decency, then stepsiblings can learn to support one another and can find adults they can count on. Under this new definition of the family as a mosaic of interrelationships, pieces of prior relationships can create a new whole.

Remarriage substitutes a more horizontal, communal set of relationships for the traditional nuclear family. Under optimal circumstances, the remarriage *huppah* grows to become a much larger tent sheltering a whole extended Jewish family.

Jewish

∧ **Marital Status**

☐ Single

☐ Not quite married

☐ Married

☐ Single again

　　☐ Widowed

　　☐ Abandoned

　　☐ Divorced

☐ Remarried

☑ Intermarried

☐ Gay or Lesbian

☐ Childless

28

Coping with Intermarriage

Jonathan D. Sarna

"AN EPIDEMIC!" This seems to be the way of apprehending the intermarriage problem in the American Jewish community. Intermarriage is viewed as a disease and studied accordingly. How many are affected? Is the rate rising? What are the hardest hit areas of the country? Are men more prone than women? What are the early symptoms? How can I protect my children? The questions are important ones, and the Jewish community's concern is fully understandable. But the disease metaphor strikes me as unfortunate. It obscures far more than it clarifies.

As I see it, intermarriage is a defect rather than a disease. It stems from our free, open, and highly individualistic society. Intermarriage must be accepted as normative—an unfortunate but inescapable result of our voluntaristic democratic system. We may seek to limit the extent of intermarriage and to mitigate its effects. To end intermarriage entirely, however, would require us to put an end to our participation in liberal society. So long as we encourage individual freedom and seek acceptance in the larger society that surrounds us, we must expect that Jews and non-Jews will meet, fall in love, and marry. Since romantic love and personal independence rank high on the list of values that Americans cherish, we must expect that Jewish opposition to intermarriage will frequently fall on deaf ears.

There is, of course, another side to this. The intermarriage rate serves as a barometer of Jewish-Christian relations. The same rising rate that now alarms us also reveals an improvement in intergroup relations, something we have traditionally found pleasing. What is more, the conditions that produce intermarriage also foster conversion to Judaism; indeed, the two phenomena rise and fall together. Of course, nothing forbids us from discouraging intermarriage and promoting Jewish communal interests. What we cannot do is prevent intermarriage. American religious tradition—a tradition based on church–state separation, freedom, and voluntarism—makes that impossible.

What intermarriage poses, therefore, is not a threat—a disease to be warded off—but a dilemma central to our existence as American Jews. What do we do when our American values and Jewish values conflict? American culture seduces us with non-Jewish partners of the opposite sex, all the while insisting that marriage is a highly "personal" decision in which love rules supreme. The state sanctions intermarriage; should clergymen refrain from performing the wedding ceremony, state officers holding aloft the banner of nonsectarianism do so gladly. Judaism, meanwhile, insists that marriage with a non-Jew is sinful, at once a violation of Divine law and an affront to Jewish solidarity. Most rabbis refuse to sanction the act, their powerlessness to stop it notwithstanding.

How have we confronted this conflict between American values and Jewish values? Over time we have evolved four basic strategies. They continue to be used today. The first two represent long-term, indirect, preventive measures aimed at keeping Jews and non-Jews apart; the second two directly counter intermarriage through the use of parental and communal pressure.

1. *Consciousness raising.* This involves making Jews aware of their distinctive identity through formal Jewish education, rituals, and practices. The Jewish community strongly supports such efforts, at home, in synagogues, in Jewish schools, and at Jewish centers in the hope that Jewishly identifying youths will select marriage partners similar in background to themselves.

2. *Self-segregation.* This delimits the Jewish universe so that single Jews are most likely to interact with singles who "happen" to be Jewish. Jewish neighborhoods, Jewish clubs and organizations, Jewish schools, colleges with high percentages of Jewish students, and that traditional social barrier—Jewish dietary laws—all function to keep Jews within the company of other Jews. "The natural course of events" takes care of the rest.

What is important about strategies 1 and 2 is that they respect the American values of personal independence and romantic love, while attempting to further Jewish values by increasing the chances that the "freely chosen mate" will be from a Jewish home. They thus aim at creating an American-Jewish synthesis by promoting Jewish ends without openly conflicting with American norms. The strategies offer no guarantee of success, however. While they may serve to limit Jewish-Christian interactions, they do not prevent them. Indeed, because these strategies work indirectly, sometimes without any mention of intermarriage, the Jew who happens to fall in love with a non-Jew may not realize how strong the community's reaction will be.

3. *Parental pressure.* This familiar strategy confronts the intermarriage problems squarely by establishing marriage to a non-Jew as an act of family betrayal. Threatened sanctions may extend from excommunication to refusal to attend the wedding to mere sadness; whatever the case, we juxtapose family loyalty to romantic love with the aim of arousing guilt and remorse.

4. *Communal pressure.* This strategy brands intermarriage as treachery toward Judaism and the Jewish people, desecration of Divine law, repudiation of Judaism's mission, and a threat to Jewish survival. A rabbi may refuse to perform the marriage, and peers may threaten social isolation.

These strategies explicitly set Jewish values ahead of American values by insisting that romantic love and personal freedom must subordinate themselves to demands for group maintenance. But although sanctioned by our traditions, these strategies no longer hold the same deterrent effect as they did in the past. The consensus that used to support strong punitive actions against the intermarried no longer exists; indeed, many view anything more than expression of parental disapproval as indefensible, incomprehensible, and almost un-American. Furthermore, we tend to balance deterrence with hope for reconciliation: "reject intermarriage, not the intermarried." Our desire for reconciliation is understandable, the more so if there is hope that the non-Jewish partner will convert and the children be raised as Jews. On the other hand, as more of us become reconciled to intermarriage, the deterrent effect weakens. In the final analysis, the twin aims of deterrence and reconciliation stand in contradiction to one another.

Given these structural tensions—identity versus assimilation, Jewish values versus American values, and deterrence versus reconciliation—we can better understand the efforts at "synthesis" attempted by a large majority of modern Jewish intermarrieds. They seek to combine both intermarriage and Judaism, and do so by converting the non-Jewish partner to Judaism, by agreeing to bring up their children as Jews, or—at the very least—by bringing elements of Judaism into their marriage ceremony.

In all three cases, intermarrying Jews seek to demonstrate some allegiance to Jewish values, as if to reassure loved ones that they have not assimilated all the way. According to available statistics, "intermarriage-in" (conversion before marriage, conversion after marriage, or an agreement to raise children as Jewish) is becoming the most common form of intermarriage, exceeding both "intermarriage-out" (conversion to the non-Jewish religion, or agreement to raise children as non-Jews) and "intermarriage-straddle" (neither side converts and children are raised with no religion or two religions). The search for synthesis explains why "intermarriage-in," especially when the non-Jewish partner converts before marriage, seemingly satisfies *both* secular pressures and Jewish ones, for it permits the exercise of American values while keeping the Jewish people intact.

The alarming intermarriage statistics frequently quoted (30–50 percent!) reveal a great deal about how to lie with statistics, but nothing at all about the future of American Jewry. They do not distinguish "intermarriage-in" from "intermarriage-out." If, as preliminary survey data suggests, one- to two-thirds of all intermarriages are "intermarriages-in," many of them with full conversion, and in addition at least one-third of "intermarriage-straddles" also yield Jewish children, then, from the point of view of numbers alone, we have nothing to fear. The gains more than compensate for losses from "intermarriages-out." Far more research needs to be done into typologies of intermarriage and into the religious character of families that result from them. Based on what we know already, however, it can safely be said that the size of the Jewish population depends far more on the birthrate than on the intermarriage rate.

All this is not to underestimate the many problems that intermarriages, even "intermarriages-in," pose. Non-halakhic conversions pose problems. Non-Jews who drift to Judaism without converting pose problems. Even "Jews by choice," converted according to *halakhah,* pose—and face—numerous problems. And, of course, intermarrieds as a group continue to suffer from a much higher divorce rate than nonintermarrieds. But so long as we view intermarriage as a disease, a pathological abnormality that can somehow be cured, we shall continue to wring our hands and never meet these problems head-on.

We must accept the fact that intermarriage, much as we oppose it, seek to prevent it, and continue to lament it, will continue to be a fact. We must realize that the intermarrying Jew need not be a traitor or rebel, but may in fact be eager to remain part of the Jewish fold. Finally, we must acknowledge that "intermarriage-in," even if it is not the same as in-marriage, can result in thoroughly committed Jews who pass on their Judaism from generation to generation.

Accepting the inevitability of intermarriage and making the best of the situation does not mean approving of it, much less making it into a virtue. It does mean coming to terms with reality. Instead of constantly proclaiming American Jewry's imminent doom, we should view problems like intermarriage dispassionately and in proper context. We can then work to manage them to the extent possible, realizing as we do so that whatever perils our free society may present, it also rewards Jews with manifold blessings.

29

Mom, We're Just Dating

Mark L. Winer

Many Jewish parents send their children a mixed message about interdating and intermarriage. When their teenagers date, most Jewish parents accept their children's romantic relationships with non-Jews. However, when asked how they would feel if their children married non-Jews, an overwhelming majority of the same parents reply that they would feel very upset. Recent sociological research—published in *Leaders of Reform Judaism: A Study of Jewish Identity, Religious Practices and Beliefs*—and *Marriage Patterns,* written by M. Winer, S. Seltzer and J. Schwager (UAHC, 1987), underscores the inconsistency of these two positions.

Evidence from this research suggests that Jewish intermarriage is part of a chain that begins with parental acceptance of interdating. Although the discovery of a causal link between interdating and intermarriage may not surprise observers of American Jewish life, it challenges the wishful thinking of many Jewish parents and their children.

Teenage dating between Jews and non-Jews seems to some a harmless expression of the happy integration of Jews into American society. A few Jewish parents even encourage interdating as a way for Jews and non-Jews to learn to live together in the modern world.

Almost no one disputes the positive atmosphere in relationships between Jews and non-Jews in America. Indeed, the rapid rise in the rate of Jewish intermarriage comprises a powerful sociological indicator of the integration and acceptance of American Jews. However, most students of American Jewry agree that the intermarriage rate constitutes a threat to the survival of Jewish distinctiveness in the United States and Canada. Since American Jews want both integration and survival, the development of strategies for accommodating both will determine the American Jewish future.

The Research Task Force on the Future of Reform Judaism was begun primarily to focus on the complex phenomenon of Jewish intermarriage. The new findings on the relationship between interdating and intermarriage come out of the first phase of the research conducted by the task force.

Among the 2,000 questionnaires analyzed, 92 percent of the respondents report that their current or most recent marriages are between born Jews. Five percent are either converts to Judaism or are married to converts. Two percent are married to non-Jews, and 1 percent have never been married.

In analyzing the differences in the Jewish backgrounds of born Jews who married other born Jews and of those who married non-Jews, the task force found nothing in the way of Jewish observance or involvement that distinguished the homes in which the two groups of born Jews were reared.

The distinction reported by the two groups lies in their parents' attitudes concerning interdating and in their dating patterns as teenagers. In contrast to born Jews married to born Jews, those who have married non-Jews are far more likely to have interdated as teenagers. Of the 700 children of both groups who have married, almost 40 percent have married non-Jews. Among the endogamous marriages in the study (born Jew married to born Jew), those who exhibit the most permissive attitudes toward their children's interdating are most likely to have children who have married non-Jews.

In reporting the findings, Union of American Hebrew Congregations research director Rabbi Sanford Seltzer underlines the complexity of the issues involved in Jewish intermarriage. He cautions against drawing definitive conclusions from the available data.

"Still," he warns, "if Reform Judaism is serious about stemming the tide of intermarriage, the permissive attitudes of Reform Jewish parents regarding the dating patterns of their children should no longer be ignored."

He also acknowledges that parental attitudes might reflect the general failure in middle-class American families to set limits on adolescent behavior.

Alan V. Iselin, chairman of the task force, emphasizes that the research indicates that "Jewish parents have not relinquished their commitment to Judaism. They still hope that if one of their children marries someone not born to Judaism, he or she will either convert to Judaism or agree to rear their children as Jews."

Iselin points out that the respondents to the questionnaire demonstrate an active involvement in synagogue activities, frequent attendance at worship services, and a high rate of ritual and holiday observance in their homes. But Iselin believes that however important these acts of formal Jewish identification are for engendering positive feelings about Judaism in their children, they cannot be effective without a reassessment of parental attitudes toward their children's interdating.

"If anything, the prevailing approach seems to convey to teen-agers that interdating and maintaining Jewish identity are perfectly compatible. This misconception needs to be addressed not only in Jewish homes but also in religious schools and in temple youth groups as well," he says.

30

Intermarriage

Joyce Eisenberg

"When my daughter Marilyn brought her Catholic boyfriend home, I wanted to tell her to walk out and never come back," recalls Hannah Minsker (not her real name), a Jewish Holocaust survivor who settled in the United States in 1948.

"I asked my daughter, 'Are you dating John because we were hidden by Christians during the war? Do you think we owe them something?'"

Hannah Minsker's family, many of whom are survivors, told her she must accept her daughter's decision: it was unthinkable to lose another family member—no matter what the circumstances.

During the past five years, Minsker has had to resign herself to her daughter's actions, step by painful step: seeing her live with her boyfriend, John; marrying him; and giving birth to a son who may not be raised as a Jew. Hannah Minsker had always believed that the children of survivors would feel obligated to carry on Judaism. But she learned to live with the death of that conviction, too. Today, Minsker says she can't help but love her 18-month-old grandson, and has come to accept, if not approve of, the marriage.

Like Minsker, the rabbinate and the Jewish community are making a slow soul-searching shift in their attitude toward intermarriage—a remarkable transition from outrage to outreach. It is a journey fueled by necessity, not by choice.

"Twenty years ago, I'd say to a Jew who married a gentile, 'You've signed your death warrant.' Now I ask myself, 'Do I have the right to cut out any other Jew?' " says Rabbi Marvin Goldman, religious leader of Adath Zion, a traditional congregation in Philadelphia.

"Intermarriage used to be like cancer: you didn't talk about it," says Lena Romanoff, director of the Jewish Converts Network, a Philadelphia-based group. "It was discussed from the pulpit, but only in terms of how to prevent it. Today, we talk about it because we have to."

Approximately 40 percent of Jews who will marry this year will choose non-Jewish mates, as opposed to 20 percent a generation ago, and 3 percent two generations ago, according to a 1984 population study by the Federation of Jewish Agencies of Greater Philadelphia in conjunction with Temple University. The study further indicated that those who intermarry tend to come from less religious homes and have received less Jewish education than those who don't. The findings reflected national trends.

"Jews have gone from Poland to polo in three generations," says Egon Mayer, professor of sociology at Brooklyn College and one of the nation's foremost authorities on intermarriage. "As we move into the mainstream and are more widely accepted by our neighbors, intermarriage results. The grandchildren of immigrants have arrived politically and socioeconomically. It's not surprising that Jews are desirable marriage partners."

Even if parents provide a child with a good Jewish education and a rich religious heritage, they cannot prevent him or her from falling in love with a non-Jew. "And when biology conflicts with theology," Mayer says, "biology triumphs."

It wasn't until the late '60s that parents and the rabbinate realized that all their outrage and exhortation hadn't stopped what demographer Mayer calls "this social drip." Their hostility instead had alienated couples who might have chosen to identify with a more receptive Jewish community.

"There has been a major attitudinal shift for the sake of Judaism," Rabbi Meyer Selekman, of Reform Temple Sholom in Broomall, Pennsylvania, explains. "If we kept our old mentality of writing off those who intermarried, we'd lose a lot of Jews."

"We noticed," says Egon Mayer, "that not all intermarriages led to assimilation. About one-third involved conversion of the non-Jewish partner to Judaism. We were witnessing something extraordinary, a reversal of previous findings that said the minority member drifted to the majority."

Today, even among interfaith marriages where there is no conversion, nearly one-third of the couples consider their children

Jewish. Many of these couples, committed to having a Jewish home and family life, are feeling their way tentatively into the Jewish community.

"The mixed-marriage couple is actually the most rapidly growing constituency of synagogue members in Reform temples," says Rabbi Richard F. Address, regional director of the Union of American Hebrew Congregations, the central body of Reform Judaism.

Egon Mayer estimates that last year there were between 400,000 and 600,000 Jewish-gentile marriages in the United States. If the current trend continues, it is not inconceivable that by the year 2050, the descendants of these intermarriages who have been raised in the Jewish faith will constitute a major group of practicing American Jews. It is these children of interfaith marriages who will determine the future viability of the American Jewish community.

Intermarriage elicits a wide range of responses among the rabbinate, from the liberal "We must keep channels open" to the hard-line "Mixed marriage is a disgrace." *Halakhah* (Jewish law) considers marriage to be a covenant between persons of the same religion, and Orthodox and Conservative rabbis refuse to officiate at a mixed marriage.

Rebecca Alpert, dean of students at the Reconstructionist Rabbinical College, says that "the majority of our rabbis don't officiate at interfaith weddings. But we might attend the civil ceremony performed by a judge to make it clear we are supportive within our ethical bounds."

The Reform movement discourages officiating at interfaith marriages, although it doesn't censure those who do, says Elliot J. Holin, associate rabbi of Congregation Rodeph Shalom in Philadelphia. "In Reform Judaism," he remarks, "each rabbi can make his own decision. At Rodeph Shalom, we will officiate at interfaith weddings because we feel it is critical to stay in touch with converts and intermarried couples."

Rabbi Mayer Selekman agrees. "I never felt good turning my back on a Jew as long as there was genuine motivation and need," he says. "I've always had the feeling that Judaism wouldn't suffer from intermarriage, that there would be a net gain." Selekman will participate in the ceremony if the couple is committed to perpetuating Judaism. He will also co-officiate with a Christian clergyman.

Selekman believes that loving our children is one of the most fundamental *mitzvahs* of Judaism. "We raise our children as Jews, and that implies that they have freedom of choice. It's each child's responsibility to make these decisions for himself."

"Parents can put a blessing or a curse on a marriage," he adds. "The latter translates as 'My children should live for me, not for themselves,' and that is a bigger impact than parents should have."

Dennis Sutnick and Marie Thompson (not their real names) met in a disco in 1975. "I knew Marie wasn't Jewish, but it didn't bother me to date a non-Jew," says Sutnick, a 37-year-old attorney. "I didn't worry about it getting serious." Sutnick had been raised in a Conservative home and was active in Jewish youth groups and his synagogue.

"When I noticed he had a *mezuzah* around his neck, I had a sinking feeling," recalls Thompson, 36, who had attended Catholic schools for sixteen years. "I wanted to marry someone Catholic, and I thought about breaking it off."

But Sutnick and Thompson fell in love and then spent the next four years figuring out how to resolve their religious differences so they could get married. With an open mind, Thompson attended Reform conversion classes, but decided that "the way I've always worshiped God was right for me."

The couple was at an impasse until Thompson agreed that she would raise their children as Jews. "That had been the one obstacle to the marriage," says Sutnick.

Thompson's parents accepted the impending union. Sutnick's father, who had been raised in an Orthodox home, "recognized that I was a big boy and could do what I wanted," Sutnick relates. "But it was quite another story with my mother, who is not observant. She refused to accept it. When I told her I was engaged, she told me not to come home for Passover."

Sutnick's mother was the only relative who didn't attend the wedding, which was held in a restaurant. A rabbi officiated.

"But when we showed up at the house for the first time a few months after the wedding," Dennis Sutnick says, "my mother pored over the wedding pictures alone in the kitchen. From that point on, she acted like nothing had ever happened. We never discussed her not coming, and since then everything has been okay."

"Weddings, births, and deaths are enormously powerful moments in the life cycle," says Sherri Alper, director of the Union of American Hebrew Congregation's regional Center for Outreach and the Family. "Jewish parents, who may not have been particularly observant, or who never objected to their children dating gentiles, may, in a moment of self-revelation, realize how important Judaism is to them." For this reason, Alper says, they may feel hypocritical and foolish about objecting to intermarriage. "I encourage parents to tell their children that they are surprised by their reactions, but that they do want to share their feelings."

Although Dennis Sutnick's mother could not discuss how she felt, perhaps intuitively she understood the distinction in Jewish law between *l'hathilah* ("at the outset") and *b'diavad* ("once it has happened"). Each of these circumstances calls for a different response. That is why some rabbis, who may refuse to officiate at interfaith weddings, endorse outreach programs.

"Outreach is predicated on the assumption that we can oppose intermarriage without rejecting the intermarried," says Rabbi Alexander Schindler, president of the Union of American Hebrew Congregations (representing the Reform movement). In 1979, the UAHC announced that it would reach out to non-Jewish spouses by providing information and referrals for intermarried couples, their parents, and their children. Soon after, the Pennsylvania Council of the UAHC established a calendar of outreach programs.

Earlier this year, the Conservative movement jumped on the bandwagon when the Rabbinical Assembly of America established its own commission on outreach. Programs are now in the planning stages.

Several hundred people attended the first Philadelphia conference on intermarriage this spring. Called "Intermarriage and Conversion: Our Challenges and Triumphs," it was cosponsored by the Intermarrieds Professional Network of the Philadelphia Chapter of the American Jewish Committee and the Board of Rabbis of Greater Philadelphia. Participants included representatives from all branches of Judaism.

Among the many deep-seated concerns expressed were: "Why is my child spiting me?" "Will our family still be together for the Jewish holidays?" "Will we dance at our grandson's *bar mitzvah?*" "What will happen to our marriage if my husband and I can't both accept our child's interfaith union?" "How can I explain to my children that I want to keep my link in the chain through my grandchildren?"

Sherri Alper believes that many parents use religion to cloak other feelings, especially those pertaining to loss. "These feelings need to be separated and identified before they can be addressed," Alper says, explaining that parents who are experiencing an empty nest as their children build separate lives for themselves, and whose own parents may be getting sick and dying, worry about the loss of a predictable family future.

"Grandparents, whose own mortality is very tangible, fervently hope that their grandchildren will be raised in a Jewish home and see themselves as Jews, thereby carrying on their values," says Rabbi Elliot Holin. "One of the definitions of Jewish *nahas* is having Jewish grandchildren."

Alper suggests that grandparents discuss the issue of religion with their children. "If a child's relationship with his *bubby* and *zayde* is satisfying," she remarks, "it can color his future decision about Judaism."

The consensus among area mental health professionals and the rabbinate is that children raised with dual religious identity usually grow up confused. "Parents must choose a religion for their children, as opposed to letting their children decide," asserts Debbie Aron, director of Jewish Family Life Education for the Jewish Family and Children's Service of Philadelphia. "Children need structure, organization, things painted black and white. They must own a religion first, before they can decide what to observe as adults."

"I wanted to start my children's Jewish education early so that they would have no identity problems," says Dennis Sutnick, whose two daughters are now 6 and 3. "Although Marie is still a practicing Catholic, we are more Jewishly observant in our home than we ever were in my family. Marie lights the Sabbath candles, and we go to my parents' house in Brooklyn for the High Holidays."

The Sutnicks also attend synagogue services together. "When my daughter first started Jewish preschool, she said to me, 'When I grow up, I'll be Catholic like my mommy,' " recalls Marie. "Now she tells us when it's time to light the *havdalah* candles."

Each year, the Sutnick family spends Christmas with Marie's parents. "I still feel the religiousness of that holiday and am glad to be there. And, I am a little uncomfortable that my children are being raised Jewish," Marie says. "It's hard for me to come to grips with all of this, with my children worshiping God in a whole other way."

Still, the Sutnicks are satisfied that they have a strong family identity and that the choices they've made are appropriate for them. Two issues remain: the children have not been formally converted, and the family has not joined a synagogue.

It is to families like the Sutnicks that the new attitude of outreach is directed. Rabbi David Teutsch, dean of admissions at the Reconstructionist Rabbinical College in Philadelphia, says that given the prevalence of intermarriage, Jewish involvement and education for interfaith families should be available. "This may encourage and facilitate the possibility of conversion and the raising of children as Jews. But even when conversion does not take place, we still believe that this is the strongest survival strategy."

Interfaith marriages may give rise to more conflicts than most, but these conflicts can be resolved. "Families have an amazing resilience," says Alper. "What is a crisis today may not be one tomorrow."

31

Peering into the Limbo of Judeo-Christian

Harold M. Schulweis

On the wake of Pope John Paul II's visit to America, a revival of Christian-Jewish anecdotes took place. One such story tells of Cohen's conversion to Catholicism, for reasons unknown. The Knights of Columbus hosted a banquet in Cohen's honor. Called upon to speak, Cohen looked at his audience, devoted lay Catholics, priests, bishops, monsignors, and began his address: "Fellow Goyim."

That genre of Jewish humor is meant to console. It insinuates that the conversion has not taken and that an ineradicable residual identity remains: a Jew remains a Jew, even after conversion.

The challenge to Jewish identity comes less from outright conversion than from surreptitious deconversion. The hyphen, not the cross, dissolves Jewish identity. The Judeo-Christian hyphen is turned into a sign of identity. While Judaism and Christianity may appear different, stripped of externalities they are the same. Blue and white light or green and red fixtures, hot-cross buns or *latkes*, they all signal the same directions.

The Judeo-Christian hyphenation is a theological triumph for those who sought to break the hyphen and free Christianity from its Jewish origins. The defenders of the Judeo-Christian link warned the church that for Christianity to sever its Jewish bonds is to attach Christianity to pagan roots. To cut the grafted branches from the good olive tree would cut off Christianity from its authenticating Jewish root (Romans 11:17). Yet for all the benefits in the grafted hyphen for Jews and Christians alike, there are serious liabilities in the assumption that deep down Judaism and Christianity are twin faiths without significant difference.

Consider the case of two attractive, intelligent, young people, very much in love, who enter my study. He, a Jew named Sam. She, a Christian named Peggy. Their object is matrimony, and the subject is a rabbi liberal enough to officiate at the mixed union or alongside a liberal priest. Neither seeks conversion. They seek an Equal Opportunity Cleric.

They each have vague sentimental attachments to the faith in which they were raised and genuine filial fidelities to their parents. They have thought out the dilemma of raising their children. They will offer them the dual advantages of two religious civilizations. "If it's a boy, we'll have him both circumcised and baptized," they agree. Far from seeing conflict in the arrangement, they are convinced that the wisdom of both Old and New Testaments will enrich their lives and confirm Malachi: "Has not one Father created us. Hast not one God made us." They see vindication in the similarities of the mother–sister traditions. Toward their own and each other's religious belief and practice, they offer benign neutrality.

The discussion wandered. At one point, possibly out of frustration, I asked them what they thought of my officiating as both rabbi and priest. They were taken aback at this bold ecumenicism. "You're not serious?" they asked. "Well, let's play it out. I know the church sacrament, the nuptial blessings, and I certainly know the seven blessings of the Judaic tradition," I said. Peggy thought such synchronistic virtuosity a bit too much. She couldn't quite conjure up the union of surplice and *tallit,* swinging rosaries and *tallit* fringes. Still, if we have one Father, why not one rabbi–priest?

They were not slow to see the *reductio ad absurdum* of my argument.

The rabbi–priest idea dropped, Peggy went on to explain that she was not a practicing Christian. Why then, I asked her, was it so important to have her child baptized? She answered with a personal anecdote of a cousin whose infant had died. "If that happened to me, I couldn't face the thought that my child was unbaptized." Unbaptized, her child would be suspended between heaven and hell, consigned to *limbus infantum.* I asked about the status of her husband-to-be. Would an unbaptized Sam be subject to limbo or damnation? Would her beloved Sam be saved? There followed a long and deep silence.

In that silence, I pondered over the neglect of Jewish theology and philosophy in Sam's life. Sam's Jewishness—he had attended a

Jewish day school and performed well at his *bar mitzvah*—amounted to casual observances of a pastiche of rituals, a vague sentimentality toward Jewishness, and an attachment to his Jewish parents.

But Judaism offered him no way of mapping the world, no distinctive view of human nature, God's character, or the quest for meaning. Sam was liberal in the manner of polytheists for whom every god is good enough. For Sam, and for Peggy as well, religions are all the same. If they appeared indifferent, it was because for them there were no true differences between the traditions. It seemed such a shame to dissolve a love because of a few ethnic residual memories. Preference for a colored Easter egg or a *seder* burnt egg, a swaying evergreen or a shaking *lulav,* are more matters of taste than of principle.

But in truth there are radical differences between Christianity and Judaism and for their sake, and that of their children, Peggy and Sam ought to understand them, for they entail world views and values that affect them more than they think.

ORIGINAL SIN AND OTHER DIFFERENCES

To begin with, Christianity is rooted in the dogma of original sin. By "original" is not meant the invention of new sins, but inherited sin (*erbsuende*) traced back to Adam and Eve's initial disobedience of God's prohibition against eating of the Tree of Knowledge. That *culpa originales* is transmitted to every living human action "by generation, not by initiation." That sin is not a consequence of an individual's choice, a congenital curse from which there is no human cure. Only by faith (*sola fide*) in the incarnation of the man-God and his unmerited kindness in dying for God's children is the stain of inherited sin wiped out. The crucified Christ is the sinless sacrifice that alone can loosen Eve's children from the grip of the Satan.

"Whoever eats my flesh and drinks my blood has eternal life and I will raise him in the last day" (John 6:53). That promise is ritualized in the eucharist, mass, or communion sacrament wherein the miracle of transubstantiation or consubstantiation takes place. The wine and wafer are transformed into the blood and flesh of Christ crucified. To what degree of literalism such transformation is understood remains a Christian debate that need not concern us here. But no matter the version of the sacrament, it is a far cry from the wine of *kiddush* that remains wine and the *hallah* of the *motzi* that remains bread.

Baptism is a sacrament critical for Christian salvation. The Roman Catholic rite of baptism includes exorcism of the Prince of darkness. The priest blows on the face of the infant ordering the spirit of Satan to depart, moistens his thumb to touch the ears and nostrils of the infant, and asks the *patrini*—the sponsors of the child—to renounce the power and pomp of Satan. Those who are baptized and who believe are saved; those who refused are stigmatized by the inherited sin that remains indelibly inscribed in the unredeemed soul. We may better appreciate Peggy's serious concern over the infant's baptism and her silence over its absence in Sam's life.

When during the trial of Adolph Eichmann, a Canadian Christian minister flew to Jerusalem to offer Eichmann's soul the opportunity to confess his belief in Christ, reporters asked him whether Eichmann's confession would save his soul. The minister affirmed that it would. Asked whether the soul of Eichmann's victims would be saved without such confession, he answered "no." "No one comes to the Father but by me," said Jesus, according to John 14:6.

For many of the Church fathers, Judaism is a vestigial anachronism, a "has been" whose purpose was that of *preparatio evangelica*, preparing the path for the good news of the advent of Christ. In the gospels of Matthew, Mark, and Luke, we read that on the day that Jesus died some forty years before the destruction of the Second Temple, the veil of the Temple was rent in twain from the top to the bottom. The Temple, the priests, the sacrificial system, and the authority of the Rabbis collapsed; the instruments for communion with God fell exclusively into the hands of the true believers in Christ crucified and resurrected.

It is noteworthy that the Christian Bible includes the Old Testament with the New Testament, but with a rearrangement of the order of the Old Testament books. The Jewish Bible (*Tanakh*) ends with the Writings, e.g., Proverbs, Psalms, and the concluding book of Chronicles, which contains a historical resume of biblical history. The last verse in Chronicles II refers to Cyrus, King of Persia, who is charged by God to build His house in Jerusalem, i.e., to rebuild the Temple. Cyrus, who in Isaiah 45:1 is referred to as Messiah—"anointed"—proclaims to the Jewish exiles: "Whoever is among you of His people may the Lord be with him. Let him go up." In the Christian reordering of the Jewish Bible, the last books are from the Prophets, specifically the prophet Malachi. Here the last verse reads, "Lest I come and smite the earth with a curse." In this manner the Christian canonizer of the Old Testament has removed the hope of Jewish return to Zion and has replaced it with threat of

Israel rejected. On that ordering of the testaments, Jesus succeeds and supplants the Hebrew prophets. With the reordering of the Hebrew texts, Israel's tragic destiny is scripturally foreshadowed. The old covenant is broken, and Israel depends for its redemption upon acceptance of the new covenant and the resurrected Savior.

And, too, the universal burden of original sin, the particularistic sin of deicide, the betrayal and killing of the son of God. The episode of the Roman procurator Pontius Pilate, washing his hands of the blood of the Jews to be crucified and the obdurate insistence of the mob of Jews crying "crucify him, crucify him," is dramatized in Easter Passion plays and in such commercial dramas as *Godspell* and *Jesus Christ Superstar.* To the contagion of the original sin is added the culpability for the rejection and mortification of Jesus. The chilling words in Matthew 27:25 put into the mouths of the Jewish mob, "His blood be on us and on our children," augurs the history of contempt for "the perfidious Jew" so virulent in the hands of the mobs as to defy even the restraints of higher church officials.

BAPTISM AND CIRCUMCISION

Sam and Peggy are oblivious to the theological, moral, and emotional contradictions in circumcision and baptism. For them, both are items of ritual choreography devoid of theological roots or psychological consequences. But baptism and circumcision are far from complementary dramas. Baptism is predicated upon an anthropological pessimism. Man is born in the womb of sin. Since there is nothing that a sinner can do in terms of works or reparation to expiate that innate and humanly ineradicable blemish, his sole recourse is to throw himself upon a supernatural Other who assumed the burden of suffering atonement for all others. For all others, the atonement is gained vicariously. As Luther expressed it, the believer becomes *velut paralyticum,* as one paralyzed, abandoning the conceit of his own deeds, utterly dependent on the self-sacrifices of the innocent lamb of God.

Circumcision is the initiation into the covenant with God and Abraham. The 8-day-old child carries no baggage of sin with him into the world. He is no alien flung into the hands of demonic powers. The Christian infant prior to his baptism is a pagan; the Jewish child is Jewish even before or without the rite of circumcision. The Jewish child is born innocent, body and soul, created and sustained in God's image. He has no need to be saved because no Satan threatens him, no eternal damnation hovers over him. As a Jew he will be raised in a tradition that mandates him to save lives, not souls.

For Christianity, man sins because he is a sinner. For Judaism, man sins when he sins. Of course, he will sin—not because he enters the world condemned as a sinner, but because he is a fallible human being and "there is no righteous human being who has done good and does not transgress" (Ecclesiastes). The sin is his or hers, the choice is his or hers, and the reparation to be done is his or hers.

No one can sin for another, cry or die for another, or absolve another. No confessors, intercessors, surrogates, or substitutes can stand in for another's turning from sin. No one can shower, bathe, clean himself that the other shall be clean. "Wash yourself clean," Isaiah addresses the penitent. "Put away the evil doings from before Mine eyes; cease to do evil, learn to do well; seek judgment, relieve the oppressed, the fatherless; plead for the widow." Communion with God is without rabbinic or priestly mediation. "Blessed are you Israel. Before whom are you purified and who purifies you? Your Father who is in heaven" (*Yoma* 85b).

The divine-human connection in Judaism is unmediated. Moreover, whereas in Christianity the relationship between self and God is a vertical relationship, the Jewish connection with God is horizontal. The horizontal human transactions that call for reparation, forgiveness, and apology for the injuries of others cannot be skipped over by a vertical leap between the individual and God in heaven, ignoring the proper relationships with God's children on earth. The prophet Ezekiel makes it clear what the truly penitent is to do: "If the wicked restore the pledge, give back what he has robbed, walk in the statutes of life . . . he shall surely live . . . none of the sins he has committed shall be remembered against him" (Ezekiel 33: 15–16).

Baptism emphasizes the paralysis of the human will, helpless without God combatting Satan. The covenant of circumcision focuses on the competence of the human being to exercise control over his life. To the sulking Cain, depressed over his act of fratricide, the Torah counsels, "Sin crouches at the door but you may rule over it."

Salvation is not for Jews alone. In Judaism, those who do not believe our way or pray our way are not threatened with divine anathema. In rabbinic literature, heaven and earth are called to witness that "whether they be gentile or Jew, man or woman, slave or free man, the Divine Presence rests on each one according to his deeds" (*Yalkut Shimoni, Tanya Debei Elijah*). The people of Nineveh (in the Book of Jonah) are spared because of their deeds, not their conversion to Judaism; because of their turning from evil ways, not their acceptance of the Sabbath and festivals. Jews do not seek to convert the world to Judaism but to convert the world to righteousness, justice, and peace.

Sam and Peggy must be given to understand that circumcision is not baptism. They are not knife or water alternatives, but ritualized dramas of values, affecting their relationships to God, world, neighbor, and self. Baptism depends upon belief in a specific divine person who walked the face of the earth. In Judaism there are no such incarnate divine beings, whether clothed as patriarchs, priests, or prophets. There is no Jewish beatification or canonization of saints, no apotheosis of blood-and-flesh heroes, no doctrine of infallibility.

The heroes of Israel are magnificent, but not so special that they are to be obeyed without question.

FAMILY TIES

Peggy spoke warmly of the Jewish family. Family is one of the consistent praises of Jewish life that rabbis hear from non-Jews. The primacy of family is not irrelevant to the horizontal theological frame of Judaism. The family and its friends are rooted in a tradition that does not tolerate the schism of love between humans and that between humans and God. Nowhere in Jewish religious literature could one find, even remotely, the approach to the family that Jesus expresses in the gospel in Luke and Matthew. "If any man come to me and hate not his father and mother and wife and children and brother and sisters—yea and his own life also, he cannot be my disciple" (Luke 14:26). In Judaism, Jews come to God through their families and friends, not through sacrifice of their relationship nor the sacrifice of self. Divinity yields its character not through the subtraction of humanity, nor through the elimination of the self, but through the love and care of human others and self. Jesus declares, "For I have not come to bring peace on earth but a sword. For I have come to set a man against his father and a daughter against her mother, and a daughter-in-law against her mother-in-law." For Jesus, the believer is confronted with a hard, exclusive disjunctive. Either heaven or earth, either Christ or family, either Jesus or self. "He who loves father or mother more than me is not worthy of me" (Matthew 10:34). In Christianity, one cannot come to the Father except through the son. In Judaism, one cannot come to the Father except through the earthly sons and daughters of one's human family.

These are not easy instructions for Peggy and Sam to hear. But it is important that the differences in their birth traditions not be trivialized. The theological differences between Christianity and

Judaism are likely to cast cultural and moral penumbra larger than they may have imagined. They may come to understand that genuine tolerance does not entail indiscriminate adoption of all faiths and that openness does not mean to reduce all traditions to sameness.

They may come to recognize conversation as not discrediting the other's faith but as flowing from an awareness of the profound dissonance between religious cultures. Their resolve to hold incompatible traditions in one household would not only distort the uniqueness of each faith civilization but compromise their own integrity. With the best of intentions, Peggy and Sam thought to offer their offspring the best of religion. But, to paraphrase Santayana, such is the attempt of those who would speak in general without using any language in particular. Judaism and Christianity are particular languages, with preciously unique syntaxes, which when thrown together produce a babble of tongues.

Sam and Peggy have important decisions to be made. If they build their lives on the narrow edge of the Judeo-Christian hyphen, they offer their children the fate of Disraeli. He became the British Prime Minister of Queen Victoria, was converted to Christianity by his father, and yet held pridefully the glories of his Jewish ancestry. Queen Victoria is reported to have asked him, "What are you, Disraeli? Which testament is yours?" He replied with sadness, "I am, dear Queen, the blank page between the Old and the New Testament."

Hopefully, Sam and Peggy will learn to recognize and respect the uniqueness and difference of the Jewish and Christian outlook and not lead their children to inherit the blank page of the testaments. For all the commonality between Christianity and Judaism, the hyphen between the cross and the Star of David is no sign of identity.

32

Intermarriage and Modern Jewish Family Life in the United States: A Research Perspective

Egon Mayer

As of the closing years of the 1980s, there are about 5.7 million Jews in the United States living in approximately two-and-a-half million Jewish households. In a 1986 survey of America's adult Jewish population, fully 18 percent of the respondents indicated that their spouses were not raised as Jews, although only 14 percent indicated that their spouses were not Jewish at the time of the survey itself. The difference between the 18 percent and 14 percent figure suggests that about 4 percent out of the 18 percent had *become* Jewish—indicating a current conversion rate of about 4/18 or 22 percent.

What these very general figures mask is a trend that suggests that the incidence of intermarriage among Jews in America has grown greatly during the past thirty years. According to demographic studies that look at the mating patterns of different age cohorts of American Jews, it appears that in the 1950s only about seven Jews out of a hundred married someone who was not born Jewish. By the 1980s that trend had increased to about thirty-five out of one hundred: a five-fold increase. Current demographic studies of American Jewish communities around the country suggest that the trend continues unabated and, indeed, is likely to be fed by its own momentum (the children who are the products of the increasing numbers of intermarriages are themselves also more likely to intermarry).

Given the age-old Jewish resistance to and fear of intermarriage, these trends have triggered a deep sense of alarm both within

Jewish families and within the organized Jewish community—within the hearts and minds of Jews who are concerned about the Jewish character of the family life of America's Jews and about the demographic survival of the Jewish people.

It is this sense of alarm that impelled the American Jewish Committee in 1975 to initiate a series of research projects, aimed at exploring the effects of intermarriage upon the Jewish family and the Jewish community. The first of these studies, conducted between 1976 and 1979, involved an elaborate survey of nearly 450 intermarried couples, of whom about 25 percent were conversionary (i.e., the non-Jewish partner had converted to Judaism); the rest were mixed marriages. Published in 1979 under the title, *Intermarriage and the Jewish Future,* the salient findings of the study were:

- Though Jews in mixed marriages very rarely relinquish their Jewish identification in any overt sense, they also do very little in their practical everyday life to actively give expression to or affirmation of that identification. When they become parents, only a minority—about 20–25 percent—will take any substantial steps to provide their children with formal Jewish education or affiliation with the organized Jewish community.
- Conversionary families are not only far more actively Jewish than mixed marriages, but are also often more actively Jewish than families in which both spouses are Jewish by birth.
- The strongest factor determining the degree of Jewishness of intermarried families—both mixed and conversionary—appears to be the strength of the Jewish commitment of the born-Jewish spouse.
- The lack of Jewish identification, affiliation, and practice among the great majority of mixed married families is very rarely a result of negative pressure by the non-Jewish spouse. Most non-Jews who are married to Jews do not identify strongly enough with their own religion of ancestry to exert such negative pressure against Judaism.
- Only a minority of the mixed married families express a desire to raise their children in a specific religion—either Jewish or Christian. Most children are raised *without any* specific ethnic/religious upbringing. Parents proclaim that they would like to "expose them to both, and let the children make up their own minds, eventually."

- Intermarriage in either of its forms, mixed or conversionary, seems *not* to produce any appreciable long-term estrangement between the intermarrieds and their parents.
- The broad range of findings in this study tend to reinforce the fear that intermarriage represents a strong challenge, if not an outright threat, to Jewish continuity. Most non-Jewish spouses do not convert to Judaism; nor does the Jewish community encourage them to do so. The level of Jewish identification and involvement in mixed married families is very low—only a minority regard their children as exclusively Jewish, and most children from such families are exposed to very little in the way of any formal Jewish education or home socialization.
- Despite the strong challenges posed by intermarriage, the study also suggests steps the Jewish community might take to ameliorate the assimilatory threat.
- The findings concerning conversionary marriages merit particular attention, since conversionary marriages compare highly favorably not only with mixed marriages, but also with typical American Jewish marriages that are between two born Jews. In some respects, there is more reason for optimism about Jewish continuity in conversionary families than in families where both of the partners are Jewish by birth.

The 1979 study concluded on a cautionary note that, while the level of Jewish involvement in mixed married families is lower than in endogamous Jewish families, it is disturbingly low in the latter as well. Only a minority are affiliated with the organized institutions of the Jewish community, and only an even smaller minority participate in its religious, cultural, and ceremonial life. Substantial segments of American Jewry do little to give outward expression to their inner sense of Jewish identification. Therefore, their capacity for transmitting Jewish identification to their children may be attenuated from one generation to the next.

The questions concerning identity transmission from one generation to the next stimulated the American Jewish Committee to sponsor a follow-up to the study of intermarried couples. In 1981–1982 it underwrote a study of the adolescent and adult children of the couples who had participated in the first study. That second study was published by the American Jewish Committee in 1983, under the title, *Children of Intermarriage.* Its salient findings, which are summarized below, both reinforced and refined the observations of the first study:

- While the overwhelming majority of the children from conversionary families considered themselves Jewish, only a minority of the children from mixed marriages did so.
- Both the children of conversionary marriages and the children of mixed marriages attached a greater significance to their "religious" identity than to their sense of "ethnic" belonging.
- The only element of group belonging that a majority of both groups affirmed was a "sense of pride in the accomplishments of Israel."
- Children of conversionary marriages were far more likely to receive a formal Jewish education and a *bar* or *bat mitzvah*, to observe Jewish holidays, and to have more Jewish ceremonial objects in their homes than children from mixed married families.
- Although the children from conversionary families were much more like typical American Jewish children than like the children from mixed marriages—so far as formal Jewish education, observance, or affiliation were involved—their attitudes toward Jewish people, Jewish social responsibility, and interdependence were not much different from those of the children of mixed married families. Both groups of children were inclined to think of their Jewishness, or absence thereof, as a "private matter" that did not involve the larger Jewish community. In short, there were greater differences between the two groups in matters of personal conduct and Jewish affiliation than in matters of attitude relating to the Jewish community.
- On the social-psychological level, neither group of respondents indicated any significant anguish or confusion about their own identities as individuals. They reported feeling comfortable with themselves as well as in the company of their families and the Jewish community as they knew it.
- The children of conversionary families reported having closer, warmer relations with their parents, particularly with their mothers, than children from mixed married families. But, in truth, neither group reported any significant impairment of relations with parents. However, the relations with grandparents appear to be more distant and tenuous for the children of conversionary families.
- As a final indication of the long-term impact of intermarriage, the study found that the children of mixed married families who themselves were married, had married non-Jewish part-

ners almost exclusively—all without conversion. Of the children of conversionary families who had gotten married, most (60 percent) married born Jews—a rate that is comparable to their age peers who were born and raised in families with two born Jewish parents.

In addition to yielding further insights into the Jewishness of the children of intermarriages, the second study also underscored the significance of conversion in assuring Jewish continuity. Therefore, in 1985–1986 the American Jewish Committee undertook sponsorship of yet another study on intermarriage, this time focusing on the dynamics and impacts of conversion. The third study availed itself of a brand-new sample of 309 respondents, selected nationally, representing the broad cross-section of non-Jewish Americans married to born Jews. Two hundred of the respondents were non-Jews who *did not* convert to Judaism, while 109 were former non-Jews who had chosen to *become Jewish*—either prior to marrying their Jewish spouses or sometime thereafter. That study was published by the American Jewish Committee in 1987, under the title, *Conversion among the Intermarried: Choosing to Become Jewish.* Its principal findings were as follows:

- Converts were far more likely to be women than men, were more likely to be people who saw themselves as religious rather than nonreligious, and were generally likely to be somewhat better educated than nonconverts.
- Converts were far more likely to be married to born Jews who were raised by Jewish parents they perceived as being religious rather than nonreligious, in contrast to nonconverts, who were more likely to be married to born Jews whose parents they perceived as being nonreligious. The former were also more likely to be married to born Jews than the latter, whose parents were first or second generation in America.
- Converts were far more likely than nonconverts to have been encouraged to convert to Judaism by their spouse or some other member of their Jewish family.
- Most of the nonconverts never actually considered conversion to Judaism, rather than having considered it and decided against it. Most reported that they did not perceive their Jewish spouses as having an interest in their converting to Judaism.

- Among the approximately sixty nonconverts who had considered conversion as a possibility, just over a half were deterred by their own religious convictions or by the feelings they had for the religious convictions of their parents. The others felt that religion was simply not important enough in their own lives or in the lives of their Jewish spouses to go through with such a fundamentally religious act.
- Somewhat surprisingly, converts reported having experienced greater resistance to their marriages from their Jewish in-laws (prior to the marriage) than did the nonconverts. To be sure, the former also reported a much greater change for the better in their relations with their Jewish in-laws than the latter group.
- On the whole, there seemed to be no great difference among the converts in terms of their self-identification or feelings as Jews, regardless of whether they converted under the auspices of the Reform, Conservative, or Orthodox rabbinate. Both their training for conversion and their sense of being part of the Jewish community were virtually indistinguishable. What differences did exist were found in the area of ritual practices, on which the three major denominations vary significantly. In short, converts resembled the "model Jew" as portrayed by the respective denominations under which they were converted.
- On virtually all indicators of Jewish identification, conduct, affiliation, and attitudes, converts resembled typical born Jews who are *affiliated* with one of the three major branches of American Judaism. The nonconverts, on the other hand, were more similar to born Jews who are *unaffiliated* or unidentified with any of the branches of the organized Jewish community.
- Although most of the converts found it easy to fit into the Jewish community, they also felt that born Jews lacked sensitivity and understanding of the unique social and emotional circumstances of converts and their families.
- Relatively few of the converts or the nonconverts reported that they experienced any Jewish outreach efforts on the part of the Jewish community. Even fewer thought that such efforts would be desirable. Most felt that whatever outreach efforts might be undertaken would have to come through the Jewish family—particularly through their spouse.
- Whether a rabbi was willing to officiate at a couple's wedding ceremony with or without the prior conversion of the non-

Jewish partner does not appear to have played a significant role in either encouraging or discouraging conversion (or in encouraging or discouraging greater Jewish identification). Only about a third of the nonconverts who were married by a rabbi felt that rabbinic officiation brought them closer to Judaism.

• Converts reported that their preparation for conversion was weighted heavily toward the academic aspects of Judaism. They felt there was little emphasis on personal counseling or the exploration of feelings and family dynamics related to the experience. They also reported few, if any, opportunities to deal with the feelings and experiences that result from their conversion to Judaism.

Taking the many personal, familial, and social characteristics of the respondents into account, it appears that conversion is the outcome of a series of confluent forces that simultaneously "pull" the individual toward Judaism and away from the religious-ethnic traditions of one's family of origin. The probability that a non-Jewish partner in an intermarriage will convert to Judaism is greatly enhanced by the effort that her/his born Jewish partner exerts in communicating the desire for that outcome. Interestingly, conversion has also been found to strengthen family ties, which ultimately also strengthens the social fabric that makes Jewish continuity possible.

Taken together, the three pioneering studies of intermarried family life have chronicled and helped shape the Jewish community's response to the profound change taking place in the structure and functioning of the modern Jewish family within the climate of the open society in America. The rapid growth in the incidence of intermarriage among America's Jews has compelled the Jewish community to raise profound questions about its own future under conditions of unprecedented freedom and general well-being. To the extent that knowledge of social science can help shape personal feelings and communal policies, research has helped change the climate of the Jewish response to intermarriage from a feeling of outrage to a desire for outreach.

33

Advice from Some Children of Intermarriage

Paul and Rachel Cowan

Editor's note: Since the writing of the Cowans' contribution, which follows a background note, Paul Cowan succumbed to leukemia on September 26, 1988. His loss is deeply mourned.

BACKGROUND: THE FRUITS OF EXPERIENCE

The following introduction to an excerpt from the Cowans' *Mixed Blessings: Marriage Between Jews and Christians* was published as a review of the book in the *Baltimore Jewish Times*, September 18, 1987.

> *If Paul and Rachel Cowan's children were to announce that they planned to marry non-Jews, their parents' advice would reflect their own experience with intermarriage. "I'm not in a position to say, 'Don't marry a non-Jew,'" said Rachel, who converted to Judaism in 1980 after fifteen years of marriage. "But they know I think the non-Jew should convert and help you have a Jewish home."*
>
> *"You can't be coercive with your children," said Paul. "You can only be a good example."*
>
> *The Cowans' new book, Mixed Blessings: Marriage Between Jews and Christians, is a distillation of the lessons of their own marriage, several friends' interfaith marriages, 300 interviews around the country, and the thirty interfaith workshops they have led since 1981. They hope the book persuades mixed couples that the interfaith nature of their marriage "needs attention instead of sliding it under the rug. This is an issue that they can explore and grow from. Many people dismiss the issue when they get married.*

*We want them to realize it can be a time bomb unless it's
addressed."*

Cowan's parents were highly assimilated Jews. Recalling his
father's inner, yet unspoken struggle with their engagement,
Cowan said that if his father had tried to dissuade Rachel and him
from marrying because of a potential interfaith conflict, it "would
only have seemed hypocritical to him." Cowan's father, the
president of CBS TV, partly saw his professional success through
the prism of someone who had shed his Jewishness.

"I have," said Cowan, "only one wish: that he would have told
us why it was so important to him.

"Yet, he was extremely generous to Rachel and treated her
not as a daughter-in-law, but as a daughter. I saw through new
eyes. What I saw seemed to me to be 'Jewish.' "

Rachel descended from Pilgrims who came over on the May-
flower. Her parents, both religious skeptics, chose Unitarianism
because its highly rational theology omitted the concept of Jesus as
the son of God. But she had, according to Mixed Blessings, "a secret
longing for the stability and mystery that religious faith offers."
She is now in her fourth year of rabbinical training at the Hebrew
Union College in New York.

Several factors moved Rachel toward conversion, notably the
desire to be theologically informed and to raise her children as
Jews. Her turn toward Judaism was also intensified by the death
of Paul's parents in a fire in 1976. The tragedy and the subsequent
outpouring of support and concern from their Jewish friends also
helped Paul realize for the first time the importance of religion and
of a religious community in the midst of great grief.

"My parents had perished," he writes. "I would perish, too.
Judaism, an imperishable, embracing force, took on a new value
for us."

In 1981, the Cowans started conducting interfaith workshops
around the country. Generally, they said, participants from the
workshops fell into four equal groups: couples in which the gentile
member converts to Judaism; couples that break up; couples in
which no conversion occurs, but the two decide to raise their
children as Jews; and couples that "muddle along as they always
have."

The hallmark of a successful interfaith marriage, said Paul, is
"the ability to confront such issues as circumcision or the Jewish
and Christian holidays in December [Hanukkah and Christmas]
and springtime [Passover and Easter]."

Often, said Cowan, "asymmetry" may mark interfaith marriages. "Jews and Christians," he said, "may have different assumptions." A Christian, for example, may consider a Christmas tree to be a Druid symbol, but a Jew can view it as a very potent Christian symbol. A Christian may simply feel ignorant about the Hebrew used in a synagogue service, but a Jew can perceive a cross in a church as symbolizing centuries of anti-Semitism.

The Cowans acknowledged that their workshops may be painful for participants. "There are a lot of tensions," said Paul. "People have called me up on Wednesday and said they can't get through the week."

But the sessions can also be "fun," he said, recalling a quip from a gentile spouse during a discussion of Christmas: "All the Jewish people here seem so threatened by Christmas. It's as if trees are going to fall on their heads or Santa Claus is going to race over them in sleighs."

"Everyone cracked up," said Cowan.

"It's also comforting to find that others are dealing with the same issues," said Rachel. "Very few people can talk about these matters with their friends in interfaith marriages. It's even harder to talk with their parents."

The Cowans' agenda for their workshops is mixed. "It would be great if they would all become Jews," said Rachel. "But we see them as individual couples. Sometimes we are drawn to one member in a couple rather than the other. Sometimes we see how they block each other from a resolution. Sometimes the Christian member has a strong faith and the Jew doesn't have any and I ask myself, 'Why should the Christian give up such conviction?' "

And one mega-goal of the workshops, added Paul, is to help parents—and their children—enjoy "the sense of wonder and transcendence" religion can engender. Toward this end, both Cowans have "a lot of faith in Judaism as a religion. We are acutely aware that this is one of the first periods since the Diaspora that Judaism can compete with other religions. In this era of choice, Judaism can compete quite well."

The advice below is taken from Children of Intermarriage, the last chapter of the Cowans' book, Mixed Blessings.

THINK ABOUT YOUR CHILD'S JEWISH STATUS

This consideration is important for couples who decide to raise Jewish children. There are now two different working definitions of

who is a Jew. According to *halakhah* (Jewish law), a child of a
Jewish mother and gentile father is a Jew by birth, while the child of
a Jewish father and gentile mother must be converted in order to be
a Jew. The Orthodox and Conservative movements of Judaism
adhere to that law. By contrast, Reform and Reconstructionist Jews
assert that if either parent is a Jew, the child is a Jew if he or she is
raised as one.

The distinction, which is hotly debated among rabbis and
Jewish leaders, is very hard for many gentiles to understand. If the
gentile mother has any doubts about raising Jewish children in the
first place, the thought that they might have to be converted adds to
her fear of separation. Many couples, even those who have decided
they want their children to be Jewish, are not willing to grant Jewish
law authority over their lives.

On the other hand, children who have not been converted often
describe the pain and anger they feel when they are told they can't
celebrate a *bar* or *bat mitzvah* in a Conservative synagogue, or join
an Orthodox synagogue, or when the traditional Jew they love refuses
to date them or marry them unless they become legally Jewish. We
have met many people who have been angry at their parents for not
making them halakhically Jewish when they were young. They feel
they would have been spared a lot of turmoil.

THINK CAREFULLY ABOUT THE
NEIGHBORHOOD YOU'LL LIVE IN AND
THE SCHOOL YOU CHOOSE FOR YOUR
CHILDREN

If you want to raise your children as Jews, don't move into a
predominantly Catholic or Protestant neighborhood. If you want to
raise your children as Christians, don't move into a predominantly
Jewish community. If you want to raise them without any religious
affiliation, don't move into an area that is primarily populated by
religiously observant people. Otherwise, they will feel like outsiders
among their friends.

BE AWARE OF THE ATTITUDES OF
SIGNIFICANT RELATIVES

Often grandparents, aunts, and uncles may be prejudiced against
the person who has married their child or sibling, or may be troubled
about their religion. Sometimes they see the grandchildren as their

allies, and seek to communicate their biases, or to convert them to the religion that they believe is true. In the South we met many couples who were confused about how to handle relatives who were born-again Christians. They didn't want to prevent a child from seeing a grandparent. But how could they stop these fervent Christians from baptizing their youngsters in their eagerness to save them from going to hell? After long discussions in their workshops, several decided that they would invite their parents or siblings to come to their home to spend time with the children, but not let the children go off to visit them.

Some children of intermarriages recalled feeling wounded and jealous when they saw how obviously their Jewish grandparents favored their cousins who had two Jewish parents over them. The cousins would be invited for all the holidays, would get more presents, and would be hugged with much warmer embraces.

BE CAREFUL HOW YOU TEACH ABOUT THE HOLOCAUST

Many parents try to create a child's Jewish identity with stories about the Holocaust. No one is served if Judaism is presented as a religion of fear: a passport to the gas ovens.

Some intermarried Jewish parents tell their children that Hitler would have considered them Jewish and killed them along with all other Jews. The reminder is supposed to give them a sense of identity. Instead, it terrifies them. They are not given any other pathway into Jewish life. With no sense of a large, vibrant Jewish community, with no larger frame of reference, they imagine the Holocaust as the terrifying sum of Jewish history, as the sole content of Judaism.

DON'T SUPPRESS A PARENT'S PAST

If the parent whose faith isn't practiced suppresses his or her ethnic background, a child can spend much of a lifetime trying to unearth it. For children idolize their parents. They fantasize about them, trying to imagine their childhoods, seeking to reconstruct important personal facts or marital bargains that seem to have been hidden.

That happened to me. From my boyhood until the day my father died, I was always aware of the fact that he had once been a Cohen and was now a Cowan, and that he had a father with a past that I wasn't permitted to know about. He and I had an unusually close relationship. We talked on the telephone several times a week, and met for lunch or supper at least once every two weeks. During the last ten years of his life, he was either bedridden or in the hospital for months at a stretch, and I visited him frequently. We always discussed political developments or trends in the arts, books he was reading, or stories I was writing. But, even though he knew how curious I was about his father, he would never describe him or discuss the Jewish aspect of his childhood.

I didn't try to provoke him to talk. I respected the fact that the mere mention of Jake Cohen's name caused him a great deal of pain. But within weeks of my father's death I set out to discover his hidden past. As I learned about it, I began to alter my picture of the Judaism my parents had transmitted to me. But I wasn't forced to choose one parent's faith or ethnicity over another's, as I might have been if my mother was a gentile and my father had concealed his history in order to placate her.

MAKE RELIGION A LIFE-STYLE, NOT A LABEL

If a religion is no more than a family label, it is not likely to mean much to children. If it seems to signal that one partner has won a marital struggle, that the other's identity has been ripped at the seams, it may provoke turmoil.

It is prudent for parents to work out ways of embodying the religion of one without hiding the other's past. Those who choose to weave Judaism into their lives display tact and foresight if they visit the Christian in-laws at crucial moments of their religious and secular year. Most of all, it is important for the couple, as a unit, to remember that they are their children's primary role models. If they embody a grudging sense that one is acquiescing to the other, they convey a negative, hostile message to their children. If they display loving sensitivity to each other's spiritual sensibilities, they convey a positive, optimistic one.

Lisa Cowan is our daughter. In 1986, she entered college. When we asked if we could interview her for the book, she laughed and said, "I don't really think of myself as the child of people with two religious backgrounds."

But then she recalled that she did have one worry when she was younger—that Rachel's parents would feel rejected. She described the episode that assuaged that fear.

"Remember when we were visiting Maggie [Rachel's mother]

one Easter when it was also Passover? We brought along enough *matzohs* for all of us, but it was before we had completely given up eating bread during Passover. Maggie brought out a plate of warm hot cross buns for breakfast. Mom picked one up. She said, 'This is my heritage!' I remember the pride on her face when she said it. I'm not sure whether she ate the bun, but I was glad to see her show pride in her past. I didn't like the feeling that she had turned her back on her family."

"Does my conversion ever trouble you?" Rachel asked.

"No! Judaism seems so normal to me that I don't quite understand people who belong to another religion. But then I think, what if Matt became a Buddhist? What if he stopped doing all the things we've been doing since we were little? No matter how much he explained it—or it helped him grow—I'd still think it was strange. So I was glad when Mom did something to show her parents that she was still proud of them and what they gave her."

When Lisa was in high school, she seldom came to synagogue with us except on the High Holy Days. But lighting candles on Friday night was special. That was a religious experience for her.

"Well, maybe not religious exactly. I don't know if I believe in God. But it was the purest form of family time I've ever known. It had a quality of . . . wholeness, which is the same kind of feeling I get when I'm in direct communication with nature or feel in communication with myself."

Then she laughed a little self-consciously. "I hate to put these things into words. It sounds so totally corny. But when I feel it, I know it."

The sense of family tradition was important to her. "This year, when I stayed at school during Yom Kippur, I went to services. It's not that I like being in synagogue that much. But I feel like I'm linked to my family."

Although she is an agnostic, she made it clear that the religion her parents chose gives her a sense of place and of internal order.

"I was a little disappointed when we stopped celebrating Christmas. Who wouldn't be? I loved all the excitement. But now I think it would be wrong to have a Christmas tree. I don't mean morally wrong. It would just feel wrong. It's the same thing during Passover. I don't eat *hametz* [leavened foods]. It's a tradition I care about. It wouldn't feel right to eat bread. It would be like eating pork."

Toward the end of the interview, we told her that a great many children of intermarried couples resent their parents' thoughtlessness or indecisiveness. If she could give us retroactive advice about her religious upbringing, what would she say?

She began to laugh. "I don't know. I can't think of anything. You're both such different people, but you share the same values. Even though you had different religions when I was born, I don't feel like the child of an intermarriage. Judaism is a part of me."

CODA

Most intermarried parents who choose to make religion a way of life and not a label begin by doing so for their children. But in fact they are untying a knot at the core of their marriage. For even if the child ultimately rejects their way of life—as some will—the husband and wife have resolved their own dilemma.

They have transformed the problem of an intermarriage into the opportunity to fashion a faith they can share for a lifetime.

Jewish

Marital Status

- ☐ Single
- ☐ Not quite married
- ☐ Married
- ☐ Single again
    - ☐ Widowed
    - ☐ Abandoned
    - ☐ Divorced
- ☐ Remarried
- ☐ Intermarried
- ☑ Gay or Lesbian
- ☐ Childless

34

Jewish and Gay

Janet Marder

Last year, on the night of his high school graduation, Robert Rosenkrantz shot schoolmate Steve Redman ten times with an Uzi semi-automatic rifle. What turns a white middle-class teenager into a murderer? In Robert's case, it was a blend of fear, rage, and desperate loneliness. Steve Redman and Robert's brother, Joey, had spied on Robert in an attempt to prove he was gay. When they caught him in a homosexual encounter, they told his parents what they had discovered. Robert testified at his trial that he had hidden his homosexuality for years for fear that he would be rejected by his family and friends. "I was not able to say 'I'm gay' until I was in custody," he admitted.

At Calabasas High School in Woodland Hills, California, where Redman and the Rosenkrantz brothers were students, hostility toward homosexuals is pervasive. "This is strictly a straight school," said sophomore Wendy Bell, 16. "If there are gay people at this school, nobody knows about it. If people found out, they would verbally torture you." Assistant Principal Robert Donahue agrees. "I think a kid who is gay is probably in the worst position of any minority." Donahue is worried that Robert Rosenkrantz's violent behavior may reinforce students' hostility toward homosexuals. "To have a young gay man go out and do what he did just confirms their attitudes that homosexuals are crazy as hell," he said.

I have been trying to imagine what it must have been like for Robert Rosenkrantz to grow up gay. I know that when I was in high school, the most painful way to insult a boy was to call him a queer or a fag—this despite the fact that few of us actually knew any lesbians or gay men. Fifteen years ago homosexuals were far less visible than they are today. Throughout my years in high school, college, and rabbinical school, I knew only generalizations and stereotypes. Most of my information came from newspapers, popular magazines, and the conversations of those around me. Thus I learned that gay people were perverted, sinful, and pathetic misfits. They dressed oddly. They molested children. They were promiscuous and hedonistic, caring only for their own pleasure; they had rejected marriage, children, and family life. They lived wretched, lonely lives, most of which they spent hanging out in bars and bathhouses, engaging in unspeakably sordid acts. Gay men were "swishy," effeminate wimps; lesbians were angry, unattractive, man-hating "dykes."

GO FOR IT

That was my education about homosexuals. Why, then, did I find myself in April of 1983 applying to be the first ordained rabbi of Beth Chayim Chadashim (BCC), a Los Angeles synagogue for gay and lesbian Jews? First, I believed that any Jewish congregation was entitled to responsible rabbinic leadership. Moreover, BCC had the support and recognition of the Reform movement. In 1973, the Union of American Hebrew Congregations (UAHC) made history by becoming the first (and only) national religious body to accept a gay/lesbian congregation. But most important was the advice of my husband, Shelly, also a rabbi. He had had professional contact with a group of BCC members who conduct monthly *Shabbat* services at a local nursing home. Shelly told me that the BCC volunteers led a service that was warmer and more spirited than any he had ever seen in a nursing home. There was clearly something special about these men and women who took such pleasure in giving. Being the rabbi of such a group, Shelly thought, would be exceptionally rewarding. "Go for it," he urged.

And so, eight months pregnant, I went to meet with the rabbinic search committee of BCC—but not without considerable anxiety. How, I wondered, could I teach Judaism honestly to a group I believed was Jewishly illicit? Leviticus 18:22 states that a man who lies with another man as with a woman has committed an abomination. Leviticus 20:13 adds that men performing such acts "shall be put to death—their blood-guilt is upon them." How could I ask gay men to love a Torah that condemns them to death? Moreover, Judaism emphasizes marriage and family as the primary means of transmitting our heritage. Could I still affirm those values while ministering to a congregation whose very existence seemed to subvert them? Finally, I was filled with doubts about my ability to counsel men and women who lived, I thought, so differently from me and everyone I knew. How would I ever understand their problems and help them? In fact, I was rather embarrassed by the concept of public displays of homosexuality; the thought of two men embracing or dancing together made me quite uneasy. Worse yet, I fully expected to hear details about my congregants' lives that would make me feel morally queasy. In other words, I wanted them to be honest with me, but I was afraid of what they might say.

Today, after three years of many trials and many more errors, I hardly recognize myself. My beliefs have changed slowly, but in profound ways that affect my entire outlook on life. My thinking has shifted most significantly in three areas: the nature of homosexuality, the role of *halakhah* in liberal Judaism, and the place of lesbian and gay Jews in our community.

SCIENTIFIC STUDIES INCONCLUSIVE

As soon as I was hired by BCC, I set out to learn whatever I could about homosexuality by reading the works of psychologists, psychiatrists, sociologists, and physicians. I also read the accounts of "insiders," such as Howard Brown's *Familiar Faces, Hidden Lives: The Story of Homosexual Men in America Today* and Evelyn Torton Beck's *Nice Jewish Girls: A Lesbian Anthology.* Even these limited forays into the subject of homosexuality showed me that scientific studies were far from conclusive. Some regarded homosexuality as physiologically based, others traced it to environmental factors; some viewed it as "curable," others as predetermined and immutable.

I began to see that the main division in studies of homosexuality is between those who classify it as undesirable, deviant behavior, regardless of origin, and those who accept it as natural, legitimate behavior in no way inferior to heterosexuality. I continued to read and learn, but I gradually found myself less interested in what the experts said, paying more attention to my own observations of the several hundred lesbians and gay men I came to know over the next few years.

The more I came to know my congregants, the less I regarded

their way of life as unethical, unhealthy, and undesirable. I realized that my initial discomfort with public displays of homosexuality arose, not from anything inherently bizarre or unnatural in that behavior, but simply from my unfamiliarity with it. One who is different provokes suspicion and, sometimes, hostility—be it a teen-ager with a pink, punk-style haircut or a traditional Jew clad in *shtreiml,* beard, and *peyot.* Once I started examining my own prejudices more carefully, I began to see nothing unnatural about my congregants' behavior; rather, I saw differences to which I quickly became accustomed. Soon I was no longer struck by the oddity of two men holding hands or dancing together; I saw, instead, their very natural need for affection and companionship.

Similarly, as I came to know my congregants as individuals, I could no longer tolerate generalizations about homosexuality as pathology or sin. Certainly I met some gay people whose lives were wretchedly unhappy. But most of the misery in their lives seemed to be the result of family rejection, social bigotry, or internalized self-hatred—not of any misery endemic to homosexuality itself. Other gay people I met acted in ways that struck me as sick or immoral. But this is no less true of the straight people I meet, and few would condemn heterosexuality as immoral—despite the high inci-dence of rape, incest, child abuse, adultery, family violence, promis-cuity, and venereal disease among heterosexuals. The sad, the sick, and the sinful are a minority in the gay community, as they are in the straight. My congregants are men and women as healthy, loving, and morally responsible as any I have known in my life.

My attitude toward homosexuality, then, has moved from tol-erance to full acceptance. I see it now as a sexual orientation offering the same opportunities for love, fulfillment, spiritual growth, and ethical action as heterosexuality. I still do not know what causes homosexuality, but I must confess that at this point I do not much care any more than I care what causes some people to have a special aptitude for music, others for baseball. I simply accept with pleasure the diversity of our species.

ROLE OF *HALAKHAH*

My changing perceptions of homosexuality forced me to confront the role that *halakhah* plays in my life as a rabbi and liberal Jew. I began an intensive study of what our tradition has to say about homosex-uality. Aside from the prohibitions in Leviticus, biblical references to homosexuality are few, and their exact meaning is not always clear, I learned.

The story of the destruction of Sodom in Genesis 19 is thought by many to reflect an abhorrence of homosexuality; in my view, it is not a comment on homosexuality per se, but a denunciation of inhospitable behavior to the stranger, as manifested in an act of attempted gang rape. (So also for the similar narrative in Judges 19.) Interestingly, Ezekiel 16:49 calls the sin of Sodom arrogance and callousness toward the poor; there is no reference to homosexual acts. The Bible (Deuteronomy 23:18) refers to a *kadesh*, or male cult prostitute, but it is not clear whether the *kadesh* engaged in homosexual or heterosexual prostitution. Another possible biblical reference to homosexuality is David's lament over the dead Jonathan: "I grieve for you, my brother Jonathan; you were most dear to me. Your love was wonderful to me, surpassing the love of women" (II Samuel 1:26). Some theologians believe this verse indicates that a sexual relationship existed between the two friends. If this is so, it would be the Bible's only favorable presentation of homosexual relations.

Nowhere in the Bible is lesbianism prohibited, or even mentioned. This may be because women are not bound by the commandment to procreate (and thus their offense is less serious), because no act of sexual penetration or "waste of semen" occurs, or because the male authors of the Bible were simply unaware of lesbianism.

Post-biblical references to homosexuality are relatively few and uniformly negative. In the *Midrash*, for example, homosexuality is called the cause of solar eclipses (*Sukkah* 29a) and the destruction of the Temple (*Tosefta Sotah* 6:9, quoted in L. Ginzberg, *Legends of the Jews*). Another midrashic passage states that Ham's sin, for which his descendants were condemned to slavery (Genesis 9:20–27), was homosexual relations with his father, Noah (*Sanhedrin* 70a). In the *Midrash* we find lesbianism prohibited. The prohibition is derived indirectly from Leviticus 18:3: "You shall not copy the practices of the land of Egypt where you dwelt, or of the land of Canaan to which I am taking you. . . ." This, according to a *midrash*, refers specifically to sexual practices: "The Egyptians used to marry a man to a man and a woman to a woman" (*Leviticus Rabbah* 23:9).

A RARE ABERRATION

The halakhic, or legal, portions of the Talmud treat homosexuality as a rare aberration. In the *Mishnah*, for instance, Rabbi Judah rules that two unmarried men may not sleep together under the same cover (*Kiddushin* 4:14), but the sages overrule him and permit it, since "Jews are not suspected of homosexuality" (*Kiddushin* 82a).

This attitude is also reflected in medieval legal materials. The greatest medieval philosopher, Moses Maimonides (1135–1204), wrote: "A Jew is not suspected of homosexuality. Therefore, a Jewish man is allowed to be alone with another Jewish man. But if one takes care not to be alone with a male . . . it is praiseworthy. An adult who commits sodomy, either passively or actively, is to be stoned" (*Hilkhot Issurei Biah* 22:2, 1:14). Rabbi Joseph Caro (1488–1575), author of the definitive legal code for traditional Jewry, was even more stringent: "In our century, when there are many lewd men around, one should refrain from being alone with another male" (*Shulhan Arukh, Even ha-Ezer* 24). A century later, however, Rabbi Joel Sirkes suspended that prohibition because "in our lands [i.e., Poland] such lewdness is unheard of" (*Bayit Hadash* to *Tur, Even ha-Ezer* 24). Homosexuality itself is not explicitly prohibited, because its author believed that such behavior was virtually nonexistent among Jews.

"SPILLING THE SEED"

Why is homosexuality rejected by our tradition? First, it is an act of "spilling the seed" in which procreation is impossible. And procreation is not merely a desirable Jewish goal, but a *Mitzvah,* a binding commandment (Genesis 1:28). As the *Midrash* says: "One who does not fulfill the commandment of procreation is like one who sheds blood and diminishes the Divine Image." Second, homosexual behavior seems to violate the natural order of being as presented in Genesis, in which woman is created to fulfill and complete man: "God said, 'It is not good for men to be alone; I will make a fitting helper for him.' Hence a man leaves his father and mother and clings to his wife, so that they become one flesh" (Genesis 2:18, 24). Third, in biblical and rabbinic sources homosexuality is associated with idolatrous pagan practices, which Jews are expected to shun. In the ancient world, as we have seen in the Sodom story of Genesis 19, homosexual rape was also a way of humiliating and degrading a vulnerable male.

Liberal Jews may analyze these reasons to determine how valid they are for us today. For traditional Jews, however, the reasons for the ban on homosexuality are not ultimately important. What matters is that the Bible forbids it and calls it "an abhorrent thing"; hence no traditional Jew can regard homosexual acts, even between consenting adults, as acceptable Jewish behavior. Writes Great Britain's Chief Rabbi Immanuel Jakobovits: ". . . Jewish law holds that no hedonistic ethic, even if called 'love,' can justify the morality of homosexuality, any more than it can legitimize adultery or incest, however genuinely such acts may be performed out of love and by mutual consent." Rabbi Norman Lamm, a contemporary Orthodox authority, states: "Compassion should be stressed for the man or woman trapped in this dreadful disease . . . the homosexual who genuinely desires to emerge from his situation ought to be helped by all the means at our disposal, whether of medicine or psychotherapy or counseling. But the compassion and help extended by society should in no way diminish the judgment that *mishkav zakhar* (male homosexuality) is repugnant. . . ."

Liberal rabbinic opinions on homosexuality vary considerably. Solomon Freehof, a prominent Reform rabbi and legal authority, calls homosexuality "a grave sin." He argues that liberal Jews are not permitted to discard the biblical prohibition of homosexuality, since it is not merely a legal enactment but reveals "a deep-rooted ethical attitude."

Hershel J. Matt, a Conservative rabbi, disagrees. He points out that the biblical prohibition of homosexuality is apparently based on the assumption that homosexuality is a free and conscious choice. The homosexual is thus one who willfully rebels against God and the Jewish people. Since, however, recent scientific evidence indicates that "homosexuality is deep seated and not something that one chooses to be or not to be," Matt suggests that it would be more appropriate to regard the homosexual as one who acts from *oness* (pronounced *oh-ness*), out of constraint and lack of freedom. Since a frequently invoked principle in Jewish law is that "in cases of *oness* the Merciful One exempts" (*Nedarim* 27a), Matt believes homosexuals should not be judged as sinners and must be treated with compassion, kindness, and friendship. He cautions, however, against regarding homosexuality simply as a valid alternative life style, for heterosexuality is clearly "the God-intended norm" and homosexuality "a sexual deviance, malfunctioning, or abnormality—usually unavoidable and often irremediable."

My study of Jewish views of homosexuality led me to a disturbing conclusion. While some rabbis urged tolerance and compassion for homosexuals, none regarded homosexuality as a fully acceptable Jewish way of life. And so I had to decide: how much did it matter to me that the voice of my tradition ran counter to the evidence of my experience and the deepest promptings of my conscience?

For me the choice was clear. I could not be guided by laws that seemed profoundly unjust and immoral. I believe, and I teach my congregants, that Jewish law condemns their way of life. But I teach also that I cannot accept that law as authoritative. It belongs to me, it is part of my history, but it has no binding claim on me. In my view, the Jewish condemnation of homosexuality is the work of human beings—limited, imperfect, fearful of what is different and, above all, concerned with ensuring tribal survival. In short, I think our ancestors were wrong about a number of things, and homosexuality is one of them.

I am also a fallible human being, and it may be that my judgments will one day be proven wrong. But for now, I have no choice but to decide for myself which parts of our tradition I hold sacred. In fact, the Jewish values and principles that I regard as eternal, transcendent, and divinely ordained do *not* condemn homosexuality. The Judaism I cherish and affirm teaches love of humanity, respect for the spark of divinity in every person, and the human right to live with dignity. The God I worship endorses loving, responsible, and committed human relationships regardless of the sex of the persons involved. There is no Jewish *legal* basis for this belief; my personal faith simply tells me that the duty to love my neighbor as myself is a compelling *mitzvah*, while the duty to kill homosexuals for committing "abominations" most certainly is not.

LIFE-AND-DEATH ISSUES

These are not academic matters; they are life-and-death issues faced by real human beings. Synagogues across the country are filled with Jews in hiding—gay men and lesbians who live in perpetual fear of the sidelong glance, the whispers, giggles, and sneers that mean someone has discovered their secret. These Jews in hiding are in the pews at *Shabbat* services, on the *bimah* preaching sermons and chanting the liturgy, in the classrooms of religious schools, and behind the principal's desk. They sing in the choir, serve on the temple board, carpool their kids to youth group meetings. In other words, wherever Reform Jews gather to pray, study, and socialize, you'll find gay men and lesbians among them.

My three years with BCC have left me at times bewildered and frustrated. I have tried to understand why liberal Jews who say they are devoted to justice and equality balk at granting justice and equality to gay and lesbian Jews. I have tried to understand why they cling so tenaciously to denigrating stereotypes about the homosexual lifestyle and its alleged threats to the purity of Jewish life. I don't understand why homophobia is the last socially acceptable form of bigotry in our country—even among Jews, who should know better. I don't know why Robert Rosenkrantz and a thousand other kids like him should have to grow up feeling desperately alone and scared to death to be themselves.

But above and beyond my moments of frustration, I feel deeply blessed to have spent the last three years of my life working with my congregation. Apart from the intrinsic joys of working with an active, questing, and spirited group, I feel grateful for the education I've been given—a chance to see with my own eyes, to make up my own mind, rather than simply swallow the judgments and slogans of others. I'm grateful also that my daughters are spending the crucial years of their early childhood in the presence of hundreds of loving gay "uncles" and lesbian "aunts." They, thank God, will grow up without the ugly myths and stereotypes that afflicted me. Perhaps that is the greatest gift I have received from my congregants.

35

A Taste of Heaven

Liz Galst

We are part of a dying art, a dying tradition: Jewish grandmothers and their granddaughters making gefilte *fish together in celebration of Passover, the season of our liberation.*

It was about this time last year that I came out to my grandmother.

You see, it was Passover. And every year at this time I uproot myself from my comfortable lesbian household in Somerville, Massachusetts, drive four hours to New York, and make *gefilte* fish with my grandmother. The traveling, of course, is a real *shlep*. But to cook with my grandmother is to taste heaven.

So there I was, with my grandmother, chopping the fish. I don't know if you know how to make *gefilte* fish, but basically what you do is put a couple of different kinds of raw fish in a wooden chopping bowl with a few ground-up carrots and onions, a little salt and pepper, *matzoh* meal, some water, and an egg. Then you chop it with a metal chopper. You chop it a lot. Then it gets kind of gelatinous, so you throw in a little more water and start chopping again. You keep doing this: chop for a while, toss in some water, and then continue chopping. Eventually, you shape this stuff into ovals and cook it for two-and-a-half hours in a pot full of fish stock and carrots.

Like I said, I was chopping the fish. My grandmother was peeling carrots with a big knife. She looked down at her hands, so I knew it was time for "The Usual Boyfriend Question," and it is this:

"Do you have a boyfriend?" It's a straightforward enough kind of a question and my grandmother likes to ask it at least three times a year. Being basically a coward at heart, I respond thrice yearly with my "Usual Boyfriend Response." "No, but I have friends who are men." For some reason, I think this will satisfy her. And God forbid my grandmother should think I'm a manhater! Sometimes, when I want to spice up my answer a little bit, I remind her that in my life, I have had a boyfriend. I neglect to mention that this was in February 1981. You see, I want my grandmother to think of me as "single." I want her to think I am currently unattached but could be swept at any moment into the world of the soon-to-be-married. I want her to know that her dreams of our shopping trip to Fortunoffs will not be shattered, that we will stroll down the aisle purchasing the kosher glass dishes with which I will begin my adult life.

Back to the fish. I am still chopping the fish. This may sound dull to you, but I love to chop the fish. It has taken me a long time to arrive at this prestigious position. As a child I was relegated to the world of carrots. I would peel them and cut them into stubby sections. My grandmother, in her special Passover housecoat, would chop the fish and gossip with my mother about friends, and about relatives whose children had become drug addicts or traveled halfway around the world to find the meaning of life. Even at a young age I sensed their sadness at broken bonds and loved ones lost to other worlds.

Now, at age 25, I am proud to still make *gefilte* fish with my grandmother. Every year I brag to my friends about it. Many Jewish women my age are unschooled in *gefilte* fish preparation (to say nothing of stuffed cabbage, borscht, *rugelakh, kreplakh,* and *tsimmes!*). Some are too busy, or not interested. Others have forgone this time-honored art out of ethical consideration for the rights of fish. My grandmother also brags to her friends and to her co-workers at the travel agency. As girls and young women before the advent of refrigeration, they shared bathtubs with whitefish and pike on their way to the slaughter. Now, many can't be bothered. "You can buy it just as good in a jar," they say. "*Rokeach* is very nice." So my grandmother and I brag. But implicit in our bragging is our knowledge that we are part of a dying art, a dying tradition: Jewish grandmothers and their granddaughters making *gefilte* fish together in celebration of Passover, the season of our liberation.

I am chopping the fish. By this point I have given "The Usual Boyfriend Answer." I am not talking. Neither is my grandmother. Chatter is an important ingredient in our production of *gefilte* fish, and it is missing. While I chop I am thinking of my grandmother and how she loved me, boisterously, in my quiet, lonely childhood home. Her hands worked my small, awkward fingers around her knitting needles as I sat with her in my grandparents' La-Z-Boy recliner. One special time, she drove me to the corner of Blake Avenue and Alabama in East New York and told me the stories of her life as a young woman and her work in the family's chicken stall there. I think back to my life in Somerville and all that I have kept from her out of fear. I am thinking of broken bonds and lost worlds. I think it's time I tell my grandmother the truth.

I swallow (swallowing can be an important part of any coming out declaration) and say, "What would you say if I said that I had a girlfriend?" To this my grandmother replies, "Do you think there's enough salt in the fish?"

DO YOU THINK THERE'S ENOUGH SALT IN THE FISH!?!!!
For this I have agonized over coming out for five years!!?!!

I wonder if my grandmother is going deaf. My grandfather, 81 years old, may he live and be well, is losing his hearing, but my grandmother? My grandmother goes on a lot of cruises for travel agents. She's a free spirit. She sits in a lounge chair on the deck of some Italian ocean liner and meets people. They converse, compare stories. All this goes on above tremendous engine noise and the crashing of waves against the hull. She hears. She's just not dealing with this.

Listen, it's not every day your oldest granddaughter tells you she's queer. I give her a few minutes. Eventually my grandmother says, "*Do* you have a girlfriend?" I tell her I don't but that I do have them occasionally. She asks me a few questions about AIDS. She asks me about having children. She is skeptical, but still she seems satisfied with my explanation of the current trend toward artificial insemination in the lesbian community. A little later I ask if she's upset that I am gay. She says, "No, but I think it's interesting that the first thing I said was, 'Is there enough salt in the fish?' "

I'm glad I came out to my grandmother. I was lucky. She did not disown me, condemn me, and best of all, she did not die of a heart attack, a method successfully employed by some people's relatives to register disapproval. She said, "You're my granddaughter and I don't love you any less. I'm 71 years old, I've learned to accept a lot of things in my lifetime. This too, I will accept." Afterward we went out to eat and my grandmother told me things I never knew: about her belief in reincarnation and her marriage at an early age. We giggled a lot.

We have been able to move on, my grandmother and I. She seems satisfied knowing she may yet see her first great-grandchild.

When and if I have the child, it will be named for my great-grandmother Sarah, the *gefilte* fish *maven*. Since I came out to my grandmother, we have become bolder with each other. "Okay, this gay movement, all right," she said to me at Yom Kippur. "But do you still have to dress like that?" You see, coming out can be a positive experience.

This year again I will *shlep* to New York and together my grandmother and I will make *gefilte* fish. I will chop, she will make sure I put in just the right amount of water; we will revel in each other's presence. Then we will bake *pesahdik* spongecake from thirteen eggs, a little seltzer, and a shredded orange, and celebrate the other miracles of Passover.

36

Interview with Rabbi David Feldman: Homosexuality

Leora Tanenbaum

Tanenbaum: Why does *halakhah* forbid homosexuality?

Feldman:[1] *Halakhah* forbids homosexuality because the Torah does. As with so many other things, the Torah prohibits or enjoins, and we then seek reasons. But as Maimonides wisely said, our acceptance of the Torah's dictates should not depend upon either our success at finding a reason or on the particular reason we do find.

Tanenbaum: When they do look for reasons in *halakhah,* one reason many cite is that it will lead to the destruction of the family. Given that intermarriage, divorce, and childlessness pose just as much of a threat to the Jewish community, why are homosexuals treated more harshly than intermarried Jews, divorced Jews, and Jewish women who postpone or forego parenthood?

Feldman: None of them should be treated harshly, that's to begin with. Then, people are not even sure what their motives are for relating harshly to anyone. Intermarriage threatens the future of the Jewish people. Homosexuals, in that they do not procreate, also threaten the Jewish family, by definition. But it all depends on how passionately or seriously one feels about those threats. One's reac-

---

[1] Dr. David Feldman is rabbi of the Jewish Center of Teaneck, New Jersey. He is the author of *Marital Relations, Birth Control, and Abortion in Jewish Law* and *Health and Medicine in the Jewish Tradition.*

tion is subconscious before he allows his conscious mind to bring better understanding and tolerance.

Tanenbaum: Do you feel that homosexuals are treated more harshly than women who choose to remain childless?

Feldman: Again you are dealing with psychology. Why do people feel threatened or uncomfortable? People feel threatened or uncomfortable in the presence of something that is alien to them or—exactly the opposite—that is close to them, so they fear they might be brought over the brink to practice likewise. A person who is not married may be in that status by choice or otherwise. So someone else in similar status may not feel threatened. They feel they can still make their own decisions. Homosexuality goes deeper. I may fear the influence; I may not be able to resist; I may be able to resist and be unhappy about it. It has to do with the wellsprings of unarticulated feelings.

Tanenbaum: Do you think there is more of a stigma attached to homosexuals than to other violators of Jewish law—for instance, those who don't keep *kashrut* or *Shabbat?* If it is all just a matter of *halakhah,* as you said, how come there isn't as much of a stigma attached to them?

Feldman: I think my answer to the previous question applies here too. It depends on the person who is doing the stigmatizing, what he or she feels threatened by. Sometimes a person seeing another in violation of *kashrut* may in fact be envious of the other's freedom, and even insecure against being tempted to do likewise. So much has to do with the stigmatizer rather than with any rational distinctions, acts, or practices.

Tanenbaum: Let's say a homosexual comes to you for guidance. He or she obeys all the *mitzvot* except the one that forbids homosexuality. This person would like to be an active contributor to the Jewish community, yet is inhibited by the community—as you said, the community that stigmatizes. What would your response be?

Feldman: My response would be the same as to any other Jew who comes in good will. All of us fall short of what we'd like to do and all of us are victims of our own shortcomings. And yet, as the *Mishnah* said, "He who does little, he who does more—they are both the same, as long as their intentions are toward Heaven." When the intent is good, everyone is to be praised for the intent. But, if I may, the burden of your questions presupposes that the onus is on those who receive or relate to homosexuals. That's one question, and all of us need to improve in how we understand, tolerate, and respect. But the issue here is not how we treat a person who lapses from one or another of the moral, ethical, or religious requirements of Judaism; the issue is whether you acknowledge a lapse, or you're trying to call homosexuality a valid alternative. That's the issue. A person who violates *kashrut* or *Shabbat* is not claiming these violations are permissible. If he or she accepts them as violations, then we tolerate the lapse. But if the claim is that they are not lapses, but equally valid, and only that the rest of us haven't reached that higher level of understanding, that's where we differ.

Tanenbaum: So you are making a distinction between those who openly flaunt their homosexuality and say this is an acceptable lifestyle as opposed to those who feel ashamed.

Feldman: No, no. Not openly flaunt . . . but claim it's permissible. It doesn't matter whether homosexuality is openly flaunted or covertly practiced. It's rather an intellectual, ideological point of view. Is homosexuality permissible and am I wrong in saying that it's not? Or is it not permissible, but that's the way he is, and accept him as a total person? I can accept the total person without denying the Torah's stand that the act is not permissible.

Tanenbaum: What about a homosexual who doesn't feel that it is permissible and therefore performs *teshuvah?*

Feldman: You mean he is no longer a homosexual?

Tanenbaum: What I meant to ask was, what about somebody who continually performs *teshuvah,* just as anyone who continually sins and asks forgiveness?

Feldman: There's no *teshuvah* unless there is a change in practice. Remember the *Mishnah,* "*Ehtah ve'ashuv*" (I will sin and repent). There is no *teshuvah* that is temporary or conditional or partial. *Teshuvah* means that you return from that way, saying it was wrong. Not that it was wrong then, and it might be right tomorrow. That's a contradiction in terms. There is a responsum that makes this and the above point much clearer. It involves a case in 1912 in which Rabbi A. I. Kook, then Chief Rabbi of Jaffa, was asked whether a *shohet* (ritual slaughterer), who was said to be homosexual, could continue as a *shohet.* Rav Kook begins with the halakhic assumption that one who violates the Torah in one way cannot be relied upon not to violate it in connection with, say, *kashrut.* But Rav Kook asks: Perhaps he's done *teshuvah?* If he's done *teshuvah*, then we accept him totally. The Talmud says that nothing stands in the way of *teshuvah*. But *teshuvah*, of course, is not temporary or conditional.

Tanenbaum: What about one who feels that he or she acts out of compulsion, *oness*?

Feldman: If the person is acting out of compulsion, then all is forgiven. In this sense, no one is responsible for acts done out of real compulsion.

Tanenbaum: Does one have to perform *teshuvah* in that case?

Feldman: It's asking forgiveness for that deed; it's not *teshuvah* in the sense of changing. We change to the degree that it is in our power to do so. Compulsion means that acting or not acting, changing or not changing, is not in your hands; it's not up to you. This is the very crux of the issue. If homosexuality is the result of compulsion, then it's not an alternate, freely chosen lifestyle; and if it's not by compulsion but is indeed a lifestyle or act of free choice, then *halakhah* calls it an immoral choice.

Tanenbaum: What are the laws regarding lesbianism?

Feldman: They differ from those regarding male homosexuality because of the absence of anal intercourse and improper emission of seed. These are two crucial factors in male homosexuality not applicable to lesbianism because of the anatomical nature of things. The only thing forbidden by the Torah, in such uncompromising terms, is male homosexual sodomy. Nothing else is so forbidden by the Torah. Male homosexual caressing, holding hands . . . none of that is forbidden. Still, the Rabbinic tradition regards lesbianism as improper, immoral, idolatrous, etc.

Tanenbaum: When David learned that Jonathan had died, he cried, *"Nifl'atah ahavat'khah li me'ahavat nashim"*—"Your love was wonderful to me, surpassing the love of women" (II Samuel 1:26). Could this be interpreted to be a favorable presentation of homosexuality?

Feldman: There is no evidence one way or the other. The verse is often cited this way, but there is no basis for reading homosexuality into it rather than mere affection. It's unlikely that the biblical narrative would be silent about an act that it condemns. The distinction between this and affection should not be blurred. There is nothing wrong with affection between two men.

Tanenbaum: With that in mind, would you counsel a homosexual to act only with affection and not on sexual impulse?

Feldman: Yes. People who are constitutionally homosexual should be counseled to indulge in affection—or rather, to be celibate. Rather than compare the homosexual deed with *Shabbat, kashrut,* or with other violations of the Torah, it is more helpful to compare it with other forbidden sexual relationships. Then he is no different from a heterosexual who has an adulterous desire—even one who is compulsive or overcome by passion. An adulterous desire is also forbidden to be acted upon. Just as heterosexuals must overcome their illicit desires, so must homosexuals from this point of view.

Tanenbaum: What is your stance toward gay synagogues?

Feldman: My problem is with condonation. The Talmud states in one particular passage that the Romans are to be praised because, even where they believed in homosexuality, they didn't solemnize the relationship; they had the good grace not to mock conventional marriage. Here, too, a gay synagogue would seem to be a public condonation of the gay lifestyle as an equally acceptable alternative.

Tanenbaum: Rabbi Norman Lamm, who regards homosexuality as a disease, has said that since capital punishment is not possible, flogging is cruel, and imprisonment counterproductive, the only method left for dealing with homosexuals is to publicly and strongly disapprove. He also advises counseling toward rehabilitation. Do you feel that his solution is an effective one?

Feldman: I guess he is strongly articulating the point just made, namely that we cannot condone the act. "Love the sinner, hate the sin" is the approach. We don't mean to condemn or even to withhold condonation from the sinner; we want to accept him or her as fully and as heartily as anyone else. And yet we are left with the burden of making the distinction between condoning the sin, in violation of the Torah that teaches otherwise, and between accepting the person, in love and understanding.

Jewish

∧ **Marital Status**

- ☐ Single
- ☐ Not quite married
- ☐ Married
- ☐ Single again
    - ☐ Widowed
    - ☐ Abandoned
    - ☐ Divorced
- ☐ Remarried
- ☐ Intermarried
- ☐ Gay or Lesbian
- ☑ Childless

37

Saying No to Motherhood

Vicki Lindner

I don't remember when I first realized I didn't have an instinctive drive to give birth to a baby. When I was a child, I played with dolls, but I saw myself not as their mother but as their creative prime mover. If someone had asked me if I expected to marry and have children, I would have said yes, because that was what all girls raised in the fifties did when they grew up. I saw no adult women in my New Jersey suburb who were doing otherwise.

When I was 28, I became pregnant while living and working in Japan. In Japan at that time, birth control pills, which I'd run out of while traveling through Asia, were illegal, and the easiest form of contraception to obtain was a cheap abortion. The father and I were in love. Months later, when our transcultural romance came to its confusing close, he looked at me with bewildered eyes and asked, "Why didn't you want to have the baby?" I'd had the nausea, lethargy, and inexplicable terror in my gut extracted like an aching tooth; I'd never thought of *it* as a child.

As I edged into my 30s, and friends began to marry and have children, no biological clock ticked inside me. Either I hadn't grown up yet or I hadn't grown up to be like other women. About the time the proverbial clock should have been sounding a shrill alarm—age 36—my younger brother married a woman who didn't opt for motherhood either. So certain was she that she wouldn't change her mind that my sister-in-law had her tubes tied before she was 30. The responsibility to carry on the Lindner genes fell to me, and I didn't want it. I *wanted* to want it; I wanted to be a normal female, part of a world of close, fertile families, joyfully reproducing themselves. Instead I was a writer living alone, creating not living beings but characters in books and short stories. On my good days, I thought of myself as a Brave New Woman in a Brave New World, paving the way for others who wished to be different. On my bad days, I felt like a neuter alien from a science fiction novel.

I'm not sure I ever chose not to have children. That is, I never sat down, counted up the minutes left on my biological clock, and said, "Do I or don't I?" Instead, I feel that my childlessness evolved from a series of life choices, which resulted in a lifestyle and personal temperament that are incompatible with motherhood. I'm not married. I live in a tiny, rent-controlled apartment in Manhattan, and I support my fiction by working as a freelance writer; my income is modest and often unpredictable. I need silence to work (actually, it would be more honest to say I love silence). I'm one of the rare people who like being alone, and I love travel and freedom, too. I want to learn instead of teach, and I am as hungry for new experience as any child; in that sense, I want to remain one. What would I be doing if I had a child? Who would I be? I must ignore the Jewish conscience that serves as an unending reminder: that the Jews are the only people on earth who are fewer in number today than they were before World War II . . . that the Jewish fertility rate is at an all-time low . . . that a loss of Jewry becomes a void in creativity in society at large. I must ignore it because if I didn't, I would be somebody different, somebody more satisfied, or less satisfied, but I would not be the person I define as myself.

Sometimes I like to get off the hook by believing that childlessness chose me. My mother's pregnancies, one of which I witnessed, were nightmares of nausea and anemia. Her mother, my maternal grandmother, died at 44 of a heart attack in the ninth month of a troubled pregnancy. When I was very young, my mother told me the story of how she had watched her mother die, gasping on the floor, and how she had run barefoot through the snow to phone the drunken rural doctor. Yet, it wasn't until I was 35 and searching for convincing reasons to explain my childlessness that I became aware of how these long-known facts (with buried significance) had made me fear pregnancy. For me, the maternal condition conjured specters of sickness and death.

As I write my reasons for choosing childlessness, I imagine my readers, who have bravely overcome their own reluctance and fears to produce lovable namesakes, saying, "What nonsense!" I imagine their faces, bemused, even angry, as they mutter, "Selfish! Neurotic!

Doesn't want to grow up! Doesn't know what she's missing. Will die alone and lonely, buried in the sheaves of a dried-up manuscript!" The truth is that I don't know whether it is the voice of my readers I hear or a voice inside myself, not yet reconciled to my unusual decision. Is it the Jewish part of me that feels guilty, the Jewish part of me that believes I had no right to make such a choice?

Recently, I held a baby at a dinner party. I was in awe. This miraculous infant of my species, so helpless, so pliable, seemed made to fit into my body's curves, to merge with them. Too young to know the difference between her mother and other women, she reached for my breast. I handed her back quickly, saying, "I don't want to get my hormones in an uproar!" The guests all laughed, but it wasn't really a joke. Having made my choice, I am afraid that what the world has told me might be true and that a force springing from my female biology, over which I have no control, might still rise up and punish me with regrets.

WHY IT'S SO DIFFICULT TO CHOOSE
CHILDLESSNESS

Traditional Jewish law and modern demographics dictate that a "good" Jew must bear children. Having one or two isn't enough anymore; because of the low Jewish fertility rate, rabbis are clamoring for at least three children per family. Not only does the childless choice flout centuries of tradition and social expectations, but also it is a relatively new option. (Birth control was not legally available until the 1930s, and abortion was legalized nationwide only in 1973.) Even though the law and medical technology have made it possible for women not to have children, society still persuades and pressures us to believe that motherhood is a duty, a virtue, and a delight—our natural calling. "To be fruitful and multiply" is, after all, the first commandment in the Bible. Few women dared to consider childlessness, or support this option, until the 1970s, when concern about the world's burgeoning population gave some a legitimate excuse to speak out. Author Betty Rollin was one. She wrote a controversial article for *Look* magazine titled, "Motherhood: Who Needs It?" Readers were outraged. "In 1970," Rollin says, "to support childlessness was equivalent to supporting communism. I wasn't antimotherhood, but I suggested that life could be good without having children. My article got more hate mail than any article *Look* had published, except for one about Hitler. People called me a monster!"

Rollin believes that it is easier to make the childless decision now than it was then. "Though pressures to have children are still very great, and there is a lot of guilt attached to not being a mother, it is not totally freakish to choose childlessness in the eighties," she says. Rollin, whose recent book, *Last Wish,* describes her terminally ill mother's suicide, believes strongly in choice—"in diversity, differences, and tolerance. Motherhood is a perfectly good choice, and nonmotherhood is a good choice too. There's no reason why we can't have both." In fact, the Zero Population Growth (ZPG) movement is popular with many young Jews, who equate new births with pollution and ecological damage. It is a paradox that they do so because they consider themselves universalists; they continue, as I do, to place the concerns of society at large before those of their own community.

WHY WOMEN CHOOSE CHILDLESSNESS

According to Jean Veevers, a Canadian sociologist who has studied childless couples, most couples who choose childlessness believe they are opting for a pleasant lifestyle over an unpleasant one. They see childraising versus a freewheeling lifestyle as an either/or choice. *Either* they can have the freedom and money to seek experience, travel, and change or quit jobs, *or* they can commit themselves to supporting a stable family. Some, who enjoy deep intimacy with their mates, fear a child's presence would sabotage it. Others think they would sacrifice important career goals for children. As Susan Brownmiller writes in *Femininity,* "Motherhood and ambition have been seen as opposing forces for thousands of years." Since studies show that most fathers shoulder little of the burden of child care, and day-care facilities are expensive and inadequate, a woman who loves her career, or who needs to earn money, might reject the time-consuming responsibilities of raising children. She may look at an exhausted "supermom" friend, struggling to work and raise a child, and say, "I don't want to take this on myself." In short, women who have decided to say *no* to motherhood do not believe kids are compatible with self-fulfillment or necessary for happiness.

According to experts, however, the childless choice is often made unconsciously, before we are old enough to form adult lifestyles and beliefs. Some choose childlessness because early childhood experiences or perceptions have made them see parenthood as unrewarding or threatening. Some view pregnancy and birth as repulsive, frightening, or, as I do, dangerous. "They do not see their bodies as being sturdy and resilient," says Lois Kennedy, a New York City psychotherapist. "They do not believe they will survive physical changes."

Others reject parenting because they feel their parents were less happy or prosperous when they had large families and devoted their lives to their offspring. Modern women may feel that their own mothers would have enjoyed richer lives if their interests and talents hadn't been submerged by domestic duties. According to Kennedy, mothers who do not see their own womanhood in a positive light, or who resent their maternal roles, communicate a negative sense of what it meant to be a woman to their daughters. These daughters often identify with their fathers and reject traditional female activities—including having children.

On the positive side, the childless may have known "Auntie Mames" who lived intriguing lives without children. They grew up more able to see themselves as nonmothers than did women without inspirational role models.

MAKING THE DECISION

The social push to have children is strong, and there are no support groups to help the childless. (The one that existed, the National Alliance for Optional Parenthood, is now defunct.) As a result, the woman who chooses childlessness chooses alone and may feel defensive, ambivalent, and confused, as friends and relatives pressure her to make a pro-baby decision. For Jews, there is the nagging feeling that one is betraying her people. Instead of regarding her choice as positive or inevitable, she is tempted to blame it on others or on herself. Some defend their own lifestyles by downgrading mothers. "Isn't it better to be doing what I'm doing," they ask, "than scraping Gerber's off the walls?" Others blame children themselves for their lack of desire to have them: kids are noisy, irritating, and expensive. Who would want one? Some say their mates would be terrible fathers. Most of the childless women I interviewed say their own negative qualities—impatience or bad tempers—would make them unfit mothers. Others ask, "Who would want to raise a child in such an unpredictable and dangerous world?" Sometimes the childless offer *all* of the above reasons.

Given the difficulties, how does a woman manage the traumatic decision-making process? Let's look at some women who made the childless choice.

PRACTICAL AND EMOTIONAL RESEARCH

Merry Bruns, a commercial model and graduate student in anthropology, presented me with the reading list and pile of books that helped her choose childlessness. "I think people should talk more openly and honestly about this issue," she says. "Most of my friends are either dying to have children or are ambivalent. I feel like I belong to a secret club."

Merry grew up "not thinking about having children." When she was 20, the "big decision" seemed "twenty-five years away. When I turned 30, my friends started having babies left and right," she says. "At my wedding, people asked not *if* we were going to have them, but *when* we were. 'I have to think about this,' I said to myself, and I researched my decision like I would a term paper." After reading extensively, Merry wrote down the reasons why she wanted a child in blue and why she didn't in black; the black column was much longer. Tops on the black list was, "I like to have complete freedom and control of my life."

Though Merry sees her decision as practical, she researched it emotionally, too. Because she is wholesome and blond, with bright blue eyes, she is often cast as a mother, holding an infant, on modeling assignments. "I would say to myself, 'On a scale of one to five, how do you feel about this baby?' " When her nephew was born, she enjoyed a special relationship with the little boy: "I'd look at Alec and ask, 'Does loving him make me want to have children?' and I'd honestly have to answer *no*. But I tried to stay in touch with new feelings."

FIGHTING URGES

Some women choose childlessness in spite of yearnings to have children. Betty Tompkins, 41, an artist who has let her clock tick with no regrets, ignored "biological urges" because they conflicted with her desire to paint. "When these urges visited, they were very strong," she says, "and I didn't want them. I'd look glowingly at some crying child in the supermarket. I'd have to wait until those feelings went away, because they never had anything to do with what was happening in my life."

Betty, like Merry, viewed her choice as a practical one that had to be weighed against other plans and obligations that, for her, came first. Like most women who choose nonmotherhood, she leads a busy, satisfying, creative life with specific goals. "It would have been naive to think I could be a full-time exhibiting painter, earn money somehow, and be a full-time mother, too," she points out. "I would have needed another day in every day to do what I'm doing and have a baby."

POSTPONING THE CHOICE

Sociologist Veevers found that many women who don't want children postpone the decision indefinitely. They evade pressures by pretending to others—and sometimes to themselves—that they may one day become pregnant. One 36-year-old woman played this complex game. "Let's say my decision is *no* until I change my mind," she says. "I think I will never make a decision *not* to have a child, until biology catches up with me."

Some women eventually realize that continued ambivalence implies a negative decision. A California woman says her husband helped her make her childless choice. "He thought having a child might be a romantic idea," she says. "I was curious. What would it be like to have a child with this man? How would it turn out? On my thirty-ninth birthday I said to him, 'I still can't decide. I'm still thinking about it,' and he said, 'Then the answer is *no.*' "

COPING WITH FEARS AND PRESSURES

The greatest fear for women who are childless by choice is that they'll regret their decision in later years. One childless woman's therapist reduced her anxiety by asking if regretful feelings had ever made her want to jump off buildings in the past. "At that point I realized regret was not a lethal emotion," she says. "Fear of regret was not a positive reason to have a child."

Most women who don't want children marry men who don't want them either. But some fear that their mates will change their minds. "I'm afraid that ten years from now he'll divorce me and have a child with a younger woman," says one woman. "Whenever we see a baby, I test the waters. I ask, 'Isn't he adorable? Don't you want to have a baby, too?' He always reassures me by saying firmly, 'No, I don't.' "

Those who pressure the childless to have children prey on such fears. These pressures prevent many women from making the childless decision or from feeling comfortable about it. The Jewish community in particular is adamant about the need to procreate. One who is childless by choice is certain to be given articles on the

"demographic problem" that are ubiquitous in the Jewish periodicals. Most of the women I interviewed confessed to feelings of guilt or
shame. Many said they felt selfish or had been told they were.
Though some labeled negative emotions as "society's trips," others
found it hard to distinguish between their own feelings and the
feelings of those who were disappointed or angry. "Almost everybody else in the world rejects your choice," says Kennedy. "That's
pretty hard to come up against and say, 'I know I'm right.' "

Why do others feel they have an obligation to convince the
childless to change their minds? According to Kennedy, those who
resort to pressure tactics may have an axe to grind. "Parents see the
childless decision as a rejection of their lifestyles and major life
accomplishment," she says. "People who love you, and who are
happy with their own babies, want you to discover this happiness,
too. They have trouble acknowledging differences and think you
can't possibly know what you're missing." Kennedy believes that no
one in our culture can raise children without ambivalence and
stress. "It's a very hard job," she says. "Parents get little help from
society. Those who experience difficulty raising children need to be
validated. They feel that you may hold them in contempt, having
made a choice that is more rebellious or creative. They will ask you
to explain, but no answer you give will satisfy them, because they
are really looking for validation."

38

Some Jews among Us—
Akarah

Sherry H. Blumberg

I sit in the synagogue. The time that I have dreaded is about to arrive. I am prepared; I have done all the crying beforehand. There can be few tears left. This is the third year—surely by now I can hear the words and sit still without tears. Now—*"peru urevu umilu et ha'aretz."* God's command to be fruitful and multiply has been given again to our people.

I am an *akarah*—a barren woman. After three years of the latest modern tests and drugs, of artificial inseminations (using my husband's sperm), of long hours in doctors' offices, of humiliating tests and frustrated hopes, and of moments of despair, I am still a barren woman. My husband is healthy; the problem is mine. We have used much of our savings, all of our patience. We have a serious operation to go through that gives us a slight chance but may cause a serious risk to my health. I no longer believe in miracles for me (even though modern medicine has worked wonders). I don't see myself as a Sarah or a Hannah who can be granted conception. I would surely offer whatever I could so that my husband could use his healthy sperm to create a child, but I've less and less hope that I will be able to conceive or carry that child.

So I sit in the sanctuary as I hear the words of God's command and I feel my emptiness. As my menstrual period comes each month, I mourn what could have been. There are no rites or ceremonies for that feeling time. Only the words *Barukh Dayan Emet* (Blessed be the Judge of Truth)—the traditional blessing for evil tidings.

Soon my husband and I will give up the infertility doctors and begin the next frustrating process of adoption. There are few babies, hardly any Jewish babies, and we are too old to go through the normal channels. We will join the many others who look for children with lawyers, doctors, rabbis, and friends. We may have to go to another country. We will spend what we need to spend. We will love any child that comes into our home as our own. I hope that the time will be soon.

WHAT DO OUR SACRED TEXTS SAY TO ME?

The hardest thing for me is confronting the tradition. There is a stigma about the *akarah*—barrenness is seen as a punishment. It sounds to me that the Barren Woman is one who has sinned or with whom God is displeased. My traditional mind asks, "What did I do?" If my reading of the *peshat* is correct, then I am being punished. I become angry at God; I scream, cry, and find little solace in prayer. I find that there are many times when I cannot call God a *Dayan Emet.* People who do not want children and who abuse children have them so easily; my husband and I, who would love and cherish a child, cannot.

And my husband—why is he being punished with me? He could, by Jewish law, seek a divorce. Although in the *Mishnah* (*Yevamot* 6:6) it says that it is the man who is commanded to reproduce and not the woman, he was furious with me when I suggested that he seek another wife. Neither of us really wants that solution. We love each other and have a good marriage. So why, I ask, is he being punished?

My rational mind says that my feelings are foolish, based on irrational ideas; the traditional materials and rabbis could not have been so unfeeling. But my feelings are my feelings. I feel the pain of emptiness, the despair of wanting to carry out the *mitzvah* and not being able.

If these feelings are not enough, there are those who say that any couple who does not have at least three children is guilty of adding to the decline of the Jewish population (ergo responsible for the demise of the Jews). When I hear that statement, I freeze. I respond with anger; what I feel is pain. Again, intellectually I know that it is not so, but I feel the numbness in my heart.

WHEN THE SAVING ACT WON'T OCCUR

There have been articles like this before, usually written by those who have had a positive result after their long frustration. I am joyful and jealous when I read those articles. For me there may be no positive result. I, and others like me, will have to confront our barrenness—even if we adopt children. Each time the story of Sarah (Genesis 11:30), Rachel (Genesis 29:31), Samson's mother (Judges 13:2), or Hannah (I Samuel 1–2) is read, I must face my own feelings of being barren, having prayed with all my heart and soul and might. In Isaiah 64:1, the charge is to "Sing O Barren One, That you did not bear, Rejoice and cry aloud . . . for more are the children of the desolate than the children of the married wife." It is very difficult to take any comfort from these words, even if they are appropriate for this time when there are so many problems for our children. It is no easier to read the book of Job (24:21) and discover that the Barren One is devoured by those who rebel against God and the light. I cry out in sorrow and in anger—I have not rebelled.

The hardest moments come, however, as I read in Deuteronomy 7:12–15: *And it shall come to pass, because ye hearken to these ordinances, and keep, and do them, that the Lord thy God shall keep with thee the covenant and the mercy which He swore to thy fathers . . . there shall not be male or female barren among you.*

Does this mean that through me God will not fulfill the covenant? How does this affect my belief in a loving and caring God? How can I try so hard to keep my part of the covenant when I cannot share in that promise? Why can't I become like the "barren woman to dwell in her house as a joyful mother of children" (Psalm 113:9)?

FAITHFULNESS WITHOUT ANSWERS

There are no rational answers to these questions; they need none. My faith and belief in the God of Israel will remain strong despite my barrenness. There are too many other miracles of living. I have found ways to serve the Jewish community and insure the perpetuation of Jewish life, even if I will always be childless. Yet . . .

So why write this article? I have tried to alert Jewish care givers, rabbis, and communal workers to be sensitive to the things they say to women and men about the requirement to *bear* children (change your words to *raise* children). I have tried to sensitize the reader to this growing problem in the Jewish community. I encourage you to hear honestly the pain and frustration of those involved in the process of infertility testing—the pain is emotional and very often financial (insurance often doesn't cover experimental procedures). Finally, I have tried to help the reader to understand that those congregants or Jews who are experiencing infertility problems may face a crisis of faith when they try to fit into the Jewish community—I still cry when the biblical portions are read.

In our tradition we praise God for both the joyous times and the painful ones. I, too, must learn to say *Barukh Dayan Emet* over and over again as these painful moments occur. If my sharing of this part of my life may help one person who feels the same way or help give the reader the insight to help another, then I can say the blessing with some thankfulness as well as pain.

39

Jewish Population Growth

Editorial from Reconstructionist

Much concern has been expressed recently in the Jewish community about the continuing low fertility rate among American Jews. It
stands at 1.5–1.7 percent, well below replacement levels. Due to low
fertility alone, Jewish population is diminished by 3.4 percent per
decade.

In response to this phenomenon, several conferences have been
held in the last year, including the National Conference on Jewish
Population Growth, which was sponsored by the American Jewish
Committee. Many of the recommendations of that Conference can be
supported with pleasure. Even if they were all implemented, however, they would be far from solving the problem. Before we offer our
own views, it is useful to summarize the Conference's proposals.

The overriding premise of the Conference was that the Jewish
community should recognize negative population growth as a serious crisis threatening Jewish survival, and that it should thus
devote substantial resources to alleviating or reversing the trend.
Specifically, it suggested three fronts on which we can be effective.

First, it called upon the Jewish community to become an active
lobbying force on the national scene in support of societal values that
are more conducive to childraising. For example, we ought to lobby
corporations to institute flex time (so that both parents in two-career
households can share in childraising), paternity leaves, and day care
centers for employees' children. In short, at a time when so-called
family values are being exalted in many quarters, the Jewish

community should ask for support of families with two working parents who share housekeeping and childraising responsibilities.

Second, the institutions of the Jewish community itself must come to the aid of parents, alleviating their financial and social burdens. Synagogues and day schools should offer substantial discounts to families with more than two children. Subsidized Jewish day care should be a communal priority. Community agencies should offer and publicize adoption services for childless couples and should devote their energies to creative matchmaking programs for Jewish singles. Rabbinic and communal exhortations to be fruitful ring especially hollow unless we are ready to assist parents after their children are born.

Third, the Conference stressed the need to change the attitudes and values of Jews of childbearing age—to cultivate the value and emphasize the satisfactions of childraising as opposed to a life devoted exclusively to self-fulfillment; to support both full-time mothers and mothers with careers who share parenting responsibilities.

While all of these suggestions are worthwhile and many, if implemented, are likely to be of assistance to those who decide to raise children, it is not at all clear that parents make their decisions about childbearing primarily on the basis of the available communal services. In addition, one can only wonder if the real crisis is statistical—in the numerical decline of the Jewish population.

If the crisis were statistical, we probably would do better to devote our resources to programs that reach out to intermarried couples and their children. They constitute a growing population pool, and most studies suggest that Jews by choice bring energy and commitment to the community, as well as numbers.

Moreover, given the percentage of American Jews who have minimal Jewish commitments, it is not clear why we should be concerned about increasing the number of Jews by birth who are not also Jewishly committed. Even if we wanted to do so, there is no evidence that we are capable of doing so. Given the low rate of affiliation and the low rate of response to the initiatives of Jewish leadership, whom can we expect to reach with our views on childbearing, and should we really expect that people will respond as we wish? Is it not the case that the real crisis of American Jewry consists of our failure to attract and hold the commitments of adult Jews? If so, our resources should be devoted to programs that increase their Jewish involvement so that, as their commitment increases in general, their values concerning childraising will also become more Jewish.

Finally, we believe that attention should be focused primarily on the question: Why have Jewish people stopped having children? Presumably, it is partly because of the economic standards we have achieved and to which we aspire. It costs more to raise children today, especially when one considers our increased standards of aspiration. For some of us, it is the cost of a separate room for each child; for others, the cost of summer camp or private college tuition; for all, the high cost of taking the family out to dinner. Are we prepared to say that it is more important to raise three or four children than it is to live as affluently as one's parents? Are we ready to risk antagonizing wealthy donors by exalting those less affluent whose largest asset is the family van? Can we imagine a UJA dinner in honor of the family with the largest number of Jewishly committed children? Even synagogues tend to choose honorees on the basis of donated wealth or time devoted *away* from one's family. What does this say about our commitment to family members? Unless we are willing to work to establish a Jewish community that offers as much esteem to full-time parents (mothers *or* fathers) as to successful professionals, we have no reason to expect that our exhortations about fertility will be credible.

If these questions are difficult to answer, it is because we are not ready to abandon the lifestyle to which we have become accustomed in America. We accept the prevailing societal values of affluence, career success, and self-actualization, all of which bear negatively upon decisions to bear children. Better child care, for example, is desirable because it is of value to working parents; it should not be expected to alter the fertility rate. For that, we need a change in our philosophies of life.

It rather seems that our energies and resources would be better spent on reviving and retaining the commitments of Jews. Let us train and finance field workers to organize new *havurot*, outreach programs that provide an orientation to Jewish living for young couples, programs offering free rabbinic consultations, heavily subsidized retreats for young singles and families in which they can experience the spirit of *Shabbat* in a liberal setting.

Perhaps it is the high cost of such programs and the way in which they threaten the turf of existing Jewish institutions that incline us to deal with less fundamental problems. If so, let us not mistake symptoms for causes. It is Jewish life itself that requires an infusion of creativity and resources. Only if the commitments of Jews are cultivated do we have reason to expect that traditional Jewish values of family life will achieve renewed popularity.

40

A Guide for the Jewish Adoptive Parent

Dan Shevitz

Our two children, Joshua Simon Luis and Noah Hernan, were born in Bogota, Colombia. Joshua was adopted at age 5 weeks, Noah at 10 weeks. We found each other through the Florence Crittendon League, a private, nonsectarian adoption agency in Lowell, Massachusetts.

The process of making our family whole was not easy. Like many adoptive parents, my wife Susan and I went through invasive, humiliating medical testing and trials, devastating realizations ("The waiting list is six years long, and it will take at least a year just to get on it"), cretinish counselors ("Wouldn't you rather travel instead?"), dead ends, disappointments, failed attempts, endless bureaucracy, moral uncertainty, self-doubt, and, of course, interminable waiting.

We worried whether our children would be accepted if they were dark skinned (they are so beautiful it's embarrassing), if they would feel completely at home in the Jewish community (who does?), whether our families would be supportive (they spoil our kids rotten). We had little encouragement from Jewish institutions and, surprisingly, found very little literature that spoke to our needs. The best help we received came from friends (actually friends of friends of friends), usually over coffee and cake, who had traveled the road before us. In this spirit I offer our road signs to those who will travel it again.

As every adoptive parent knows, the joys of welcoming a new

member of the family, of caring and nurturing, of giving and sharing love, rank among the greatest of joys. Whether the impetus for adoption be the inability to have biological offspring, or the desire to give a home to a needy child, the result is the same: the deep realization that the family has been blessed. A Jewish family will naturally turn to the tradition in search of an expression of its feelings of joy and thanksgiving and to make the child's rite of passage into a new family.

It might come as a surprise to learn that adoption, as a legal institution, does not exist in Jewish tradition, at least not in the same way that it is understood in civil law. But the lack of a formal, traditional adoption ceremony does not indicate an indifference to the need to express the emotions attendant upon the adoption experience. Nor does the Jewish tradition lack material; Jewish history, law, tradition, and practice are filled with examples of caring for and nurturing of children who do not share a biological relationship with their families. However, as in so many other areas, the Jewish approach differs from that of the ambient culture. While it is clear that the sources examined here will not necessarily address all the concerns of the adoptive family, it is hoped that they can be useful in creating a Jewish context for the adoption process.

ADOPTION IN THE JEWISH TRADITION

Adoption as a legal institution was rare in biblical and rabbinic literature. The Bible contains several incidents of foster care that, though not the equivalent of adoption, are noteworthy. Most famous of these cases is that of Moses, who was raised by Pharaoh's daughter. Later rabbinic sources praise this pagan woman for her piety and note that Moses' name was given to him by his foster mother; his Hebrew name, presumably given to him at birth, is not remembered. Ruth's son Oved was nursed, and perhaps raised, by her mother-in-law Naomi. The biblical verse says: "And Naomi took the child, and laid him in her bosom, and became a nurse to him. And the neighbors named him, saying 'a son has been born to Naomi.' " In this case, though the biological mother is still alive and presumably involved in childrearing, the grandmother has assumed some legal, fiduciary relationship to the child. Esther, orphaned at an early age, is raised by her cousin Mordecai. Though no formal adoption is indicated, Mordecai displays more than avuncular concern for her well-being and education. We may also note that similar foster-relationships, characterized either by rights of inheritance or by a fiduciary bond, exist between grandparent and grandchild, master and servant, and employer and employee.[1]

Rabbinic law describes no formal adoption procedure. Rather, the Rabbinic court provided for the care of needy children by the appointment of a legal guardian, an *apotropos,* who was responsible for the child's economic and educational welfare. An *apotropos* was appointed for orphaned children, for an *asufi* (foundling—a child with no known parents), and occasionally when biological parents were incapable of providing adequate care. It was considered meritorious to take into one's house children in need of care and to raise them along with one's own family.[2]

There are crucial differences between the Jewish and civil institutions of adoption. While Jewish law recognizes the possibility of creating a facsimile of parental and filial obligations that could approximate those in a biological relationship, the natural bond between parent and child cannot be legally severed. Though a child might be physically removed from the biological parents, some legal relationship to them was preserved.

Nevertheless, adoptive parents may create, with a vow, something very much like a series of parental obligations.[3] Even if the parents made no vow, rabbinic courts viewed the existence of a de facto parent–child relationship as sufficient evidence that an unexpressed vow had been taken. These assumed obligations were legally enforceable, not retractable, and even incumbent upon the adoptive parents' heirs. The child so adopted assumed filial duties to the new parents by virtue of the accepted principle that it is appropriate to acknowledge and reciprocate the gifts we receive. According to the Rabbis, even the rights of inheritance can be created artificially. Though by biblical law an adopted child does not inherit from

----

[1]See Exodus 2:10; Ruth 4:16–17; Esther 2:7,15; Genesis 48:5–6, 50:23, 15:2–3, 16:2, 30:3,29–31; I Chronicles 2:35–41. For Rabbinic examples, see *Sanhedrin* 19b, *Megillah* 13a, *Esther Rabbah* 2:17.

[2]For a thorough treatment of the halakhic intricacies of adoption, see Gershon Felder, *Nahalat Zevi,* vol. 1 (New York, 1972). See also *Shulhan Arukh, Even ha-Ezer* 114, HM 60, 207; Ben Zion Uziel, *Piske Uziel,* #64; Moshe Feinstein, *Iggrot Moshe, Yoreh De'ah* 161. Characteristic of the authority given the court is this statement found in *Teshuvot ha-Rashba ha-meyuhasot laRamban,* #38: "The court must always adhere scrupulously to what, in each circumstance, is most advantageous to the orphan, for the court is the father to all orphans, and must pursue their benefit."

[3]Arthur Jay Silverstein, "Adoption in Jewish Law," *Connecticut Bar Journal,* 1974, 48:73–82, and references there.

adoptive parents, the father may indicate in his will that his adoptive children shall receive full and equal shares of his estate. Some authorities go further and state that if the father has publicly assumed parental obligations, he is deemed to have agreed to entitling his adoptive children, even should he die without a will.[4]

INFERTILITY AND ADOPTION

While historically the function of adoption was to provide a home or insure the status of needy children, today many additional motives exist. The desire of childless couples to raise and nurture a child are often intense. Since searching for "adoptable" children is often the first recourse of infertile couples, we should consider, briefly, some Jewish issues associated with infertility.

The charge to "be fruitful and multiply" (Genesis 1:28) was the first commandment given to the first man and woman in the Garden of Eden. Fertility was a sure sign of divine blessing. Infertility was a bitter curse for Sarah and Abraham, Rachel and Hannah. Pseudore-medies for this affliction were at a high premium. Infertility had legal ramifications also: it was grounds for divorce, and sometimes an impediment to marriage. Though according to the accepted view one son and one daughter were sufficient to satisfy the requirements of the commandment, Jews were nonetheless enjoined not to desist from reproduction as long as they were physically able.[5]

Notwithstanding all of this, it would be a mistake to speak in terms of a "right" to children. Though throughout the ancient world parents exercised enormous authority over children, Jewish law denied parents absolute power over their progeny. Rabbinic law spells out in detail the obligations incumbent upon parents toward their children, and the limitations of their authority; the Jewish courts even reserved the right to remove children from their homes if it was deemed to be in their best interests.

Furthermore, in a curious wrinkle of rabbinic legislation, the commandment to have children is not incumbent upon women. Though a man must search for a wife willing to bear children, no woman is likewise obliged to accept the responsibility to do so. These limitations upon parenthood must be stressed, particularly because

---

[4]See Gerald Bildstein, *Honor thy Father and Mother: Filial Responsibility in Jewish Law and Ethics* (New York: Ktav, 1975).

[5]D. Feldman, *Marital Relations, Birth Control, and Abortion in Jewish Law* (New York: New York University Press, 1968).

of the widespread opinion that every couple is entitled to children, regardless of whether they are suited to this sensitive role or not. Adoption agencies, too, are often more concerned with pleasing clients by trying to meet rigid specifications of age, sex, color, size and health than with placing children who are in urgent need of care.

ADOPTION MARKETS AND OTHER OPTIONS

There exist, in many countries, both black markets and gray markets for procuring healthy white infants. The term black market in adoption refers to practices that include high-pressure tactics designed to induce biological mothers to surrender their children, kidnapping and trafficking in human lives, deception, fraud, and child abuse. In this market, the buyer will pay several thousand dollars for delivery of a baby, no questions asked.

The gray market generally involves a third-party intermediary, usually a lawyer or doctor, who locates biological mothers wishing to surrender their children and matches them with prospective adoptive parents. In some states, this kind of referral is legal and is usually accompanied by the requirement that a licensed social service agency certify the adoption. Once the parents have located the baby, the state asks the agency to evaluate the health of the child and the fitness of the potential adoptive parents. This is called a "tagged" or "identified" adoption. The fees involved may be negligible, or can include the not so inconsequential expense of doctors' fees, health care fees, and insurance for the biological mother, fees for counseling, travel expenses, and other costs.

How does Jewish tradition relate to these two options? There can be no doubt that use of the black market for adoption should definitely be avoided. Though the desires of the adoptive parents may be noble, there can be no justification for the blatant immoral and illegal practices involved. Human lives cannot be bought and sold.

Similar problems may or may not exist in the gray adoption market. Prospective adoptive parents who turn to this option may want to consider these questions:

Have all fees been specified in advance, and are they reasonable and usual?

Has confidentiality been maintained, including the anonymity of the biological and adoptive parents?

Has the biological mother been given adequate time after the birth of the child to reconsider?

Is the biological mother secure from all forms of pressure or material inducements that might influence her decision?

Has the consent of the biological father also been obtained?

Have the biological parents received sufficient professional counseling to aid them in their decision?

If the biological mother is Jewish, a confidential record of the child's history should be kept by the adoptive family's rabbi.

It is clear that unless there is an identified child in need of a home—such as a relative or friend suddenly orphaned—it is best to turn to a reputable adoption agency, which will ensure that the rights and responsibilities of all parties concerned are recognized and respected. Where agencies are not able to help, it is possible to turn to a trustworthy lawyer, doctor, or rabbi for arranging an identified adoption. Local or state adoption services, and support groups for infertile and/or adoptive couples, may be able to supply the names of experienced professionals.

Other options are available to the prospective adoptive parent, many being the result of advances in reproductive technology. These include artificial insemination, either from the husband or from an anonymous donor; surrogate mothering, in which a "host" mother, inseminated with the husband's sperm, brings the child to term, and then surrenders it to the biological father and/or his wife; in vitro fertilization, where the ovum is fertilized in a laboratory culture and reimplanted in the uterus of the mother. Although an analysis of these methods is beyond the scope of this chapter, it can be said that many of the problems of black and gray market adoption exist in these procedures, too. Furthermore, the long-term implications of these high-risk reproductive techniques have yet to be analyzed. Prospective adoptive parents should carefully consider the ethical questions attendant upon these choices.

ADOPTION OF A JEWISH CHILD

A determination of the child's status must be made. Is the child known to have a Jewish mother?[6] If the father is known, was his relationship with the mother either incestuous or adulterous? In the absence of any evidence, we may presume that the child of a Jewish mother is legitimate.

---

[6]Traditionally, a child is Jewish if the mother is Jewish. Current Reform practice allows for an indeterminate status for a child with one Jewish parent; the status is determined by the extent of Jewish observance and education in the home.

Since the legal bonds between biological parents and children cannot be severed by adoption, the prohibitions of incestuous marriages obviously still apply between the adopted child and any biological relatives. That is why it is necessary that a confidential record of the particulars of the adoption be kept by a rabbi or Jewish service organization to insure that the improbable event of such a union does not occur. Male children of a Jewish mother should be given a proper *brit milah* (ritual circumcision) on or after the eighth day, and, if first born to their Jewish biological mothers, should be redeemed in a *pidyon ha-ben* ceremony on or after the thirty-first day.[7]

Any name given by the child's biological parents should be retained, though with an additional name added at the *brit milah, pidyon ha-ben*, or other naming ceremony.[8] Formally, the child should retain the patronym of the biological parents when called to the Torah and in Jewish legal documents. However, if adopted at such a young age that the child is not likely to remember the biological parents, Jewish practice allows the child to be called after the adoptive parents. Since the status (Kohen, Levi, Yisrael, etc.) of the adoptive parents is not conferred upon the adopted child, care should be taken not to include the descriptive title (if any) of the adoptive father in the child's name. In some communities, to better avoid confusion, the word *ha-megadlo* (who has raised him) is inserted in documents after the adoptive father's name. It is omitted when the name is being read aloud, such as in a *get* (bill of divorcement) or *ketubah* (Jewish marriage contract).[9] Though the child's filial obligations toward the biological parents are not diminished, no affront to the biological father's honor is implied by using the adoptive father's patronym.

In many ways, rabbinic *aggadah* equates the nurturing of a

---

[7]If the son is born to a Jewish father and mother, the redemption must take place on or after the thirty-first day. If the child's biological mother only is not Jewish, there is no *pidyon ha-ben*. If the child's father is gentile but his mother is Jewish, there are differing options. See Tur, *Shulhan Arukh Yoreh De'ah* 305, and *Arukh haShulhan*.

[8]Since the adoption creates a new parent–child relationship, but does not destroy the old one, it would be unseemly to attempt to eclipse the biological identity by removing a name. Adding an additional name, even a primary name that would take precedence over the given name, is more appropriate.

[9]M. Steinberg, *Responsum on Problems of Adoption in Jewish Law* (London: Office of the Chief Rabbi, 1969).

child to giving birth. A few examples of this attitude will suffice to show how seriously the rabbis took the adoptive relationship:

> And her neighbor named the child, saying, "A son has been born to Naomi." Did Naomi bear him? Surely it was Ruth who bore him! But Ruth bore and Naomi raised him; therefore he was called after Naomi.
> Rabbi Samuel b. Nahmani quoted Rabbi Jonathan: He who teaches Torah to the son of his neighbor, Scripture ascribes it to him as if he had begotten him, for it says: "Now, these are the generations of Aaron and Moses"; and later it is written, "These are the names of the sons of Aaron"; this teaches us that Aaron begot them but Moses taught them; therefore they are called by his name.[10]

Though there were some objections among later authorities to calling the child after the adoptive father because this might be seen as an entitlement to an inheritance when the father had no such intention, this is a minority view that is not followed by current rabbinic authorities.

ADOPTION OF A NON-JEWISH CHILD—
CONVERSION

There exists an element of Jewish tradition—strongest in biblical times, but present also in later periods—that focuses on the racial and biological aspects of Jewish peoplehood. Nevertheless, the strongest single aspect of Jewish self-definition has always been the covenant. This means the bonds of promise, service, and expectation between God and Israel that makes one a true member of the Jewish community. The convert to Judaism, having voluntarily come into that covenant, enjoys a noble station. Although, traditionally, converts to Judaism retain some minor technical disadvantages vis-à-vis born Jews, there should be no question as to their Jewish status. Maimonides, in his poignant and moving letter to Ovadiah the Proselyte, declares that the convert must pray "God of our Ancestors, Abraham, Isaac, and Jacob" in the daily liturgy. Even though the convert may not share a biological kinship with the Patriarchs, he or she is a spiritual descendant of them, and is an equal member of the Community of Israel.

---

[10]*Sanhedrin* 19b. See also *Genesis Rabbah* 46:5: "The one who raises [the child] is called father, and not the one who begets."

It must be stressed that there are no objections to adopting a non-Jewish child; in fact, it is halakhically preferable, since the problems of potentially incestuous marriages do not arise. Nor should there be any religious impediment to adoption because of color or race; the overriding concern should be the needs of the adoptive child. However, the child must be formally converted to Judaism.

If the child's mother is not Jewish, the child is considered not Jewish and must be converted (see footnote 6). If there is no evidence of the mother's status, we presume that she is a member of the majority community in her place of residence. Therefore, in most domestic and international adoptions, if we have no information about the mother, we may assume that she is not Jewish, and the child must be converted.

When a child converts to Judaism, the procedure differs from the adult's discipline because a young child does not have the ability to study or freely accept the principles of Jewish life. Instead, the *Bet Din* may act as surrogate for the child and, by substituting the *Bet Din*'s consent for the child's, proceed immediately to *brit milah* and *mikvah.* In this case, the court invokes the principle that a privilege may be conferred on an individual without requiring assent.[11] For an older person this principle could not be used. Once having experienced a life without the demands and rigors of Jewish responsibilities, an adult may not consider it a privilege to be so obligated; thus, the adult candidate must make a freely determined decision. Obviously, in the event that the child is of intermediate age—from preschool age through adolescence—a case-by-case determination must be made.

According to most rabbinic authorities, a child may not be converted without the tacit acquiescence of the biological parents (at least one of them). If they were known to refuse permission, conversion would be impossible. However, it is assumed that if a child has been surrendered to an adoption agency, or even to a third-party intermediary, without contrary instructions, then the biological parents tacitly agree to whatever the child's providers deem to be in the child's interest.

The *brit milah* is performed as soon as possible after the boy's eighth day of life. If the eighth day is a Sabbath or holiday, it is postponed. Likewise, the *brit* is postponed if the boy's medical

---

[11]*Ketubot* 11a and commentaries.

condition so warrants, until the doctors are satisfied that there is no medical reason for delay.

If the boy has already been circumcised soon after birth in a nonreligious context, then a token ritual circumcision is performed by the *mohel*. A drop of blood is drawn from the penis; otherwise the ritual is the same. Even if the adoptive parents are not concerned with this ritual, it is entirely possible that when the boy matures, it will be a concern to him. In such cases—and there are many like it—the boy must "re-do" his circumcision as an adult. Though this is not painful, it can be awkward; it is much kinder to have it done correctly as early as possible.

After the wound of circumcision has healed, an appointment is made at the *mikvah* for ritual immersion.

Though the conversion is not complete without the *mikvah*, there is no reason to schedule it hastily. Some pediatricians prefer to wait until the child is at least 6 months old. Parents should discuss the medical aspects of both *brit milah* and *mikvah* with a sympathetic doctor.

NAMES

After the immersion, a Hebrew name is given to the child; this may be done at the *mikvah*, at home, or in the synagogue. Many adoptive parents may wish to use this ceremony as an opportunity to celebrate with friends. Many naming ceremonies for daughters have been created in recent years, some of them quite elaborate. Adoptive parents may want to consider involving family and friends in a home-based celebration welcoming their new daughter.

There are many traditions concerning names, not all of them consistent. A Hebrew name consists of a surname and a patronym, such as Shlomo *ben* David (Solomon, son of David). In some communities, the child's mother's name is also used. Though there was at one time a tradition to give all converts the surname Abraham, Sarah, or Ruth, this is no longer practiced in all quarters, and many think that any Jewish surname is appropriate. For adult converts, it is a tradition to adopt the patronym of the Patriarch Abraham (and in some communities, Mother Sarah), who is the spiritual father of all converts. Is this rule to be followed for small children, or may they be called after their adoptive parents?

As with a native-born Jewish adoptee, the convert may use the patronym of the adoptive parents. The appelation "son (or daughter) of Father Abraham (and Mother Sarah)" is only necessary when there is fear that there will be no other reminder of the child's conversion. As long as the *Bet Din* and parents are in agreement that the child's status as a convert will not be concealed, there is no need to exclude the adoptive parents' names from the child's.

There is a dissenting tradition among the codifiers of Jewish law, which requires that the status of both converted and Jewish-born adoptees be preserved in their name. The reasons for this are not only to guard against the possibility of incestuous marriages but for the child's protection.[12]

RENUNCIATION

The Talmud states that when a child is converted with the surrogate assent of the rabbinic court, the child has the right to reject the privilege conferred and to renounce Jewish identity when mature. There are three important considerations: At what age can the child renounce his or her Jewish identity? Is the renunciation effective retroactively? Is the right always available?

There is considerable discussion in the halakhic literature on these issues. Most authorities agree that the age of majority is 13 years for a boy and 12 for a girl, although some rule that the age may be younger if the child can make a reasoned judgment. All agree, though, that once the age of renunciation is reached and the child has not renounced his or her Jewish identity, the right to do so is past and can no longer be invoked.

More important, there is no consensus as to whether the renunciation is only from that moment on, or if it retroactively annuls the conversion. The question hinges on whether this renun-

---

[12]There is also the problem of *halitzah.* According to biblical and Rabbinic law, if a couple is childless at the time of the husband's death, the wife is obliged to marry her husband's brother. This is called *yibum,* or levirate marriage. Alternatively, she may be released by a ceremony called *halitzah,* in which both she and her brother-in-law participate. However, if the husband is survived by biological children, the levirate obligation is not activated; in fact, a marriage between the widow and her deceased husband's brother is forbidden. Since adoptions cannot create a biological relationship, the presence of adopted children would not exempt their mother and her brother-in-law from the need to perform *halitzah.* The gravity of this situation and the possibility of confusion make it imperative that the child's adopted status not be concealed from any of the parties involved, especially the child.

ciation reflects a sudden change of heart, or if it comes at the end of a long period of vacillation, confusion, or apathy. In the former case, the renunciation should affect only the future, whereas in the latter, it should serve to indicate that the process of conversion was never satisfactorily completed. Therefore, if a child has not assumed an independent Jewish identity by the time of *bar* or *bat mitzvah,* and has not been given any Jewish education, a rabbinic court may well be obliged to rule that the conversion was incomplete. It behooves adoptive parents, therefore, to seriously consider the need to inculcate a positive Jewish identity in their children, and to make available to them the spiritual treasures of Jewish tradition.

There is a further complication. The right to renounce the decision of the court to confer Jewish status upon the child is predicated on the child's knowledge of the court's action. If raised in the knowledge of the adoption and conversion, the child is able to affirm or renounce his or her Jewishness. However, if the child's origins have been concealed, there is no such possibility. Consequently, though the right to renounce would normally expire at the age of majority, the clock continues to tick, so to speak, until the child knows of the conversion. Should that knowledge be withheld, the Jewish status of the convert, even through adulthood, is in jeopardy. It is conceivable that an adult, just learning that she was adopted and converted, could undo not only her status but that of any children she might have had.

MAKING IT PERSONAL

Though Jewish tradition places primary importance on the rights and welfare of the adopted child, the spiritual treasures shared by the whole family should not be overlooked. Any of the ceremonies involved in an adoption—*brit milah, mikvah,* naming, *pidyon haben*—may serve as the occasion for celebration and thanksgiving.

There is an atavistic belief in some communities that adoption is a source of embarrassment and must therefore be concealed. Adoption celebrations might therefore have another, pedagogic function: to educate one's friends and family about the source of blessing, occasion for pride, and opportunity for holiness that attends an adoption. As long as there are children in need of homes, and loving homes in need of children, adoption should be encouraged as an act of commitment and love.

41

And Baby Makes Two: Single Mothers by Choice

Ruth Mason

Bonnie Bergman was always independent. She left for California right after college and spent six summers traveling alone through Europe. "I had gotten all that out of my system," says the Brooklyn-born teacher. "I had done it all, I had my career . . . but I wasn't a mother.

"People said, 'What can you do about it? You're not married.' I said, 'I can do something. It *is* in my control.' " So two weeks before her 36th birthday, Bonnie told her gynecologist she wanted to be artificially inseminated. She left it to him to match her with an appropriate donor. "All I know about him is that he is a Jewish doctor, is musical, is easy-going, and has a very high IQ," Bonnie says. Later she nods toward 3-year-old Jessica and says, "Look at her. He must have blue eyes." Bonnie is naturally curious about the man who fathered her child but doesn't want to meet him. "That would defeat the whole purpose." As for Jessica, she knows she doesn't have a daddy.

"It doesn't seem to have affected her at all. She says, 'Oh, well, I have a Mommy.' "

Having a child alone was hard in the beginning, Bonnie admits. There's no one to take over a midnight feeding, and Jessica was pigeontoed and bowlegged and went through six sets of casts. Bonnie has no siblings, but a cousin acted as her labor coach, and her mother helped out after Jessica's birth.

The apartment Bonnie and Jessica share is full of a mother's loving touches. Jessica sleeps in a white canopy bed that Bonnie never had. Jessica's paintings are mounted on colored construction paper, and hanging on the walls are professional, framed photographs chronicling her first three years. It's a room devoted solely to games and toys.

Bonnie still wants to get married but is more relaxed about it. She also has less time to date. Bonnie is direct and unhesitating, tempering her quick speech with an urban sense. "I'm not a women's libber. I believe in equal pay for equal work, but I still like a man to be a man. I like being a woman and like a man to open the door for me—but also to respect my independence. Men fall into two categories now: Some feel what I did is wonderful and brave. Others can't handle it at all, in which case they're not for me."

Man or no man, "I'd still be sitting here at 39, so I'm glad I did it. When I hit 35, it really started to bother me. There was no man in my life at the time, and I always thought I'd have a child. I'd been thinking about it since I was 30, and it became firmer and firmer in my mind: Having a child was more important to me than getting married. And I wouldn't get married just to have a child.

"It's not for everyone," Bonnie cautions. "I have the time, the money, the emotional stability—and a lot of love to give."

OTHER METHODS

Some women desiring a child believe artificial insemination is the least complicated method. Others choose a male friend by whom to get pregnant. Some call this brave and unconventional; maybe it's thoughtless and selfish. But whatever the label, one thing is clear: The number of Jewish single women having children is growing.

Four years ago, Jane Mattes, a New York psychotherapist who was the single mother of a 2-year-old boy, invited several other single mothers over for coffee. That gathering turned out to be the founding meeting of Single Mothers by Choice, a 500-member, New York-based organization with chapters around the country. In New York, most of the members are Jewish.

"I really wanted to be part of a family," said Jane, "so I had one by myself."

DEFIANCE

Who are these women who are defying thousands of years of tradition, not to mention their own parents' wishes? They are, for the most part, well-educated women in their 30s and 40s who have established careers, emotional stability, and savings accounts, but no potential husband. Some are divorced, others have been through unsuccessful relationships. Almost all see single motherhood as second-best. They would rather be married but don't want to grow gray waiting for Mr. Right to come along.

Lee Blumer, 41, was married for eight years to a man who didn't want children. "It's one of the main reasons we didn't stay together," she says. In her late 30s, she "fell into the arms of an emotionally broken Polish political refugee artist" who went on a drinking binge when he found out she was pregnant with her son, Alexander. Shortly afterward, he was out of Lee's life. Despite his reaction, Lee says, "I never thought about not having the baby."

Now a music publicist in New York, Lee says, "I was always a little avant garde. I went to Africa for a year when I was 18 instead of going straight to college and was the first kid on my block to be affected by the '60s. But I never thought I'd do something like this."

She knows she chose a difficult path, but she considers herself blessed. Her friends and family have been helpful and supportive. "I'm not out there by myself."

As a child, Lee cut Sunday school. Her parents paid only lip service to *Yiddishkeit,* despite the fact that her father was raised in a hasidic home in Poland. Though she flirted with Christianity, she's thinking of sending Alexander, now 2, to a yeshivah. "I'd like very much to expose Alexander to the right kind of Jewish identity in a way I wasn't. There are some fundamental traditions in Judaism that are liberal, kind, and humane. That's the kind of Judaism I'd like to expose him to."

While other Jewish single mothers say they stay away from synagogues because they fear they'd feel out of place, Lee has no discomfort. "I'm not embarrassed about doing this. I don't feel I did anything that anyone can judge me about."

Lee and others like her are, in part, the casualties of demographic trends. There are simply more single women than single men—and among Jews, the gap widens. More Jewish men than women intermarry, and most men still marry younger women. Single women who are becoming mothers belong to a generation that postponed marriage and childbearing. When they began to feel the pressure of the biological clock and saw no marriage partner in sight, they were forced into unilateral action.

CAUTION

Single Mothers by Choice is quick to warn potential mothers that single motherhood is not for everyone. In fact, they don't advocate single motherhood: "In general, our members feel that a good marriage is preferable to raising a child as a single parent." They simply offer themselves as a resource and information center. They discourage anyone who has serious doubts or does not seem financially or emotionally ready for the responsibility.

"Single parenthood," the organization says, "is difficult enough for the woman who is sure and prepared."

Manhattan psychologist Dr. Elan Golomb agrees that it takes a special person to make a good single mother. "If a woman is overly susceptible to what society thinks, she will pass her feelings on to the child, who will then feel inadequate." But, she adds, "The truth is, traditional nuclear families have raised a lot of neurotic people."

Most of the women interviewed for this article thought long and hard before deciding to become mothers. They read and they planned and they saved.

"I spent four years exploring the idea of single parenthood," says Lila Suna, 38. "I joined discussion groups and read everything I could get my hands on. I met with a psychiatrist at one point to talk out some issues and see if this was real or just some fantasy. It was a major undertaking and I owed it to the child to think the decision through thoroughly."

At 20 months her son, Kenneth, is too young to ask why he doesn't have a father, but Lila already knows what she will answer when he does. "I don't want to lie to him. I plan to tell him that I wanted a child very, very much and wasn't lucky enough to have a relationship at that point."

Some single mothers choose a godfather for their child; others try to actively involve uncles and grandfathers in their child's life.

"At some point a child needs a male model," says Golomb. "But it's quite disputable that a child needs a father in order to be emotionally healthy. In some South Seas cultures, an uncle plays a more important role than the father."

WHERE'S POPPA?

When Jane Mattes's son Eric was 4, he went through a period of asking why he didn't have a daddy. "It wasn't anything terrible," says Jane. "He was just a little confused. I think he was looking to me to see if he should be upset about it or if it was okay. In our workshops, we tell people that whatever they say, they should be comfortable with it."

According to Jewish law, a child born to a single woman is not considered illegitimate. An illegitimate child (or *mamzer*) is the product of certain forbidden unions, such as that of a married woman and a man other than her husband. But while there may be no halakhic problems, single parenthood is far from being socially acceptable. In the family-centered Jewish tradition, these options are frowned upon. Parents worry not only about how their daughters and grandchildren will cope without husbands and fathers, but about what the neighbors will think.

Bonnie Bergman's father didn't speak to her for three months when he found out she was pregnant. Bonnie says he was concerned about his friends and neighbors. But Bonnie is his only child and 3-year-old Jessica his only grandchild and the apple of his eye. He and Bonnie's mother come to Brooklyn from their Florida home to visit their daughter and grandchild "every chance they get."

THRILLER

Jane Mattes says, "[my mother was] actually thrilled. But she had a little trouble about whether to lie or tell the truth to her circle." But the truth was told, and to Jane's surprise, they accepted it. Although she can't know what was said privately, they told her, "It's nice you settled down."

Like Jane's mother, some parents are accepting—even philosophical—from the start. One grandmother explained, "Many actresses and other celebrities are having babies on their own, so we see and hear and read about it. In today's world, nothing is shocking. When my daughter told me she was pregnant, I took it as a matter of course. This wasn't always acceptable, but if you can't find the right man, at least you should be happy from a child—and a man will come."

It's too soon to tell whether most single mothers by choice will marry eventually, but many hope to. They see themselves as having reversed the order of things. As Lila put it, "There's a limit to the number of years in which you can have a child, but there's no limit to when you can meet someone."

Although the government does not know how many single mothers choose to have children, a recent report from the National Center for Health Statistics says that one baby in five is born to an unmarried woman. Birth rates for unmarried women in their 30s and 40s continue to increase as they have for the past decade.

THE NEXT STEP

Jane Mattes attributes the growth in deliberate single motherhood in large part to the women's movement. "When single women began to become financially successful, they realized they could also be the head of a household better than a divorced woman who hadn't planned on living alone. It seems like the next logical step. If you can afford it, why not have a child without a man?"

While their numbers are growing, women having children on their own are still a shadow phenomenon in the Jewish community. Many single mothers stay on the fringes for fear of ostracism.

Bonnie Bergman's daughter was named at *Shabbat* services at a *shul* in Brooklyn. But a Manhattan rabbi approached by a single mother who wanted to do the same suggested naming the baby during a weekday morning *minyan*, a decidedly less public event. If single mothers' ranks keep swelling and if more of them turn to the Jewish community, synagogues and other institutions will have to begin to examine and come to an understanding of this new type of Jewish family.

Epilogue

Which is the greater contributor to Jewish survival, Family or Community? One third of Jews in the latter part of the twentieth century find themselves in alternative style families: single, divorced, widowed, childless, gay, and lesbian. The intact two-parent family with mother at home and father at work is no longer the model. The two chapters in the epilogue highlight the issues addressed in this book in elegant form. They provide the necessary summation, even though they leave us with more questions than answers.

42

Family, A Religiously Mandated Ideal

Susan Handelman

"A Jew today," someone wrote, "is anyone who has Jewish grand-children." The words sting—perhaps more than any others in our painful debates about Jewish identity.

Of course, the definition is only metaphorical. Innumerable Jews are unable to have children; others have chosen not to have them. Many have intermarried; others are unmarried by choice or fate. And many now openly prefer erotic relationships with members of their own sex. Rare, indeed, is the Jew today who can be certain of having Jewish grandchildren.

But Jewish families have never had it easy. Even in the best circumstances, many might agree with George Burns: "One of the secrets of a long, happy life is having a large family—especially when they live in another city."

It's no news that alternate lifestyles, assimilation, challenges to traditional Jewish authority, and demographic changes have all ravaged the Jewish family. One now hears the argument that the traditional Jewish emphasis on the family is obsolete because it excludes large numbers of Jews from Jewish life. Some feminists claim that the traditional nuclear family is a repressive, patriarchal institution whose ideology has helped to exclude women from full participation in Jewish institutional life. Homosexuals argue for the validation of their lifestyle. Singles often feel hurt and condescended to by a community that sees them as unfulfilled and not full adults as long as they are unmarried.

The other side argues that the family is the foundation of Jewish life and guarantor of Jewish survival, that the first *mitzvah* is "be fruitful and multiply," and that attacks on the Jewish family emanate, not from a depth of true Jewish commitment and understanding, but from an all too American ethic of self-gratification, narcissism, and antinomianism. Being Jewish is not to be defined by whatever makes one feel good and self-justified. The lifestyles of Jews should not determine the Jewish style of life.

My aim here is not to engage directly in the difficult issues of Judaism and homosexuality, or the challenges of feminism, or the problems of singles in the Jewish community. But these questions have raised for me a deeper, underlying question: Beyond all the usual platitudes, *why* is the family so important in Judaism?

DEMANDING CONTINUITY—AND MORE

To define a Jew as someone who has Jewish grandchildren—for all its irony—strikes me as conceptually profound. It defines a Jew in terms of family—but not *immediate* family. It validates not only biological self-reproduction but a spiritual continuance beyond the immediate and across time. The Jew is not defined by how Jewish she or he may feel, or how many *mitzvot* they may perform, or how much money they give, but their ability to *embody* (literally, in children) and *transmit* Judaism so vitally that these children choose to remain Jewish and are able, in turn, to pass on that spark to their own children. "Three is a *hazakah*," as Jewish tradition says. In other words, only when something is done three times does it have the element of surety, permanence—only then can one trust its stability. Grandchildren are the third generation; they confirm the Judaism of the first generation. Transmission requires a biological next generation, but that is not enough; biology is shaped by spirituality, self is pulled toward other, the blindness of the present toward a vision of the future.

This is not to argue that simple survival is what being Jewish is all about. Yet, beyond all the obvious reasons for our contemporary stress on "survival" (the decimation of the Jewish population in the Holocaust, the continuous threats to Israel, declining birthrates and intermarriage), Judaism seems strangely obsessed with this theme and with the idea of family from the beginning. Why?

OUR GOD'S CONCERN WITH HISTORY

The book of Genesis, for instance, is a book all about families, barren wives, sibling rivalries, destructions by flood and fire, constant threats to the process of transmission and continuity. These themes are narrated in part to demystify nature as an autonomous controlling force and stress the then revolutionary idea that the One God is in control of both nature and history.

And history is meaningful in Jewish thought precisely because God is passionately involved in it, a "God of pathos" as Heschel wrote, not the static, emotionless, ahistorical God of the Greeks. Just as God, the ultimate model, is intensely involved with the quarrels of families from Cain and Abel to the conflicts between the families of nations, so, too, are the biblical heroes and heroines deeply involved with—in fact, defined by—the problems of their own families. Families are the great scene of spiritual struggle; both then and now, they are the paradigms of intimate connection and intense ambivalence. Unlike their Greek counterparts, biblical heroes do not attain identity and glory in solitary combat away from their families; their problems are deeply domestic.

It's no accident that the critical test of Abraham was precisely the command to sacrifice his son . . . and not to be tempted in the wilderness, like Jesus, or have to sacrifice himself. For the son was not his alone, and the crisis was not only personal; it was collective. The call to Abraham was for him to become a great nation; it was not a private covenant with a single person. Judaism, unlike other religions, does not advocate or promise salvation to individuals. The covenant is made not with Abraham alone but with all his descendants, the family that was to grow into the nation that Moses led to Sinai. And the revelation at Sinai again was collective, to an entire people, not to individuals.

Is this obsession with family the remnants of primitive tribalism? Is the focus on survival the result of a desert mentality and the tribulations of exile? And what does all this have to do with our modern need for individualism and self-definition?

THE PRIMAL ACT OF KEEPING COVENANT

The family is central to Judaism, I think, because it is central to Jewish ideas of God, creation, covenant, and history. The biological family reminds us that we, like the world, are created; we are not inevitable, necessary, autonomous. We are an effect of someone else's will—and in the best case—someone's desire to give to an other. We have a history. The creation of another human being echoes and partakes of God's creation of the world—it, too, is a something from nothing, an act of faith and hope . . . and something else, perhaps. Isaac Bashevis Singer once said, "Humanity could not have gone through all its suffering and problems and crises without a sense of humor. The very fact that we are here shows that our grandparents and parents had a sense of humor."

To refuse to give birth to the next generation is to refuse to continue God's creation, and thus also to refuse to live in history, and thus also to deny the covenant. For the covenant is *collective* and *historical.* Torah is a guide and inheritance to a people who were to journey not just in space to the Promised Land—but in *time,* through the travails of history. History—the physical turmoil of this world, of its passions, temptations. "The Torah," as the book of Deuteronomy says in a famous passage, "is not in Heaven." "Every descent," the Jewish mystics say, "is for the purpose of an ascent." The soul's descent into the scrappy physical world and the people's wanderings through the course of history enable a great spiritual blossoming— and thus the Talmud compares the Jewish people to the olive: only when squeezed does it give forth oil.

This world, daily human relationships, are the scene of divine action, by both God and Israel. The world is not an allegory; spirituality is not elsewhere. The Jew is engaged in sanctifying this physical world and mundane historical time. That is why memory is so important to the Jews—it is the sanctifying and linking of past, present, and future. In Jewish time, the past remembers the future. Memory, said the Baal Shem Tov, is the secret of redemption.

GENERATION: JEWISH RESPONSIBILITY

And to put it simply—there is no physical future, no history without physical reproduction. The family is the unit that creates life, welcomes and protects it, is intimately involved with it, and there-fore is the most powerful agent of transmitting personal and collec-tive Jewish memory. That is why there is such an emphasis on generations in the Bible, why teaching and learning are so highly valued—because they are acts of transmission to and reception and renewal by the next generation . . . of the heritage, of the gift. The threat to the covenant is that there will be no one, or the wrong one, to carry it on into history. Perhaps that is one of the meanings of the famous *midrash* that when God was about to give the Torah He asked for guarantors who would keep it. It was not enough for the Jews themselves to pledge to keep it; only when they said, "Our children will be our guarantors," did God agree to reveal it.

Just as the children were pledged before they had any choice in the matter, the self is not an isolated, autonomous, totally free creation, despite the dogmas of pop American psychology. The family is a covenant. For in the family, we are continuously reminded of, obligated to, intruded upon and pained by, delighted and pleased with others. We are in constant dialogue—even if it is angry. True, one can divorce a husband or wife. But however severe the alienation may be, a child's biological bond to a parent is indissoluble. As Robert Frost once put it, "Home is the place where, when you have to go there, they have to take you in." In this way, familial relations are a microcosm, training ground, reminder, and enactment of the Jewish people's intimate and tempestuous relations to God; why, after all, are we called the "children" of Israel, the "children of God"? The prophets, of course, exploit the full implications of these metaphors: In the book of Jeremiah, God may angrily "divorce" the Jewish people as his unfaithful "wife" who has played harlot (Jeremiah 3:8) but then cries yearningly for their redemption: "Return, O backsliding *children*" (Jeremiah 3:14).

THE INTEGRITY OF TRADITIONAL SEX VALUES

Thus I will speculate that one of the reasons Jewish tradition opposes homosexuality is that there can be no next generation from that kind of union—no biological child; therefore, no history, no future, no covenant. Now, of course, Jewish tradition holds that one who teaches another's child is as if s/he gave birth to that child. And this is a great value—but Judaism, unlike Christianity, does not allegorize away the physical commandments of the Torah and seek salvation in another world. The ideal Jewish saint is not an ascetic, or one who, as in other religions, attains purity by removal from the community, or from the demands of a family, or the physical world. For these struggles are the deepest spiritual struggles. The secrets of the *kabbalah* were to be taught only to married men. And the *kabbalah* itself describes the various aspects of God's mystical inner being (the configurations of the *sefirot*) in terms of family metaphors, "father, mother, son, daughter."

I once heard a founding member of the *havurah* movement discuss why he no longer agreed with the radical revisions made in the language of the *siddur*. The rationale had been to take out the crude and offensive anthropomorphisms and the sexist biases: "God as a King, Father, Warrior, etc." "I have a love/hate relationship with the traditional *siddur*," he said, "but I realized that our most primal and intimate human emotions are evoked by much of this language—especially our relations with our families, and that to expunge this language and these human feelings, as ambivalent and archaic as they may be, is to cut us off from achieving the most intimate relationship with God."

Thus the traditional Jewish advocacy of marriage, childbearing, and heterosexuality, I think, should not be mistaken for a repressive patriarchy, an intolerance of lifestyles, a primitive tribalism, or outmoded ideology. Now Jewish tradition clearly teaches that a Jew is a Jew no matter what, that every Jew is holy and part of the Jewish community. I am in no way arguing for the exclusion of those with alternate views from the Jewish community or synagogue. And I do not want to minimize in any way the personal pain this position may cause to homosexuals, to singles, to the childless—but that pain is not a persuasive argument for change . . . only for compassion and extra warmth.

OUR JEWISH DUTY WAS—AND IS—CLEAR

The family can indeed be a repressive institution—as can any relationship that is distorted—but I have tried to argue here that the Jewish concept of family is distinctive and absolutely integral to Judaism; it is not reducible to a bourgeois societal arrangement or lifestyle. It is deeply theological. One is free to make other choices. But what will be the grounds and values on which those choices are made? For the freedom to make choices should not be confused with the freedom to remake Jewish tradition into one's own image . . . with only one's present in mind. The ultimate ground of value in Judaism is not the autonomous self, but the personhood bestowed by being in and continuing God's creation and covenant.

Rabbi Michael Brooks once said that having children made him relate to God a lot better. "How so?" I asked. "Because now I understand what it is like to create something you have no control over," he answered. This is ironic and also very wise. Having children is indeed an aspect of being made in the image of God. For God's creation as an act of God's free will gives us free will and so makes our very actions in history meaningful . . . and makes the Torah ours, to be renewed in every generation. A child is both oneself and completely *other*. Similarly, in the process of transmission, Torah is the same and other—wholly accepted, and also changed and enlarged through newness of the next generation. As the Talmud says, "Even the innovations that a brilliant student will one day teach in front of his master were already given at Sinai." In this sense, the Latin-American writer Borges said that Jews alone produced grandchildren, whereas in the secular Western tradition of writing and texts, "The nights of Alexandria, Babylon, Carthage, Memphis have never succeeded in engendering a single grandfather." Although no one can guarantee it, it is our obligation to try to make sure that we do have Jewish grandchildren.

43

Family or Community?

Martha A. Ackelsberg

I find Susan Handelman's chapter (see chapter 42) on the place of families in Judaism profoundly disturbing. In the guise of making a theological argument, she makes a biologically reductionist claim that takes as a model for all time the specific conditions of the earliest period of Jewish history. In consequence, she ignores the crucial importance of community in Jewish history and religious life. I believe, however, that if family has been important in Jewish history, it is as a means toward the creation and preservation of the community. It is the community, then, that ought to be the focus of our concerns. The question for contemporary Jews should be: What are the ways in which that community may be sustained and strengthened?

FAMILY AND THE PATRIARCHS

Susan Handelman's portrait of the centrality of the family in the life of the patriarchs is certainly a true one. The central concern of the patriarchal narratives in the book of Genesis is family. The major triumphs and tensions of the book all focus on essentially domestic intrigues: who will inherit, who will carry the blessings (of God and of the patriarchs themselves)? But family is central in these narratives, I would argue, not because the Bible is trying to teach us about the importance of generational connections, but because, in the early period of the establishment of the people, family was coextensive with community. And it is the community, and not the family, that is to carry the burden of Jewish continuity for the generations to come.

For the image of family, while central in the patriarchal period, is surely *not* the controlling image for the rest of the biblical narratives. Once the tribes settle in Egypt, and, most certainly, once the people stand at Sinai, the central tensions and confrontations are *communal,* not familial. Moses is known not as the father of the Jewish people, but as the lawgiver, the one who molded them into a community and interceded with God on their behalf. The central conflicts in his life were not familial (certainly not in the domestic sense), but communal. Joshua, Deborah, Isaiah, Jeremiah, Ezra, Nehemiah, Mordecai, Esther, and an entire host of biblical heroes and heroines are accorded that status in our tradition not because of their familial accomplishments, surely not because they generated Jewish grandchildren, but because they made crucial contributions—defined in nonbiological ways—to the continuity of the Jewish people.

COMMUNITY AND CONTINUITY

The real issue around which Handelman's arguments about the place of families in Judaism turn is the continuity of the Jewish community/people. What sustains it? What contributes to its growth? Here, as Susan Handelman herself acknowledges, the tradition has been clear: while biological reproduction is important, it is not viewed, and never has been viewed, as the *sole* form of contribution to Jewish continuity. In her words, "Jewish tradition holds that one who teaches another's child is as if s/he gave birth to that child." Yet, in her next sentence she attempts to rob that statement of its force by adding, "Judaism, unlike Christianity, does not allegorize away the physical commandments of the Torah and seek salvation in another world." Is that what it is to devote a life to Jewish teaching and learning? Is that the way we remember Rabbi Akiba, Maimonides, Rashi, Joseph Caro, or any of the other great Jewish teachers and codifiers? Their contribution to the continuity of Jewish tradition and Jewish peoplehood is clear and undebated. Their status as biological producers of Jewish grandchildren seems quite beside the point.

Our own communal/religious history provides us, then, with a variety of models of fulfilled Jewish living, including many models of what we might call "grandparenting" in a nonbiological sense. Why should we insist now on the eternal validity of a much more narrow definition—one that identifies being a Jew, or contributing to Jewish survival, with biological reproduction in the context of a heterosexual nuclear family?

COMMUNITY, OPPORTUNITY, AND OBLIGATION

I firmly agree with Susan Handelman that "the ultimate ground of value in Judaism is not the autonomous self, but the personhood bestowed by being in and continuing God's creation and covenant." But, as I have tried to argue, our tradition does not define our participation in creation and in the covenant solely in terms of the nuclear family. Instead of giving us a theological defense of the family in Judaism, Susan Handelman has given us a thoroughly modern defense of the "heterosexual bourgeois nuclear family lifestyle," rooted in a reductionist vision of what constitutes generational continuity. But, as I have argued elsewhere,[1] understandings and definitions of what constitutes a family and what obligations its members owe to one another have changed dramatically over the centuries, in the Jewish community as much as in the secular world. Not only is the vision she offers us much narrower than that which Jewish tradition provides; it is also a profoundly, and unnecessarily, limited view of who is a good Jew.

Her biological analysis is seriously flawed in a number of important respects. On the one hand, *biological* continuity is surely not the only kind of continuity there is: as we have seen, people can contribute to communal continuity in other than biological ways. On the other hand, even in terms of biological continuity, reproduction is surely possible outside the nuclear family context.

To define a Jew as one who produces Jewish grandchildren, in the literal sense in which Handelman clearly means us to apply it, is foolish, if not inconsistent. Many Jews who are childless (whether now or in earlier times) find themselves without children not because they "refuse to give birth to the next generation," but because the circumstances of their lives do not allow them to do so: they may be physically unable to bear children, they may lack the economic means to rear them properly, they may not have appropriate heterosexual partners, they may lack the social supports that would enable

---

[1]Martha A. Ackelsberg, "Families and the Jewish Community: A Feminist Perspective" (*Response* 14:5–19, 1985).

them to bear and raise children in the absence of such a partner. Others may have Jewish children, but be unable, despite their best efforts, to guarantee that those children will remain committed Jews and themselves have children who will remain committed Jews. Ought we to leave such people feeling they are any the less Jews because they do not have control over the choices of their children and children's children?

COVENANT—INCLUSIVE RELATIONSHIP

Furthermore, even if we turn to generativity in the biological sense, heterosexual nuclear families are not the only contexts in which continuity can be assured. And, with respect to "convenanting," I agree that making long-term commitments to love and care for others is important; Judaism does not share the liberal individualism so characteristic of contemporary American society. But heterosexual nuclear families are not the only contexts in which people can or do covenant, nor are they the only units in or through which people may express love or long-term care and commitment. As all too many studies unfortunately attest, for many women and children, families are often the last place to go for such nurturance.

A more appropriate definition of what constitutes Jewish continuity would not only relieve the "pain" of exclusion for many such people; it might well make possible their biological contribution to the next generation! For, as it is important to note, while biological reproduction is not the only form of reproduction, it is also the case that not only heterosexual nuclear families give birth to biological children. With a more open attitude on the part of the Jewish community, many of those who are now single or not heterosexually partnered might well be encouraged, or enabled, to have biological children, and make an effort at generating those grandchildren that Handelman claims to value so fully.

In sum, while I agree that, as Jews, we share an obligation (and, I would see it, an opportunity) to "be fruitful and multiply," to contribute to the continuity and the deepening of our tradition and values, it seems to me foolish and self-defeating to define those obligations in narrow, biological terms. Our tradition is too rich, the community too varied, to claim that all that matters (or that what matters most) is simply biological reproduction. If there is a theological imperative in Judaism, it demands not the blind reproduction of families but that we be a holy nation. That is not to imply that a concern for reproduction is irrelevant: we must continue to exist if we are to fulfill our religious obligations. But it is to insist that there are many ways to contribute to that continuity, whether biologically or spiritually, outside the framework of the so-called traditional nuclear family. To deny that diversity is to ignore the lessons of our own history and, it seems to me, to threaten the very continuity of the community and traditions we wish to sustain.

Afterword: Critical Choices and Change

This anthology has endeavored to explore the many choices and resultant impact of a changing society on Jewish life in this last decade of the twentieth century.

In past generations of this century, Jewish coupling leading to marriage and children reflected the first commandment in the Torah, *"peru urevu"*—"be fruitful and multiply." Our sages taught that this *mitzvah* superseded all the other *mitzvot*. The family was the core of Jewish life—the repository from generation to generation of the Jewish ethos, the protector and source of stability of the young, the instiller of Jewish self-esteem and confidence enabling one's children to strive inexorably toward their dreams—in short, an admired model for other subcultures to emulate. Indeed, "Jews by choice" often have chosen Judaism and to marry Jews because of their respect for and desire to be part of the close, warm, supportive system known as "the Jewish family."

But as this ethos was affected by increasing numbers of choices wrought in part by the women's movement—career paths to individual fulfillment often with resultant postponement of marriage and children, childlessness or single by choice, and increasing divorce rate—the joy and gratification of earlier marriage and family life became less assured.

As Hadassah, the largest women's Zionist organization, we acknowledge with concern the trends and the forces of change that are threatening our future viability. Will there truly be one-third less of us in year 2010, as has been predicted? We believe that we can serve as an instrument in this period of societal change, to ensure that there will be strong and committed Jewish families raising Jewish children with positive self-esteem and faith in the future.

Throughout this book and its accompanying program guide (available through Hadassah's Order Department), we have striven to illuminate Jewish family values even as we delineate the social forces that undermine them. We acknowledge, too, that some current choices are considered by many to be departures from Jewish morality. We hope, however, that through Jewish education, our outreach programs to singles, career women, the young, intermarrieds, dual-career couples, and others disengaged from Jewish life, we can serve as a catalyst and an advocate for setting new paths to Jewish survival.

We seek to bring Jewish people together through seminars and educational events; study groups for members, couples, and youth; Kallot; social activities; travel programs; parent education programs; advocacy of child care services; and outreach to the intermarried.

Hadassah's Jewish Education program is part of Hadassah's commitment to informed action, to meet challenges through study and an integrated approach, which involves many of Hadassah's programs. Although no single organization (even one as visionary as Hadassah) can singlehandedly affect demographic trends, we can employ our vast network of members and supporters to create new opportunities for the unaffiliated to enter into Jewish life and help ensure its continuity into the twenty-first century. Thus we hope that through this book—its collective wisdom and insights—a new generation can determine its choices for a fruitful Jewish life.

Ruth G. Cole
National Jewish Education Chair

Resources

SINGLE

Below is a list of Singles Programming Resources and Dating Services. For additional listings see *Jewish and Female: A Guide and Sourcebook for Today's Jewish Woman* by Susan Weidman Schneider (a Touchstone Book published by Simon and Schuster Inc.).

Singles Programming

National Jewish Outreach Program, Inc.
475 Fifth Avenue, Suite 1810
New York, NY   10017
(212) 725-1690
    Not exclusively for singles.

Lincoln Square Synagogue
200 Amsterdam Avenue
New York, NY   10023
(212) 874-6100
    An Orthodox synagogue that offers a wide variety of courses and lectures for singles and married alike, of all ages.

Sutton Place Synagogue
235 East 51st Street
New York, NY   10021
(212) 593-3300

  This synagogue sponsors separate High Holiday services and meals for singles. Also sponsors periodic all-singles Shabbatons.

Singles Programs
Group Services Department
92nd Street YM/YWHA
1395 Lexington Avenue
New York, NY   10028
(212) 427-6000

  In addition to specific singles programs, the Y offers a wide range of cultural and educational programs.

Adas Israel Congregation
2850 Quebec Street NW
Washington, DC   20008
(202) 362-4433

  Sponsors a highly successful program for Jewish singles.

National Commission on Singles
United Synagogue of America
Tom Kagedan, Coordinator
155 Fifth Avenue
New York, NY   10010
(212) 533-7800

  Contact this office for information on singles programs in Conservative synagogues in your area.

New York Metropolitan Region
United Synagogue of America
Bruce Greenfield, Executive Dir.
155 Fifth Avenue
New York, NY   10010
(212) 533-7800

New Jersey Region
United Synagogue of America
Sherri Kirschenbaum, Singles Coordinator
910 Salem Avenue
Hillside, NJ 07205
(201) 353-7877

Pacific Southwest Region
United Synagogue of America
Linda Zweig, Singles Coordinator
15600 Mulholland Drive
Los Angeles, CA
(213) 879-2013

Union of American Hebrew Congregations
838 Fifth Avenue
New York, NY   10021
(212) 249-0100
　　　Contact for information on singles programming in Reform congregations in your area. (Also see list of selected UAHC regional outreach coordinators listed in this guide under INTERMARRIED.)

New Jewish Agenda
1123 Broadway, Rm. 1217
New York, NY   10010
(212) 620-0828
　　　An organization created by progressive Jews, which sponsors groups and discussions for singles. Contact this office for the location of the chapter nearest you.

Single Mothers By Choice
P.O. Box 1642
Gracie Square Station
New York, NY   10028

Mr. Dan Laufer
Harvard/Radcliffe B'nai B'rith Hillel
Young Adult and Graduate Students Society
74 Mount Auburn Street
Cambridge, MA   02138
(617) 495-4696
　　　This is just one of many programs run by B'nai B'rith Hillel Foundations located on college campuses all over the country. Contact the national B'nai B'rith offices for more information:

B'nai B'rith Hillel Foundation
1640 Rhode Island Avenue NW
Washington, DC   20036
(202) 857-6600

Dating Services/Matchmaking

Bobbie Goldfarb, Sandy Olkon, & Jean Bundt
The Jewish Dating Service
6009 Wayzata Boulevard
St. Louis Park, MN   55416
(612) 542-9790
        This service's clients are Jews from all backgrounds. They are primarily college-educated singles in their 20s and 30s.

Education Alliance West
Compatimates
51 East 10th Street
New York, NY   10003
(212) 420-1150
        A Jewish dating service that specializes in selective introductions made by caring, trained professionals.

Jewish Dating Service
Cheryl Dritz, Director
Leo Yassenoff Jewish Center
1125 College Avenue
Columbus, OH   43209
(614) 231-2731

United Synagogue of America Pacific Southwest Region runs a computer dating service for New York, Phoenix, and southern California. Call 1-800-451-9609.

Aish HaTorah
Jewish Computer Dating Service
1671 East 16 Street, Suite 209
Brooklyn, NY 11229
(718) 336-7911

National Directory of Jewish Singles
1947 Ocean Avenue
Brooklyn, NY   11230

Chutzpah Unlimited
P.O. Box 2400
Chicago, IL   60690

Kesher
National Office
Mrs. Irene Barun
1624 46th Street
Brooklyn, NY   11204
(718) 853-6448
This is the address of a totally volunteer organization whose goal is to help Orthodox singles find partners. It has chapters in many North American cities and states including: New York City, Long Island, New Jersey, Baltimore, Chicago, San Francisco, Los Angeles, Florida, and Toronto.

Union of Orthodox Congregations
Marriage Commission
45 West 36th Street, 9th Floor
New York, NY   10018
(212) 563-4000
Conducts a two-faceted program: a dating service for singles and workshops for singles to discuss values clarification and the expectations that dominate the thinking of many singles.

Rabbi and Rebbetzin Daniel Fingerer
1709 Avenue J
Brooklyn, NY   11230
(718) 376-4088
Presently, only deal with Orthodox singles but are contemplating interviewing single Jews from all backgrounds. Rabbi and Rebbetzin Fingerer conduct unique workshops for singles, as well as offer *shadkhan* services. They have also developed a program called TAME (Torah and Marriage Enrichment), which provides both singles and married couples opportunities to explore what a Jewish marriage ideally should be. The TAME program draws on Torah and resources available from the field of marital counseling.

Ms. Beth Morris
916 North Belgrade
Silver Spring, MD   20902
(301) 649-7333

Private matching of modern Orthodox singles, primarily young professionals.

Rabbi Yeheskel and Mrs. Pearl Lebovic
Likrat Shiduch-Matchmaking Service
7 Kissel Lane
Morristown, NJ   07960
(201) 285-1769
Rabbi and Mrs. Lebovic see their work as a service to the community and as such require only a small initial fee. They provide their service to Jewish singles of all backgrounds.

Rabbi Martin Siegel
Zedek Marriage Bureau
5885 Robert Oliver Place
Columbia, MD   21045
Works with Jewish singles from all backgrounds.

Lincoln Square Synagogue
Shadchen Committee
200 Amsterdam Avenue
New York, NY   10023
(212) 874-6100

Mimi Teplow
270 Buckminster Road
Brookline, MA   02146
(617) 731-5380

Ms. Judi Ehrlich
New Possibilities
126 Billings Street
Sharon, MA 02067
(617) 784-7980

Judith Moss
4520 North Meridian Avenue
Miami Beach, FL 33140
(305) 534-2458

Telephone Hotlines

Jewish Singles Partyline: (212) 753-7282

Jewish Singles Date Phone: Men call (212) 755-3009. Women call (212) 755-3008.

Jewish Talk: 1-900-999-0900 ($0.95/minute)

Singles Travel

United Synagogue Singles Travel
155 Fifth Avenue
New York, NY   10010
(212) 533-7800

American Jewish Committee
165 East 56 Street
New York, NY   10022
(212) 751-4000

American Jewish Congress
Stephen Wise Congress House
15 East 84 Street
New York, NY   10028
(212) 879-4500

Jewish National Fund
Mission Desk
42 East 69th Street
New York, NY   10021
(212) 879-9300

Young Israel
Achva for Young Adults
3 West 16th Street
New York, NY   10011
(212) 929-1525
    For young adults 22–29 years old.

Zionist Organization of America
Leadership Mission
4 East 34th Street
New York, NY   10016
(212) 481-1500

UJA Singles Mission
Department of Overseas Programs
United Jewish Appeal
1290 Avenue of the Americas
New York, NY   10104
(212) 980-1000

NOT QUITE MARRIED

Engaged Couples Seminar
Jewish Community Center
60 South River Street
Wilkes Barre, PA   18701
(717) 824-4646
    A course that is broad in scope and open only to those planning
marriage.

MARRIED

Marpeh Clinic
1967 Turnball Avenue, Suite 28
Bronx, NY   10473
(212) 597-3434
    The Marpeh Clinic is a unique outpatient service geared toward
providing a wide range of counseling and mental health services for
the observant Jew and his or her family.

TAME
Rabbi and Rebbetzin Daniel Fingerer
1709 Avenue J
Brooklyn, NY   11230
(718) 376-4088
    TAME stands for Torah and Marriage Enrichment. It is a
program developed by the Fingerers that consists of workshops for

married couples (and singles) to explore what Jewish marriage
ideally should be. It draws on Torah and on the most current
resources in the field of marital counseling.

Jewish Marriage Encounter
c/o Laurie and Bob Brussel
365 Woodmere Boulevard
Woodmere, NY   11598
(516) 374-6430
     A specifically Jewish wing of the marriage encounter move-
ment. This grass-roots organization leads weekends around the
nation, conducted by a rabbinic couple and a lay couple. Contact this
address for addresses of groups located in your area.

Marriage Encounter
National Office
Chuck and Sandy Ogg
4704 Jamerson Place
Orlando, FL   32807
     A nonprofit organization whose goal is to assist couples in
discovering their marriage through mutual trust and dialogue. Couples of all faiths and those with no religious affiliation are welcome to
share in this experience. Workshops are held countrywide.

"In Support of Marriage"
Group Services Division
92nd St. YM/YWHA
1395 Lexington Avenue
New York, NY   10028
(212) 427-6000
     This is a course that focuses on "two major areas of concern and
potential conflict in a relationship—sex and money."

Making Marriage Work
The University of Judaism
Dept. of Continuing Education
15600 Mulholland Drive
Los Angeles, CA   90024
(213) 476-9777
     A course for Jewish couples preparing to marry or recently
married. Run by a rabbi and a marriage counselor, the ten-session

program discusses money, sex, career–family conflicts, in-laws, remarriage, and more.

In almost all Jewish communities today, there are counseling services for engaged couples and married couples. For a detailed listing of Jewish family and children's agencies across the continent, see *Jewish and Female: A Guide and Sourcebook for Today's Jewish Woman* by Susan Weidman Schneider (a Touchstone Book published by Simon and Schuster Inc).

SINGLE AGAIN—WIDOWED

The Widow's Center
Temple Isaiah
10345 West Pico Boulevard
Los Angeles, CA   90064
(213) 277-2772

Phylliss Solow
20613 Callon Drive
Topanga, CA   90290
        Solow, a gerontologist, is the designer of widow-to-widow support group programs in Los Angeles County.

Widow-to-Widow
Mayer Kaplan Jewish Community Center
5050 Church Street
Skokie, IL   60076
(312) 675-2200
        This organization is for widows over 40.

Westchester Jewish Community Services, Inc.
172 South Broadway
White Plains, NY   10605
(914) 949-6761
        This agency runs a number of different programs for widows and widowers. The support groups require nominal fees and are led by professionals. Descriptions of some of the programs follow:

1. For widows and widowers of all ages there is a mutual support group that meets twice a month on Sunday evenings, 12 months

a year. The evening is divided into two parts: The earlier part is a bereavement group for the newly widowed and for people who are having trouble coping. The second portion of the evening is social, educational, and entertainment oriented.

2. There is another group that is specifically for widows and widowers with school-aged children. It meets every Wednesday night during the school year. A parents' group meets separately from groups for children who have lost their parents.

3. There is also a group for people who are not-so-newly widowed (minimum of a year) and want a professionally led support group. It meets every other Monday evening.

Widow-to-Widow
YM/YWHA and NHS of Montreal
5500 Westbury Avenue
Montreal, Canada H3W2W8
(514) 737-6551

Robin Siegel
c/o Jewish Family Service of Orange County
12181 Buaro Street, Suite G
Garden Grove, CA   92640
    Siegel did her Master's thesis at the Hebrew Union College-Jewish Institute of Religion on Jewish widows.

Women in Transition
125 South 9th Street
Philadelphia, PA   19107
(215) 922-7177, administrative offices
(215) 922-7500, 24-hour hotline
    Provides a full range of services to women of diverse ethnic, racial, and economic backgrounds, including individual, couple, and family counseling support groups and workshops. Programs are available for women experiencing separation, divorce, domestic violence, drug and alcohol abuse, and (re)entering the workforce. Some services are provided free of charge; others are provided on a sliding fee scale.

SINGLE AGAIN—ABANDONED AND DIVORCED

Agunah, Inc.
463 East 19 Street
Brooklyn, NY 11226

(718) 859-4896 (10 AM to 5 PM)
(718) 282-9805 (evenings)

Bet Din
Rabbinical Council of America
1250 Broadway, Suite 802
New York, NY   10001
(212) 594-3780
　　　To locate a *bet din* for a divorce, consult a local rabbi or contact this Orthodox national organization for a referral to local resources.

Bet Din
Rabbinical Assembly of America
3080 Broadway
New York, NY   10027
(212) 749-8000
　　　To locate a *bet din* for a divorce, consult a local rabbi or contact this Conservative national organization for a referral to local resources.

G.E.T. (Getting Equal Treatment)
P.O. Box 131
1021 Avenue I
Brooklyn, NY   11230
　　　This organization is focused on raising consciousness about the issue of *gets* through lecturing and other tactics.

REWARDS Program
Jewish Community Center
7900 Northaven Road
Dallas, TX   75230
(214) 739-2737
　　　Jewish women in Texas seeking to cope with their divorces may turn to this one-on-one counseling program.

"Growth Beyond Divorce"
Jewish Community Center
4800 East Alameda Avenue
Denver, CO   80222
(303) 399-2660
　　　For men and women who want to get beyond their divorce, the Denver Jewish Community Center offers this program.

"Facing the Problems of Divorce"
YM/YWHA
1395 Lexington Avenue
New York, NY   10028
    New York City's 92nd Street Y support group for separated and
divorced people.

Jewish Family Service
1610 Spruce Street
Philadelphia, PA   19103
(215) KI 5-3290
    Counseling for parents, children, and even grandparents who
are trying to cope with divorce is available to the Jews of Philadelphia.

Single Parent Family Center
YM/YWHA
45-35 Kissena Boulevard
Flushing, NY   11355
    A multiservice center for parents with children under the age
of 18.

Orthodox Single Parents Center
Boro Park YM/YWHA
4912 14 Avenue
Brooklyn, NY   11219
(718) 438-5921
    Part of a growing recognition that divorce is a growing reality in
the Orthodox community.

National Havurah Coordinating Committee
270 West 89 Street
New York, NY   10024
(212) 496-2960
    or
9315 SW 61 Court
Miami, FL 33156
(305) 666-7349
    Single-parent families may feel more welcome in a *havurah* as
opposed to a large synagogue congregation. Contact this national
office for information on the *havurot* in your area.

Women in Transition
125 South 9th Street
Philadelphia, PA   19107
(215) 922-7177, administrative offices
(215) 922-7500, 24-hour hotline
     Provides a full range of services to women of diverse ethnic, racial, and economic backgrounds, including individual, couple, and family counseling support groups and workshops. Programs are available for women experiencing separation, divorce, domestic violence, drug and alcohol abuse, and (re)entering the workforce. Some services are provided free of charge; others are provided on a sliding fee scale.

REMARRIED

Stepfamily Association of America
602 East Joppa Road
Baltimore, MD   21204
(301) 823-7570
     The Stepfamily Association of America, Inc. is a focus for national advocacy related to the needs of stepfamilies. The goal of this organization is to expose myths, educate society, and provide information that will improve the chances of success for remarried families. They accomplish this by various means, including: local chapters, a stepfamily bulletin, an annual stepfamily conference, and educational resources. Contact this office for information on the chapter nearest you. They will also be able to provide you with a catalogue of educational resource materials that contains titles for stepparents, children of stepfamilies, and professionals.

Stepfamily Association of America, Metropolitan Chapter
Ms. Rebecca Ehrlich
Jewish Board of Family and Children's Services
120 West 57th Street
New York, NY   10019
(212) 582-9100
     This is the New York City area chapter. It is a self-help support group run by the participants under the guidance of a professional. Meetings are held on the second Tuesday of every month.

Jewish Board of Family and Children's Services
120 West 57th Street

New York, NY   10019
(212) 582-9100, ext. 196
      For therapeutic treatment for problems relating to remarriage
and blended families, contact this agency.

Jewish Family Life Education Program
Jewish Board of Family and Children's Services
120 West 57th Street
New York, NY   10019
(212) 460-0900
      For speakers on a variety of topics relating to remarriage and
blended families, contact this program.

INTERMARRIED

Intermarriage Groups

Rabbi Irwin Fishbein
Rabbinic Center for Research and Counseling
128 East Dudley Avenue
Westfield, NJ   07090
(201) 233-0419

Conversion Course Office
New York Federation of Reform Synagogues
835 Fifth Avenue
New York, NY   10021
(212) 249-0100

Dr. Egon Mayer
903 Park Avenue
New York, NY   10021

Rabbi Burt Siegel
445 East 65 Street, Apt. 4-A
New York, NY   10021
(212) 570-9047

Interfaith Couples Workshop
Family Life Education
Jewish Social Services Agency
6123 Montrose Road
Rockville, MD   20852
(301) 881-3700

This is just one of many such programs offered around the country. Contact your local federation or Jewish Community Center to find out about similar offerings in your area.

Intermarriage Programs of the United Synagogue of America
Committee on Intermarriage
United Synagogue of America
155 Fifth Avenue
New York, NY   10010
(212) 533-7800

Project Joseph
New Jersey Region
United Synagogue of America
910 Salem Avenue
Hillside, NJ   07205
(201) 353-7877

Union of American Hebrew Congregations

The UAHC (Reform) has Regional Outreach Coordinators, located throughout North America, who can provide information regarding interfaith marriages, programming for intermarrieds, and introduction to Judaism programs. A number of the regional coordinators are listed below. For a complete listing contact: UAHC, 838 Fifth Avenue, New York, NY   10021.

Canadian Council
Rabbi Daniel Gottlieb
534 Lawrence Avenue West, 205
Toronto, Ontario
Canada M6A 1A2
(416) 787-9938/8200

Southeast Council
Rabbi Rachel Hertzman

UAHC
Doral Executive Office
3785 NW 82nd Avenue, Suite 210
Miami, FL   33166
(305) 592-4792

Southwest Council
Rabbi Lawrence Jackofsky
UAHC
12700 Hillcrest Road, Suite 180
Dallas, TX   75230
(214) 960-6641

Midwest Council
UAHC
10425 Old Olive Street Road
Suite 205
St. Louis, MO   63141
(314) 997-7566

Pacific Southwest Council
Arlene Chernow
UAHC
6300 Wilshire Boulevard, Suite 1475
Los Angeles, CA   90048
(213) 653-9962

Great Lakes Council
Mimi Dunitz
UAHC
100 West Monroe Street, 312
Chicago, IL   60603
(312) 782-1477

GAY OR LESBIAN

For a more complete listing of Gay/Lesbian resource groups as well
as Gay/Lesbian synagogues, see *Jewish and Female: A Guide and
Sourcebook for Today's Jewish Woman* by Susan Weidman Schneider (a Touchstone Book published by Simon and Schuster Inc.).

Lesbian and Gay Jewish Activists
511 Capp Street
San Francisco, CA   94110

Jewish Parents and Friends of Gays
Charlotte K. Hoffman
3536 Chevy Chase Drive
Chevy Chase, MD   20815
(301) 652-7975

Lesbian and Gay Rights Task Force
New Jewish Agenda
150 Fifth Avenue
New York, NY   10011
(212) 620-0828

Women's Center
243 West 20th Street, 3rd Floor
New York, NY   10011
(212) 741-9114
        For Jewish lesbian events.

Zionist Union of Gays, New York
c/o CST
P.O. Box 1270, G.P.O.
New York, NY   10116

CHILDLESS

Adoption Resources

Rabbi Reuven Simons
Emergency Council of Jewish Families
2 Penn Plaza
New York, NY   10001
(212) 244-3100
        Contact for information on becoming a foster parent or if you
know of a child who needs placement.

Foster Homes/Adoption Information
Jewish Child Care Association
345 Madison Avenue
New York, NY   10017

(212) 371-1313
Contact Ms. Metric.

Vista Del Mar Child Care Services
3200 Motor Avenue
Los Angeles, CA   90034
(213) 836-1223

Louise Wise Services
12 East 94 Street
New York, NY   10028
(212) 876-3050
    This agency offers services such as counseling for unwed parents, residential care for women, plus adoption placement and postadoptive services for adoptees, birth parents, and adoptive parents.

Children's Home Society
800 Northwest 15th Street
Miami, FL   33125
(305) 324-1262
    Since the elimination of adoption facilities at the Jewish Family Services of Dade County, this nonsectarian agency has worked with Jewish families who want to place Jewish children in Jewish homes, or who are looking for Jewish children to adopt. They try to place children in Dade County Florida first; if that is not possible, they place them in other Florida counties. They do not handle out-of-state adoptions.

"A Rabbi's Guide to Adoption"
Central Conference of American Rabbis
790 Madison Avenue
New York, NY   10021
    A useful resource.

Pregnancy Loss Counseling
Jewish Women's Resource Center
National Council of Jewish Women—New York Section
9 East 69 Street
New York, NY   10021
(212) 535-5900

Peer-counseling in a Jewish context for women and couples dealing with miscarriage and stillbirths. They also conduct a Pregnancy After Loss Program, for pregnant women who have had a miscarriage in the past.

"The Report on Foreign Adoption"
International Concerns Committee for Children
911 Cypress Drive
Boulder, CO 80303
    This report is available for $15.

OURS Inc.
3307 Highway 100 North, Suite 203
Minneapolis, MN   55422
(612) 535-4829
    This organization also publishes a magazine.

North American Council on Adoptable Children
P.O. Box 14808
Minneapolis, MN   55414
(612) 644-3036

Latin American Parents Association
Box 72
Seaford, NY   11783

For Jewish Adoptive Parents

Stars of David
c/o Phyllis Nissen
Temple Shalom Emeth
14-16 Lexington Street
Burlington, MA   01803
(617) 272-7454

Single Mothers By Choice
Jane Mattes
PO Box 1642
Gracie Square Station
New York, NY 10028
(212) 988-0993

Glossary

Abbah: father

Aggadah: homiletical *Midrash*

Agunah: (pl. *agunot*): a woman who does not know whether her husband is dead or alive

Akarah: barren

Al het: a prayer said on the Day of Atonement in which one asks God's forgiveness for a long list of sins

Aliyah: the act of settling in the land of Israel, considered by some to be a commandment

Almanah: a widow

Am Kadosh: a holy nation (refers to Israel)

Arayot: forbidden sexual relationships

Aufruf (Yid.): the bridegroom's *aliyah* to the Torah on the sabbath prior to his wedding

Ayshet ish: the wife of a man

Baba Batra: a talmudic tractate of the order *Nezikin* that deals with laws of property ownership, inheritance, and preparation of legal documents

Ba'al teshuvah: one who has successfully repented of his sins, or one who becomes a religious Jew

Badhan: a joker

Bar mitzvah (fem. *bat mitzvah*): a Jew who has taken on the responsibilities of an adult, or the ceremony, usually at the age of 13, at which the Jew becomes a full-fledged member of the community

B'diavad: after the event

Ben: son

Berakhah: a blessing
Bet Din: a tribunal empowered to make legal decisions
Biah: sexual union
Bimah: raised platform found in many synagogues
Brit: a covenant
Brit milah: the ritual circumcision of a Jewish boy on his eighth day
Bubby (Yid.): grandmother
Da'at: knowledge
Daven (Yid.): to recite one of the proscribed services
Dayan Emet: a name for God meaning the Judge of truth
Eretz Yisrael: the land of Israel
Erusin: betrothal (engagement)
Esther Rabbah: rabbinic exegesis on the book of Esther
Evenha-Ezer: a book of halakhic rulings by the Raban (Rav Eliezer ben Nathan of Mainz) who lived from c. 1090 to c. 1170
Ezer k'negdo: companion; help-mate
Galut: exile from Israel; the diaspora
Gaon: literally a genius; a leader of a Jewish community by merit of his scholarship
Gefilte fish (Yid.): chopped fish, traditional appetizer, usually made from carp, white fish, and yellow pike
Genesis Rabbah: an exegetical verse by verse commentary on the entire book of Genesis
Get (pl. *gittin*): a writ of divorce
Gittin: a talmudic tractate of the order *Nashim* that deals with the laws of the *get*, a document of release (usually of divorce)
Haggadah: a book read at the Passover seder that includes an account of the exodus from Egypt
Halakhah: normative Jewish law
Halakhic: according to, or abiding by normative Jewish law
Halitzah: a ceremony that nullifies the obligation of a man to marry his brother's childless widow
Hallah: a braided loaf of bread, usually eaten on the sabbath and holidays
Hametz: leavened food, which is forbidden on Passover
Hanukkah: holiday beginning on the 25th of the Hebrew month of *Kislev*, celebrating the Jews' victory over the Greeks
Ha-Shem: God (literally the name)
Hasidim: members of a movement that began in the 18th century. It emphasizes spirituality over unrelenting dogmatism.
Havdalah: the ceremony at the conclusion of the sabbath and festivals, separating a holy day from a regular one, using wine, spices, and candle
Havurah (pl. *havurot*): a community or group
Hazakah: a precedent
Hesed: righteousness
Herem: excommunication from the Jewish community, proclaimed by a community leader or leaders

Het: a sin according to Jewish law

Heter: a permission obtained from a rabbinic authority

Hilkhot Issurei Biah: law of forbidden sex

Hillel: an early rabbinic sage who founded a school of sages (d. 10 c.e.)

Hirhurim: thoughts, meditations

Hukkah: law, custom

Huppah: a canopy under which Jewish couples are married

Ima: mother

Kabbalah: Jewish mystical movement

Kaddish: Aramaic prayer recited by congregations and mourners

Kashrut: Jewish dietary laws

Kavanah: intent; also a feeling of spirituality which is desirable when praying

Kedeshah: female prostitute

Kedushah: holiness; also refers to a section of the *amidah* prayer

Kedushat Yisrael: the holiness of Israel

Kesef: money

Ketubah: a marriage certificate, often elaborately decorated

Ketubot: a talmudic tractate of the order *Nashim* that deals with marriage laws

Keva: fixed, set

Kiddush: a blessing of sanctification; the phrase is commonly used to denote the blessing over wine

Kiddush ha-Shem: the sanctification of God

Kiddushin: talmudic tractate in the order *Nashim* that deals with marital laws; the marriage ceremony

Kinyan: symbolic transfer of ownership

Klal Yisrael: the community of Israel

Kof et yitzreinu: overcome evil inclination (lust)

Kohen (pl. *Kohanim*): priest of the Jewish temple cult, or their descendants

Kovesh et yitzro: one who conquers or controls his impulses

Kreplakh (Yid.): a meat dumpling

Lashon ha-ra: gossip or other hurtful talk

Latkes (Yid.): potato pancakes traditionally eaten on Hanukkah

Letov lakh (f.): for your benefit

Leviticus Rabbah: rabbinic exegesis on the book of Leviticus

L'hathilah: from the beginning

L'havdil: a phrase meaning "to differentiate," usually said after comparing something holy to something profane

Lulav: four types of branches that Jews carry and bless on Sukkot in commemoration of the temple ceremony

Malkhut: a kingdom

Mamzer (pl. *mamzerim*): a child born of an adulterous or incestuous relationship

Maimonides, Moses: (1135–1204) a prominent Medieval scholar from Spain. His works include *Mishneh Torah,* a legal code, and *Moreh Ne-*

vuhim, a philosophical treatise.

Matzoh *(matzah):* unleavened bread eaten on Passover in commemoration of the bread baked by the Jews hastening to leave Egypt.

Mazal tov: literally (your) good luck; congratulations

Megillah: talmudic tractate in the order *Moed* that deals primarily with the reading of Esther on Purim

Mehitzah: the divide between the men's and women's sections of traditional synagogues

Mehutanim: the father and mother of one's son-in-law or daughter-in-law

Mentsch (Yid., pl. *mentschen):* a good, decent person

Mentschlikheit (Yid.): humanity, humanness

Meraglim: spies, or the spies sent by Moses to scout the land of Canaan

Mezuzah: an encased scroll containing the *Shema* prayer, found on the doorposts of Jewish houses

Mi-d'oraita: (a commandment) of biblical origin

Midot: extent (measure, pl.)

Midrash: exegetical material on the Bible, both legal and homiletical

Mikvah (pl. *mikvaot):* a ritual bath, used for purification

Mishkav zakhar: male sodomy

Mishnah: a collection of oral laws compiled by Rabbi Judah ha-Nasi (136–220 c.e.) that form the basis of the Talmud

Mishneh Torah: a legal code, written by Maimonides, containing all the laws in the Torah

Mitzrayim: Egypt

Mitzvah (pl. *mitzvot):* a commandment

Minyan: ten Jews (traditionally adult males) needed for public prayer

Mohel: one who performs ritual circumcisions

Motzi: a blessing thanking God for bringing forth bread from the earth

Nahas: pleasure

Nedarim: talmudic tractate in the order *Nashim* that deals with the law of vows

Nibul peh: obscene language

Niddah: talmudic tractate in the order *Tohorot* that deals with laws of uncleanness

Nissu'in: marriage

Oneg Shabbat: a sabbath celebration

Oness: rape

Palgah gufah: a half being

Pesah: festival beginning on the 15th of the Hebrew month of *Nisan,* celebrating Israel's redemption from slavery

Pesahdik (Yid.): kosher food to be eaten on Passover

Peshat: the clear or literal meaning (often of a biblical selection)

Perutah: a coin

Peru urevu: the commandment to "be fruitful and multiply"

Peyot: sidelocks worn by religious Jews

Pidyon ha-ben: ceremony in which a father redeems his son from God by giving money to a descendant of a temple priest

Pilagshut: concubinage

Purim: holiday falling on the 14th of the Hebrew month of *Adar,* which celebrates the Jews' triumph over the wicked Haman in ancient Persia

Ravak: bachelor

Rugelakh (Yid.): rolled pastries filled with raisins and nuts

Sanhedrin: talmudic tractate in the order *Nezikin* that deals with courts and capital punishment

Seder: the service recited in the home on the first evening(s) of Passover, as well as the accompanying meal

Sefirot: kabbalistic concept of emulations of God

Shabbat: Saturday, the Jewish sabbath

Shadkhan: a matchmaker

Shalom bayit: peace in the household, for the sake of which certain sacrifices are appropriate

Shammai: an early rabbinic sage who is known to be strict and uncompromising. Shammai and his school often disagreed with Hillel and his school.

Shavuot: a festival held on the 6th of the Hebrew month of *Sivan,* celebrating the receiving of the Torah at Mt. Sinai.

Shema: a central prayer of biblical origin

Shetar: a formal legal document such as a betrothal agreement

Sheva berakhot: seven blessings recited at a marriage ceremony and celebration; also, celebrations held in honor of the newlyweds following the wedding day

Shevirat ha-kelim: breaking of dishes at the signing of a marriage contract

Shivah: the seven initial days of mourning following the death of an immediate relative

Shlep (Yid.): to travel a long distance or carry a heavy load

Shohet: one who slaughters animals for eating according to Jewish dietary laws

Shtreiml: hat worn by some religious Jews

Shul (Yid.): synagogue

Shulhan Arukh: a concise legal code written by Joseph Caro in the 16th century

Siddur (pl. *siddurim*): a Jewish prayerbook

Siman tov: a good sign or omen

Simhat ishto: his wife's happiness

Sofer: a Jewish scribe

Sotah: a talmudic tractate found in the order *Nashim,* most of which deals with laws concerning adultery

Sukkah: a makeshift hut in which families eat, study, and sometimes sleep during the holiday of Sukkot

Sukkah: talmudic tractate in the order *Moed* that deals with laws of Sukkot

Sukkot: festival beginning on the 15th of the Hebrew month of *Tishrei.* A

thanksgiving festival that also commemorates Israel's wanderings in
the desert.

Taharat ha-mishpahah: family purity

Tahor: pure

Takkanah: a rabbinic amendment or addition to *halakhah*

Tallit: a fringed shawl worn by Jews (traditionally male) during prayer

Talmud: a compilation of rabbinic teachings, comprised of the *Mishnah*,
which expands on the Torah, and the *Gemmara*, which expands on
the *Mishnah*

Tameh: impure; profane

Tanakh: an acronym for the Hebrew Bible; (Torah, *Nevi'im, Ketubim)*

Tanya Debei Elijah: a book of responsa written by Elijah ben Benjamin
Ha-Levi (d. after 1540)

Tena'im: conditions; terms

Teshuvah: the process of repentance

Tohara: purification

Torah she-be'al peh: the Talmud's oral law as opposed to the Bible's

Tosefta sofah: appendix supplement to the *Mishnah*

Tsimmes (Yid.): a sweet stew (usually made with carrots, prunes, and
honey)

Tzarah d'gufah: her physical misfortune

Tzedakah: righteousness; charity

Tzniyut: appropriate modesty and decorum in dress and behavior

Tzuris (Yid.): trouble, problems

Ulpan (pl. *ulpanim*): institute teaching Hebrew to adults

Yalkut Shimon: comprehensive midrashic anthology covering the entire
Bible

Yatom: an orphan

Yesod: foundation; basis

Yetzer ha-ra: the impulse that pulls one toward evil (lust)

Yevamot: a tractate of the Talmud, found in the order *Nashim* that deals
with, among other things, the laws of *yibum*

Yibum: the obligation of a man to marry his brother's childless widow

Yiddishkeit (Yid.): Jewishness

Yihud: consummation of a marriage immediately following the wedding

Yihus: relationship; connection

Yoma: a tractate of the Talmud, found in the order *Moed* that deals with
laws of *Yom Kippur*

Yom tov: a Jewish holiday on which work is forbidden

Zayde (Yid.): grandfather

Z'nut: improper sex

Zohar Hadash: the fifth volume of the kabbalistic *Zohar.* It is a collection
of sayings and texts found after the main body of the *Zohar* was
printed.

Bibliography

SINGLE

Books and Articles

Auerbach, Marilyn Iris. "Single but Equal." *Jewish Woman's Outlook* (Spring 1985):5, 10.

Axelrod, Toby. "Back to the Future: New Twists in Matchmaking." *The Jewish Week*, 201:5:30, 40, 42.

Barkas, Janet. *Single in America.* New York: Atheneum, 1980.

Biale, Rachel. *Women and Jewish Law: An Exploration of Women's Issues in Halakhic Sources.* New York: Schocken Books, 1984.

Bluestone, Naomi. "Sunset, Sunset: The Life of Jewish Singles." *Moment* 2(1):22.

Blumengarten, Louis H. "I'm Ready But What Can I Do?" *Sh'ma* (January 1978).

Davis, Hanna B. "Toward a New Understanding of Jewish Men." *Genesis 2* (March 1982).

Filsenburg, Rosa. "The Noah Syndrome." *Davka* (Winter 1975).

Fishman, Sylvia Barack. "Heaven Can't Wait: Jewish Marriages." *The Jewish Week* (July 1, 1988):21.

Gordon, Suzanne. *Lonely in America: A Portrait of Americans—Young, Old, Married, Single, in Groups and Alone.* New York: Simon and Schuster, 1976.

Handelman, S. "Stranger in a Strange Land: Plight of the Single Orthodox Woman." *Jewish Observer* 1983;17:17–21.

Harris, Marylou. "The Men Are Not Always Nice." *Present Tense* 1977; 4:13–16.

Hartman, Susan. "Arranged Marriages Live On." *The New York Times* (August 10, 1988): C12.

Hofstein, Saul. "Perspectives on the Jewish Single Parent Family." *Journal of Jewish Communal Service* 1978;54:229–240.

Jacobs, Betty. "Thou Shalt Get Married (Already!)." *Moment* 1988;13:26–31.

Jacobs, Phil. "Singles and Their Personal Vendettas." *Baltimore Jewish Times* (June 11, 1982).

Jolles, Andrea. "The Singles Plight." *The Jewish Week* (October 7, 1983).

Klein, Judith Weinstein. *Jewish Identity and Self-Esteem: Healing Wounds Through Ethnotherapy.* New York: American Jewish Committee.

Lebovitz, Yehuda. *Shidduchim and Zivugim: The Torah Perspective on Choosing Your Mate.* Southfield, MI: Targum Press, Inc., 1988.

Levine, Shlomo. *The Singular Problems of the Single Jewish Parent.* New York: United Synagogue Commission on Jewish Education, 1981.

Listfield, Stephen Chaim. "Turning Singles Into Spouses." *Moment* 1988; 13:20–25.

Milton, Mimsi. "Single By Choice?" *Baltimore Jewish Times* (June 19, 1987):64–65ff.

Pash, Barbara. "The Marriage Connection." *Baltimore Jewish Times* (February 13, 1987):80–82.

Polonsky, Linda. "Their Community Work Proved to be a Labor of Love." *The Jewish Week* (January 23, 1987):27–28.

Rosove, J. L. "A Synagogue Model for the Single Jew." *Journal of Reform Judaism* 1986;33:29–36.

Shapiro, C. "Shadchanim-Matchmakers." *Jewish Observer* 1985;18:31–38.

Silverberg, David. "Anatomy of a Singles Group." *Baltimore Jewish Times* (January 12, 1979):46ff.

Yager, Jan. "Single and Jewish: Conversations with Unaffiliated Jewish Singles." American Jewish Committee (1986).

Zelizer, Viviana A. "The Unmarried Jew: Problems and Prospects." *Conservative Judaism* 1978;32:16–21.

Pamphlets

Singles Program Directory. Individual copies available for free. Published by the National Commission on Singles, United Synagogue of America, Tom Kagedan, Coordinator. 155 Fifth Avenue, New York, NY 10010.

Five Model Programs—A Handbook. 16 pages. $2.00. Published by the Commission on Singles, United Synagogue of America, Tom Kagedan, Coordinator. Edited by Rabbi Robert Rubin.

Videotapes

"Ethnotherapy With Jews." 42 min. A videocassette and discussion guide. Based on *Jewish Identity and Self-Esteem: Healing Wounds Through Ethnotherapy,* a pioneering study of the forces shaping Jewish identity, based on group-encounter dialogues and research findings on positive and negative feelings toward Judaism and Jewishness. Rental $50. American Jewish Committee, 165 East 56th Street, New York, NY 10019.

NOT QUITE MARRIED

Books and Articles

Baum, Charlotte, Hyman, Paula, and Michel, Sonya. *The Jewish Woman in America.* New York: New American Library, 1977.

Biale, Rachel. *Women and Jewish Law: An Exploration of Women's Issues in Halakhic Sources.* New York: Schocken Books, 1984.

Borowitz, Eugene. *Choosing a Sex Ethic.* New York: Schocken Books, 1969.

Brewer, Joan Schere. *Sex and the Modern Jewish Woman: An Annotated Bibliography.* Fresh Meadows, New York: Biblio Press, 1986.

Chipman, Jonathan. "Sex and the Tradition: A Rejoinder." *Response* 1977;34:103–106.

Dresner, Samuel H. and Sherwin, Byron. "Before Marriage—Pre-Marital Fidelity." *Impact* 1978;Winter:4–18.

Geller, Laura, and Koltun, Elizabeth. "Single and Jewish: Toward a New Definition of Completeness." *The Jewish Woman: New Perspectives,* ed. Elizabeth Koltun, pp. 43–49. New York: Schocken Books, 1976.

Gittlesohn, Roland. *Love, Sex and Marriage: A Jewish View.* New York: Union of American Hebrew Congregations, 1980.

Gordis, Robert. *Love and Sex: A Modern Jewish Perspective.* New York: Farrar, Strauss, & Giroux, 1978.

Lamm, Maurice. *The Jewish Way in Love and Marriage.* New York: Harper and Row, 1982.

Mayer, Barbara. "Sex and the Jewish Girl." *Cosmopolitan* 1970;169:68–74, 175.

Milton, M. K. "Unmarried Couples—New Etiquette Meets Jewish Tradition." *Baltimore Jewish Times* (March 9, 1979).

Schneider, Susan Weidman. *Jewish and Female: Choices and Changes in Our Lives Today.* New York: Simon and Schuster, 1984.

Schwartz, Tony, et al. "Living Together." *Newsweek* 1977;90:46–50.

Videotapes and Films

"Living with Peter." 22 min. (1973). This is an informal, candid, autobiographical documentary of two grandchildren of European Jewish immigrants to America—worldly, college-educated people, whom all of us immediately recognize—who have chosen to live together without being married. Even though the film deals casually with the issues it raises, it is a good discussion starter. Rental $25. Miriam Weinstein, 36 Shepard Street, Cambridge, MA   02138.

"We Get Married Twice." 22 min. (1973). Is a sequel to "Living with Peter." Miriam and Peter decide to get married, first in their hip, unauthoritarian casual ceremony; then for the second time in a very formal fashion organized by and to suit the tastes of Miriam's parents. The two films taken together should spark a lively discussion. If time permits the showing of only one film, the second, properly introduced, is the more revealing. Rental $25. Miriam Weinstein, 36 Shepard Street, Cambridge, MA   02138.

MARRIED

Books and Articles

Bernard, Jessie. *The Future of Marriage.* New York: World Publishing Co., 1972.

Biale, Rachel. *Women and Jewish Law: An Exploration of Women's Issues in Halakhic Sources.* New York: Schocken Books, 1984.

Baum, Charlotte, Hyman, Paula, and Michel, Sonya. *The Jewish Woman in America.* New York: New American Library, 1977.

Borowitz, Eugene. *Choosing A Sex Ethic.* New York: Schocken Books, 1969.

Bulka, Reuven P. *Jewish Marriage: A Halakhic Ethic.* Hoboken, NJ: Ktav, 1986.

Davidovich, David. *Jewish Marriage Contracts Through the Ages.* New York: Adama Books, 1985.

Deburger, James E. *Marriage Today: Problems, Issues and Alternatives.* New York: Schenkman, 1977.

Diamant, Anita. *The New Jewish Wedding.* New York: Summit Books, 1985.

Dresner, Samuel H., and Sherwin, Byron. "Before Marriage—Pre-Marital Fidelity." *Impact* 1978;Winter:4–18.

Eider, Shimon D. *Halachos of Niddah.* Lakewood, NJ: Halacha Publications, 1981.

Feldman, David M. *Marital Relations, Birth Control and Abortions in Jewish Law.* New York: Schocken Books, 1974.

Furstenberg, Rochelle. "The Modern Mikveh." *Hadassah Magazine* 6:22–23, 36–37.

Ganz-Ribner, Mindy. "Observance Despite Reservations." *Sh'ma* (January 9, 1980).

Garfiel, Evelyn. *The Marriage Service.* New York: United Synagogue of America, 1964–1975.

Geller, Laura. "Mikveh is not a Mitzvah for Me." *Sh'ma* (January 9, 1980).

Gittelsohn, Roland B. *The Extra Dimension: A Jewish View of Marriage.* New York: Union of American Hebrew Congregations, 1983.

Glen, Jacob B. "Sex and Marriage in Judaism." *The Jewish Forum* (February 1961):21–22.

Goldstein, Elyse M. "Take Back the Waters: A Feminist Reappropriation of Mikvah." *Lilith* 1986;15:15–16.

Goodman, Phil and Goodman, Hanna. *The Jewish Marriage Anthology.* Philadelphia: The Jewish Publication Society of America, 1965.

Gordis, Robert. "The Jewish Concept of Marriage." *Judaism* 2:225–238.

_____. *Love and Sex: A Modern Jewish Perspective.* New York: Farrar, Straus & Giroux, 1978.

Green, Alan S. *A Celebration of Marriage: When Faith Serves Love.* New York: Collier Books, 1979.

Greenberg, Blu. *How to Run a Traditional Jewish Household.* New York: Simon and Schuster, 1985.

_____. "Integrating Mikveh and Modernity." *Sh'ma* (January 9, 1980).

_____. "Marriage in the Jewish Tradition." *Journal of Ecumenical Studies* 1985;Winter:3–20.

_____. *On Women and Judaism.* Philadelphia: Jewish Publication Society, 1981.

Kaplan, Joseph C. "Discussing Niddah, Mikveh, Family Purity." *Sh'ma* (January 9, 1980).

Lamm, Maurice. *The Jewish Way in Love and Marriage.* New York: Harper & Row, 1982.

Lamm, Norman. *A Hedge of Roses: Jewish Insights into Marriage.* Spring Valley, NY: Philipp Feldheim, 1977.

Meiselman, M. *Jewish Woman in Jewish Law.* Library of Jewish Law Ethics. Vol. 6. Hoboken, NJ: Ktav, 1978.

Raphael, Mar Lee, ed. *Approaches to Modern Judaism.* Chico, CA: Scholars Press, 1983.

Routtenberg, Lilly S., and Seldin, Ruth R. *The Jewish Wedding Book: A Practical Guide to the Traditions and Social Customs of the Jewish Wedding.* New York: Schocken Books, 1969.

Strassfeld, Sharon, and Green, Kathy. *The Jewish Family Book.* New York: Bantam, 1981.

Videotapes and Films

"A Seal Upon Thy Heart." 30 min. 16 mm film. $45 rental. Share the experience of a young couple that has chosen to embrace a modern Jewish lifestyle. They show, in a personal way, how and why "Jewish marriage means more than just owning a *ketubah* and silver candlesticks." A timeless classic produced in 1978. Alden Films, 7820 20th Avenue, Brooklyn, NY 11214, (718) 331-1045. Also available for purchase ($69.50) in videotape from the Board of Jewish Education of Greater New York, 426 West 58th Street, New York, NY 10019, (212) 245-8200.

"Mikva, Marriage, and Mazel Tov." 18 min. 16 mm film. $35 rental. Presents to a young couple the historic significance of the *mikvah* and the application of the laws of the Torah to marriage. Thought provoking while entertaining. The traditional Jewish marriage, the two weeks of abstinence, and the requirement for restraining and admissibility are thoroughly explained. It is useful to students of folklife, Jewish history, and to general audiences for its religious and social implications. Alden Films, 7820 20th Avenue, Brooklyn, NY 11214, (718) 331-1045.

"In Her Hands: Women and Ritual." 20-min. videotape. A woman's look at a woman's ritual, presented from the point of view of two women—one married and one single—in Brooklyn's Syrian Jewish community. Contact: Dr. Faye Ginzberg, New York University, Dept. of Anthropology, 25 Waverly Place, New York, NY 10003, (212) 998-8558.

SINGLE AGAIN—WIDOWED

Book and Articles

Dahl, Dolores. *Suddenly Alone: A Progression of Emotions Embraced by a Widow on the Path of Healing.* Lebanon, OR: Single Vision, 1987.

Filsenburg, Rosa. "The Noah Syndrome." *Davka* (Winter 1975).

Foehner, Charlotte, and Cozart, Carol. *Widow's Handbook: A Guide for Living.* Golden, CO: Fulcrum, Inc., 1987.

Gantz, Paula. "Our Golden Years." *Lilith* 1983;10:6–9.

Grollman, Earl A. *Concerning Death: A Practical Guide for the Living.* Boston, MA: Beacon Press, 1974.

_____. *Living, Where a Loved One Died.* Boston, MA: Beacon Press, 1987.

Hensley, J. Clark. *Coping With Being Single Again.* Nashville, TN: Brondman Press, 1978.

Kreis, Bernardine, and Pattie, Alice. *Up from Grief.* New York: Walker and Co., 1984.

Kushner, Harold S. *When Bad Things Happen to Good People.* New York: Schocken Books, 1981.

Silman, Roberta. *Boundaries.* Boston: Little Brown, 1979. (fiction)

Singer, Lilly, Sirot, Margaret, and Rodd, Susan. *Beyond Loss: A Practical Guide Through Grief to a Meaningful Life.* New York: E. P. Dutton, 1988.

SINGLE AGAIN—ABANDONED AND DIVORCED

Books and Articles

A Feminist Handbook on Separation and Divorce. New York: Charles Scribner, 1975.

Ain, Stewart. "Controversial Bill Provokes Heated Debate." *Jewish World* (August 5-11, 1983).

American Jewish Committee, Institute of Human Relations. *Service Providers Look at Divorce and the Jewish Family: A Consultation.* New York, 1983.

Amram, David Werner. *The Jewish Law of Divorce.* New York: Hermon Press, 1975.

Belt, Anita. "Jewish Single Parent." In *Jewish Family Book,* ed. Sharon Strassfeld and Kathy Green, pp. 23–31. New York: Bantam, 1981.

Benson, Paulette, and Bissell, Sherry. *Divorce and Jewish Life and Tradition.* Denver: Alternatives in Religious Education, 1977.

Berman, Gerald S. "The Adaptable American Jewish Family: An Inconsistency in Theory." *Jewish Journal of Sociology* 1976;18:5–16.

Biale, Rachel. *Women and Jewish Law: An Exploration of Women's Issues in Halakhic Sources.* New York: Schocken Books, 1984.

Bissell, Sherry. "My Divorce and My Community." *Sh'ma* (April 1978).

Bubis, Gerald B. "The Single Parent Family." *Reconstructionist* (February 1976):7–10.

Chelms, S. "Personal Advice for Jewish People." Leo Baeck College Lectures. *European Judaism* 1985;19:7–13.

Chiger, M. "Ruminations over the Agunah Problem." *The Jewish Law Annual* 1981;4:207–225.

Cottle, Thomas J. "Divorce and the Jewish Child." New York: American Jewish Committee, 1981.

Dick, Judah. "Is an Agreement to Deliver or Accept a *Get* in the Event of a Civil Divorce Halachically Feasible?" *Tradition* 1983;Summer: 91–106.

Donelson, Kenneth, and Donelson, Irene. *Married Today, Single Tomorrow.* New York: Doubleday, 1969.

Eisenstein, Ira. "A New Approach to Jewish Divorce." *Journal of Divorce* 1983;Summer:85–90.

Feldman, David M. *Marital Relations, Birth Control and Abortion in Jewish Law.* New York: Schocken Books, 1968.

Filsenburg, Rosa. "The Noah Syndrome." *Davka* (Winter 1975).

Fried, Jacob, ed. *Jews and Divorce.* New York: Ktav Publishing House, 1968.

Friedell, Steven F. "Enforceability of Religious Law in Secular Courts—It's Kosher but is it Constitutional?" *Michigan Law Review 1641* (1973).

Friedman, Nathalie with Rogers, Theresa F. "The Divorced Parent and the Jewish Community." New York: American Jewish Committee, 1985.

_____ . "The Jewish Community and Children of Divorce: A Pilot Study of Perceptions and Responses." New York: American Jewish Committee, 1983.

Gershenfeld, Matti. "Planning for Single Parents." In *Proceedings: Consultation on Single Parent Families,* ed. National Jewish Welfare Board, pp. 23–26.

Gershfield, Edward M. "The Jewish Law of Divorce." New York: National Council of Jewish Women, 1967.

Gertel, Elliot. "Jewish Views on Divorce." New York: American Jewish Committee, 1984.

Grade, Chaim. *The Agunah.* New York: Twayne Publishers, 1974. (fiction)

Greenberg, Blu. *How to Run a Traditional Jewish Household.* New York: Simon & Schuster, 1983.

_____ . *On Women and Judaism.* Philadelphia: Jewish Publication Society of America, 1981.

Greenberg, Simon. "And He Writes Her a Bill of Divorcement." *Conservative Judaism* 1970;24:75.

Grishaver, Joel Lurie. "From Ketubah to Get." *Keeping Posted* 1981;23:6–8.

Grollman, Earl A., ed. *Explaining Divorce to Children.* Boston: Beacon Press, 1969.

Harris, Monford. "Toward a Theology of Divorce." *Conservative Judaism* 1969;23:33–44.

Haut, Irwin H. *Divorce in Jewish Law and Life.* New York: Sepher-Hermon Press, 1983.

Hentoff, Nat. "Who Will Rescue the Jewish Women Chained in Limbo?" *The Village Voice* 1983;28:6.

Hofstein, Saul. "Perspectives on the Jewish Single-Parent Family." *Journal of Jewish Communal Service* 1978;54:229–240.

Hunt, Morton, and Hunt, Bernice. *The Divorce Experience.* New York: McGraw-Hill, 1977.

Jacobs, Phil. "When 'Happily Ever After' Turns into the Nightmare of Divorce." *Baltimore Jewish Times* (March 11, 1988):56–60.

Kamen, Marcia. "Wednesday the Rabbi Called at My Divorce." *Ms.* 1974;2:14–15.

Lamm, Norman. "Recent Additions to the Ketubah, A Halakhic Critique." *Tradition* 1959;2:93.

Lauter, Evelyn. "The Family in Transition: A Search for New Answers." *The Reconstructionist* (January 1980).

Levine, Shlomo D. *The Singular Problems of the Single Jewish Parent.* New York: United Synagogue Commission on Jewish Education, 1981.

Lookstein, Haskel. "Jewish Divorce: Solutions to the Problem." *The Jewish Week* (February 6, 1987).

Neff, Carol. "Socializing, Support, and Shabbat." *National Jewish Monthly* 1979;93:20–22.

Novak, David. "The Agunah, or the Case of the Uncooperative Husband," In *Law and Theology in Judaism,* ed. David Novak. New York: Ktav Publishing House, 1974.

_____ . "Annulment in Lieu of Divorce in Jewish Law." *The Jewish Law Annual* 1981;4:188–206.

Oles, Miriam. "Getting a *Get:* Some Experiences." In *The Second Jewish Catalog,* ed. Michael Strassfeld and Sharon Strassfeld, pp. 121–122. Philadelphia: Jewish Publication Society of America, 1976.

Osofsky, Bracha. "Kol Isha Progress on the *Get* Problem." *Lilith* 1983;10:4–5.

Rackman, Honey. "Getting a *Get:* How Some Husbands are Blackmailing Their Wives and Getting Away With It." *Moment* 13(3):34–41.

Rakeffet-Rothkoff, Aaron. "Annulment of Marriage within the Context of Cancellation of the *Get*." *Tradition* 1975;15:173–185.

Schwartz, S. H. "Conservative Judaism and the Agunah." *Conservative Judaism* 1982;Fall:37–44.

Seltzer, Sanford. "Some Suggested Guidelines for School and Synagogue." New York: Union of American Hebrew Congregations.

Siegel, Seymour. "Divorce." In *The Second Jewish Catalog,* ed. Michael Strassfeld and Sharon Strassfeld, pp. 108–121. Philadelphia: Jewish Publication Society of America, 1976.

Weinberger, Bernard. "The Growing Rate of Divorce in Orthodox Jewish Life." *Jewish Life* 1976;Spring:9–14.

Weiss-Rosmarin, Trude W. "The Agony of the Agunah." *Conservative Judaism* 1965;20:51–53.

_____ . "A Grain of Truth." *Jewish Spectator* (March, 1968):30–33.

Videotapes and Films

"The Empty Chair." 22 min. (1981). In this poignant drama, members of a divorced, single-parent family struggle to maintain their integrity as a family while observing Jewish tradition on Pesah. Purchase, $79.50. Board of Jewish Education Greater New York, 426 West 58th Street, New York, NY 10019.

"Family Life Forum" is a series of 15 programs, each 28 minutes long. A talk-show format focuses on vital human concerns and experiences. 5. Divorce, 6. Single Parenting, 8. Week-end Parenting, and 9. Remarriage are available as a package. Rental of VHS 1/2"—$35/show, 3/4"—$40/show. Jewish Board of Family and Children's Services, 120 West 57th Street, New York, NY 10019.

"Chris and Bernie." 25 min. (1975). A beautiful documentary about two 25-year-old divorced working women with young children. Seeking mutual support systems, they move in together, but still face the particular problems of the single parent. The picture focuses on a variety of important questions concerning the special needs of these parents. Rental, $35. New Day Films, P.O. Box 315, Franklin Lakes, NJ 07417.

"The Greenberg Family." 60 min. (1977). This film is a part of the series "Six American Families" broadcast on national television. It is a study of the single-parent family in which the other parent is very much an active participant. It examines the mother as a single parent, and the father as the weekend parent. Rental, $35. Syracuse University Film Center, 1455 East Colvin Street, Syracuse, NY 13210.

"Not Together Now: End of a Marriage." 25 min. (1974). This film focuses on both the single mother and the single father. What is particularly interesting is that this is one of the very few films dealing with the vulnerable single father. The film drags at some points, but gives an excellent overall picture of the single parent. Rental, $40. Polymorph Films, 118 South Street, Boston, MA   02111.

REMARRIED

Books and Articles

Appelman, Harlene. "Yours, Mine and Ours." *Hadassah* 1986;7:40–41.

Belovitch, Jeanne. *Making Remarriage Work.* Lexington, MA: Lexington Books, 1987.

Eisenstein, Elizabeth. *The Step Family: Living, Loving and Learning.* Boston, MA: Shambhala Publications, 1985.*

Keshet, Jamie K. *Love and Power in the Stepfamily: A Practical Guide.* New York: McGraw-Hill, 1986.*

Levine, Shlomo D. *Yours, Mine and Ours: A Guide to Remarriage and Stepparenting in a Jewish Mode.* New York: United Synagogue of American Commission on Jewish Education, 1981.

Messinger, Lillian. *Remarriage: A Family Affair.* New York: Plenum Press, 1984.*

Ricci, Isolina. *Mom's House, Dad's House: Making Shared Custody Work.* New York: Macmillan, 1980.*

Stuart, Richard B. and Jacobson, Barbara. *Second Marriage: Make it Happy! Make it Last!* New York: Norton, 1985.*

Visher, Emily and John. *Stepfamilies: Myths and Realities.* Secaucus, NJ: Lyle Stuart (Citadel Press), 1980.*

Videotapes and Films

"Family Life Forum" is a series of 15 programs, each 28 minutes long. It uses a talk-show format to focus on vital human concerns and experiences. Shows 5. Divorce, 6. Single Parenting, 8. Week-end Parenting, and 9. Remarriage are available as a package. Rental of VHS 1/2"— $35/show, 3/4"—$40/show. Jewish Board of Family and Children's Services, 120 West 57th Street, New York, NY   10019.

---

*Available for purchase from the Stepfamily Association of America, 602 East Joppa Road, Baltimore, MD   21204, (301) 823-7570.

INTERMARRIED

Books and Articles

Barron, Milton L. *The Blending American: Patterns of Intermarriage.* Chicago: Quadrangle Books, 1972.

Belin, David. *Why Choose Judaism: New Dimensions of Jewish Outreach.* New York: Union of American Hebrew Congregations, 1985.

Berman, Louis A. *Jews and Intermarriage: A Study in Personality and Culture.* New York: Thomas Yoseloff, 1968.

Besanceney, Paul H. *Interfaith Marriages: Who and Why.* New Haven: College & University Press, 1970.

"Children of Mixed Marriage: Are They Jewish? A Symposium on Patrilineal Descent." *Judaism* 1985;34:3–135.

Cohen, J. Simcha. *Intermarriage and Conversion: A Halakhic Solution.* Hoboken, NJ: Ktav, 1987.

Colman, Hila. *Mixed-Marriage Daughter.* New York: Morrow, 1968.

Commission on Reform Jewish Outreach. *Jewish Parents of Intermarried Couples: A Guide for Facilitators.* New York: Union of American Hebrew Congregations, 1987.

_____ . *Times and Seasons: A Jewish Perspective for Intermarried Couples, A Guide for Facilitators.* New York: Union of American Hebrew Congregations, 1987.

Cowan, Paul, and Cowan, Rachel. *Mixed Blessings: Marriage between Jews and Christians.* New York: Doubleday, 1987.

Crohn, Joel. *Ethnic Identity and Marital Conflict: Jews, Italians and Wasps.* New York: American Jewish Committee, 1986.

D'Antonio, M. "Jewish Husbands, Christian Wives (and vice versa)." *Present Tense* 1985;13:5–9.

Edelheit, Joseph E. "Are We Ready for the New Jewish Community?" *Journal of Reform Judaism* 29 (Winter 1982).

Eichhorn, David M. *Conversion to Judaism: A History and Analysis.* New York: Ktav, 1966.

_____ . *Jewish Intermarriages.* Satellite Beach, FL: Satellite Books, 1974.

Eisenstein, Ira. "Intermarriage." United Synagogue of America.

Ellman, Yisrael. "Intermarriage in the United States: A Comparative Study of Jews and Other Ethnic Religious Groups." *Jewish Social Studies* 1987;49:1–26.

Frideres, J. S. "Jewish-Gentile Intermarriage—Definition and Consequences." *Social Compass* 1974;21:69–84.

Friedman, Edwin H. *Generation to Generation: Family Process in Church and Synagogue.* New York: Guilford Press, 1985.

Gittelsohn, Roland B. *Love, Sex and Marriage: A Jewish View.* New York: Union of American Hebrew Congregations, 1980.

Goldenberg, Naomi. "A Response to Anne Roiphe on the Jewish Family: The Problem of Intermarriage." *Tikkun* 1986;2:118–120.

Gordis, Robert. "To Move Forward, Take One Step Back." *Moment* 1985;11:58–61.

Gruzer, Lee F. *Raising Your Jewish/Christian Child: Wise Choices for Interfaith Parents.* New York: Dodd, Mead, 1987.

Huberman, Steven. *New Jews: The Dynamics of Religious Conversion.* New York: Union of American Hebrew Congregations, 1979.

Jacobs, Phil. "Sorting Out the Issues of Intermarriage." *Baltimore Jewish Times* (September 30, 1988):56–59.

Jacobs, Sidney, and Jacobs, Betty. *1222 Clues for Jews Whose Children Intermarry.* Culver City, CA: Jacobs Ladder Publications, 1988.

Jolles, Andrea. "Intermarriage: For Better or For Worse." *Jewish Monthly* (January 1988):8–11.

Kaplan, L. "Mutual Respect." *Reconstructionist* 1985;51:16–17.

Kirschenbaum, Carol. "A Late Believer." *Savvy* (November 1986):26.

Klausner, Abraham J. *Weddings: A Complete Guide to All Religious & Inter-faith Marriage Services.* Columbus, OH: Alpha Publishing Co., 1986.

Kling, Simcha. *Embracing Judaism.* New York: Rabbinical Assembly, 1987.

Kukoff, Lydia. *Choosing Judaism.* New York: Union of American Hebrew Congregations, 1982.

Lamm, Maurice. *The Jewish Way in Love and Marriage.* New York: Harper & Row, 1982.

Luey, H. S. "Please Don't Blame Our Marriage." *Reform Judaism* 1986;14:32–33.

Luka, Ronald. *When a Christian and a Jew Marry.* New York: Paulist Press, 1973.

Maller, Allen. "Why Jewish Women Marry Gentile Men." *Women's American ORT Reporter* (March/April 1977).

Massarik, Fred. "Rethinking the Intermarriage Crisis." *Moment* 1978;3:29–33.

Mayer, Egon. *Children of Intermarriage.* New York: American Jewish Committee, 1983.

_____ . "Confronting Irish Roses." *Haddasah* 1986;67:28–29.

_____ . *Love and Tradition: Marriage Between Jews and Christians.* New York and London: Plenum Press, 1985.

Mayer, Egon, and Scheingold, Carl. *Intermarriage and the Jewish Future.* New York: American Jewish Committee, 1979.

Mirsky, Norman. "Mixed Dating, Mixed Mating, Mixed Marriage." *Moment* 1980;5:62–63.

Moskowitz, Moshe A. "Intermarriage and the Proselyte: A Jewish View." *Judaism* 1979;23:423–433.

"Non-Jewish Spouses to be Welcomed as Full Members in Many Reform Synagogues." *The Jewish Week-American Examiner* (October 5, 1980).

Ostling, Richard N. "The Intermarriage Quandry." *Time* 1988;120:82.

Pelcovitz, Ralph. "The Intermarriage Issue: Crisis and Challenge." *Jewish Life* (October 1973):38–47.

Reuben, Steven Carr. *But How Will You Raise the Children? A Guide to Interfaith Marriage.* New York: Pocket Books, 1987.

Rosenberg, Roy A. *Happily Intermarried: Authoritative Advice for a Jewish Christian Marriage.* New York: Macmillan, 1988.

Rosenthal, Gilbert. *The Jewish Family in a Changing World.* New York: Thomas Yoseloff, 1970.

Sandmel, Samuel. *When a Jew and a Christian Marry.* Philadelphia: Fortress Press, 1977.

Seigel, Robert A. *Intermarriage: A Guide for Jewish Parents.* Miami: Rashi Press, 1979.

Seltzer, Sanford. *Jews and Non-Jews: Falling in Love.* New York: Union of American Hebrew Congregations, 1975.

_____. *Jews and Non-Jews: Getting Married.* New York: Union of American Hebrew Congregations, 1984.

_____. "The Psychological Implications of Mixed Marriage," *Journal of Reform Judaism* 1985;32.

Shanks, Hershel. "Rabbis Who Perform Intermarriages—Who They Are and Why They Do It." *Moment* 1988;12:14–19.

Siegel, Morton K. "Convert: Genuine Jew?" United Synagogue of America.

Silver, Marc. "Intermarried Couples Who Cope." *The National Jewish Monthly* 92:10–16.

Spiegel, S. "Outreach to Interfaith Couples." *Journal of Jewish Communal Services* 1985;62:182–183.

Stern, Elizabeth G. (Leah Morton). *I am a Woman—And a Jew.* New York: Schocken Books, 1926 (reprint ed., 1969).

Stiller, Nikki. "The Shiksa Question." *Moment* 1980;10:6.

Strassfeld, Sharon, and Green, Kathy. *The Jewish Family Book.* New York: Bantam, 1981.

Videotapes and Films

"Choosing Judaism: Some Personal Perspectives." 28 min. Explores issues of conversion from the points of view of four Jews by choice and of one Jewish parent whose child intermarried. Available in 16 mm film and video format from the Union of American Hebrew Congregations, 838 Fifth Avenue, New York, NY   10021.

"Ethnotherapy With Jews." 42 min. A videocassette and discussion guide. Based on *Jewish Identity and Self-Esteem: Healing Wounds Through Ethnotherapy*, a pioneering study of the forces shaping Jewish identity, based on group-encounter dialogues and research findings on positive and negative feelings toward Judaism and Jewishness. Rental, $50. American Jewish Committee, 165 East 56 Street, New York, NY   10019.

"Intermarriage: When Love Meets Tradition." 28 min. Documentary focusing on five interfaith couples in a candid, poignant, and balanced portrait of the problems they face. Available in film and video: $250 per videocassette; $30 per video rental. Direct Cinema Limited, P.O. Box 69799, Los Angeles, CA   90069.

"Parents and Ethnicity." 30 min. How ethnic, cultural, and religious traditions influence family life and parental expectations. With discussion guide. Rental, $50. American Jewish Committee, 165 East 56 Street, New York, NY   10019.

"The Myth of the Melting Pot Marriage: Ethnotherapy with Jewish-Gentile Couples." 30 min. This videocassette presentation maps the terrain of interpersonal and identity issues in Jewish/non-Jewish marriages and is intended to help professionals as well as the intermarried and their families in identifying and dealing with the ethnocultural consequences of intermarriage. Rental, $50. American Jewish Committee, 165 East 56th Street, New York, NY   10019.

"This Great Difference." 13 min. Trigger film focusing on interfaith dating couples and the decisions they face. Excellent for use with youth groups. Available in film format. Direct Cinema Ltd., P.O. Box 69799, Los Angeles, CA   90069.

"Where Judaism Differed." Series of 5 hour-long videocassettes. Exploration of Judaism's relationship to paganism, Hellenism, Christianity, Islam, and modernity. Purchase of all five, $200. Rental per cassette, $50. American Jewish Committee, 165 East 56 Street, New York, NY   10019.

"Lisa's Dilemma." 6 min. (1981). This is a trigger film to promote discussion about the effects of intermarriage on the children of such unions. This short, insightful look at the generation produced by intermarriage should be a useful programming tool for discussions on Jewish identity and intermarriage. Rental, $12. Toronto Jewish Congress, 150 Beverly Street, Toronto, Ontario M5T 1 Y6, Canada.

"Rachel." 3 min. (1974). A trigger film that presents the extreme case of alienation from the Jewish marriage ethos. We see a middle-aged man observing what appear to be traditional Jewish mourning rites for his daughter. Only in the last shot do we learn that she has not died, but married in church. The film comes with a kit of teaching materials on the subject of intermarriage. Rental, $6; purchase, $55. Jewish Media Service, Institute for Jewish Life, 65 Williams Street, Wellesley, MA   02181.

GAY OR LESBIAN

Books and Articles

"Abraham" and "Sarah": "Two Perspectives on Being Gay." *Jewish Currents* 30(1)1:18–20.

Arich, Aliza, and Hannah. "A Feeling of Family: Boston Gay and Lesbian Jews Attend World Conference." *Gay Community News* (August 29, 1981).

Baetz, Ruth. *Lesbian Crossroads: Personal Stories of Lesbian Struggles.* New York: William Morrow, 1980.

Bauman, Batya. "On Coming Out Gay." *Lilith* 1976;1:9–10.

Beck, Evelyn Torton, ed. *Nice Jewish Girls: A Lesbian Anthology.* Waterloo, MA: Persephone, 1982.

Becker, Robin. *Backtalk.* Cambridge, MA: Alicejames Books, 1982.

Berzon, Betty, and Leighton, Robert, ed. *Positively Gay.* Millbrae, CA: Celestial Arts, 1979.

Biale, Rachel. *Women and Jewish Law: An Exploration of Women's Issues in Halakhic Sources.* New York: Schocken Books, 1984.

Bloch, Alice. "Scenes from the Life of a Jewish Lesbian." In *On Being a Jewish Feminist: A Reader,* ed. Susannah Heschel, p. 177. New York: Schocken Books, 1983.

Chutzpah Anthology: "Dilemma of a Jewish Lesbian." San Francisco: New Glide Publications, 1977, pp. 30–31.

Epstein, Louis M. *Sex Laws and Customs in Judaism.* Rev. ed. New York: Ktav, 1967.

Gordis, Robert. *Love and Sex: A Modern Jewish Perspective*. New York: Farrar, Straus & Giroux, 1978.

Gordon, Eric. "Being Jewish and Gay: A Conference Report." *Jewish Currents* 1986;40(6):14–15.

Heschel, Susannah, ed. *On Being a Jewish Feminist*. New York: Schocken Books, 1983.

Katz, Judith. "Nadine Pagan's Last Letter Home." *Sinister Wisdom* 19 (1982).

Klepfisz, Irena. "Anti-Semitism in the Lesbian/Feminist Movement." *Off Our Backs* (April 1982).

Lamm, Maurice. *The Jewish Way in Love and Marriage*. New York: Harper & Row, 1982.

_____ . "Judaism and the Modern Attitude to Homosexuality." In *Encyclopedia Judaica Yearbook* 1974, pp. 194–205. Jerusalem: Keter, 1974.

Lowenstein, Andrea Freud. *This Place*. Somerville, MA: Summerhouse Press, 1982.

Malcolm, Sarah. "I Am a Second Generation Lesbian." *Ms.* 1977;7:13–16.

Matt, Herschel J. "Sin, Crime, 'Sickness or Alternative Life Style'?: A Jewish Approach to Homosexuality." *Judaism* 1978;27:13–24.

Mehler, Barry Alan. "Gay Jews." *Moment* 2:22.

Rabinowitz, Mayer E. "Homosexuality and the Halakhah." *Reconstructionist* 51 (October-November 1985).

Rankin, M. "Let the Day Come Which is all Shabbat: The Liturgy of the 'Gay-Outreach' Synagogues." *Journal of Reform Judaism* 1986;33:69–73.

Schwartz, Barry Dov. "Homosexuality—A Jewish Perspective." *United Synagogue Review* (Summer, 1977):4–5ff.

_____ . *The Jewish View of Homosexuality*. Thesis, Jewish Theological Seminary of America, New York, 1979.

Sh'ma: A Journal of Jewish Responsibility 1980;11:1–8.

Silverstein, Charles. *A Family Matter: A Parent's Guide to Homosexuality*. New York: McGraw-Hill, 1977.

Sinclair, Jo (pseud. for Ruth Seid). *The Changelings*. New York: McGraw-Hill, 1955. Reprinted by Feminist Press 1983 (fiction).

Soloff, Rav. A. "Is There a Reform Response to Homosexuality?" *Judaism* 1983;32:417–424.

Tilchen, Maida. "JEB Talks—Picturing Lesbians." *Gay Community News* (August 8, 1981).

Toder, Nancy. *Choices*. Watertown, MA: Persephone Press, 1980.

Umansky, Ellen M. "Jewish Attitudes towards Homosexuality: A Review of Contemporary Resources." *Reconstructionist* 51 (October-November 1985).

Audiotape

"Jewish Lesbian Culture and Anti-Semitism in the Lesbian Community." A presentation by Minneapolis Jewish Lesbians. Available from: Radical Rose Recordings, BDO 1, P.O. Box 8122, Minneapolis, MN 55408.

CHILDLESS

Books and Articles

Adelman, Penina V. "Prayer to Rahmana, Mother of Wombs." *Reconstructionist* (June 1985):26–27.

Alpert, Rebecca. "A Prayer On the Occasion of Miscarriage or Abortion." *Reconstructionist* (September 1985):4.

Bayer, Linda. *The Blessing and the Curse.* Philadelphia: Jewish Publication Society, 1988.

Callaway, Mary. *Sing, O Barren One: A Study in Comparative Midrash.* Atlanta, GA: Scholars Press, 1986.

Diamant, Anita. "The Newest Jewish Faces." *Hadassah* 1988;5:17–19.

Faux, Marian. *Childless by Choice: Choosing Childlessness in the Eighties.* Garden City, NY: Anchor Press, 1984.

Gittelsohn, Roland. *The Extra Dimension: A Jewish View of Marriage.* New York: Union of American Hebrew Congregations, 1983.

Gold, Michael. *Adoption and the Jewish Couple.* New York: United Synagogue of America.

_____.*And Hannah Wept: Infertility, Adoption and the Jewish Couple.* Philadelphia: Jewish Publication Society, 1988.

Greenberg, Blu. *How to Run a Traditional Jewish Household.* New York: Simon and Schuster, 1985.

_____. "ZPG: Feminism and Jewish Survival."*Hadassah* 60:12–13, 27–29, 33–35.

Kanigel, R. "Will Jewish Baby Boom Babies Ever Have Their Own?" *Jewish Monthly* (June/July 1983):9–12.

Laiken, Deidre. "Adoption: One Couple's Story." *New Woman* (May 1987):125–129.

Salkowitz, Tracy. "Hannah Cried . . . But I Got Hormone Shots." *Moment* 1988;9:32–35.

Strassfeld, Sharon, and Green, Kathy. *The Jewish Family Book.* New York: Bantam, 1981.

Index